Window
Eleven Septembers

Reiner Leist

Window

Eleven Septembers 1995–2005

Essays by
Ludger Derenthal
Jonathan Santlofer

MUSEUM FÜR FOTOGRAFIE

SMB Kunstbibliothek
Staatliche Museen
zu Berlin

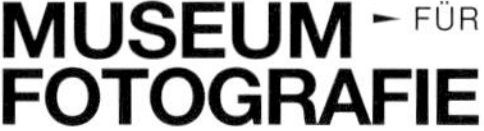

PRESTEL

Munich · Berlin · London · New York

For Gerda and Jürgen Leist

Window to the World
Ludger Derenthal

Since March 1995, Reiner Leist has photographed the view from his apartment window on the 26th floor of a commercial building on New York City's Eighth Avenue. The scene is of the architecture of downtown Manhattan. To the left, at 34th Street, sit One Penn Plaza and the round structure of Madison Square Garden; in the center at a distance stand the skyscrapers of the financial district, once including the World Trade Center—in the axis of the nearly always crowded Eighth Avenue—as well as the rooftops of smaller buildings; while on the right is the old New Yorker Hotel. The view is cropped by the window's frame and objects of daily use on the table close to the window, constituting each photograph's foreground.

When in New York City Reiner Leist photographed daily, whenever he got around to it, at all times of day, despite weather conditions and positions of the sun. He used a 19th-century full-plate camera loaded with 8x10-inch black-and-white negatives. During the course of the decade he acquired a certain routine: placing the camera on the kitchen table, opening the window, focusing, measuring the light, inserting the negative and finally making the exposure, followed by the jotting down of date and time in his journal. These tasks became a small ritual, a performative act, representing something of a break in a busy New York work day.

Reiner Leist has made roughly 2,200 exposures in this way during the last eleven years. They document the everyday, a changing Manhattan, as well as the big historical *cesura,* the destruction of the World Trade Center. Leist's serial way of working is inscribed in the technical medium of photography. And, of course, none of the images are ever the same. On the contrary, the point of view is always taken afresh and the ever-changing new gaze from the window onto the city charges the images with a rich diversity, demanding ever more comparison.

The window view is the oldest motive of photography. The apparently eight-hour exposure Nicéphore Niépce made from the window of his manor in Chalon-sur-Saône 1826-27, the very first surviving photograph, a heliograph, bears mention here. Niépce was looking out into an open field, framed on both sides by buildings, a constellation that Leist picks up again. Also worth noting is Louis-Jacques-Mandé Daguerre's view onto the Boulevard du Temple in 1839, the year photography's invention was announced. No single detail from the street scene Daguerre photographed from his apartment window was lost. The exposures were so exact that they naturally aroused enthusiasm in his contemporaries. Using long exposure times, he captured not only place but time. The at first paradoxical result was that the houses, but not the moving carriages and people, were pictured. The only exception was an idle man getting a shoeshine. In March 1839, Samuel Morse saw the daguerreotype and noted with surprise: "Objects moving are not impressed." Only later, in the serial photographs of Eadweard Muybridge and Étienne-Jules Marey, who examined the physiological foundation of bodily movement in animals and humans through scientific experiments, that motion found its photographic representation. The two separated time into fractions of moments, which could be reassembled in portfolio plates and simultaneous exposures. It was around 1930 that Alfred Stieglitz began capturing the long flow of time, the constant change a city undergoes from season to season. In a photographic series of New York City, taken from the window of the Shelton Hotel, he captured the constant building up and tearing down of urban building blocks. Stieglitz's fascination was with the clear cubes and contours of skyscrapers as the sun lit them from the side; he looked for images that would transform the city into a landscape of shapes. Stieglitz's view onto the towering structures was determined by the rhythm of the city: He followed the growth of the steel skeletons day and night, grabbing ever new, almost cinematic views from the depths of the street canyons with his 8x10-inch camera. He avoided indicating his own point of view, allowing the camera, without the context of the window frame, to seemingly float above the city and the everyday, solely dedicated to the patterns of light and shade on the buildings.

The New York photographs by Reiner Leist appear simultaneously casual and overwhelming when viewed in their totality. The exposures are created with a certain degree of routine assurance; the artist was always certain that the city would offer a worthwhile image. In this way the photographer became a documentarian, but he had to give his project an artistic shape. It is only the series that allows the observer to recognize the city's changing face. Photographs, which are focused in their essence on the moment, no matter how long that may be stretched, can only tell of a long process when aligned like words that form a sentence. It was by accident that Reiner Leist was not in the city on September 11, 2001; in the absence of an image from that day we find a void in the historic center of the work. But this seems adequate to his approach, and furthermore, the consequences of the intrusion of history into the long flow of the city's time are visibly catalogued by each consecutive photograph.

To develop a book and an exhibition from this enormous accumulation of photographs required extensive conceptual preparations. In the beginning, the images were made without any particular intention—they were primarily based on one man's enthusiasm for the grandiose view from his breakfast table. Later, a goal emerged: all "windows" in a large-scale installation. The Kaisersaal (Emperor's Hall) of the Museum for Photography in Berlin was destroyed during World War II and has never been restored. The resulting ruinous charm of the space, with its raw brick walls and high open ceiling, makes it an ideal one for exhibiting all of Leist's photographs. Its cavernous depth makes the project's evolution become acutely visible. This brave undertaking's stringency and its long development are the keys to the presentation concept. Reiner Leist manufactured black-and-white transparencies in an 8x10-inch format identical to his negatives. Not only does this process retain the impressive format of the original negatives, but it also maintains a traditional and common principle of translation, the images mirroring the process with which they were made in the first place.

Each individual transparency is placed into a light-box. A group of ten light-boxes, representing a single day on the calendar over the span of a decade, are stacked in a vertical tower, the first year topped by each subsequent one. In this way, the chronology is perfectly maintained: each year occupies one rung. For every day without an image, a darkened box fills the gap. Visitors to the Kaisersaal will be completely surrounded by the installation, which will line all four walls of the space. The course of one year can be followed horizontally. The very same day can be compared over ten years when viewed from bottom to top, or vice versa. When viewed at close-range, the high quality of the film format and the reproduction process become remarkably clear. Each photograph is characterized by precise drawing and sharpness, rich in detail and contrast. The enormous volume of material, on the other hand, stands for the strict completion and presentation of the entire project.

For exhibitions at the Julie Saul Gallery in New York and Galerie Walter Storms in Munich, Leist searched for ways to show the piece in smaller spaces. He edited the work down to size by choosing individual months, maintaining the light-box format for the New York presentation, while exhibiting various "test" images and light-boxes from throughout the process in Munich. The collective view reports on both the changes and constants in America's largest metropolis through the decade. The same is true for this book's presentation of *Window*, a bisection of all of the September months from 1995 until 2005. But in the book, the individual image takes center stage. The volume again presents each image printed in the 8x10-inch format, page by page adding up to something like a contact sheet of the exposure, each photograph standing on its own, commented on only by the printed date. Like an oversized flipbook, it allows the days to pass quickly or slowly by the eye of the observer. Small details like a steadily emptying fruit bowl in the foreground, a rooftop canopy covered by a tarp during a renovation, or the constantly changing advertising banners on Madison Square Garden gain weight and importance as one reads in them the passing of time.

Only the attentive observer will notice the interruption between the years—though, of course, all will anticipate the censure of September 11, 2001. Reiner Leist did not photograph during September 2000, and did not create images on 1-10 September 2001, so the book preserves no immediate "before." Thrust into the center of that tumultuous month, one sees only the dust- and smoke-clouds that obscured the radical destruction and metamorphosis of the city in the days following. In viewing the photographs of those "after" days, the observer becomes more and more focused on the sky above New York, increasingly and symbolically occupied, at first by the traces of circling helicopters, in the following years by searchlights that later conceded to the darkness of night and less glaring remembrance of the attack's victims. A void in history, at least where this work is concerned, gives way to a jarring, unstoppable period, reminding the observer that time may slow, but it never halts.

Reiner Leist's view from the window stands in a long art-historical tradition that got its theoretical foundation from Leon Battista Alberti, who once said that painting is an open window to the world. Photography finds its historical beginnings as *camera obscura,* in the desire to fix this view onto the world, freezing it mechanically. The chosen cutout of the world transforms the scene into an image, something that can be appropriated and defined. But the visible border also has meaning: On this side of the window's frame resides your own, somewhat manageable world; on the other side starts the larger, the alien, world, which you'll never contain but can endlessly explore. In Leist's work the window frame itself is only photographed in rare cases; the softly fading black vignetting of the old lenses and the strict lines of the negative's frame border the scene instead. His photographs provide an exact demarcation between the private and the public, with the always out-of-focus, banal objects that move in and out of the foreground symbolizing a certain buffer between he who lives inside and that which happens out. The relationship between the worlds on either side of that glass pane comes into play over and over again; at times the foreground, occupied by a vase, bowl, or candle, becomes so much the view that the city is nothing but a background. But so much more often, the view is searching; the camera, high in the sky, dares to float outside, onto the architecture, soaring above the city. This metropolis that in the 20th century represented the dream of western civilization like no other became, in the 21st, the symbol of its endangerment. Reiner Leist opens with his photographs a wide-open window to this city and to this world.

September 1, 1995

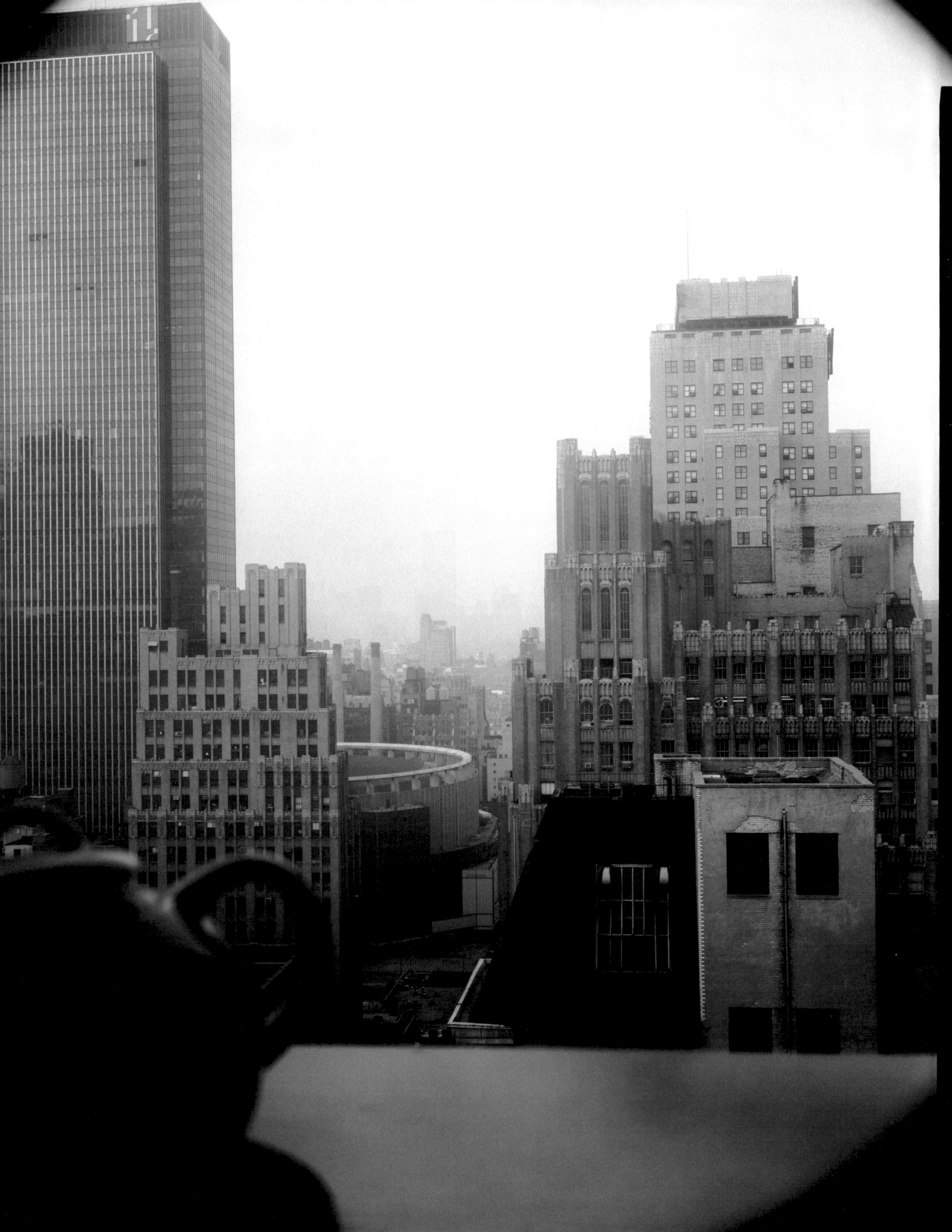

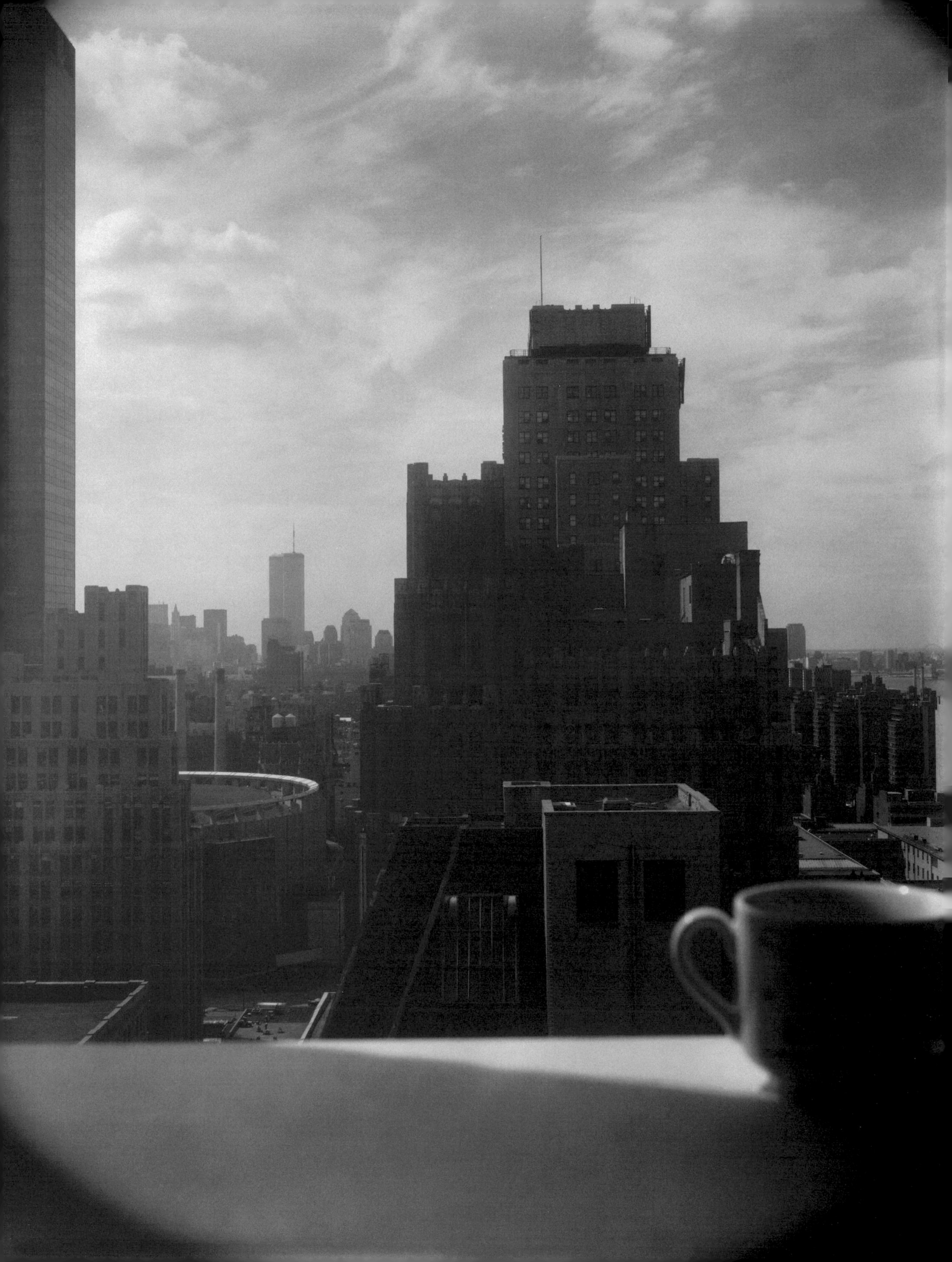

September 3, 1995

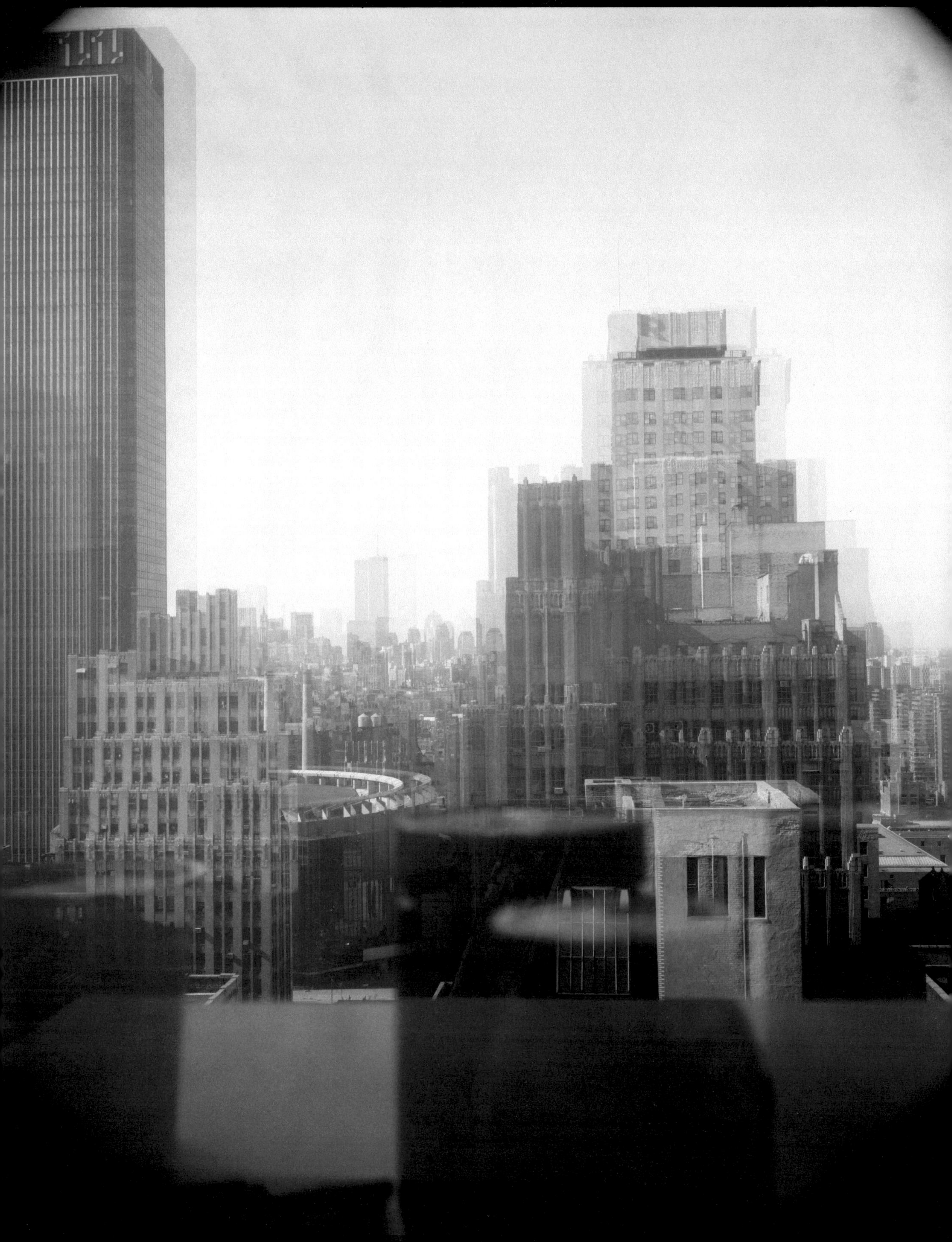

September 4, 1995

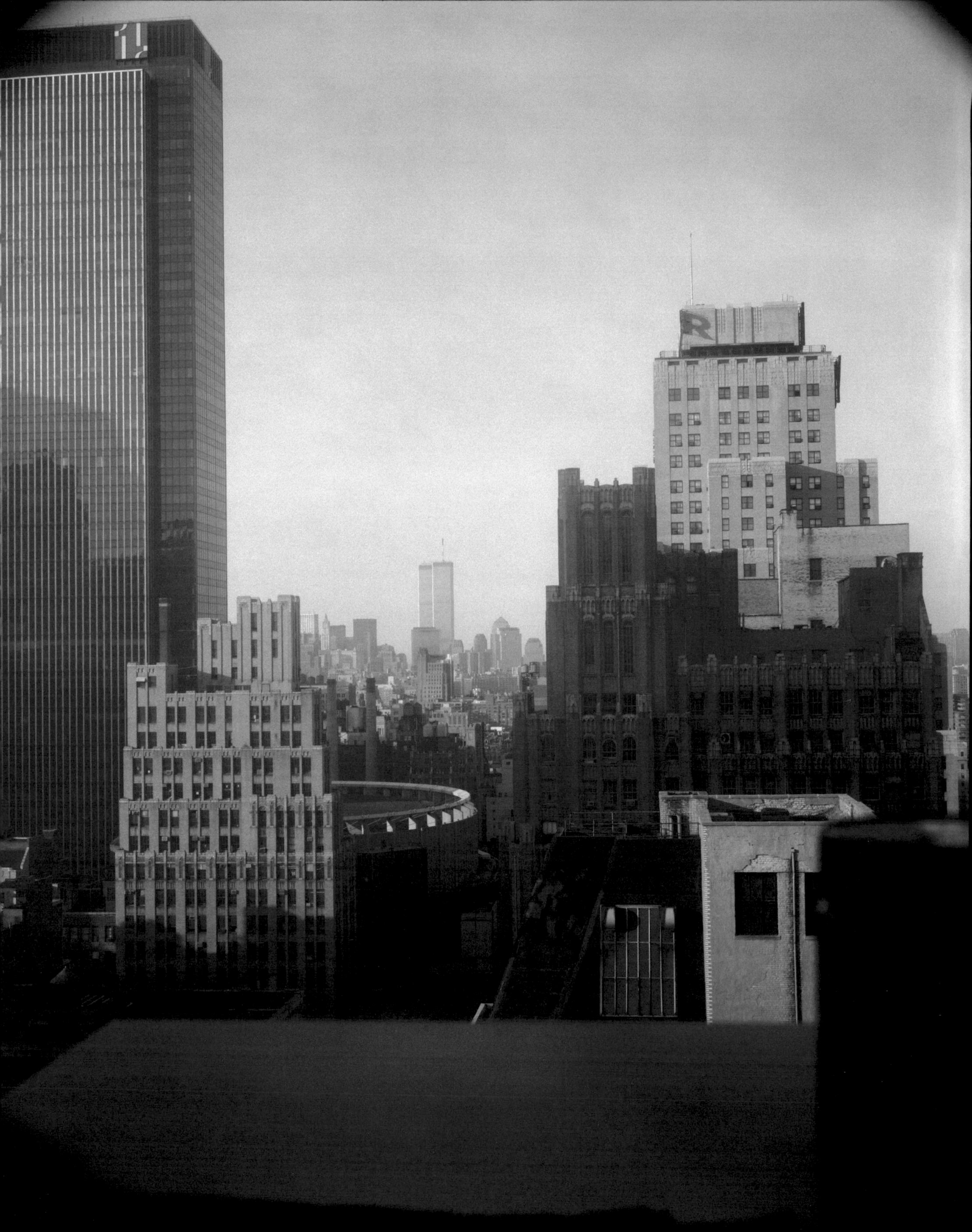

September 5, 1995

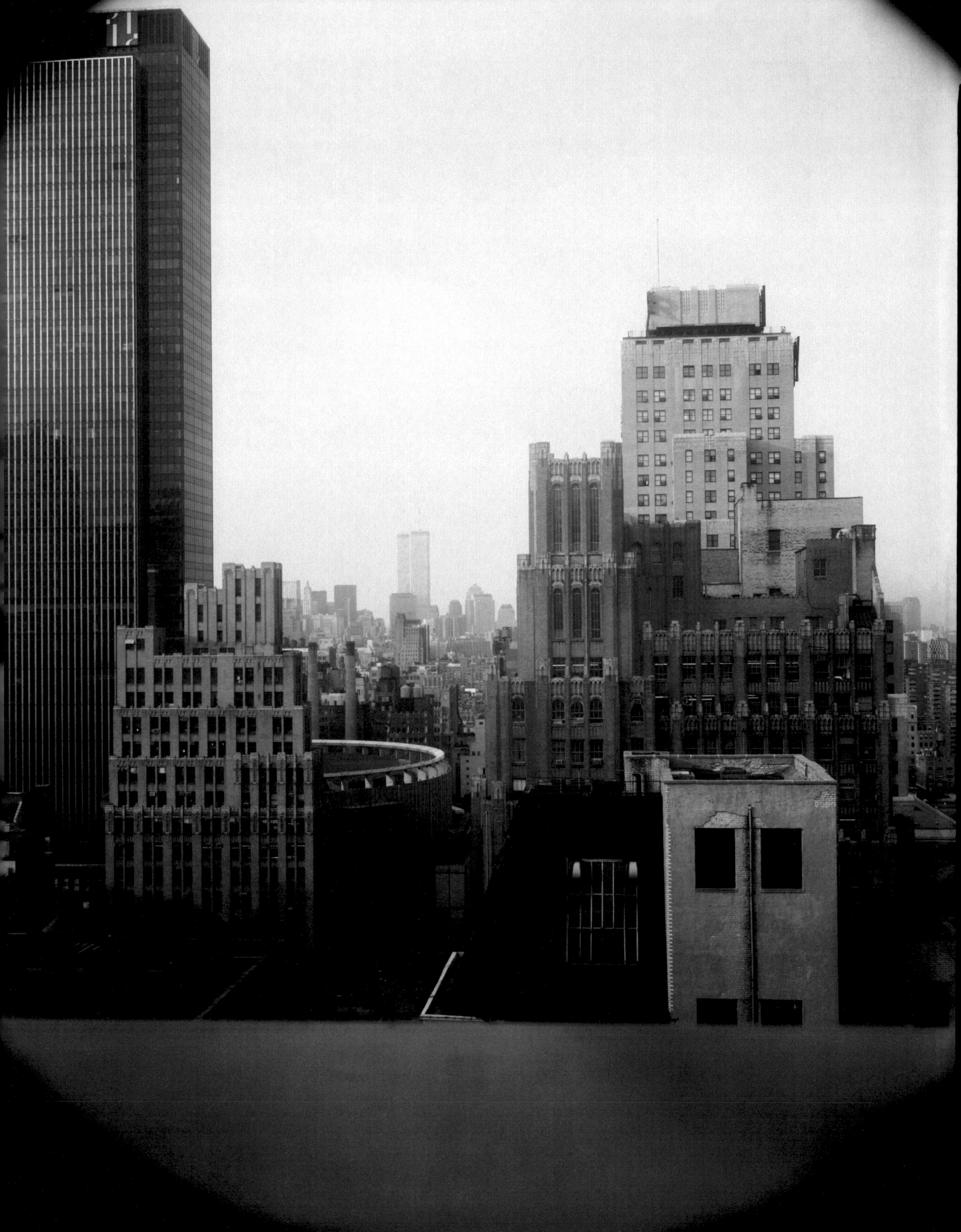

September 6, 1995

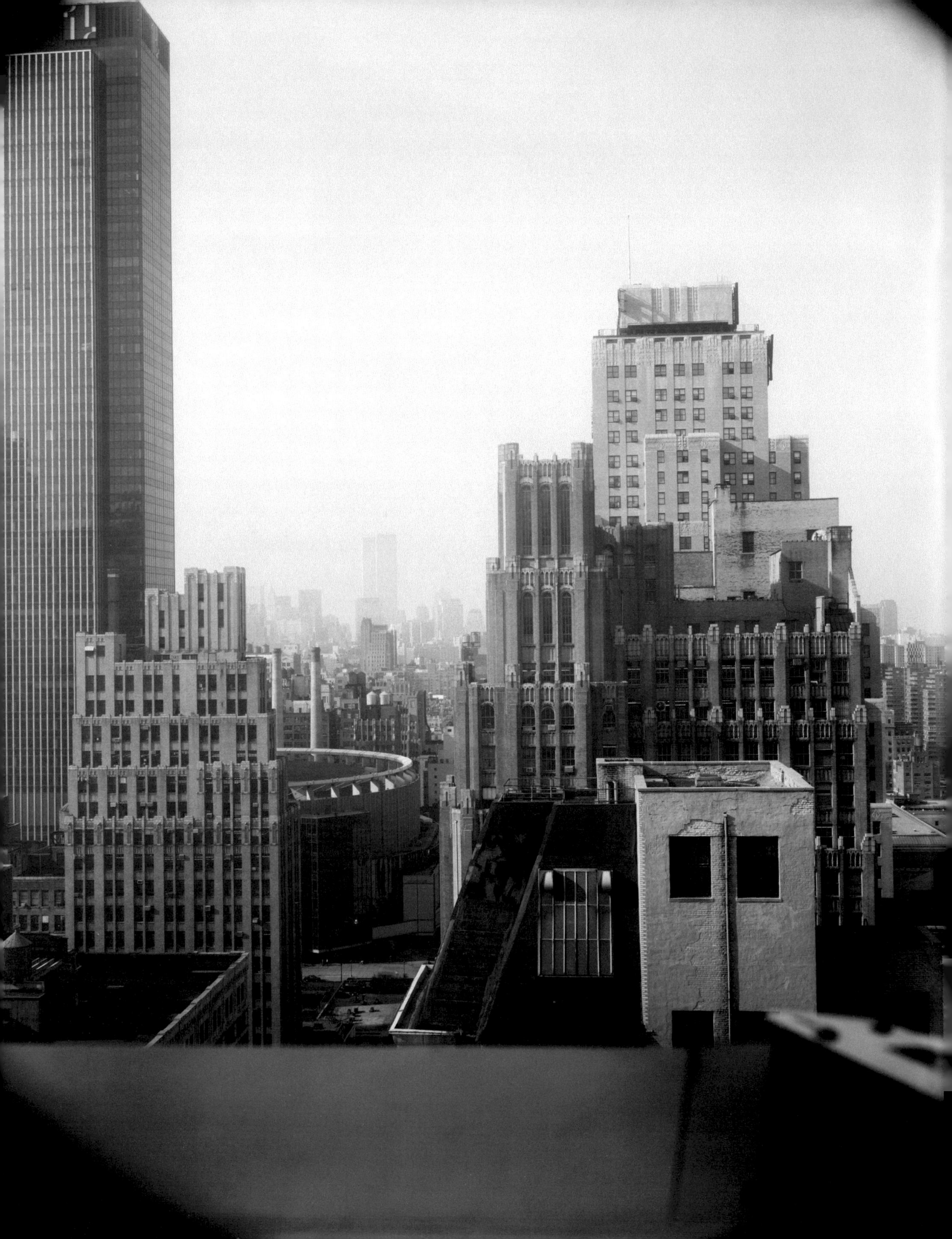

September 7, 1995

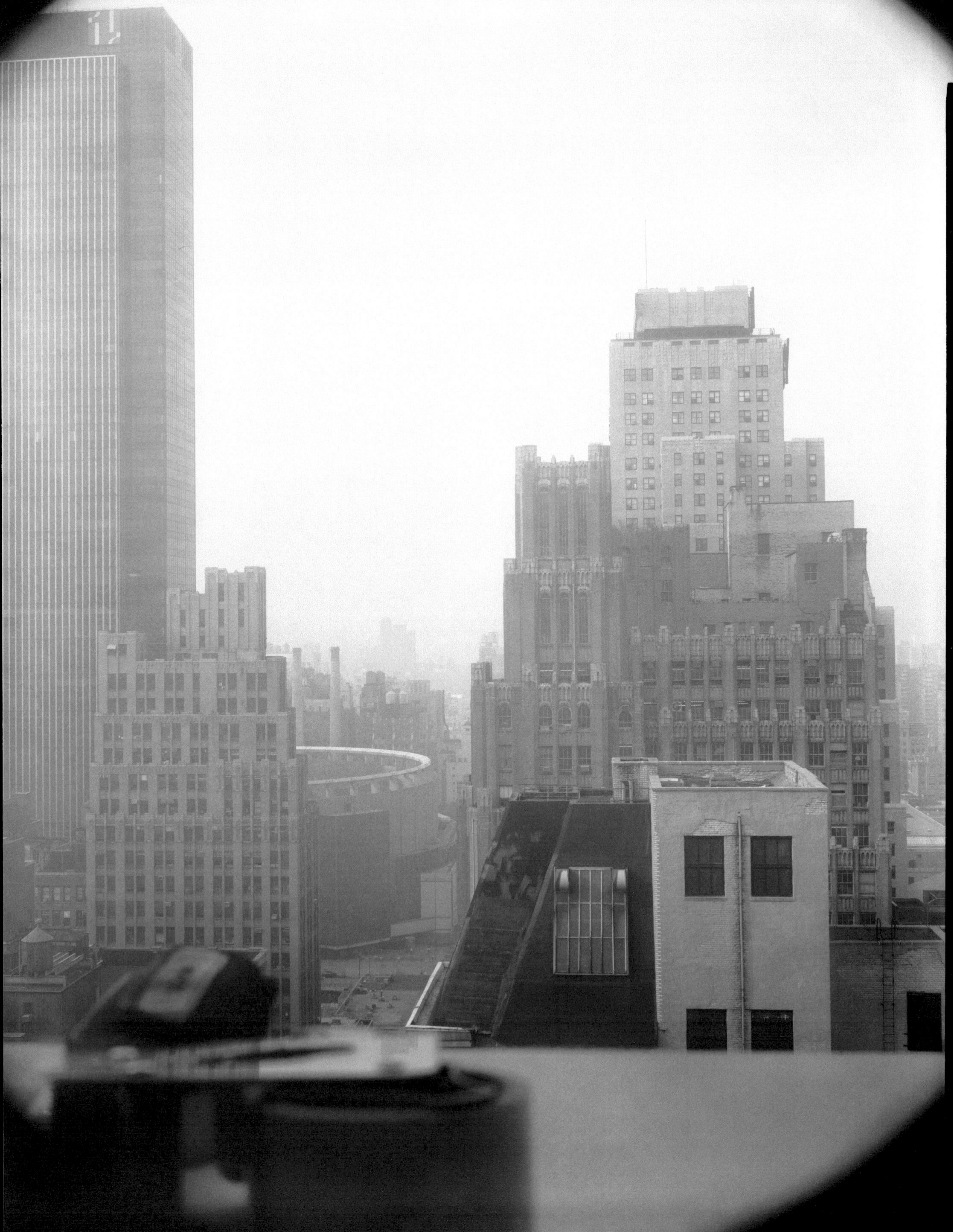

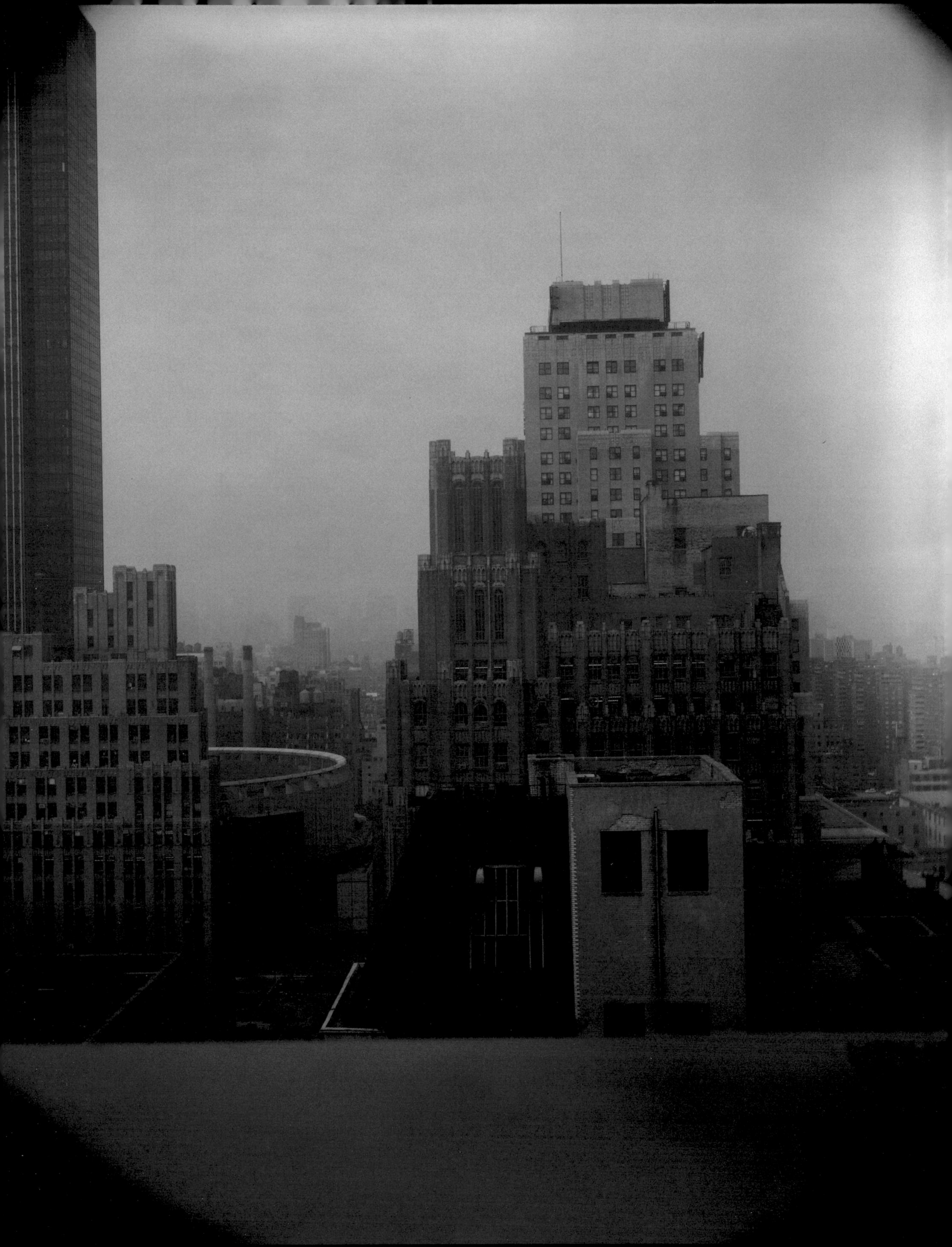

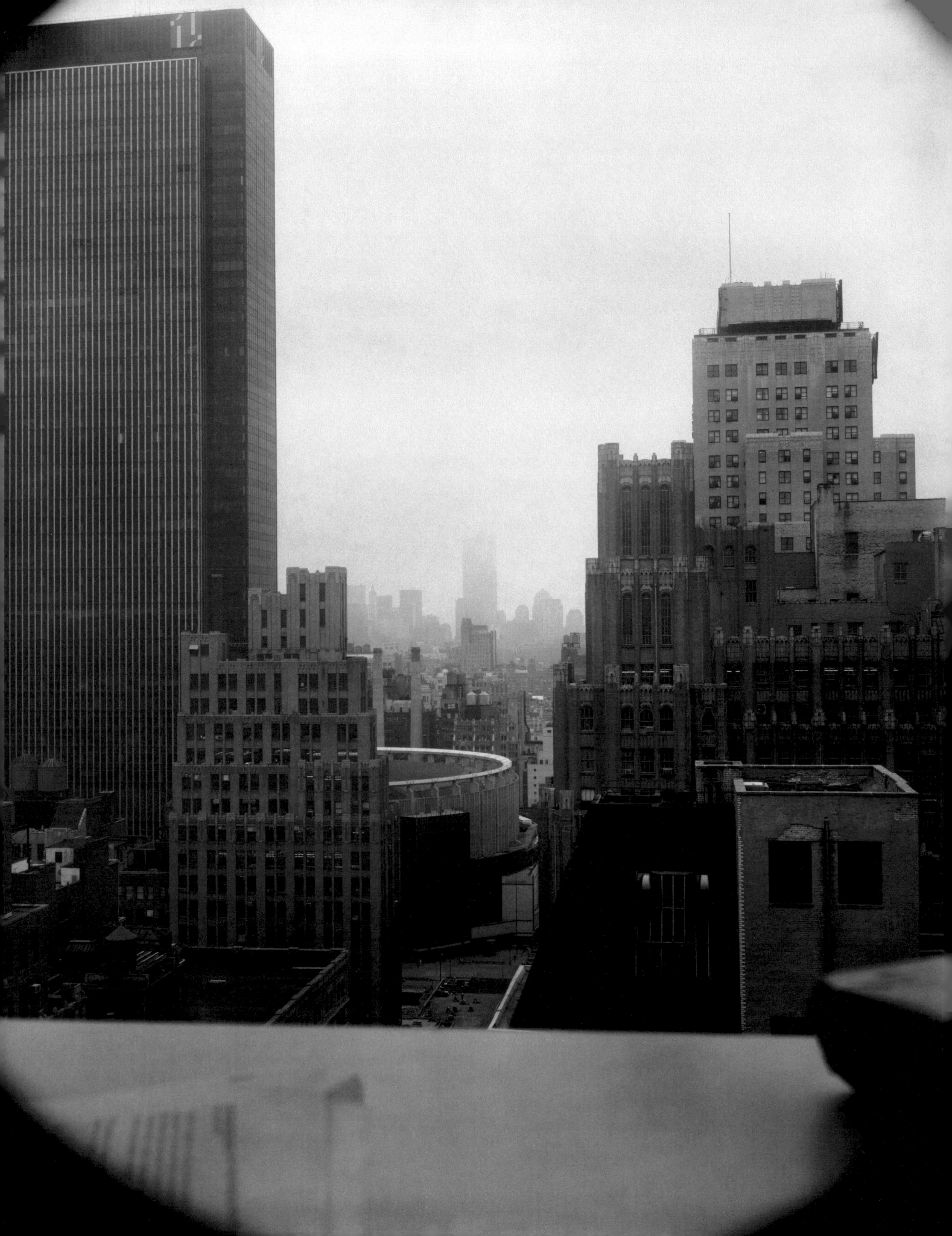

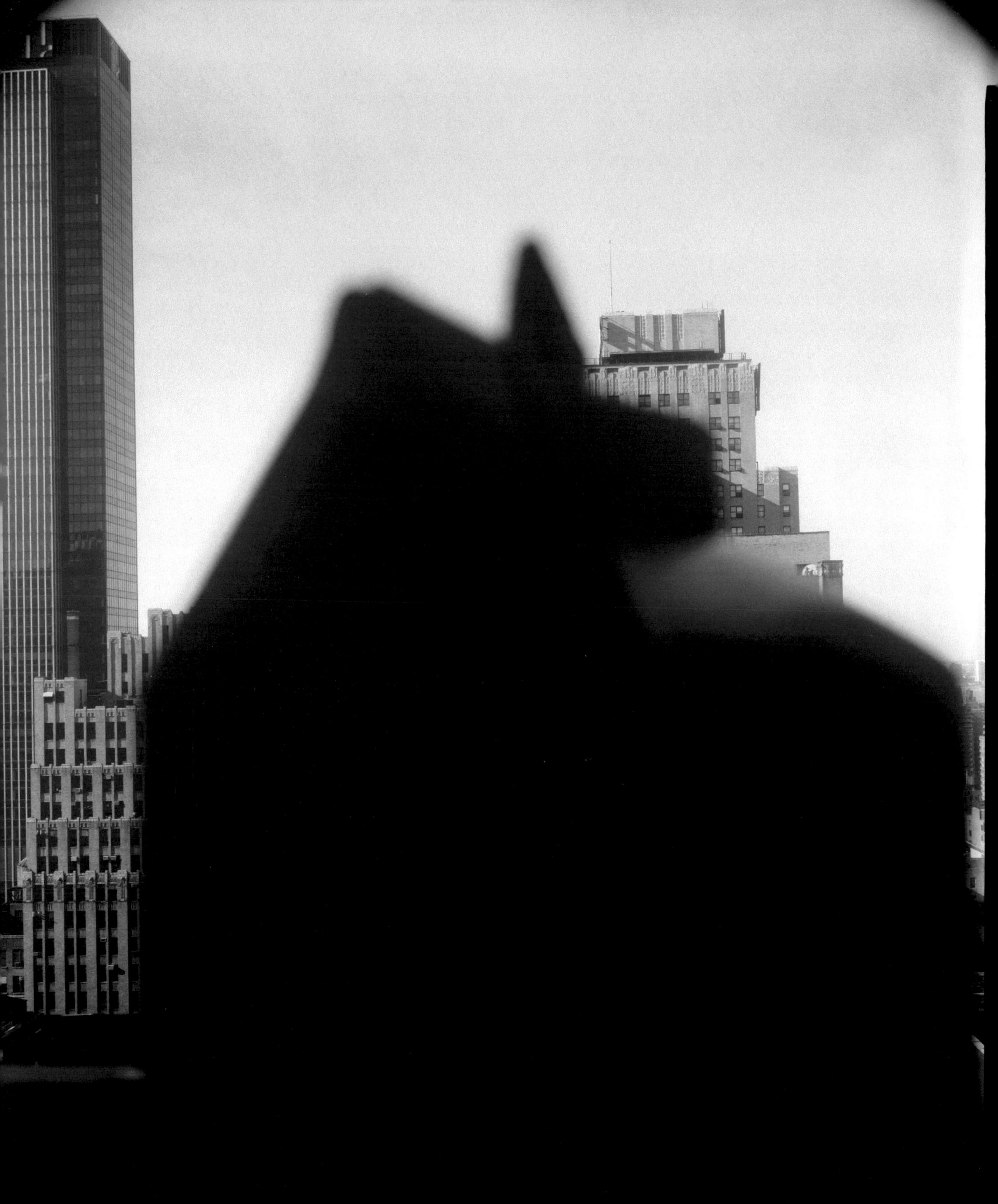

September 11, 1995

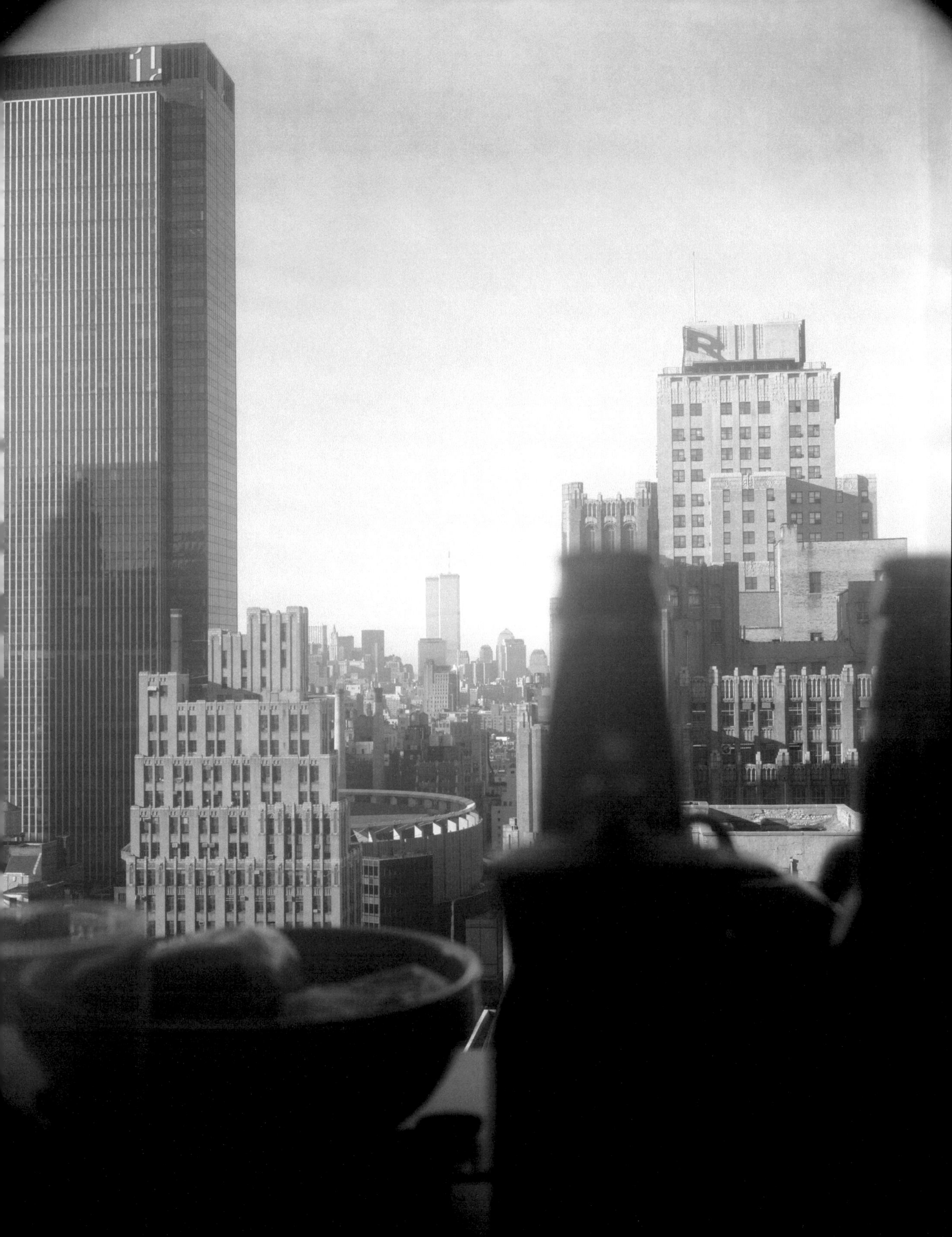

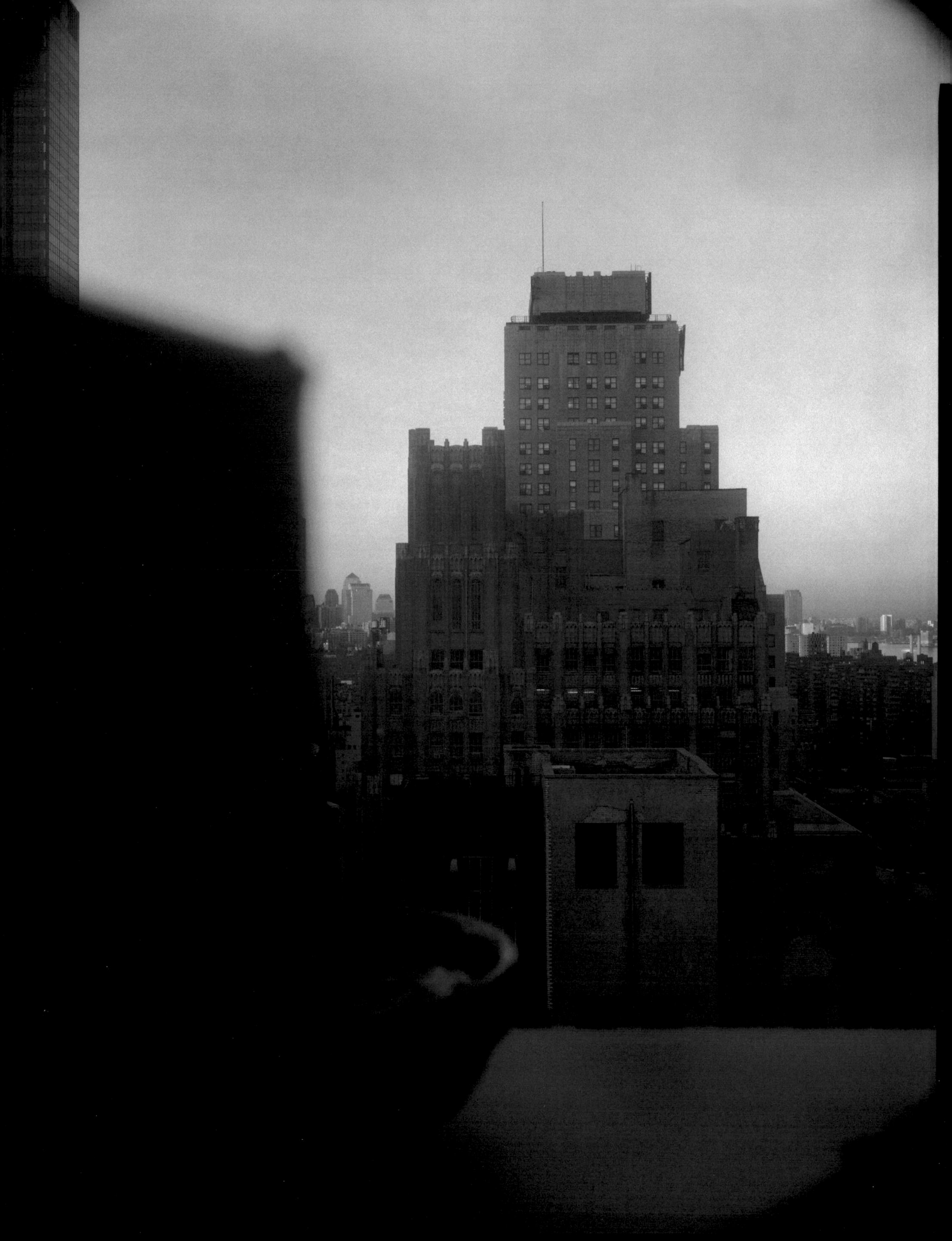

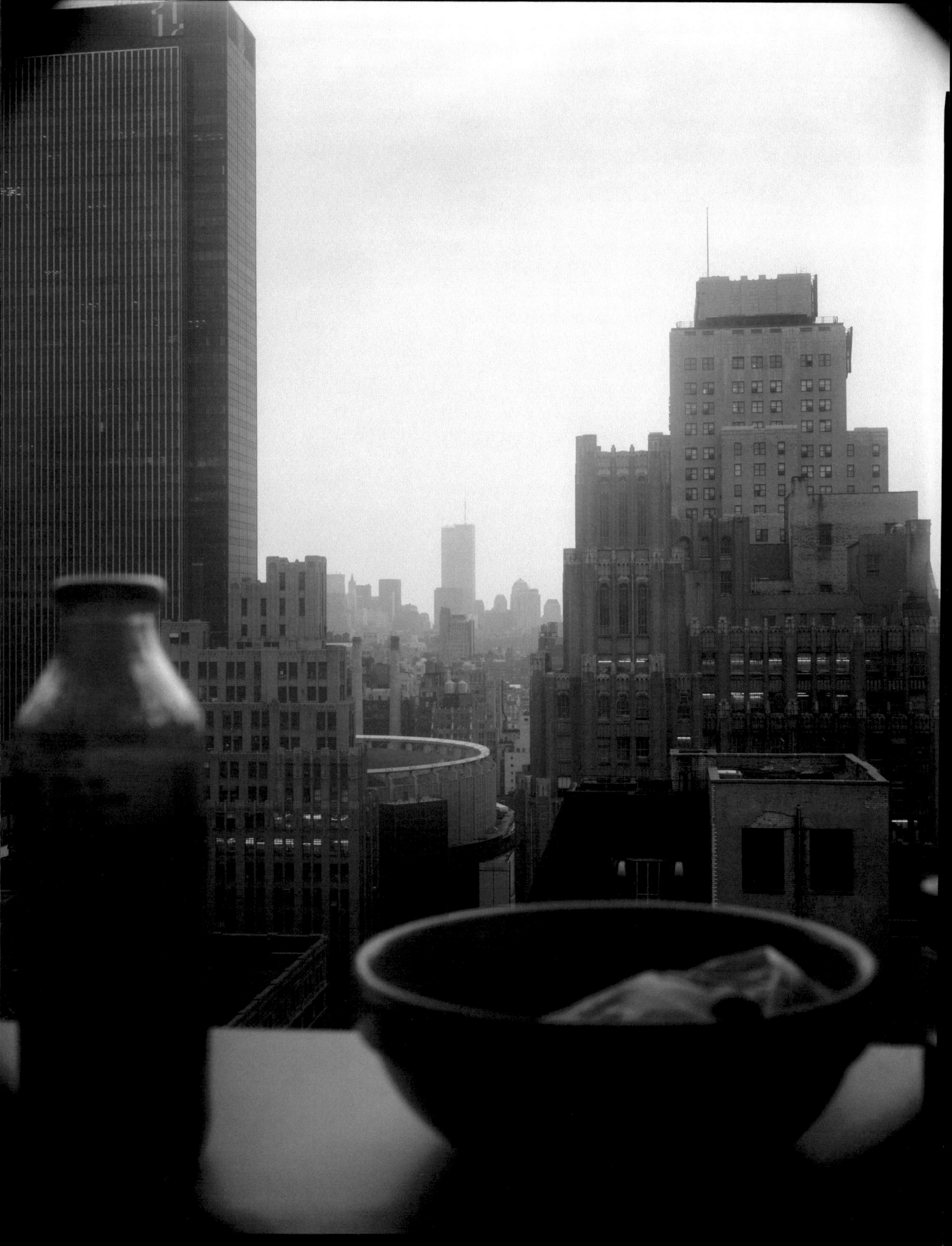

September 14, 1995

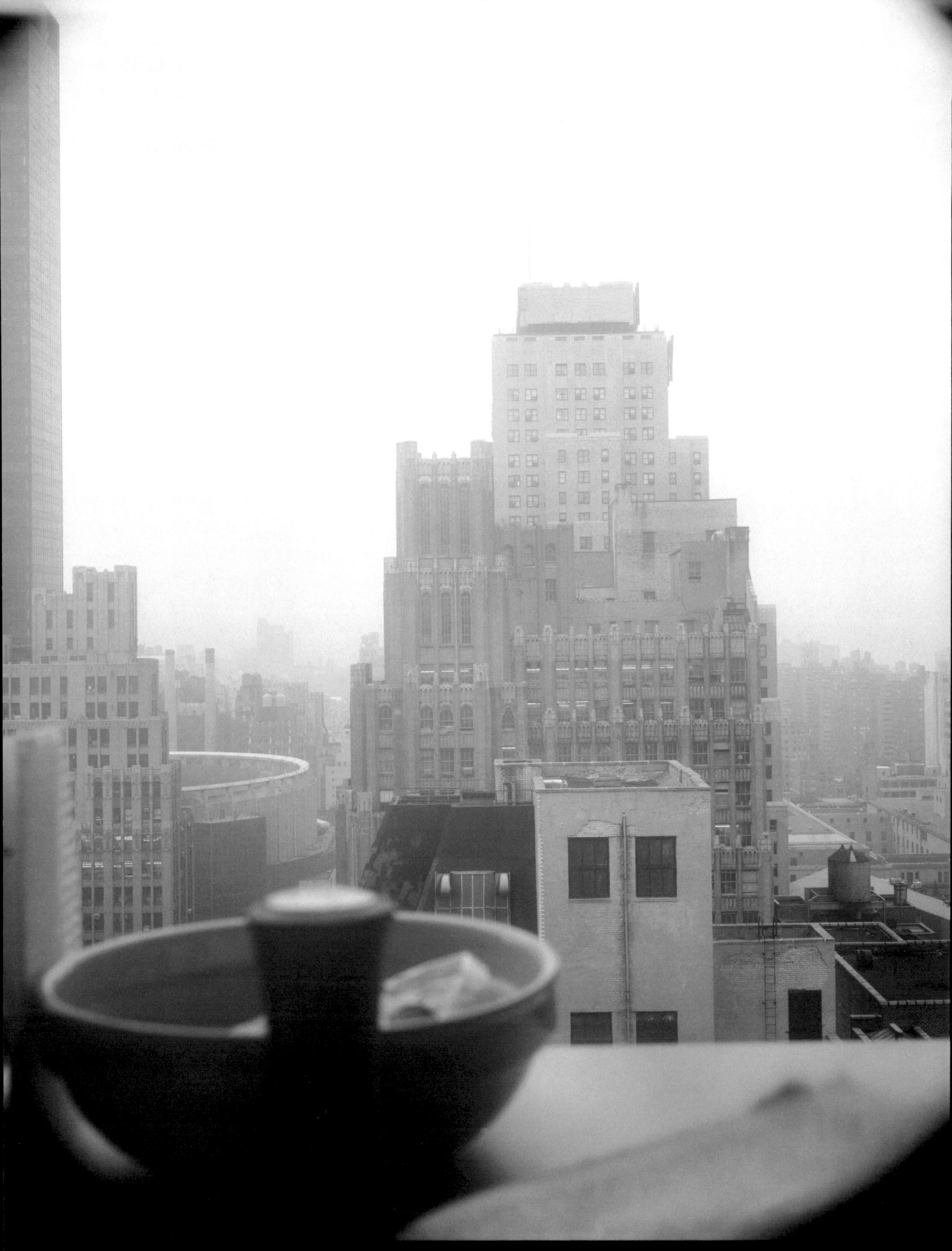

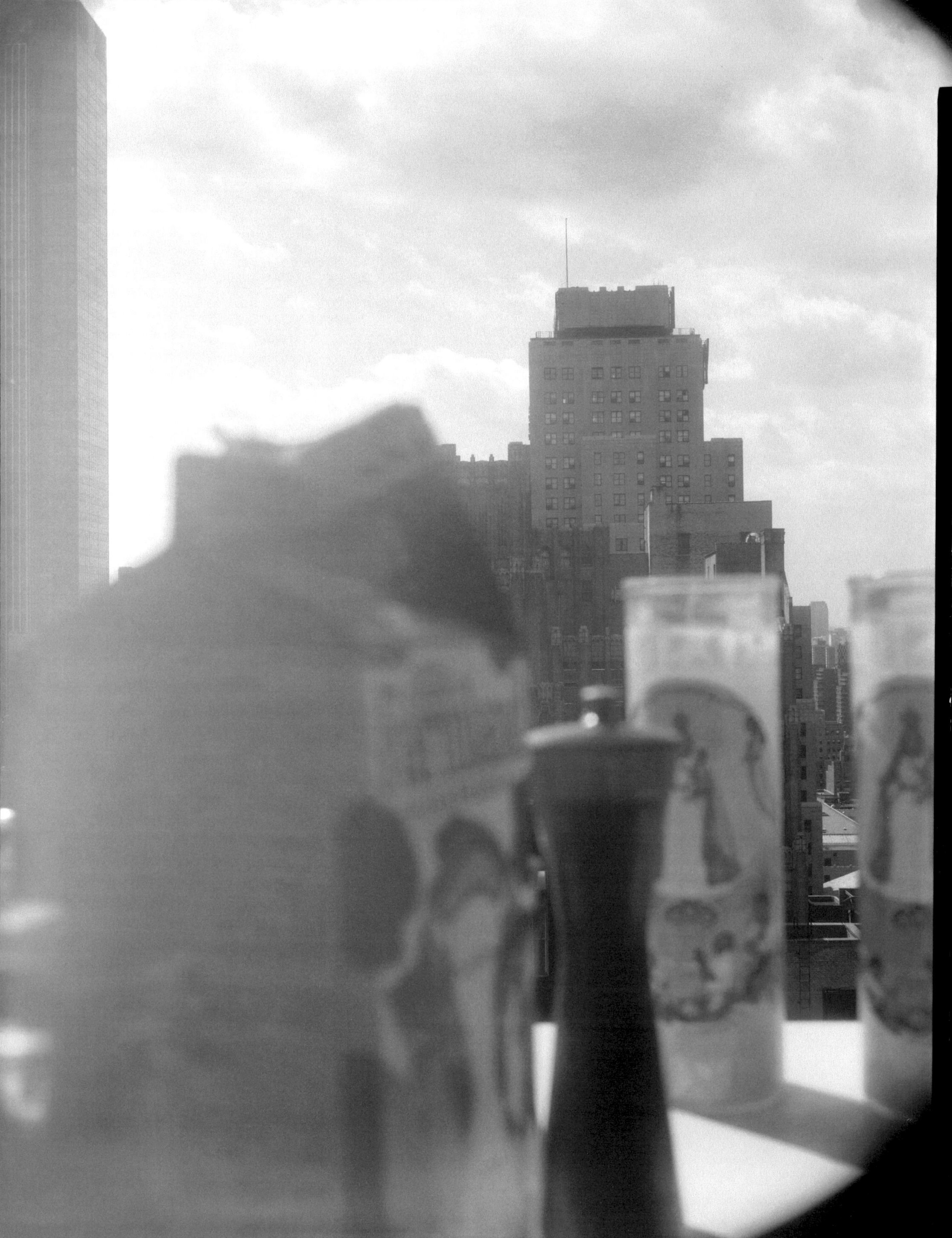

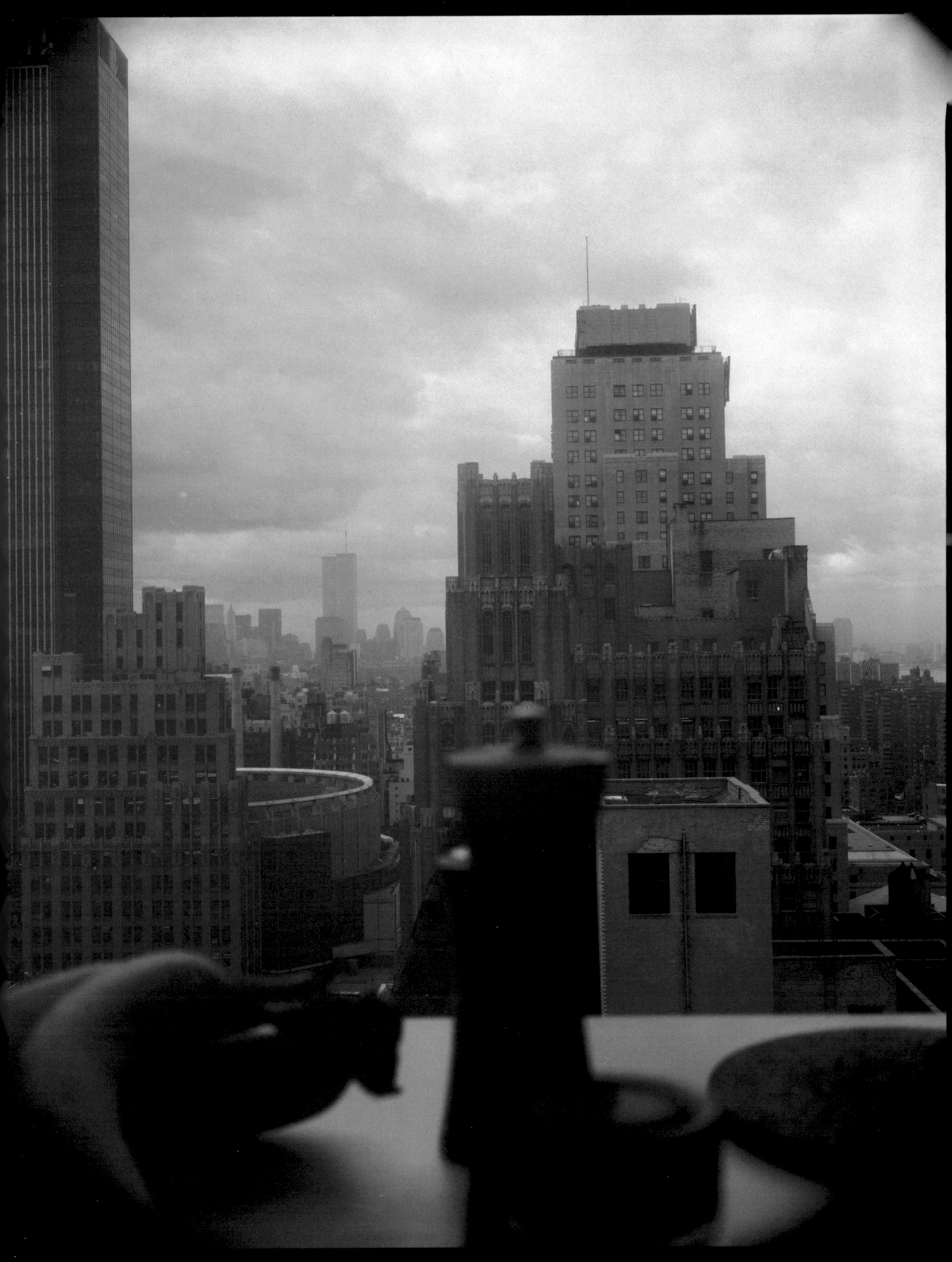

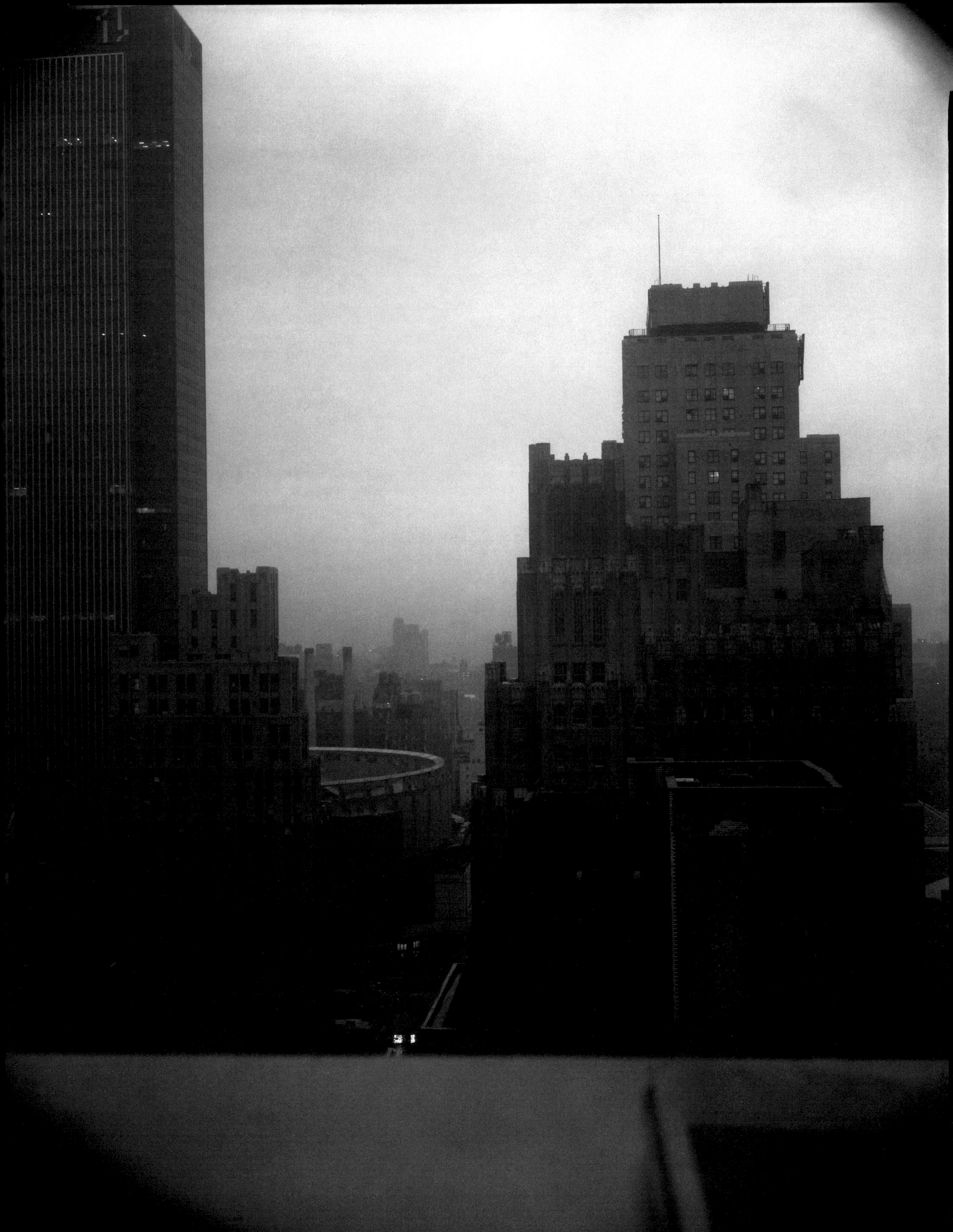

September 18, 1995

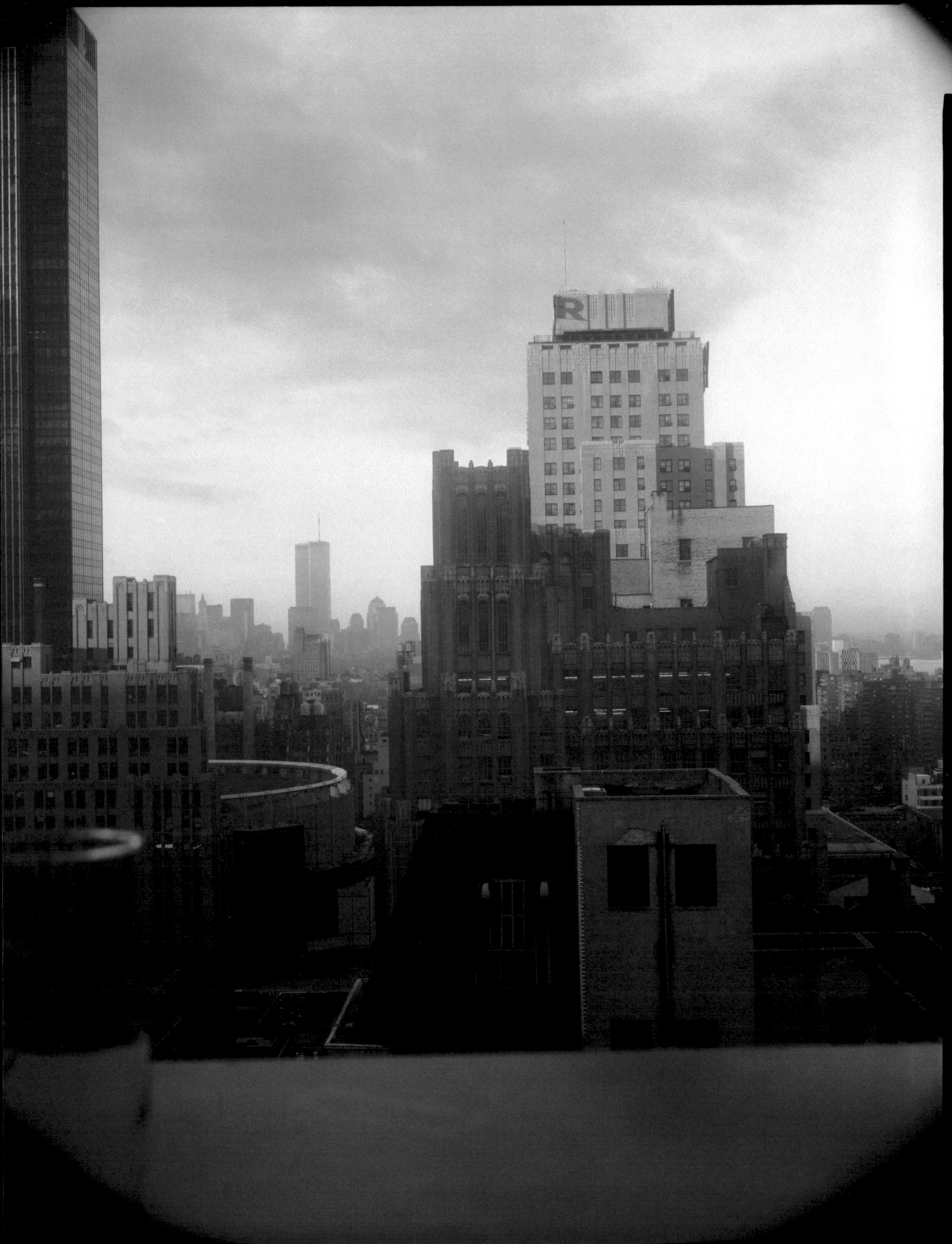

September 19, 1995

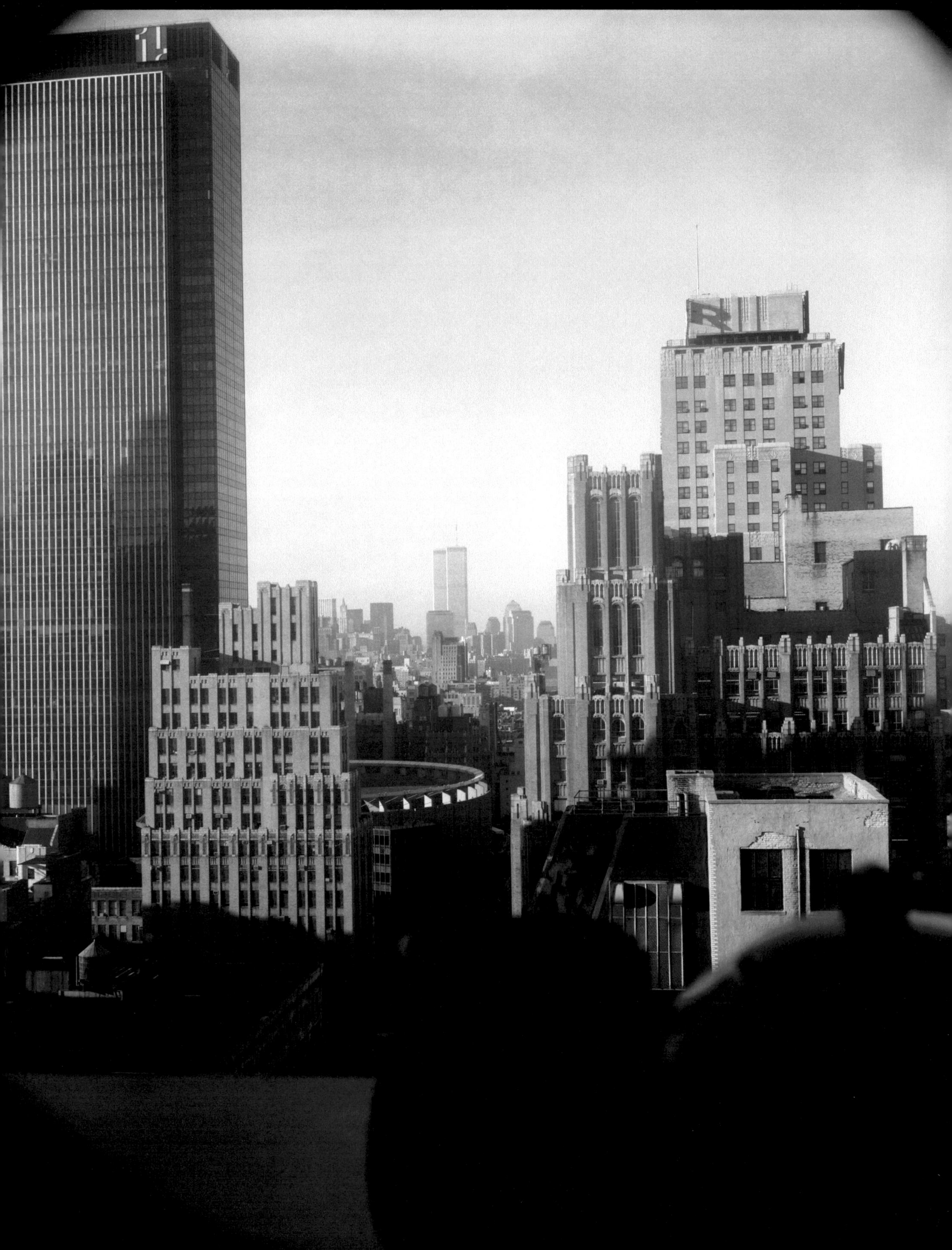

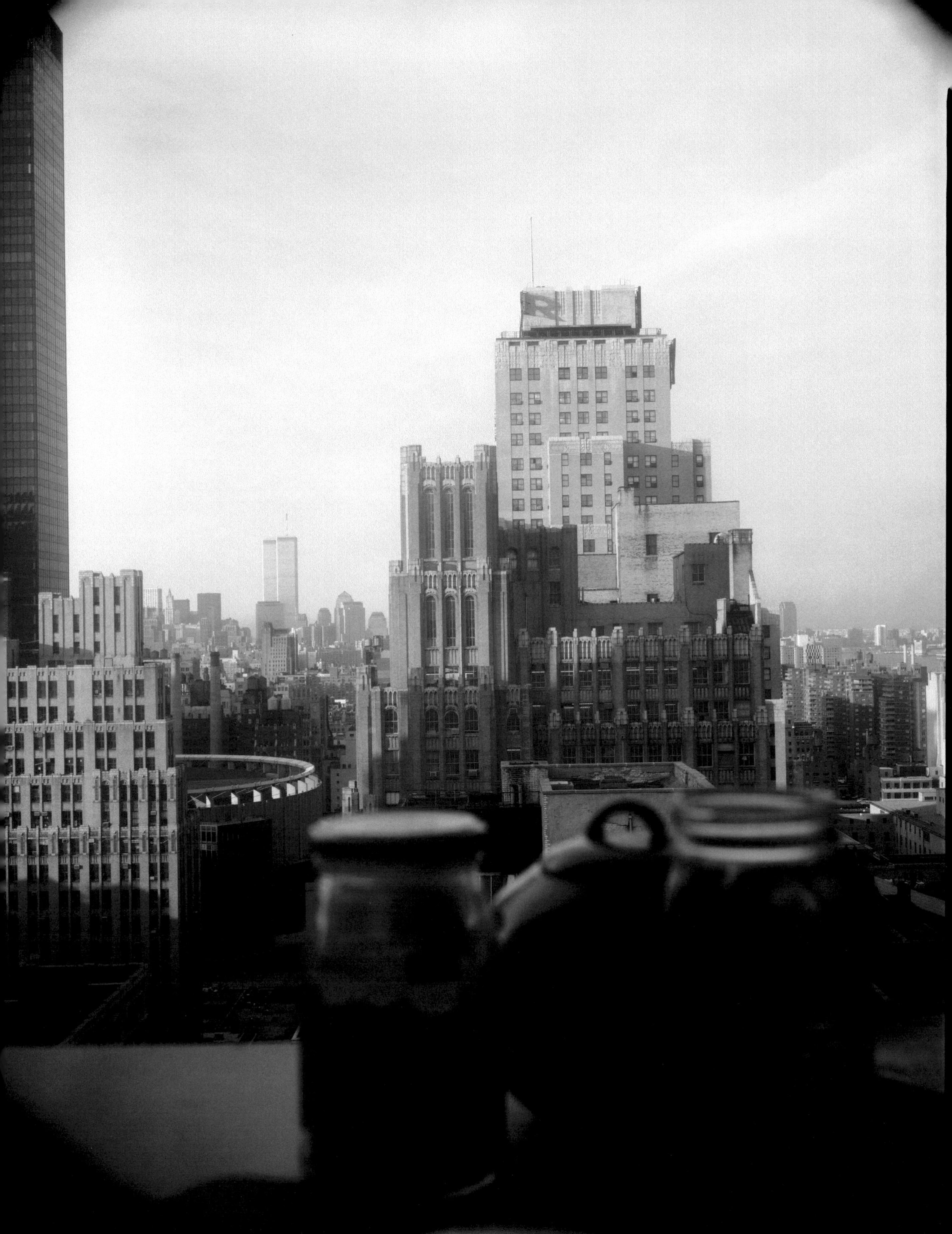

September 21, 1995

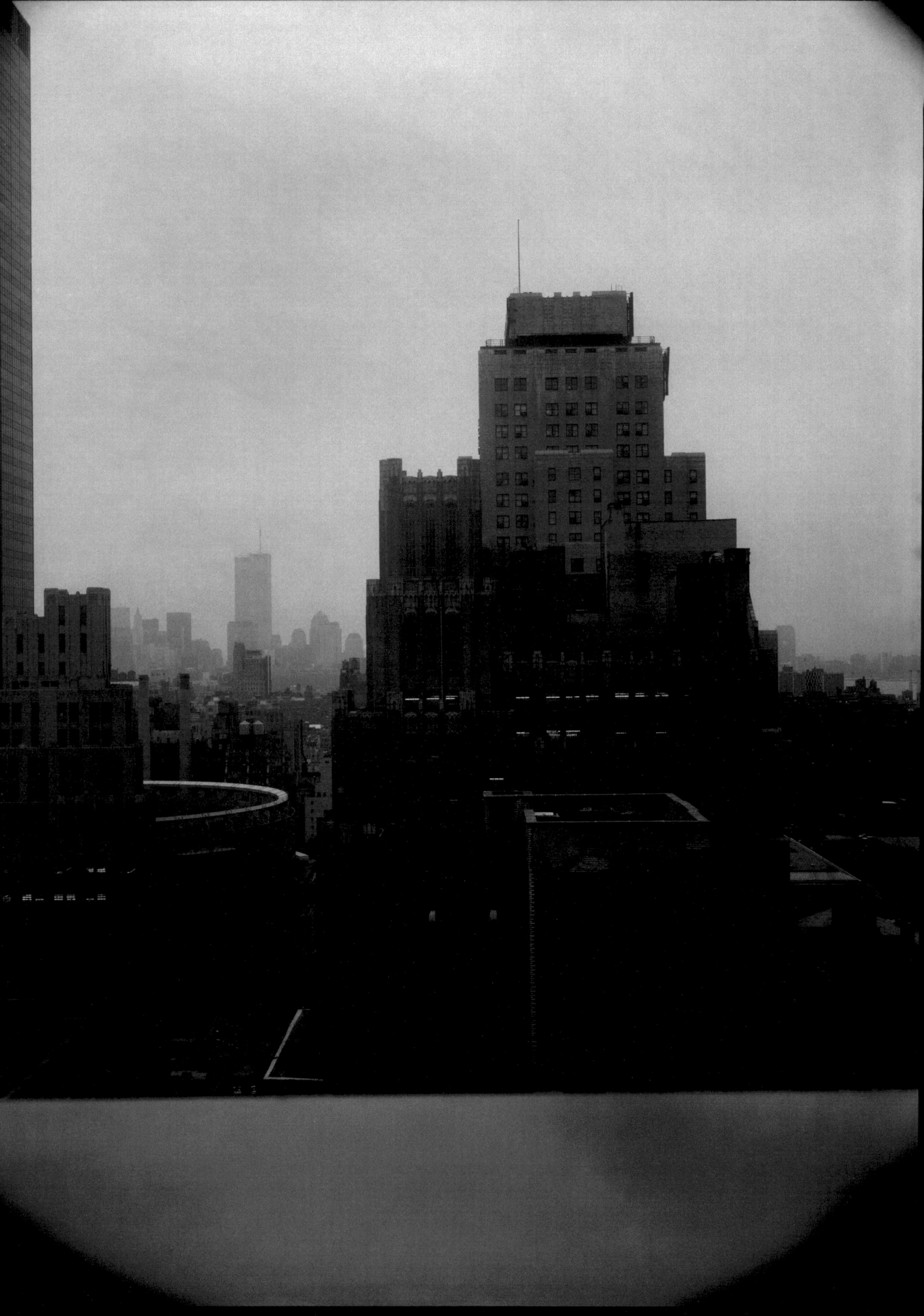

September 22, 1995

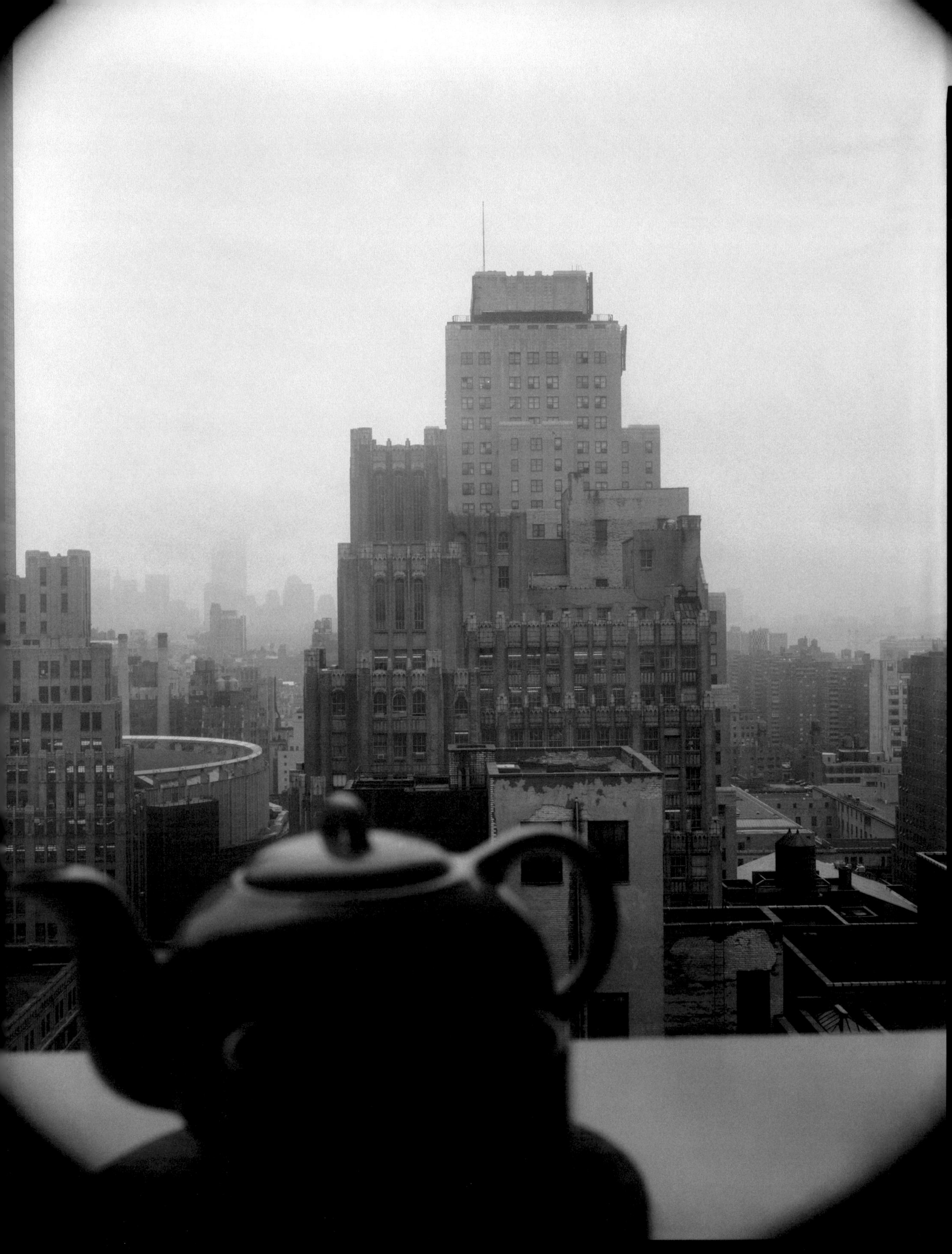

September 23, 1995

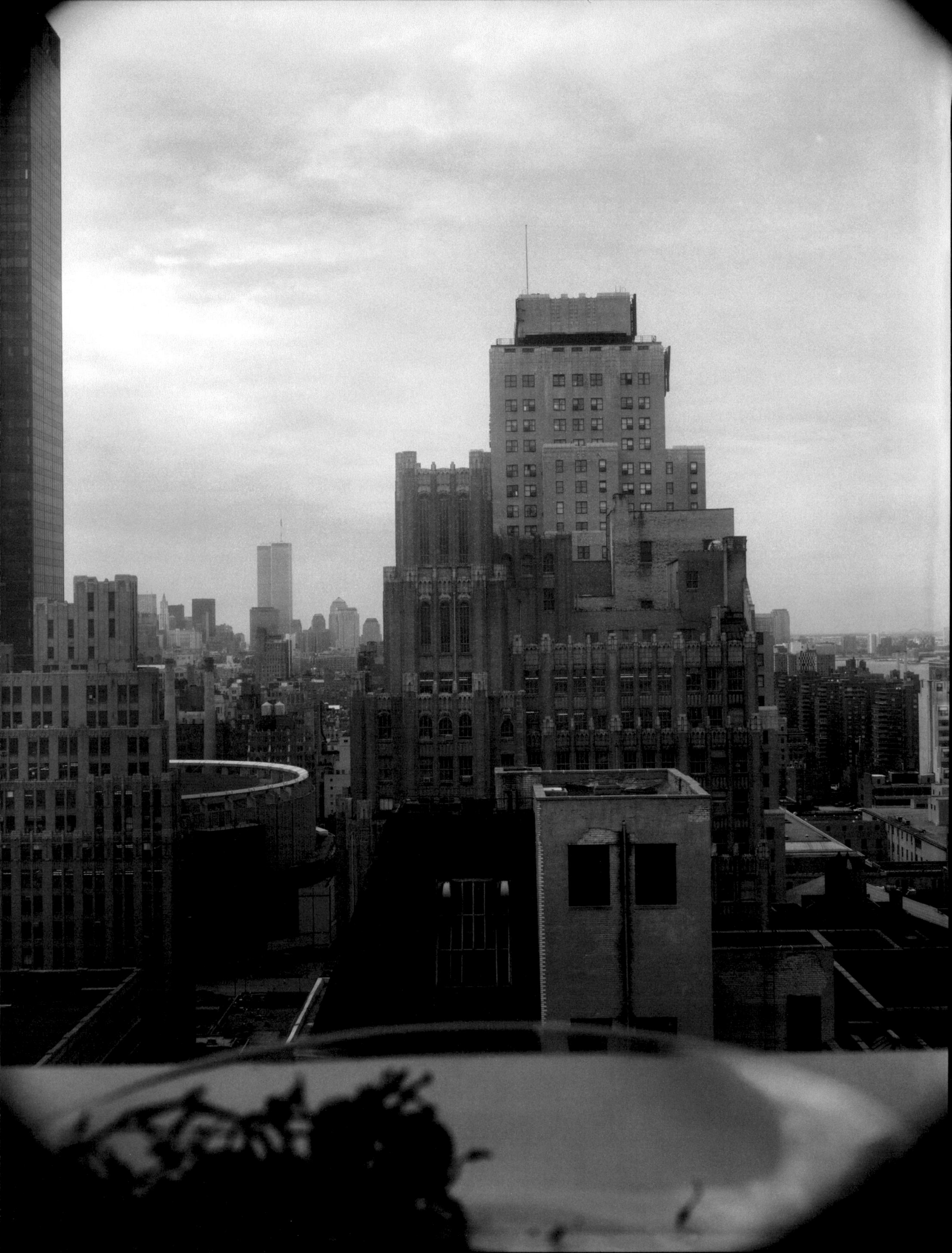

September 24, 1995

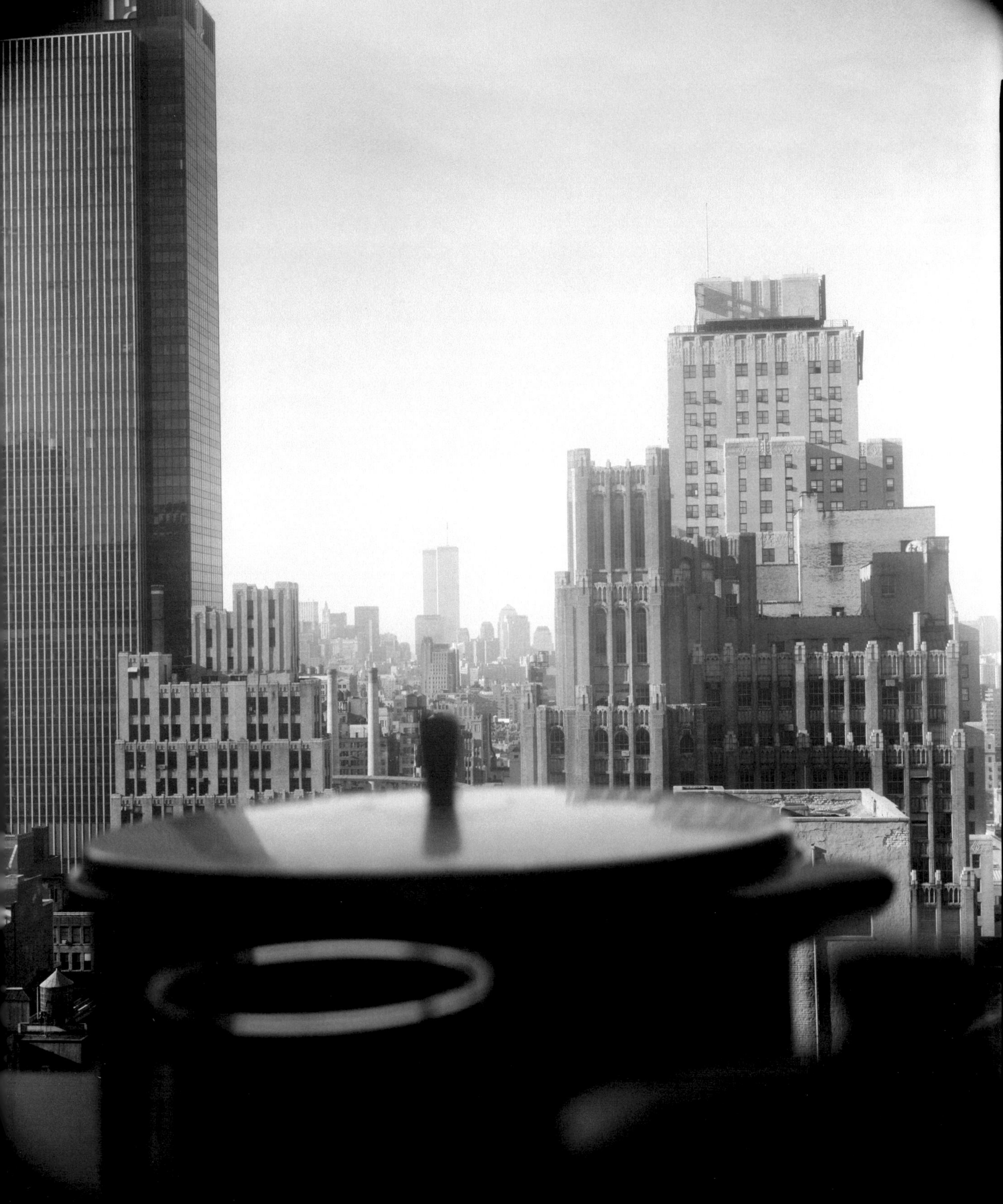

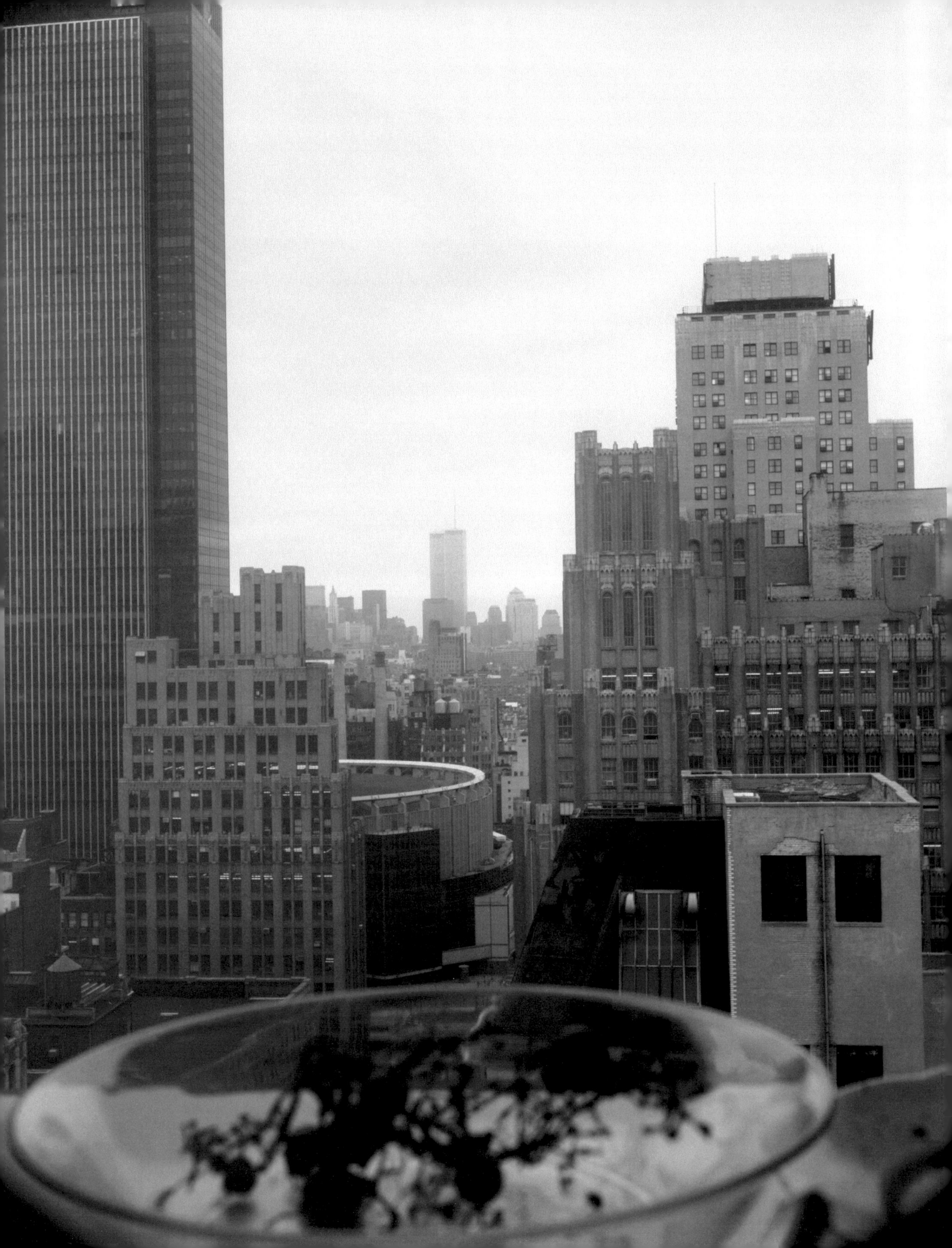

September 26, 1995

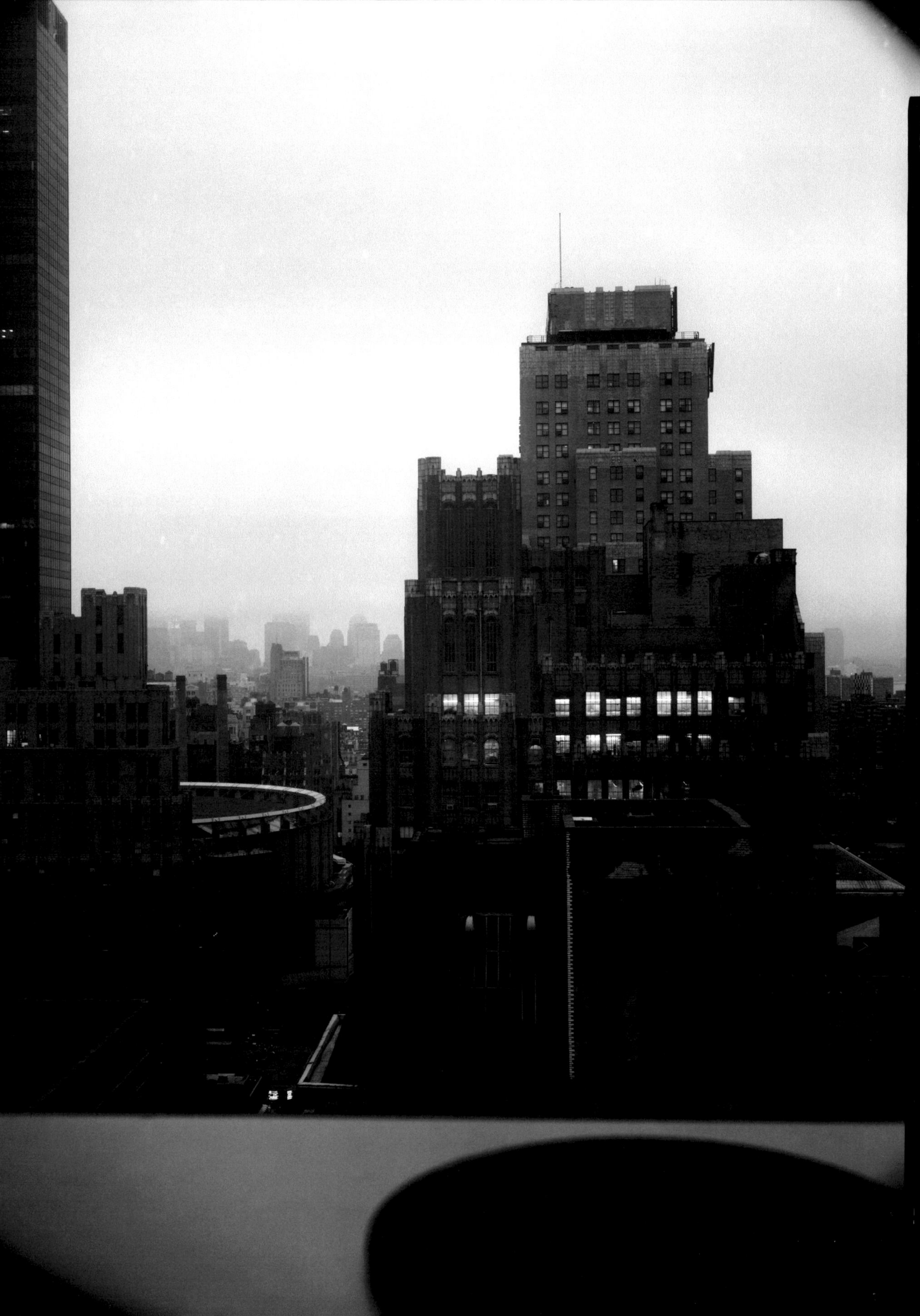

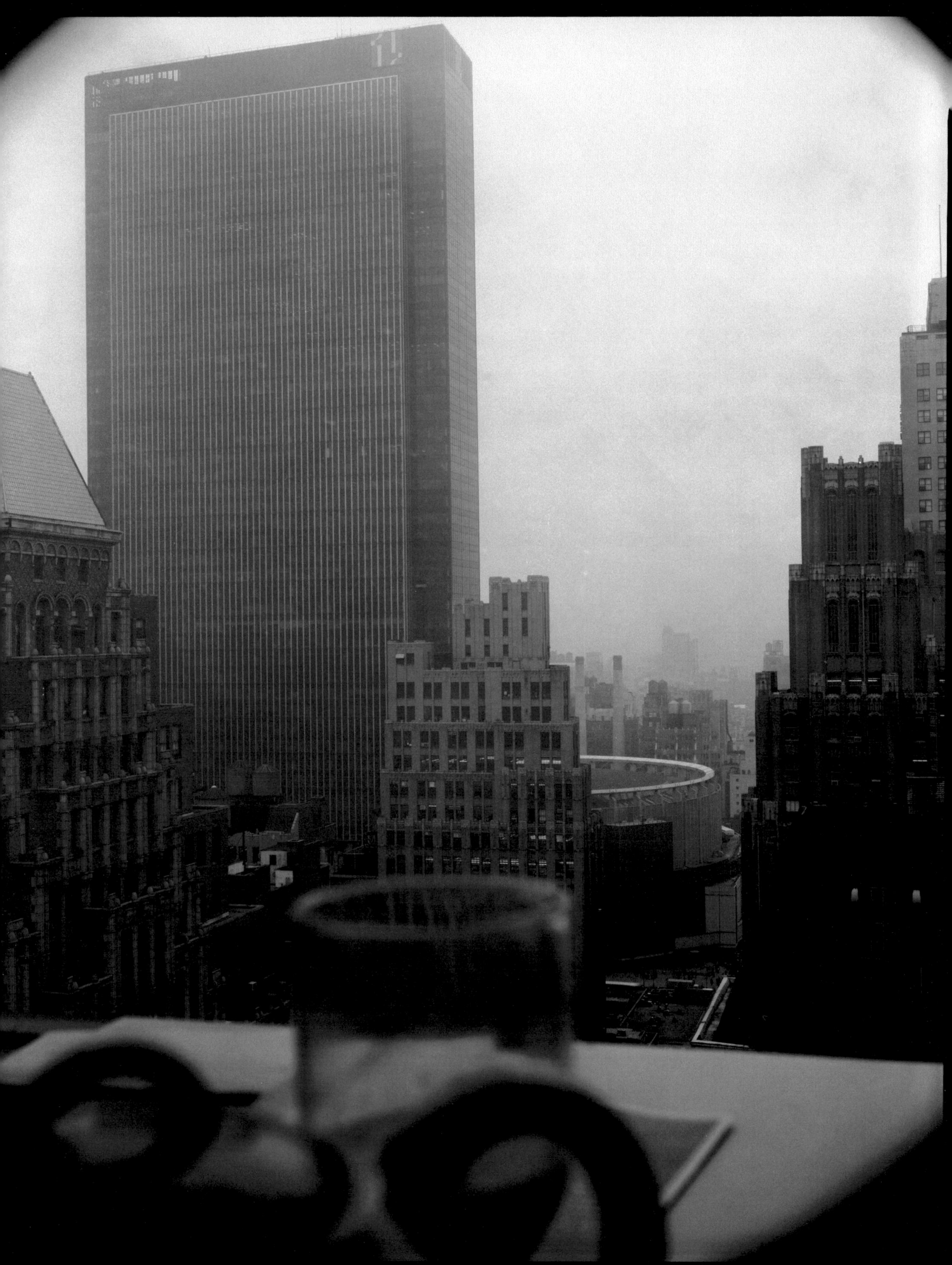

September 28, 1995

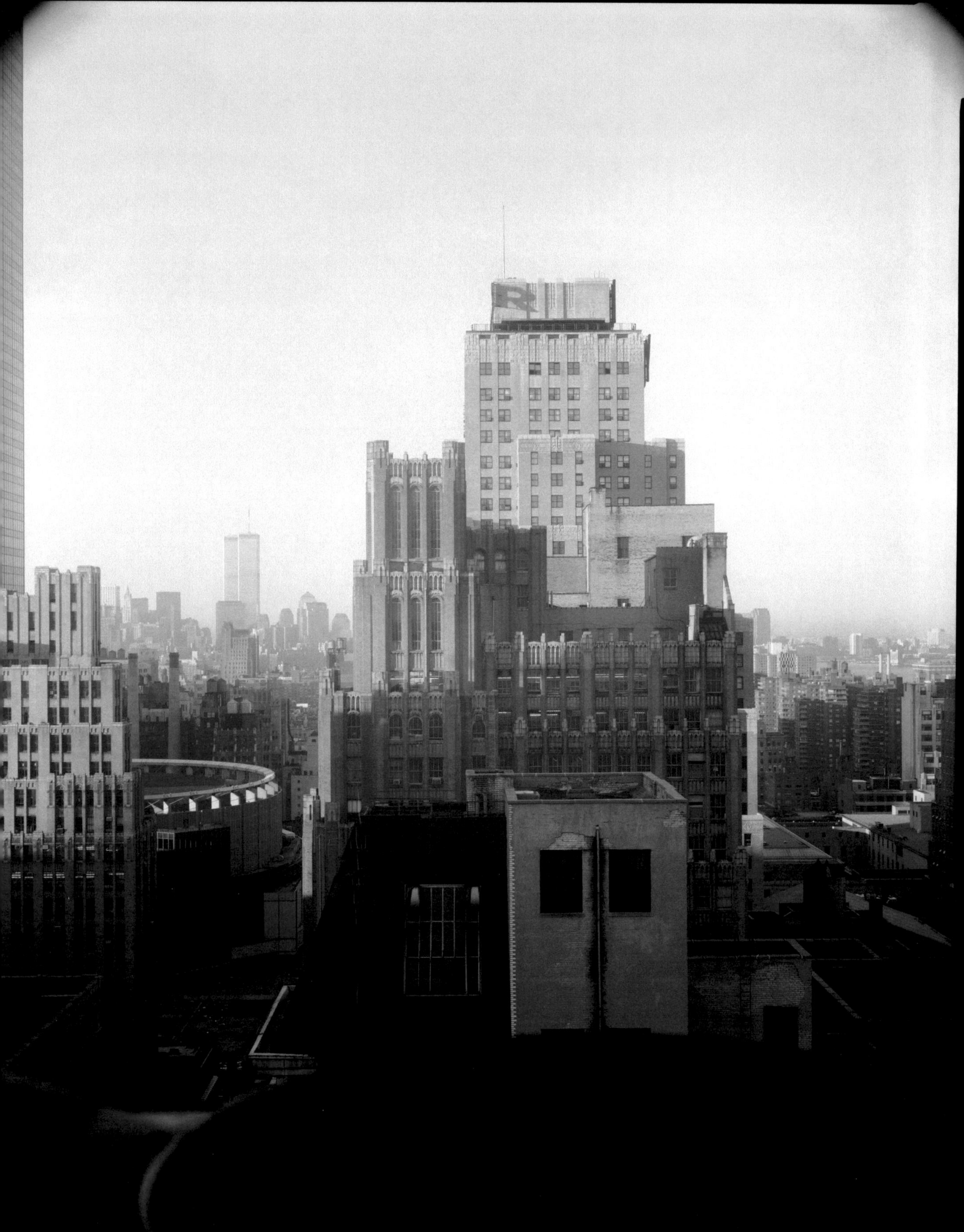

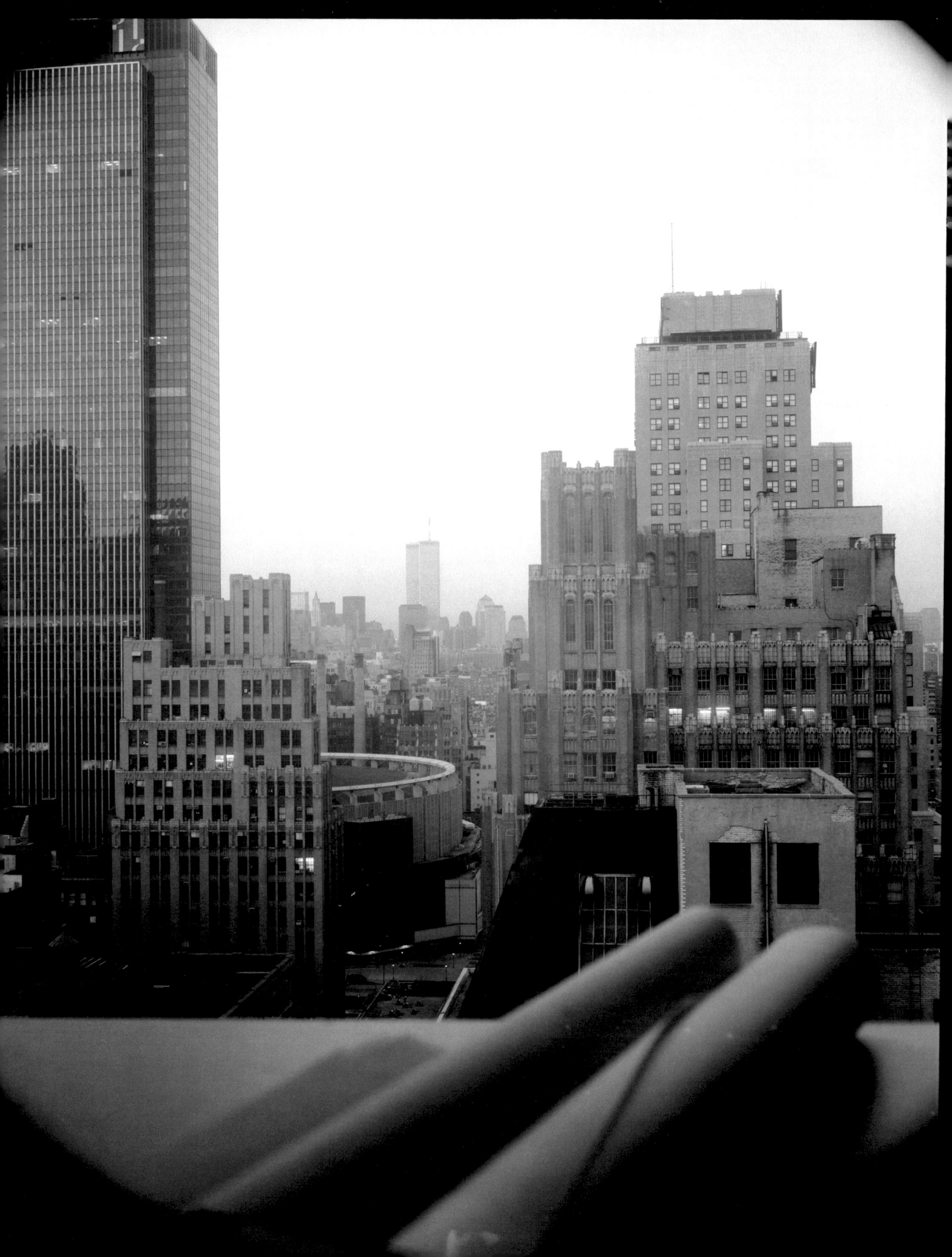

September 30, 1995

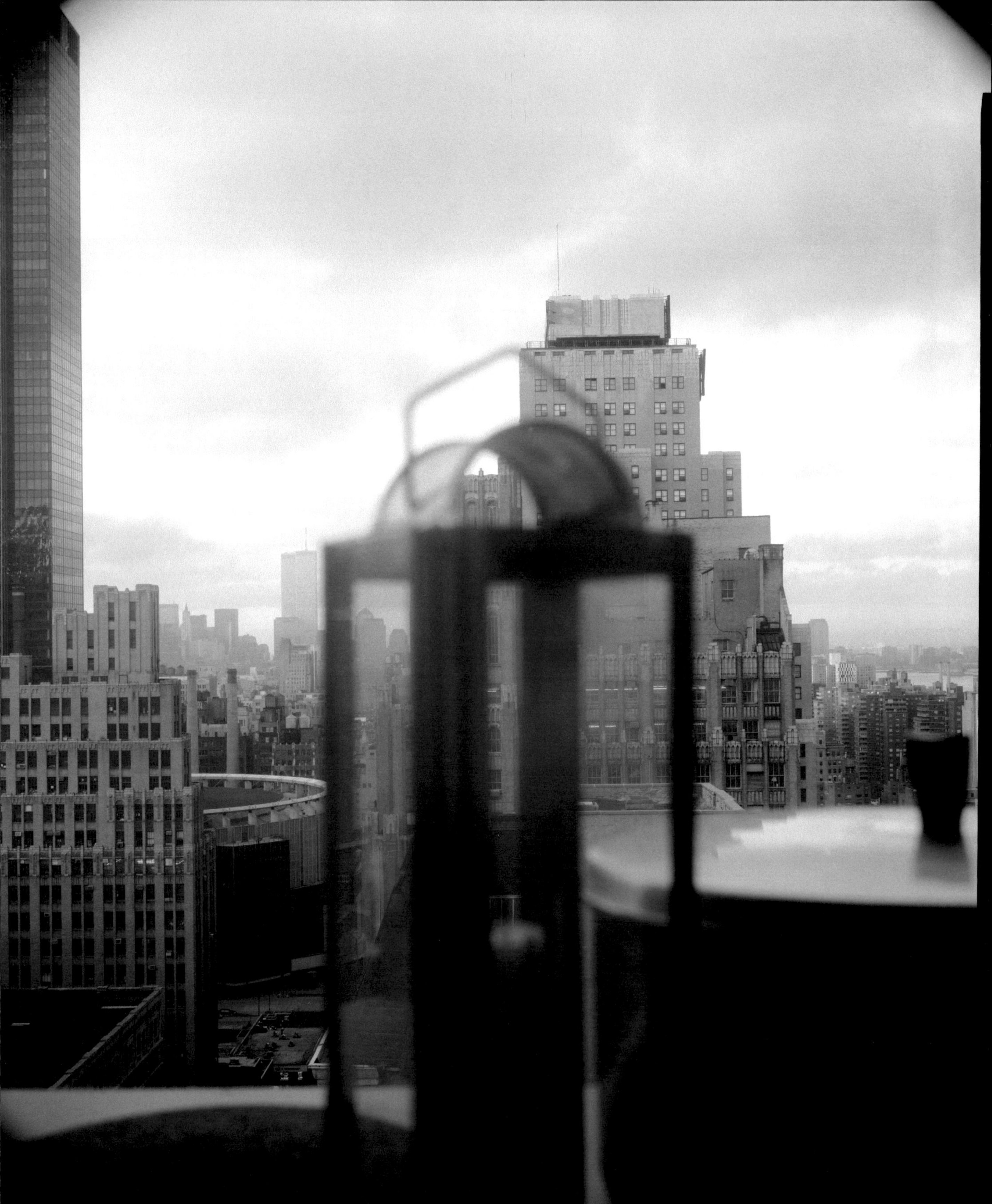

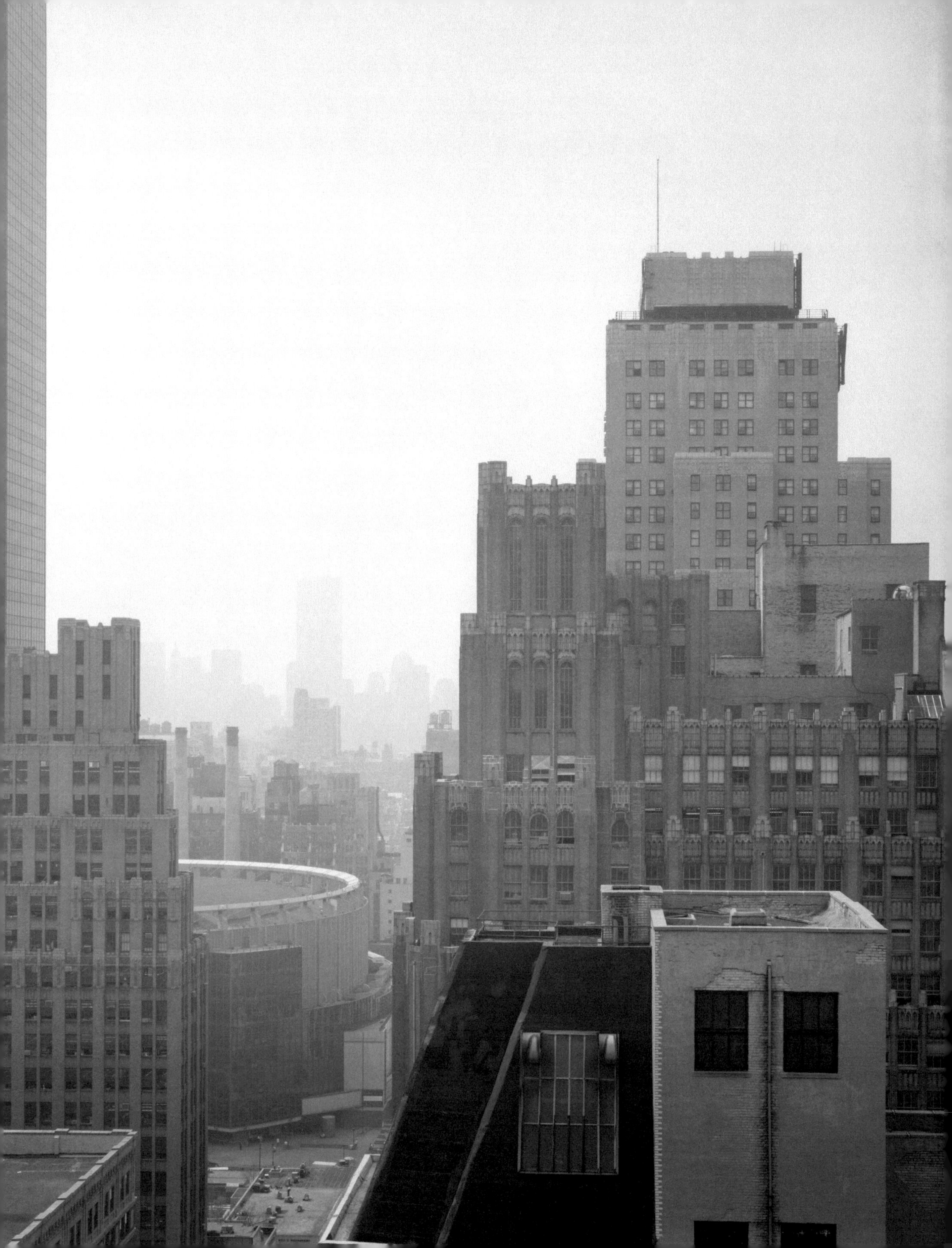

September 6, 1996

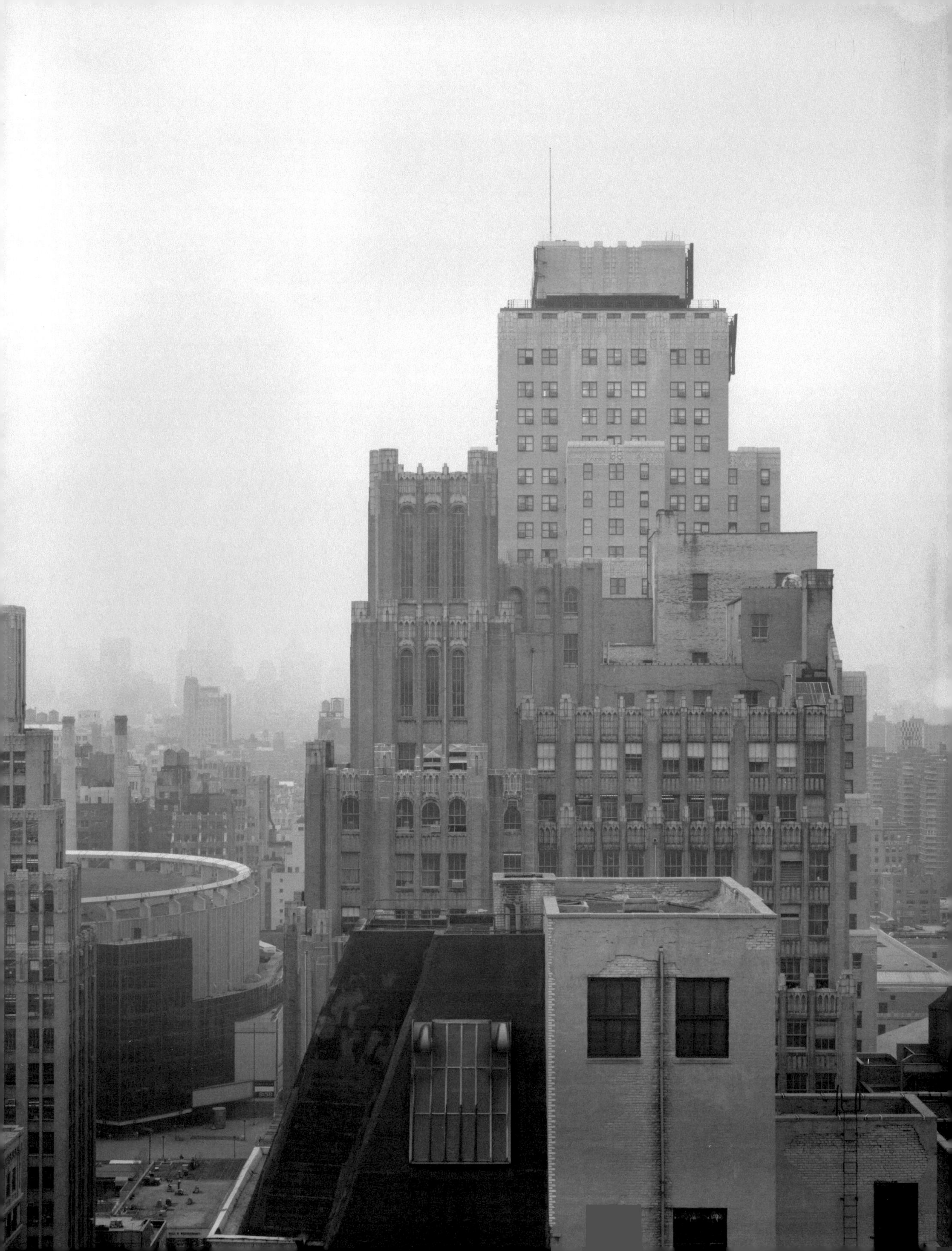

September 7, 1996

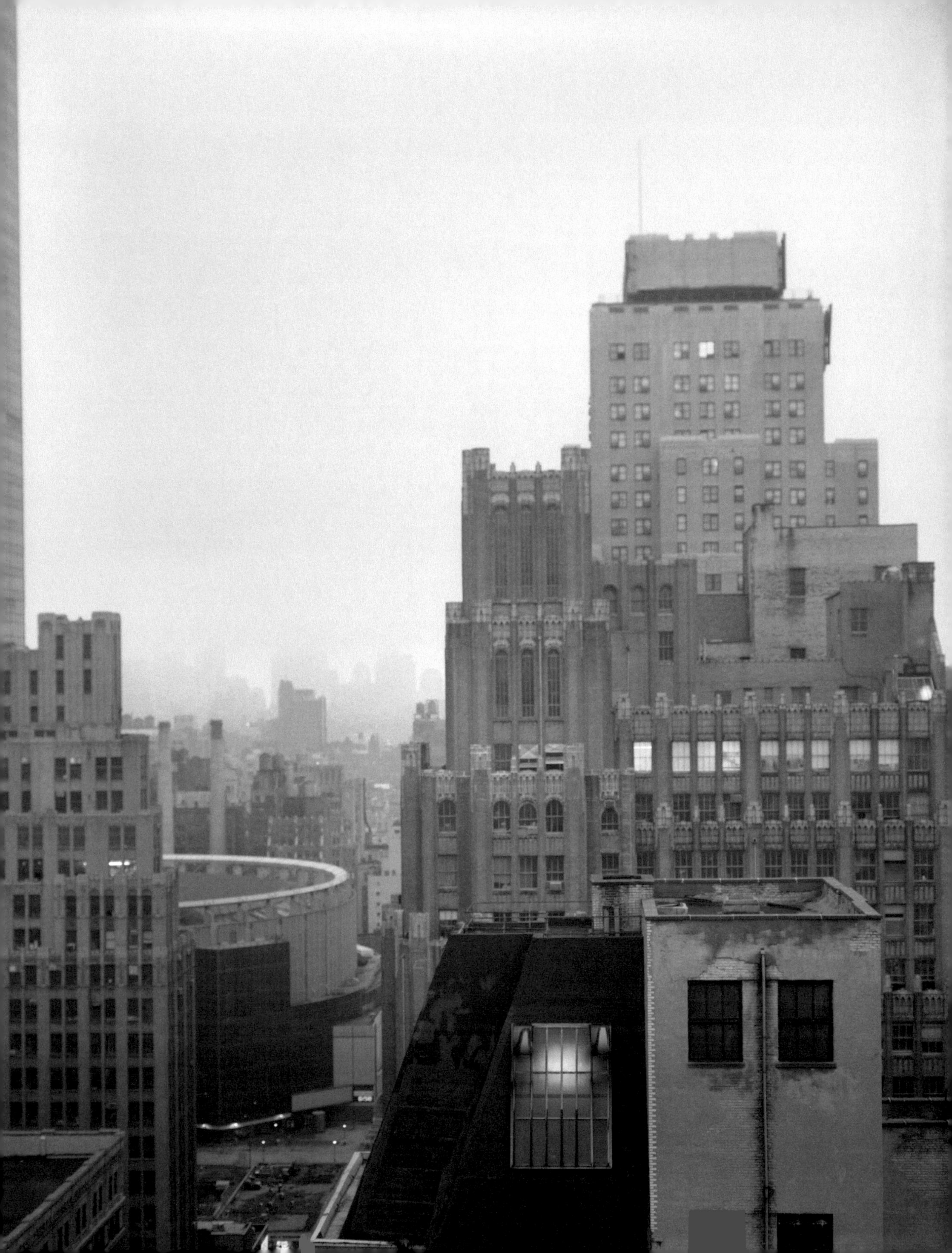

September 8, 1996

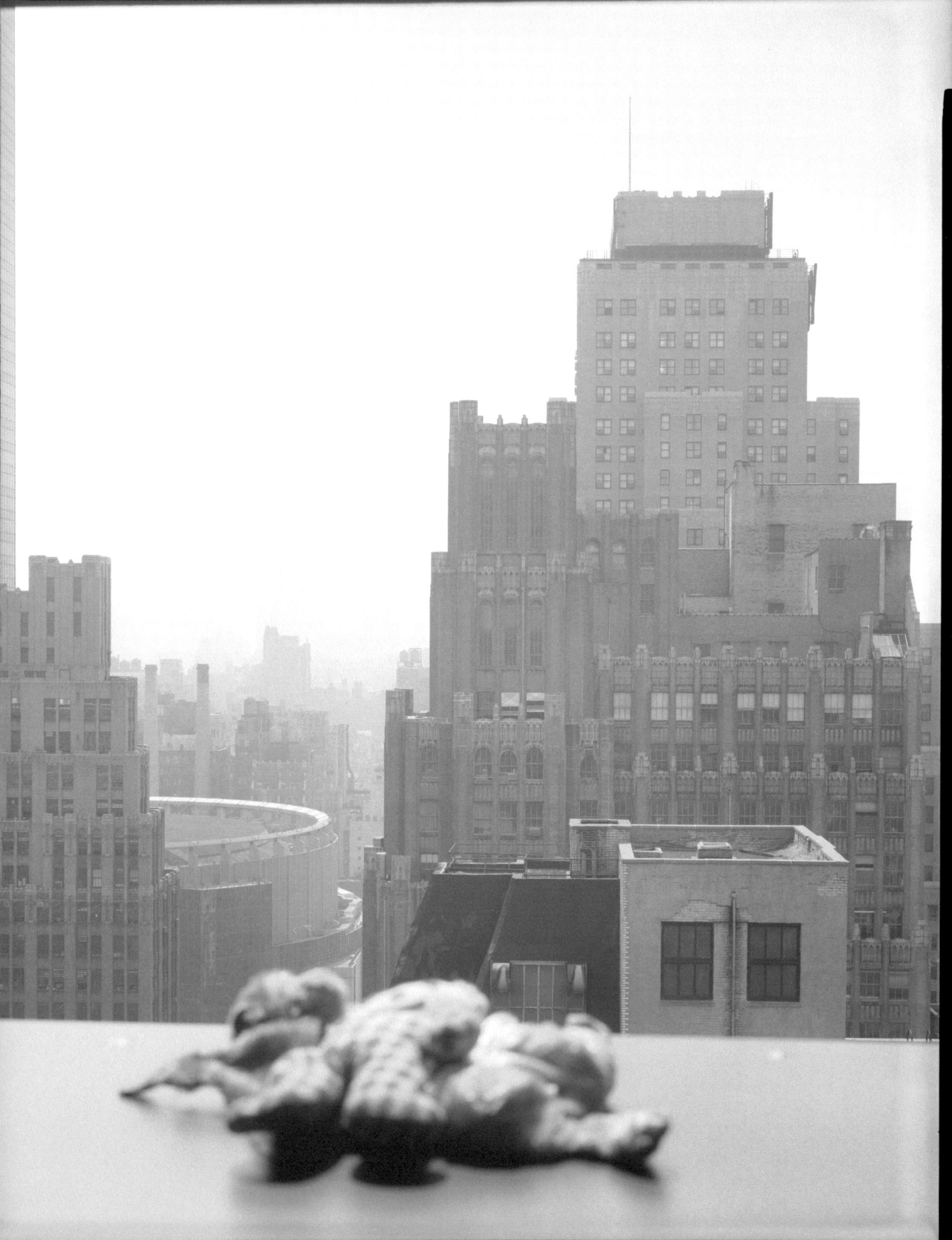

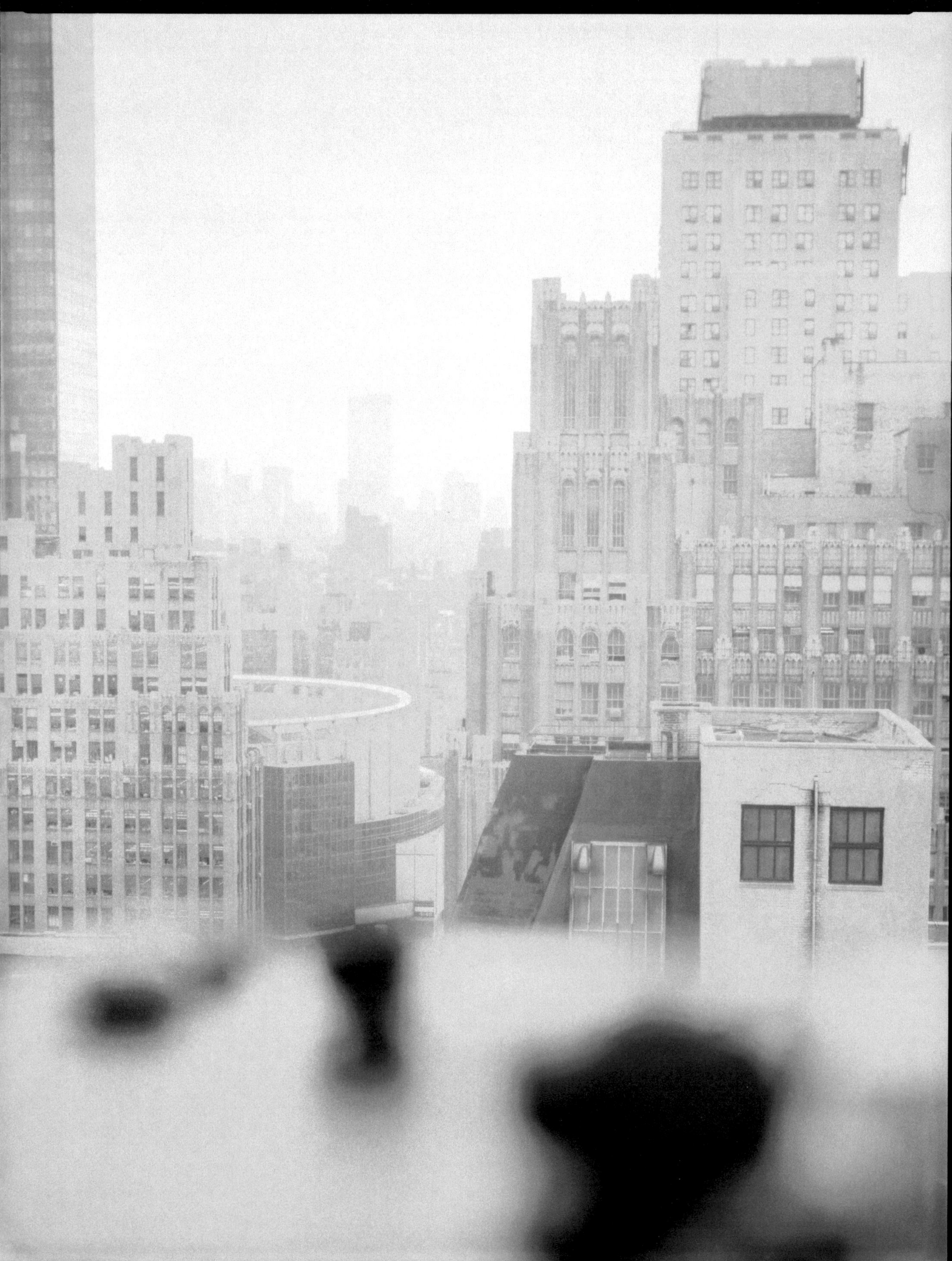

September 10, 1996

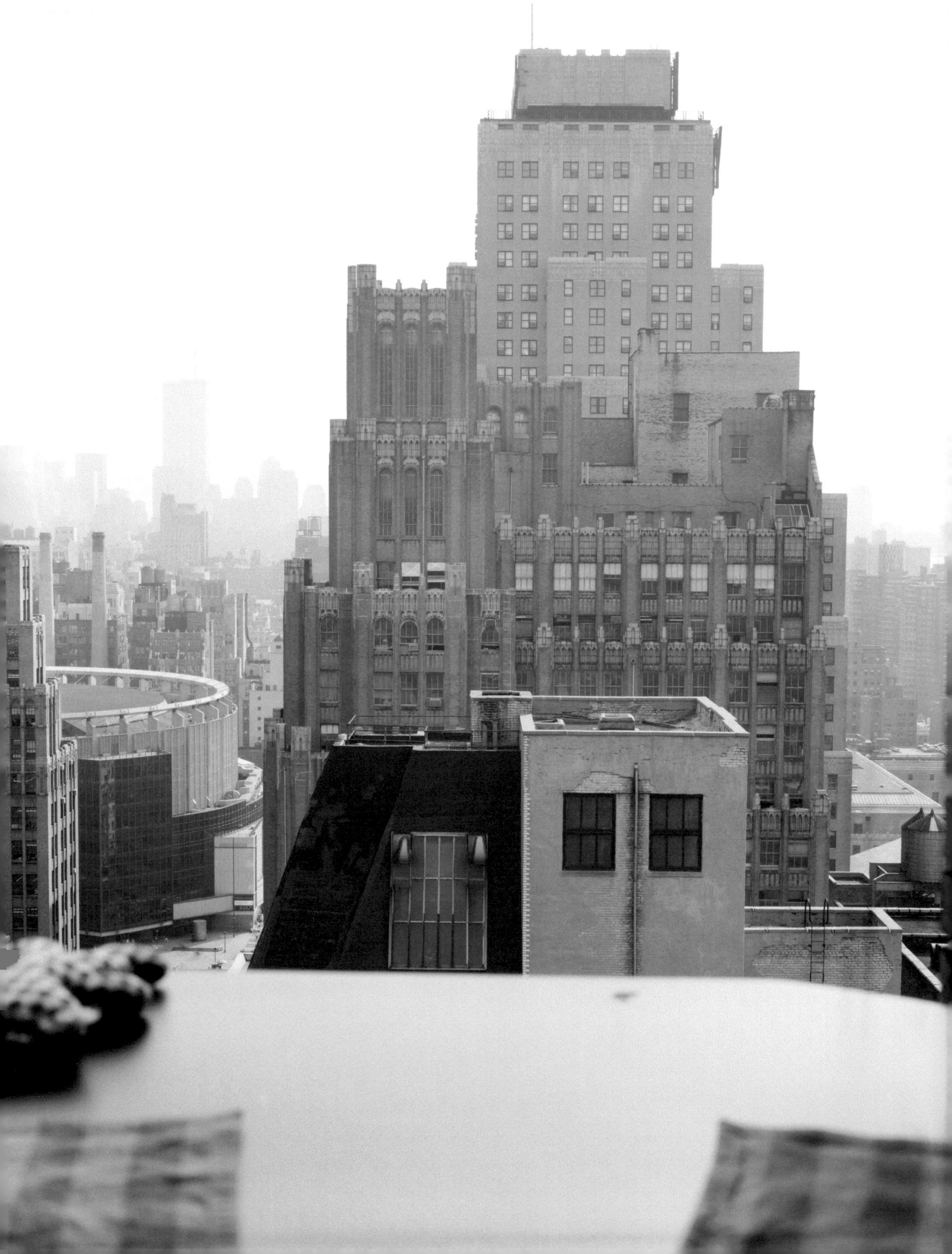

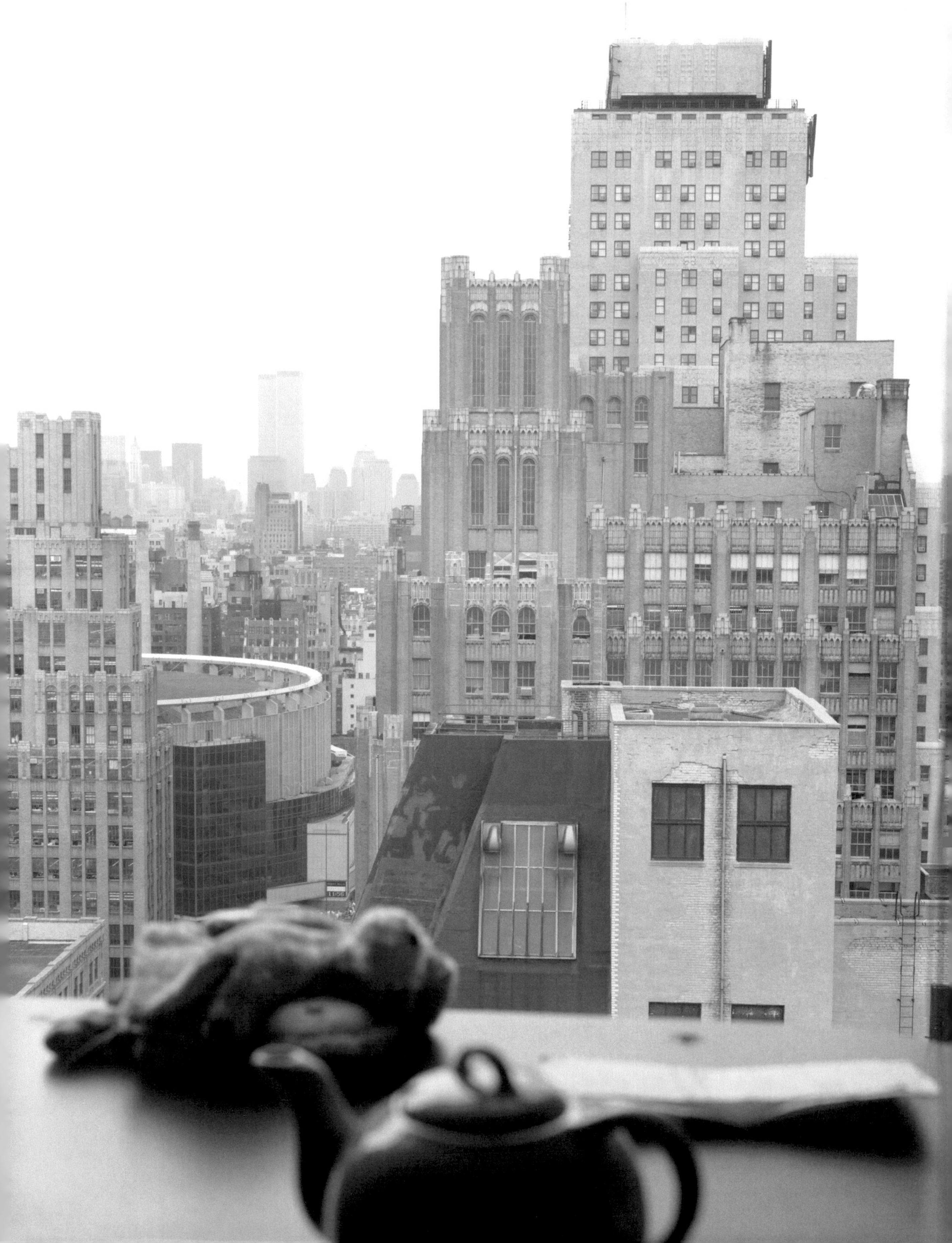

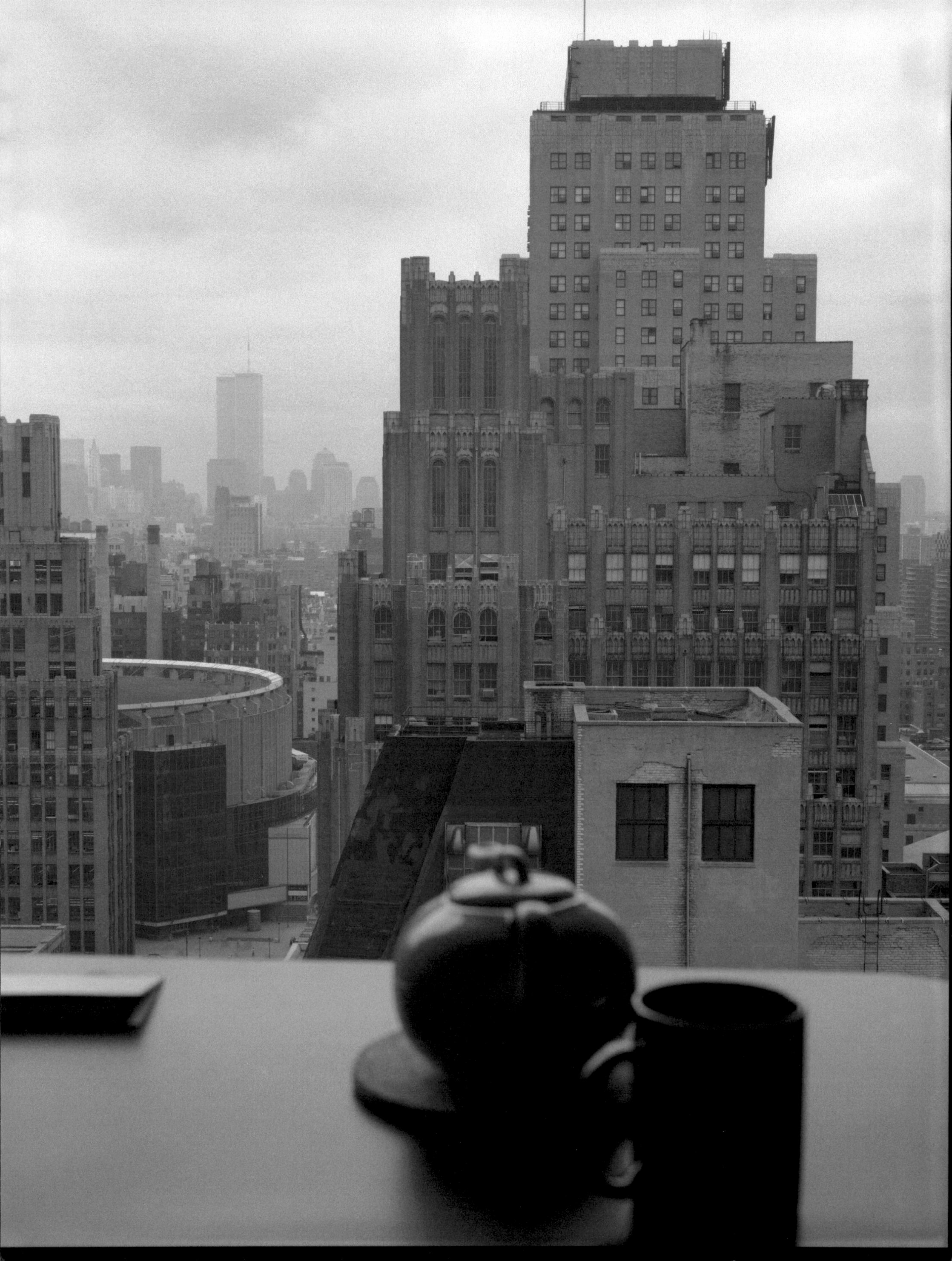

September 13, 1996

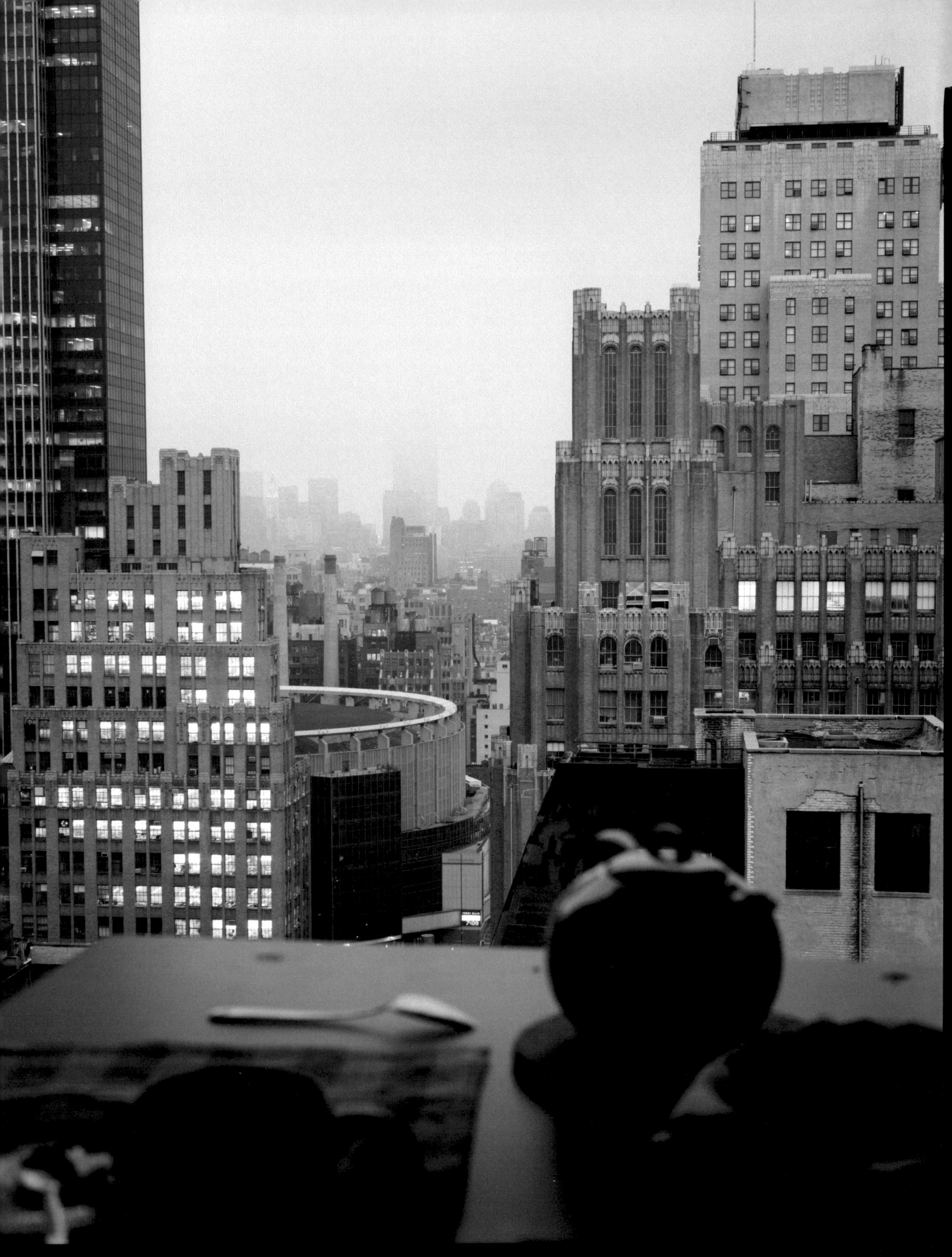

September 14, 1996

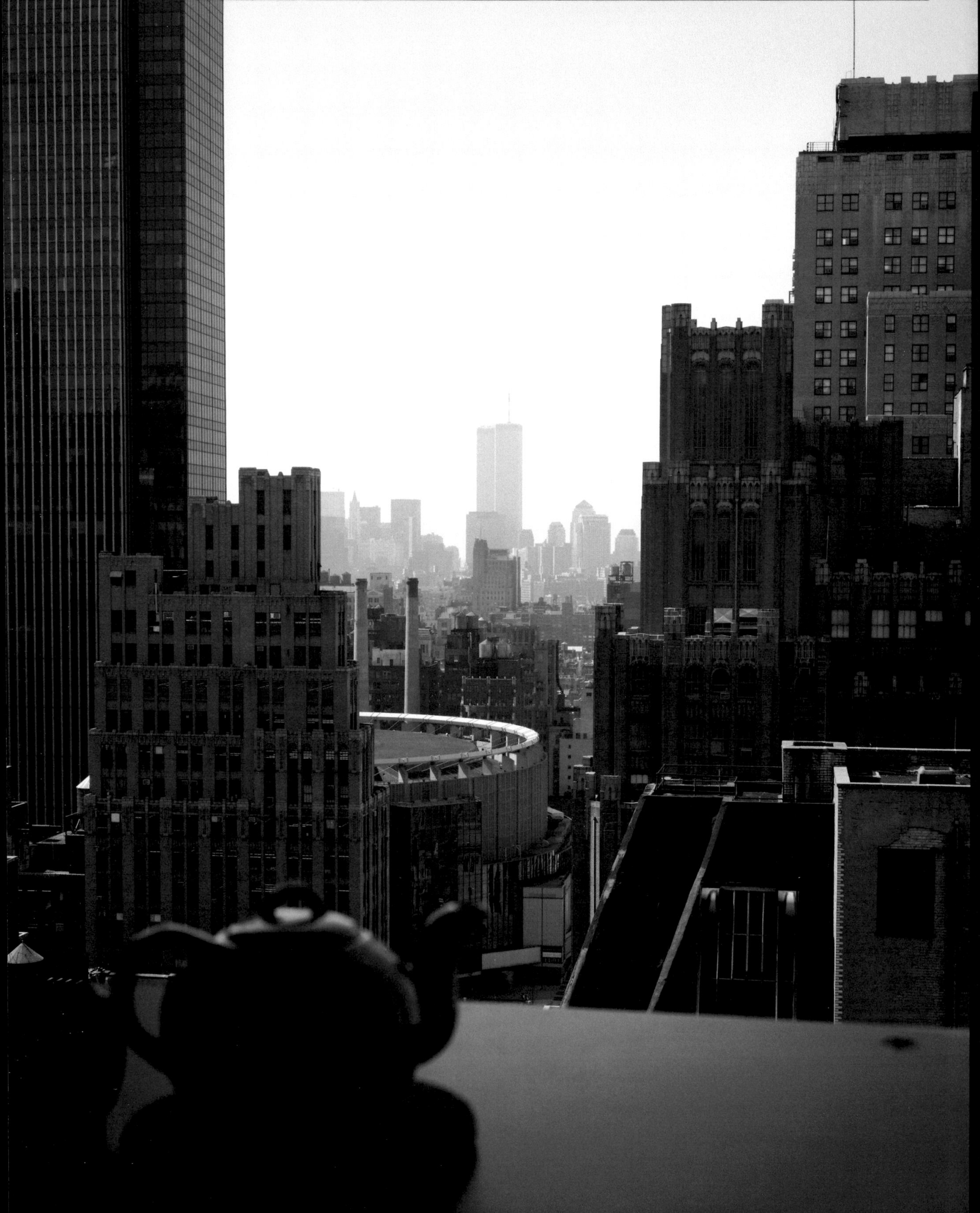

September 15, 1996

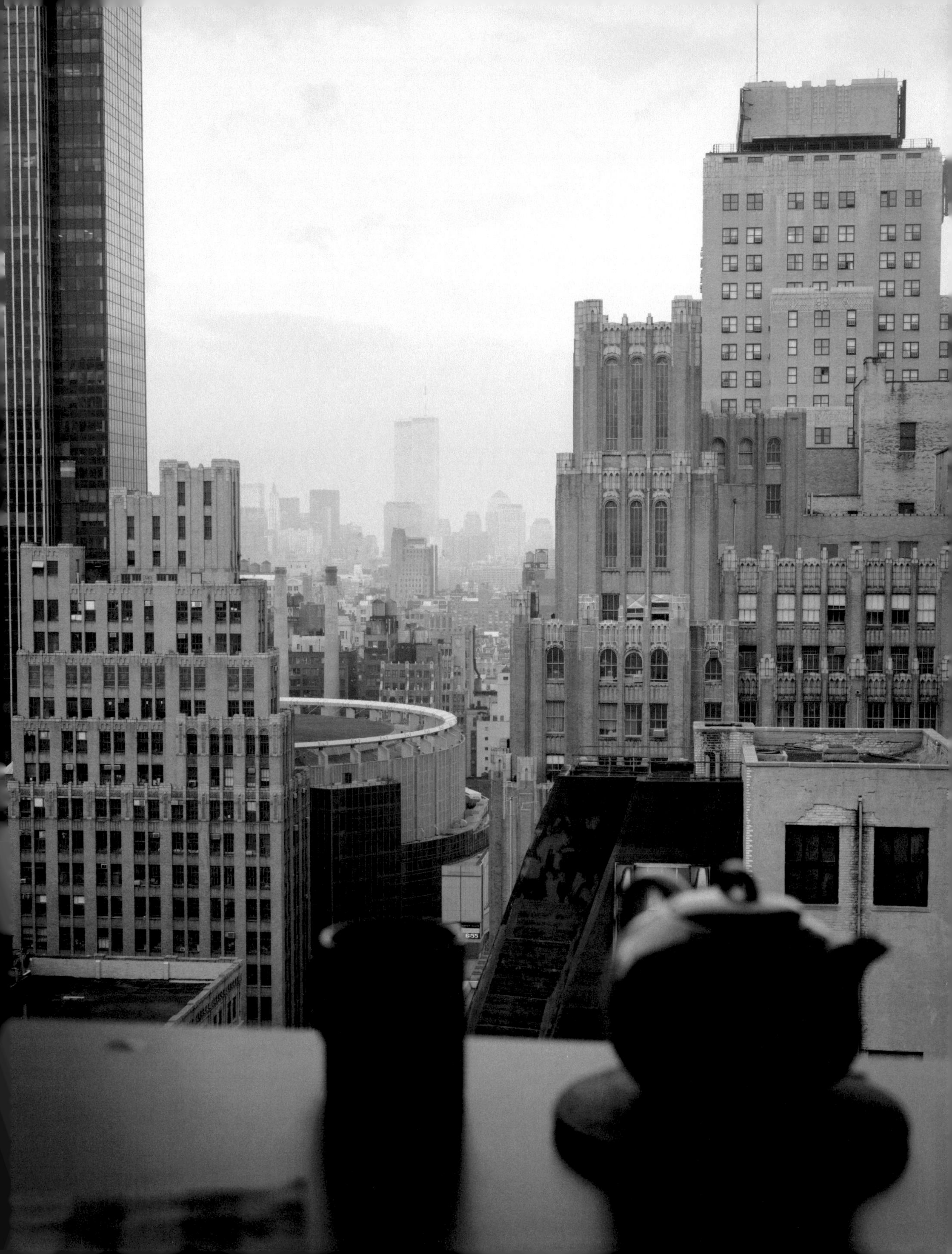

September 16, 1996

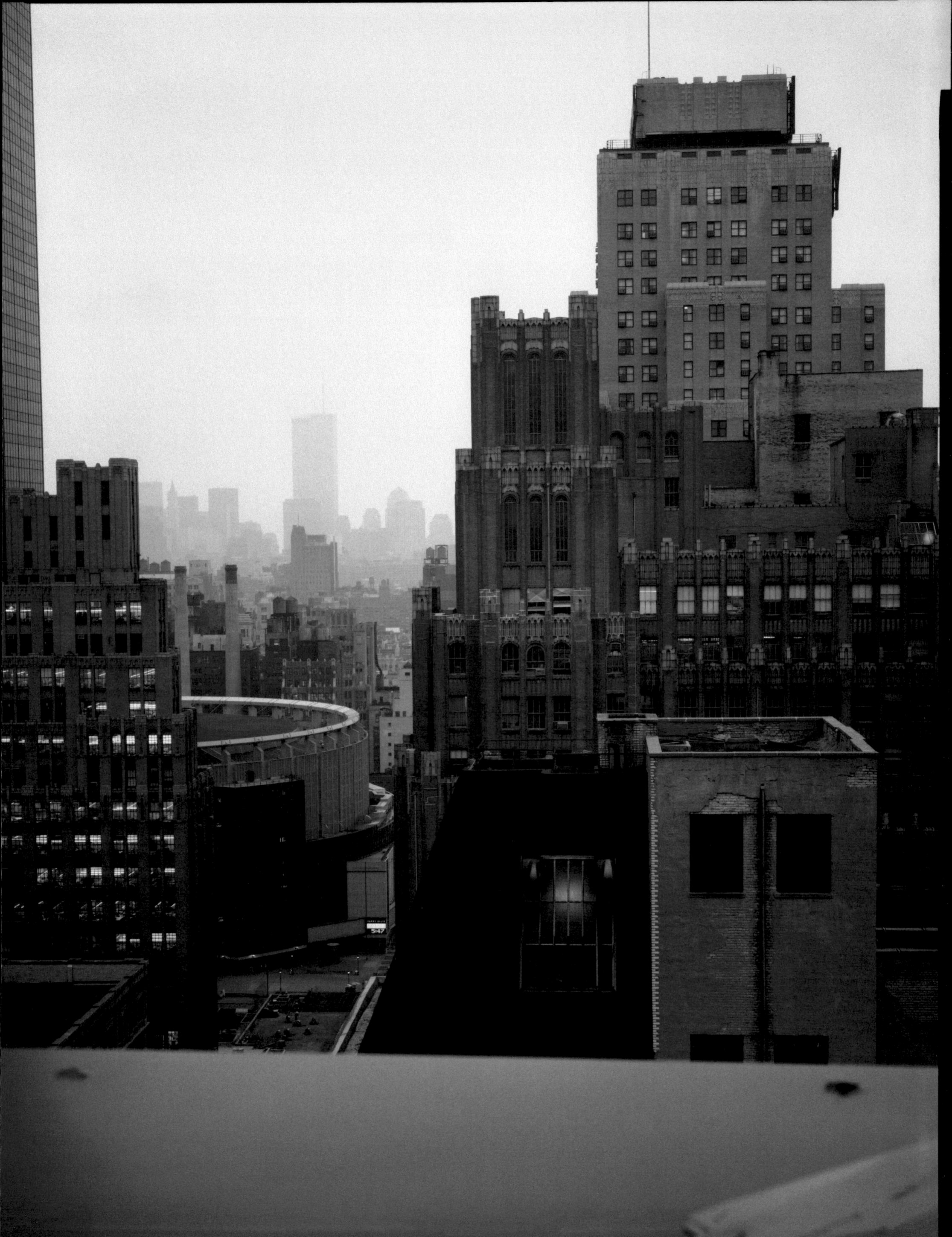

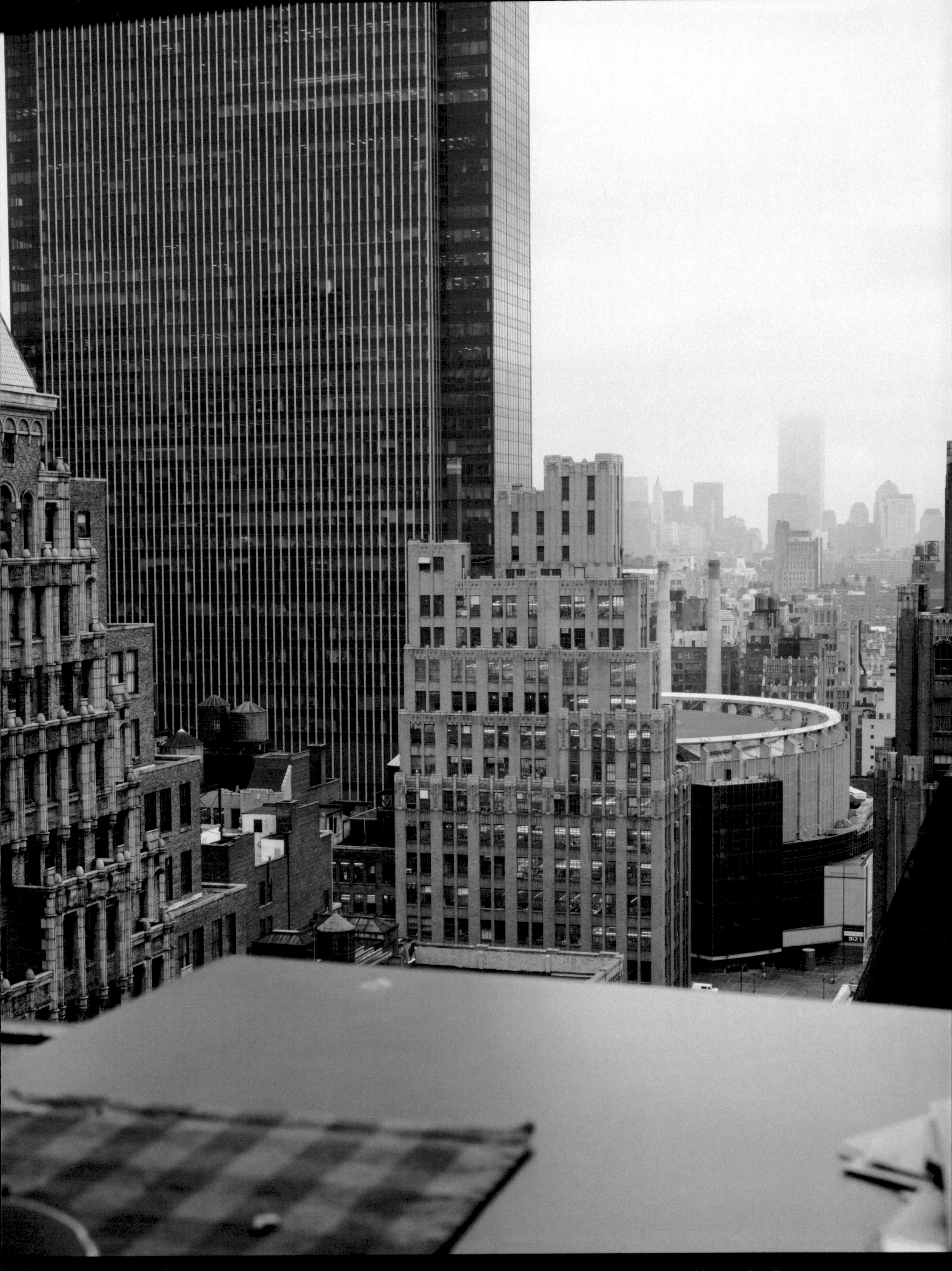

September 18, 1996

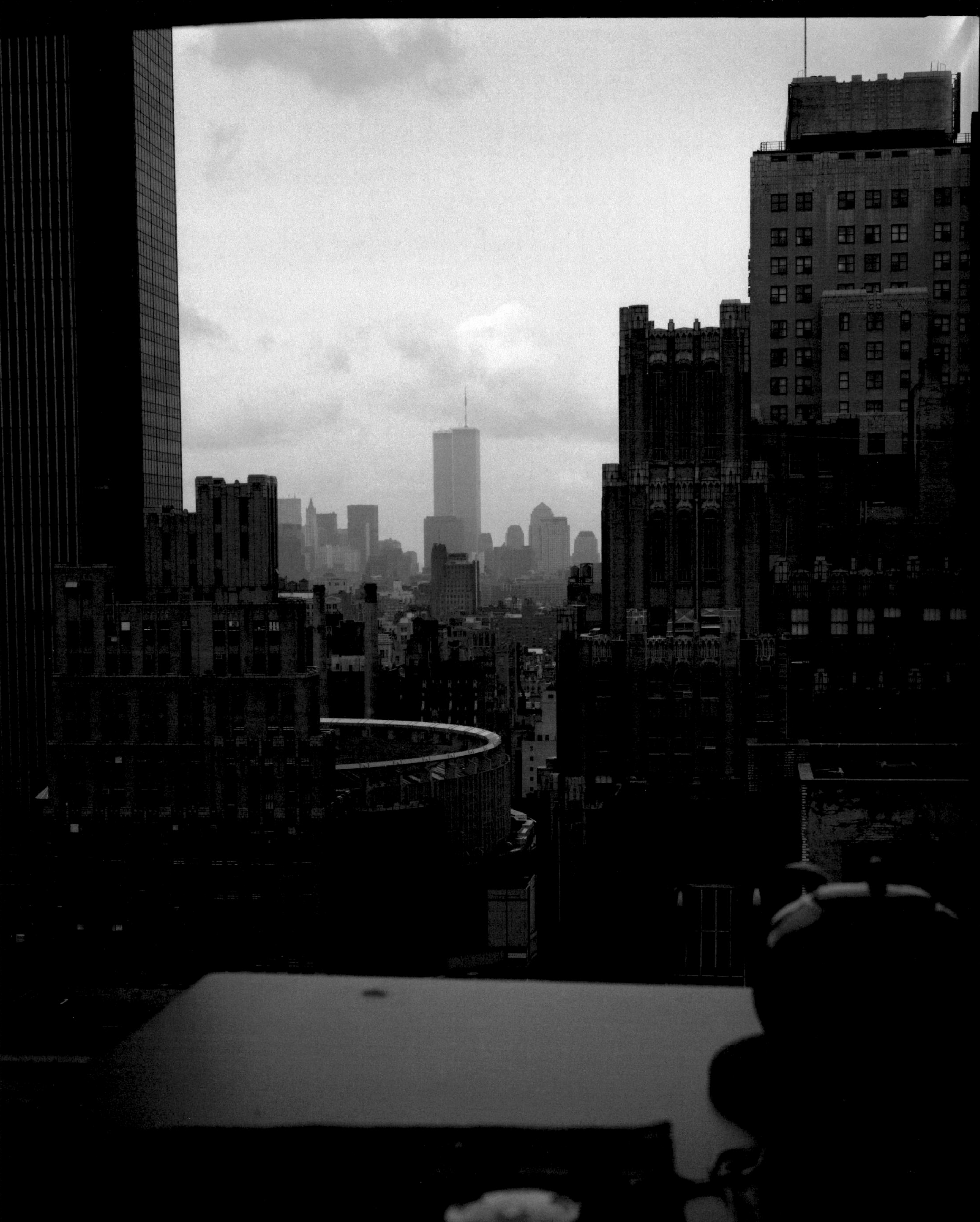

September 19, 1996

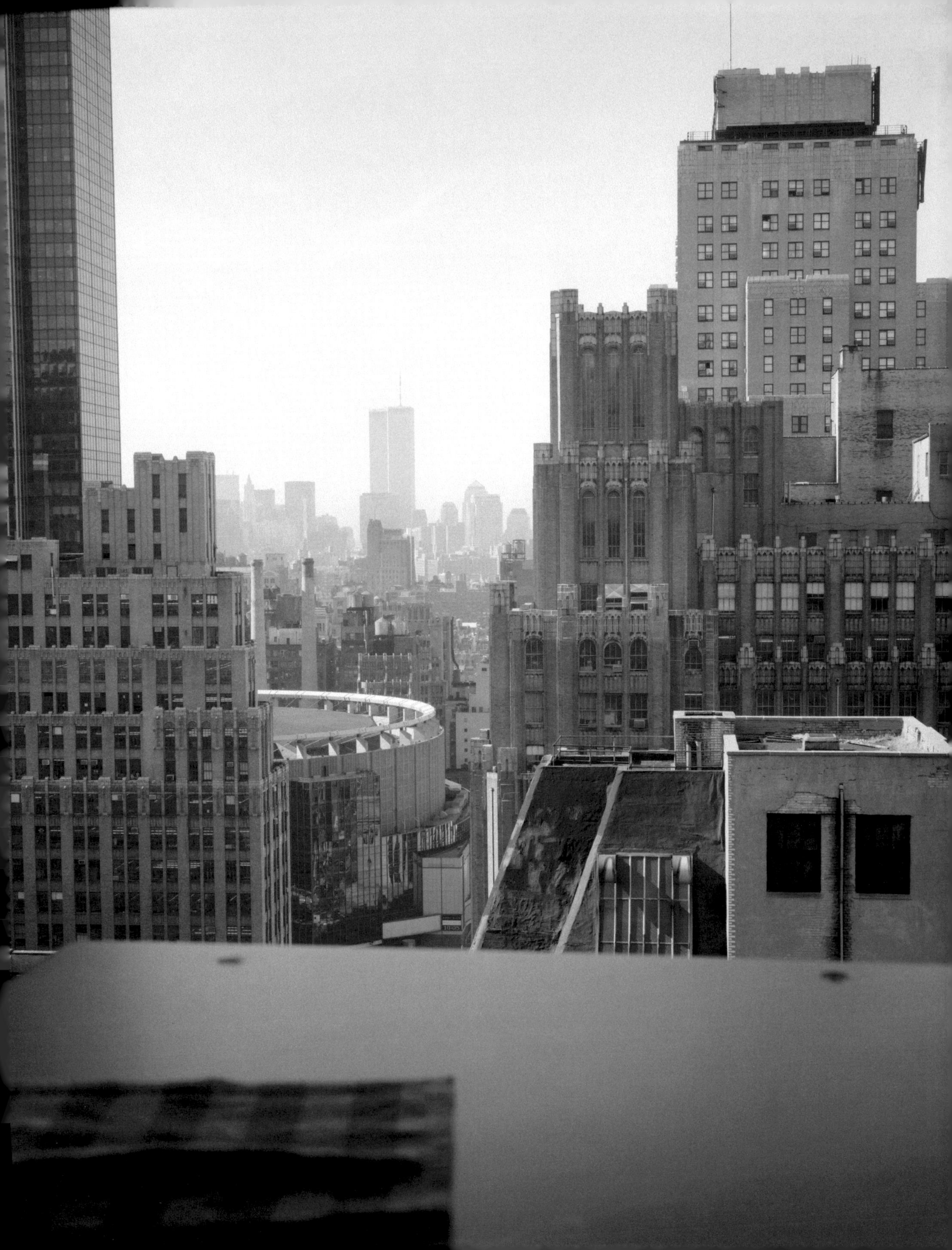

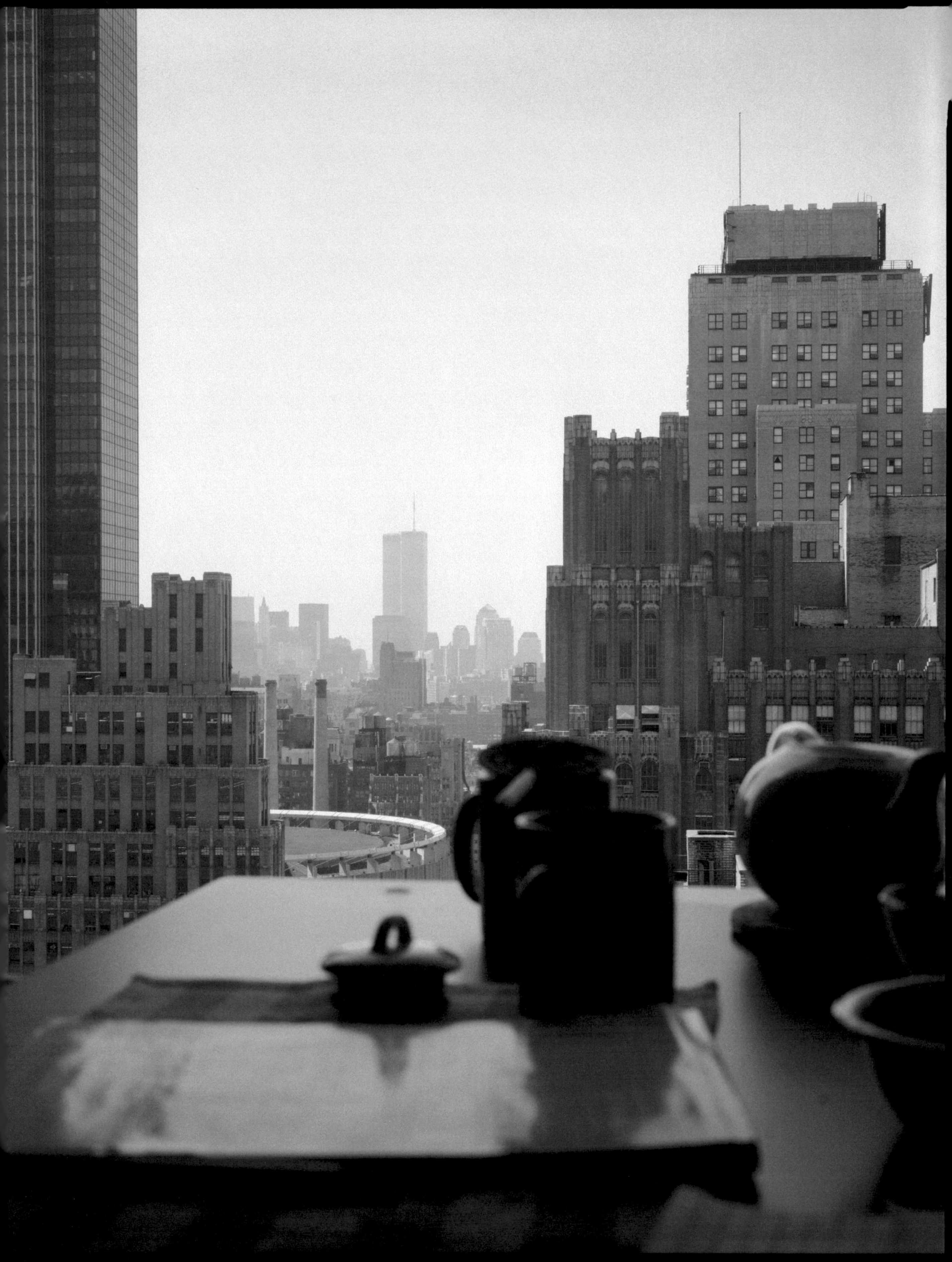

September 21, 1996

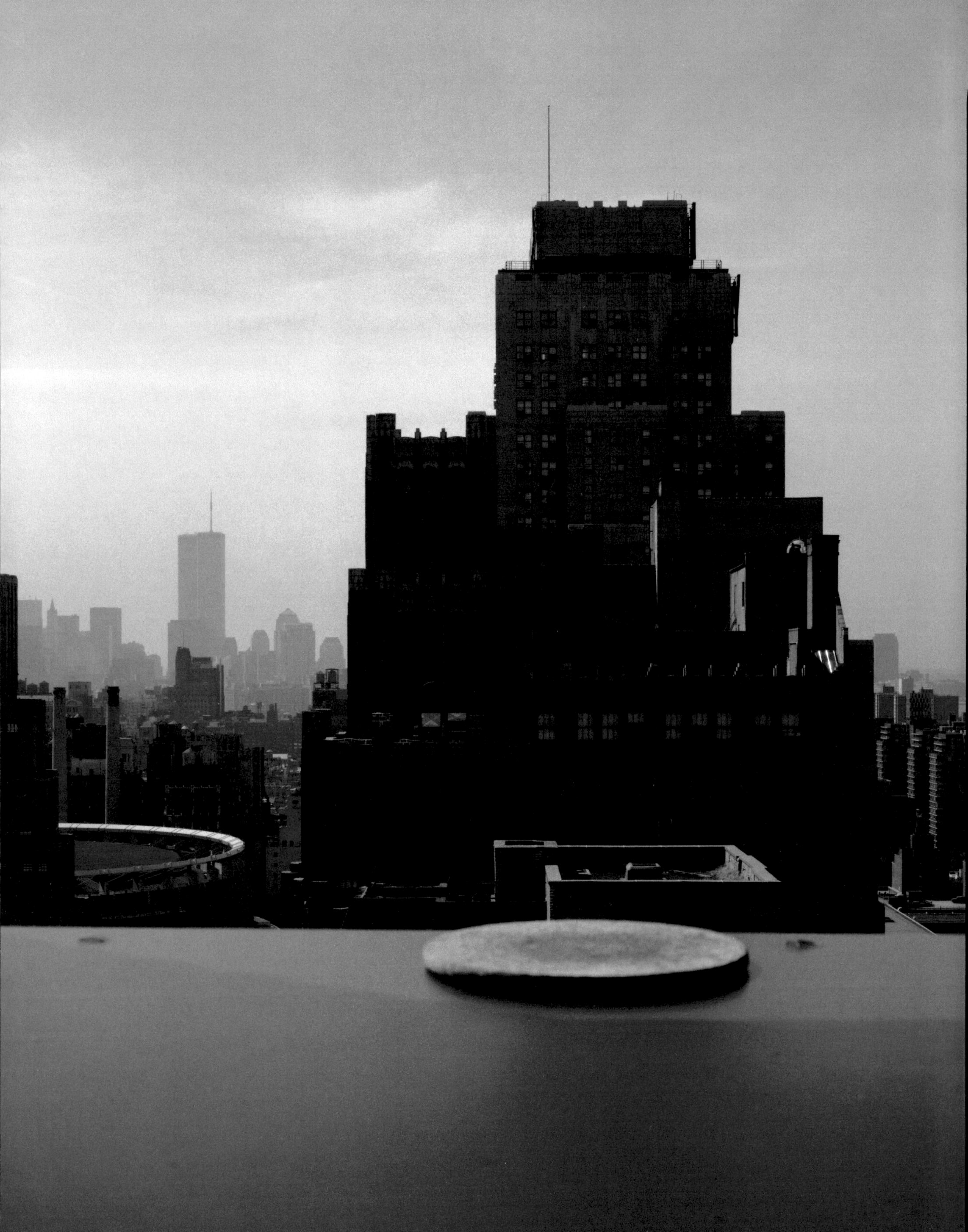

September 22, 1996

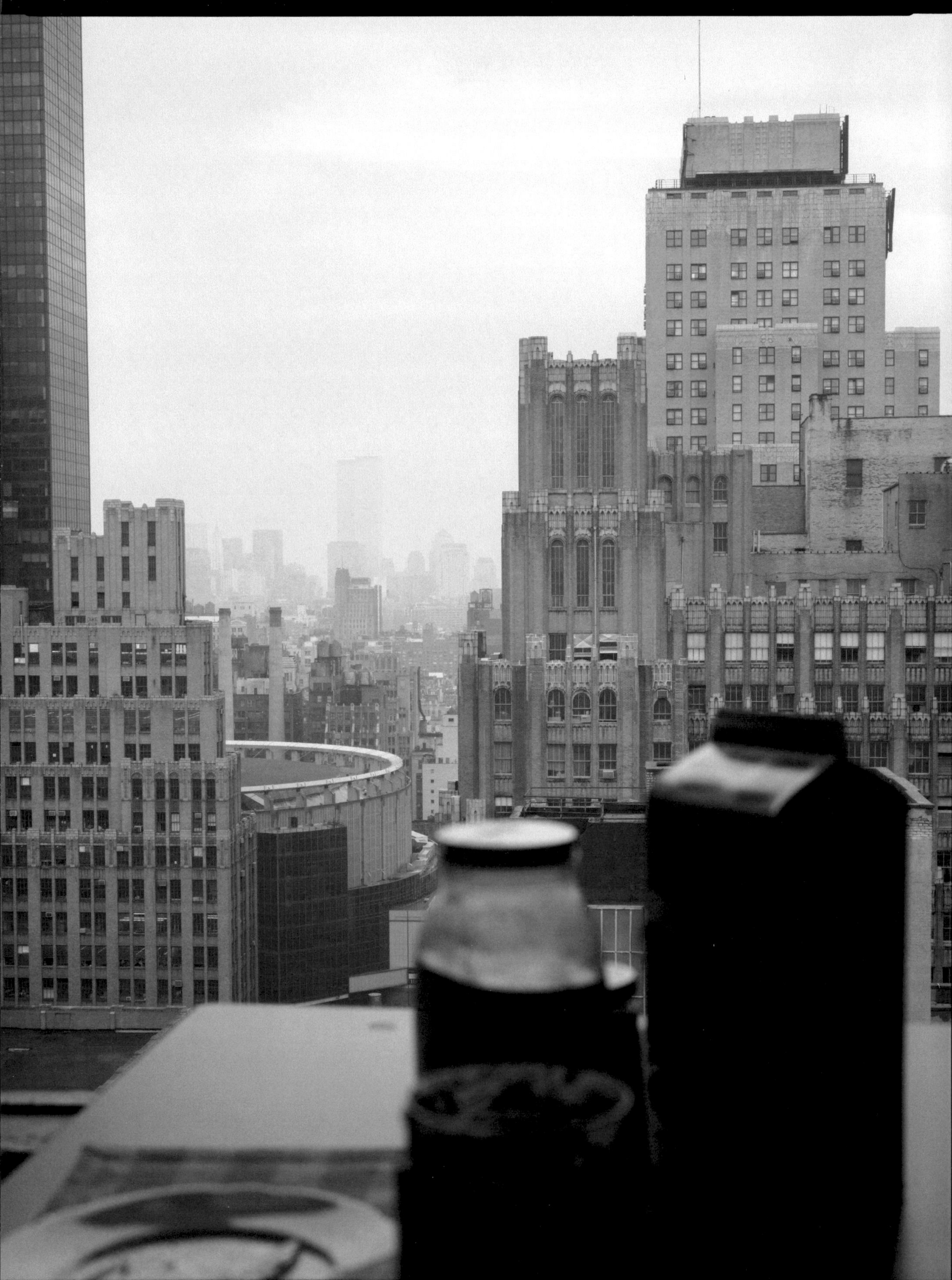

September 23, 1996

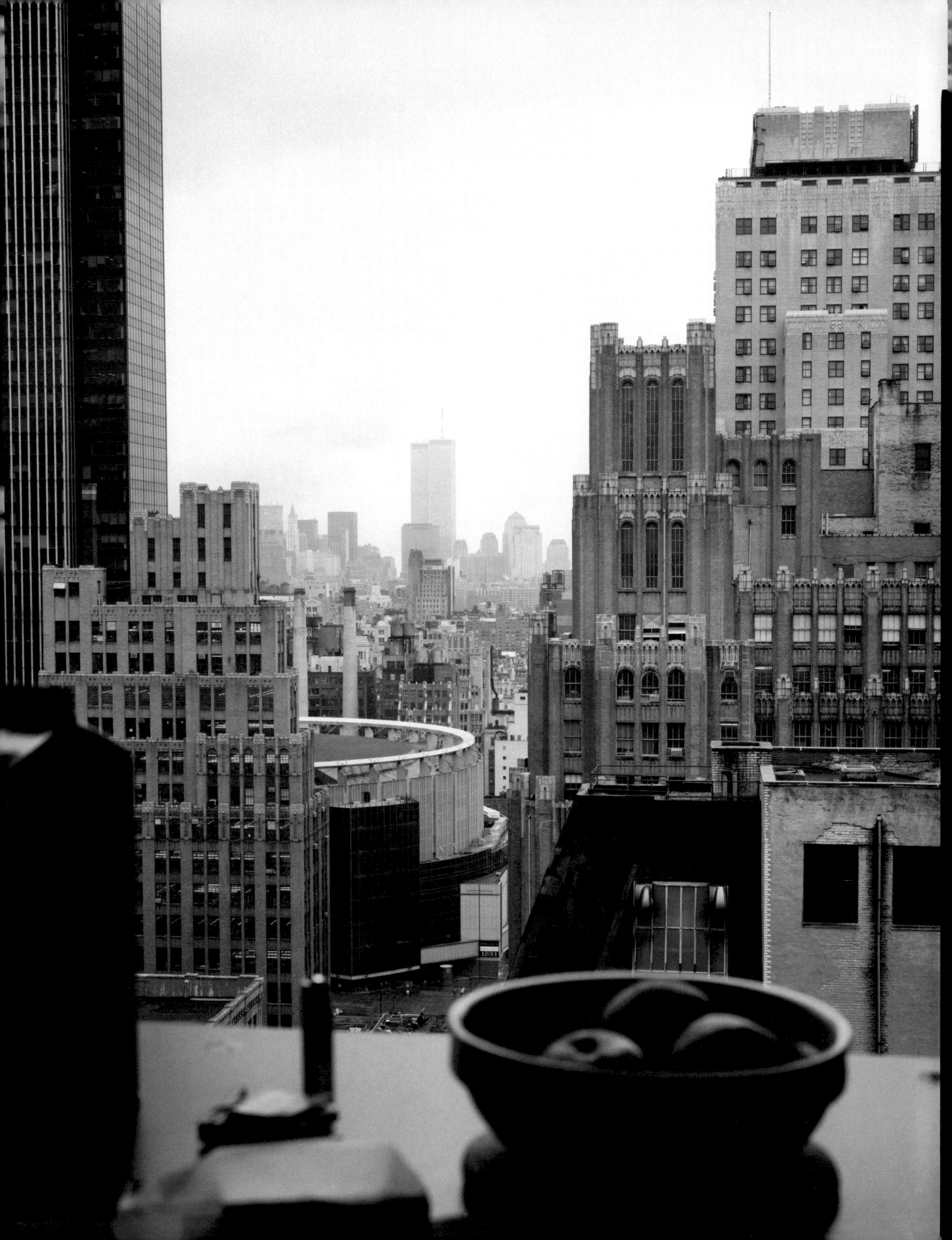

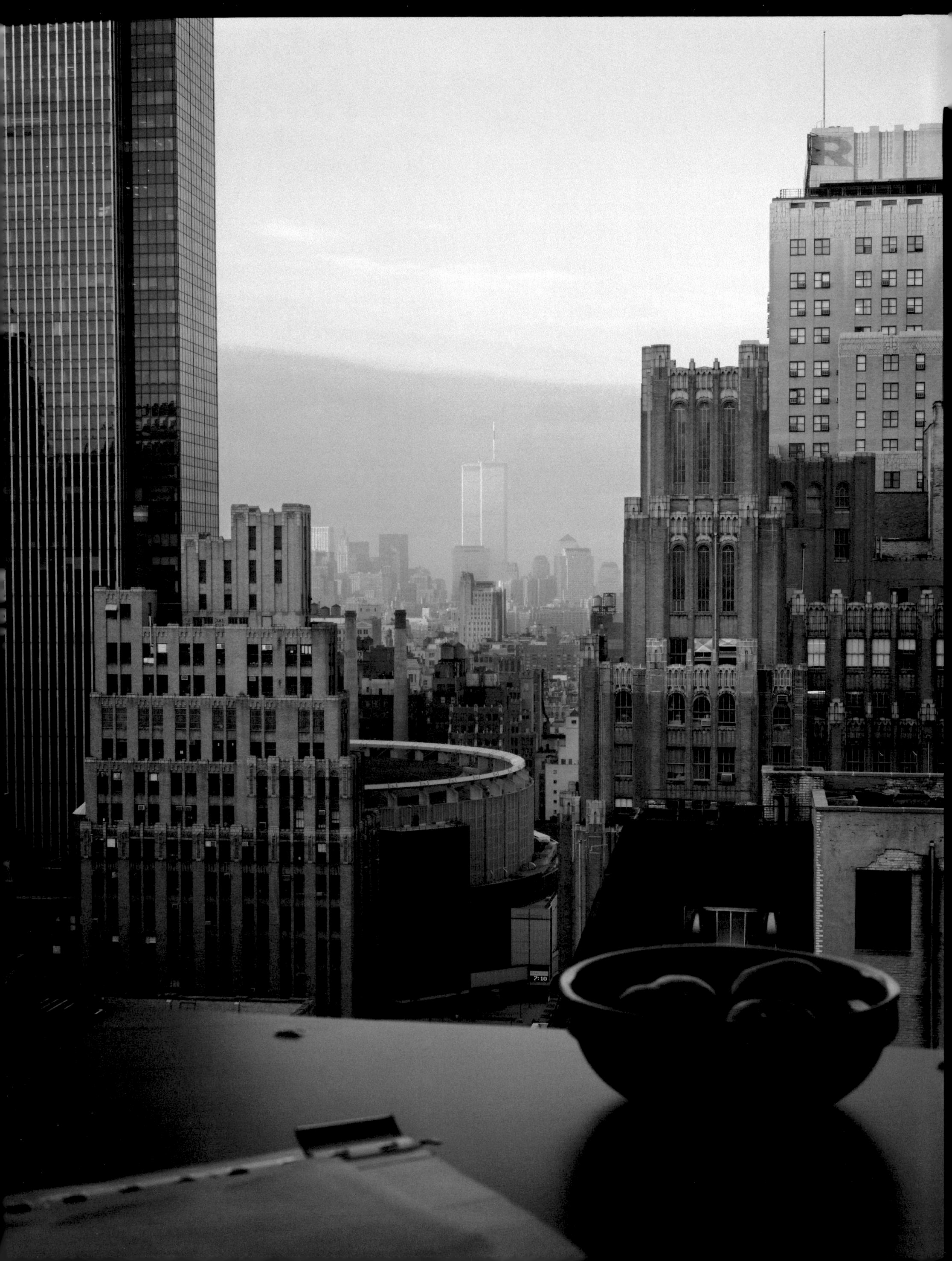

September 25, 1996

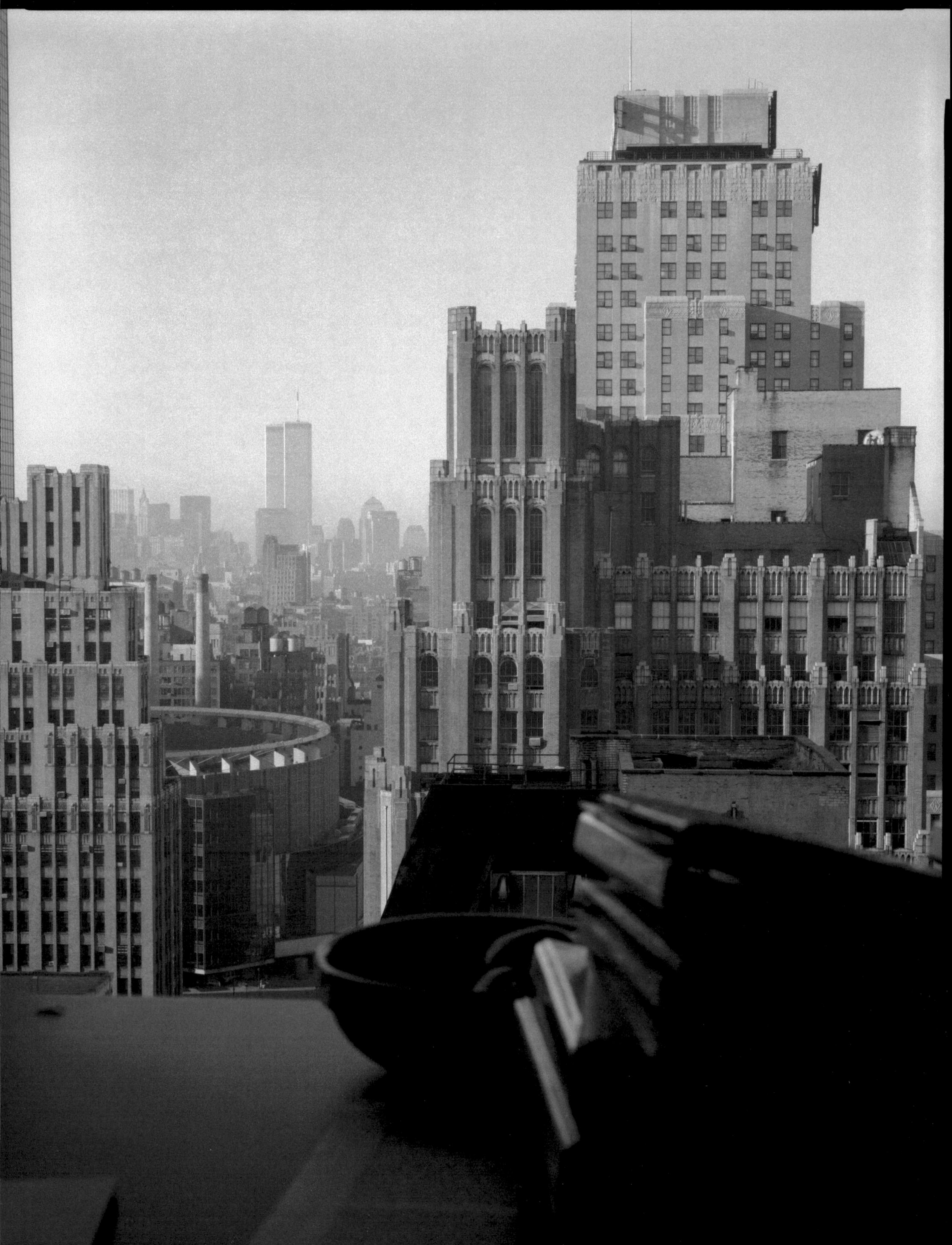

September 26, 1996

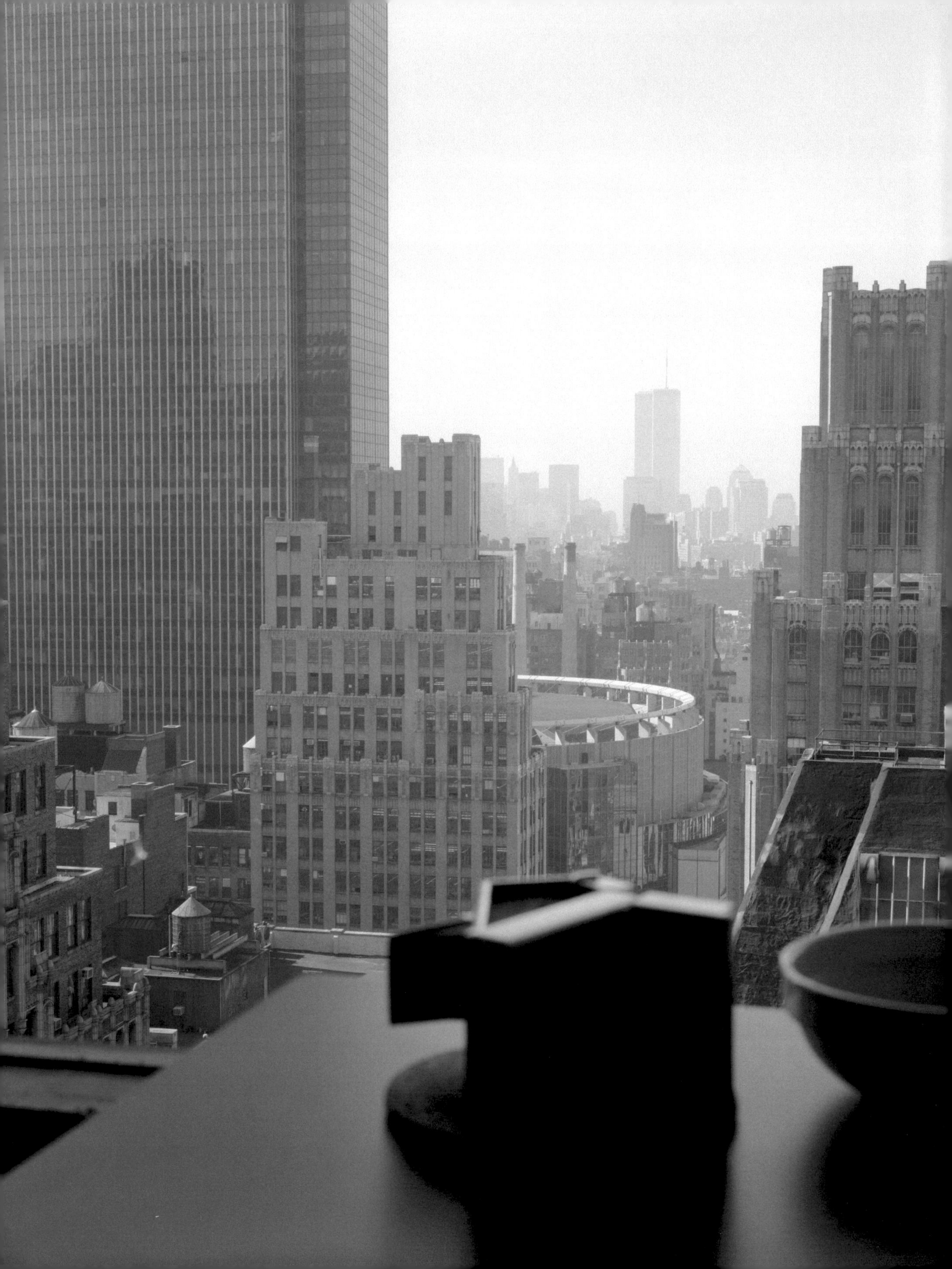

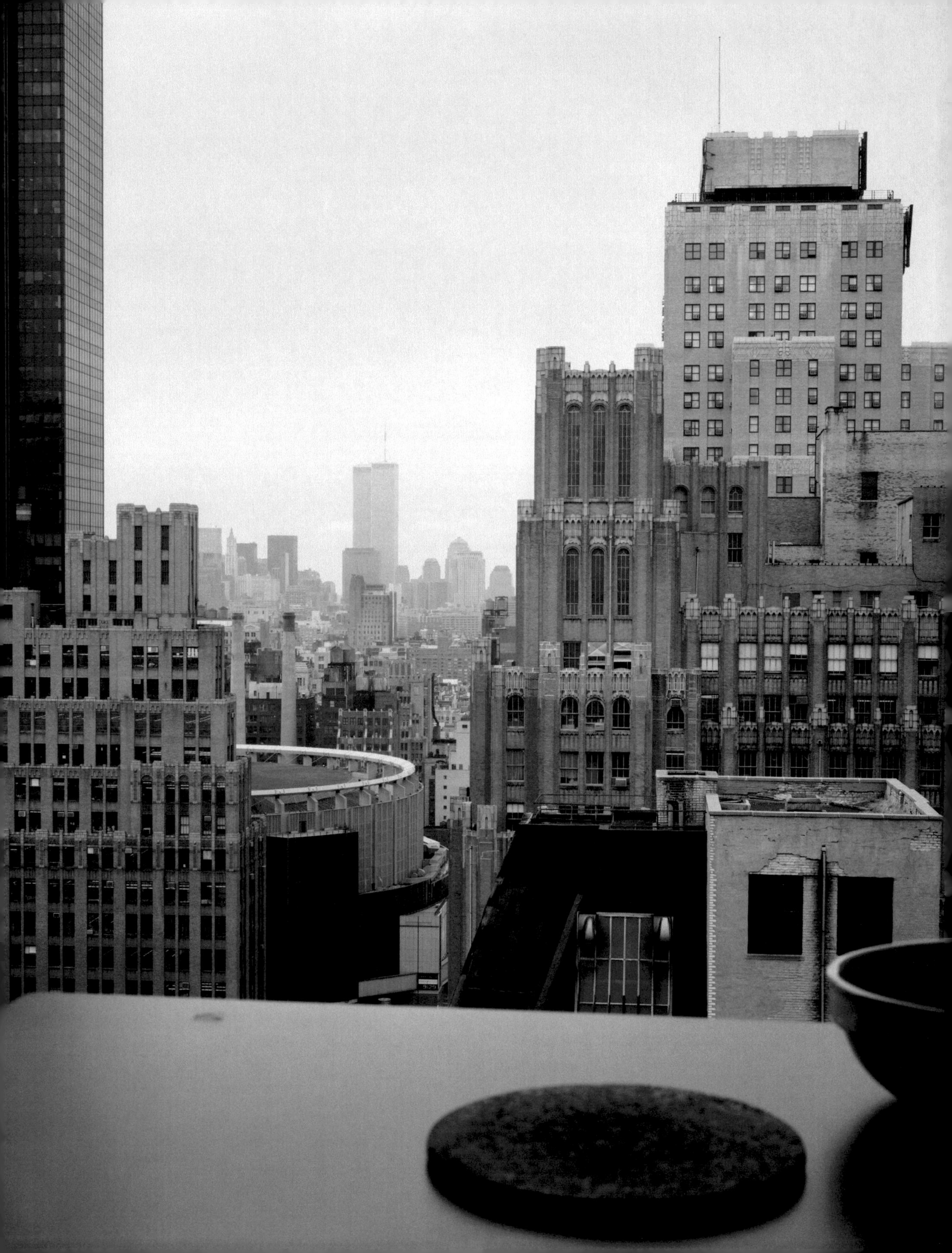

September 28, 1996

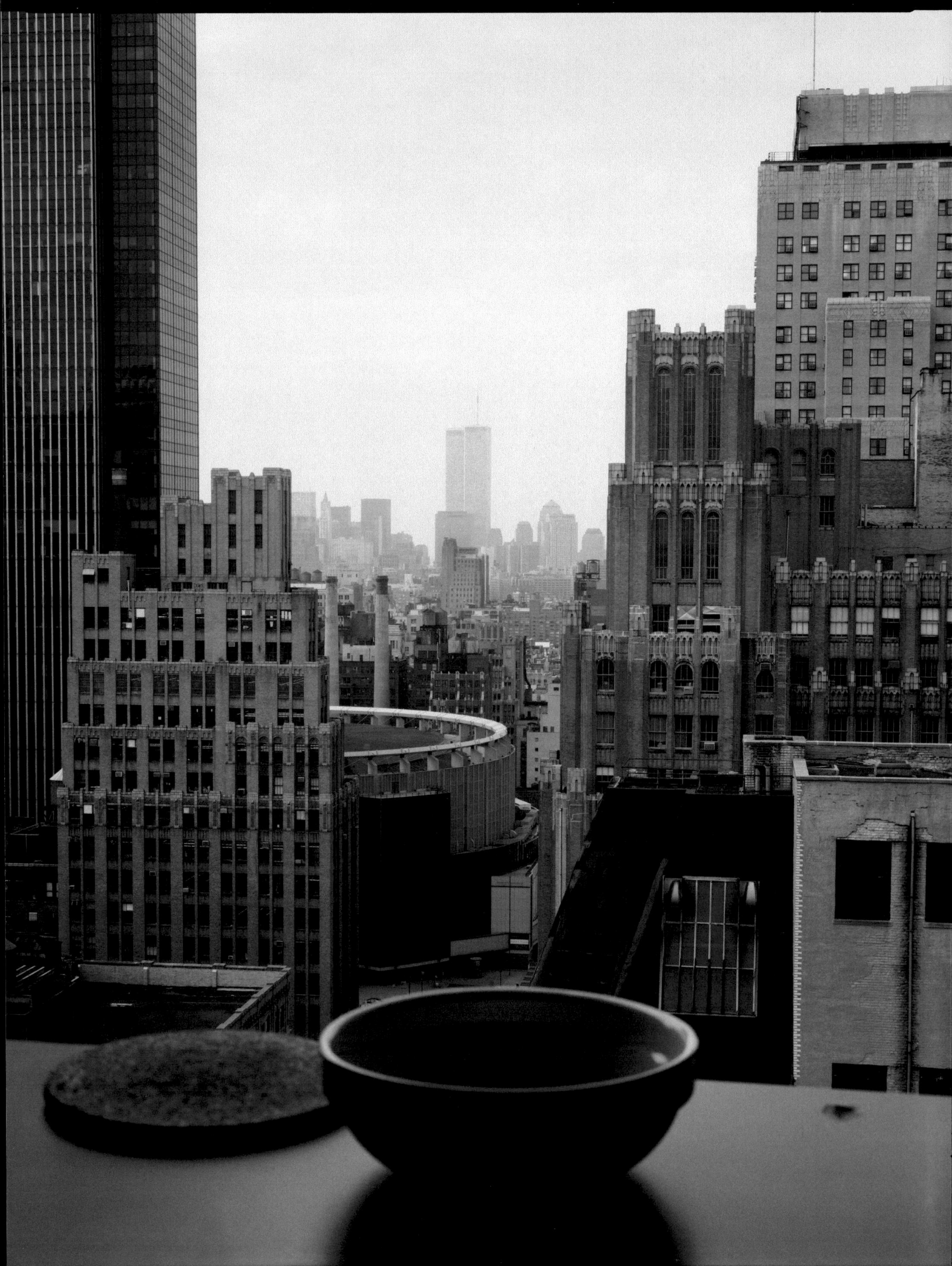

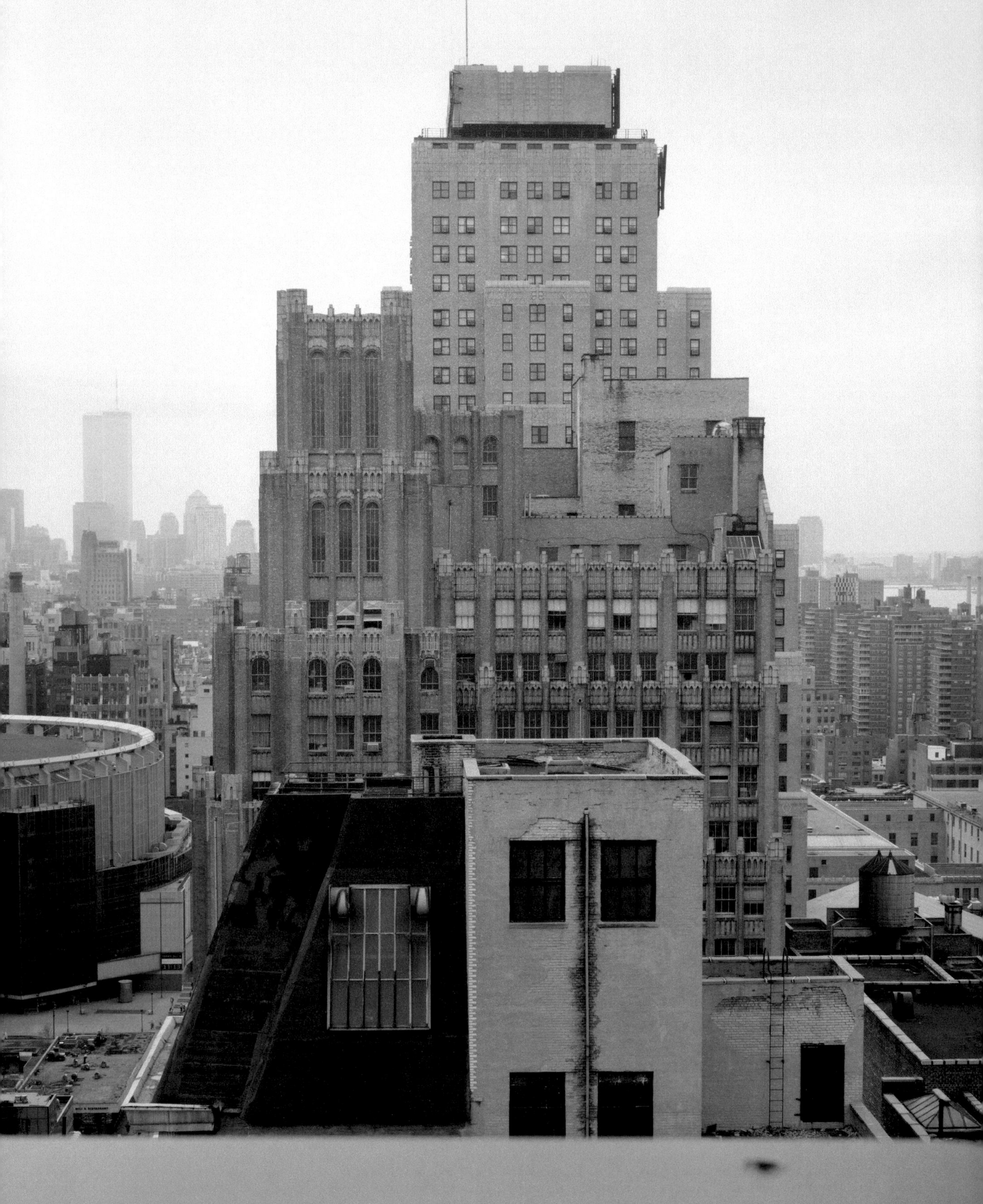

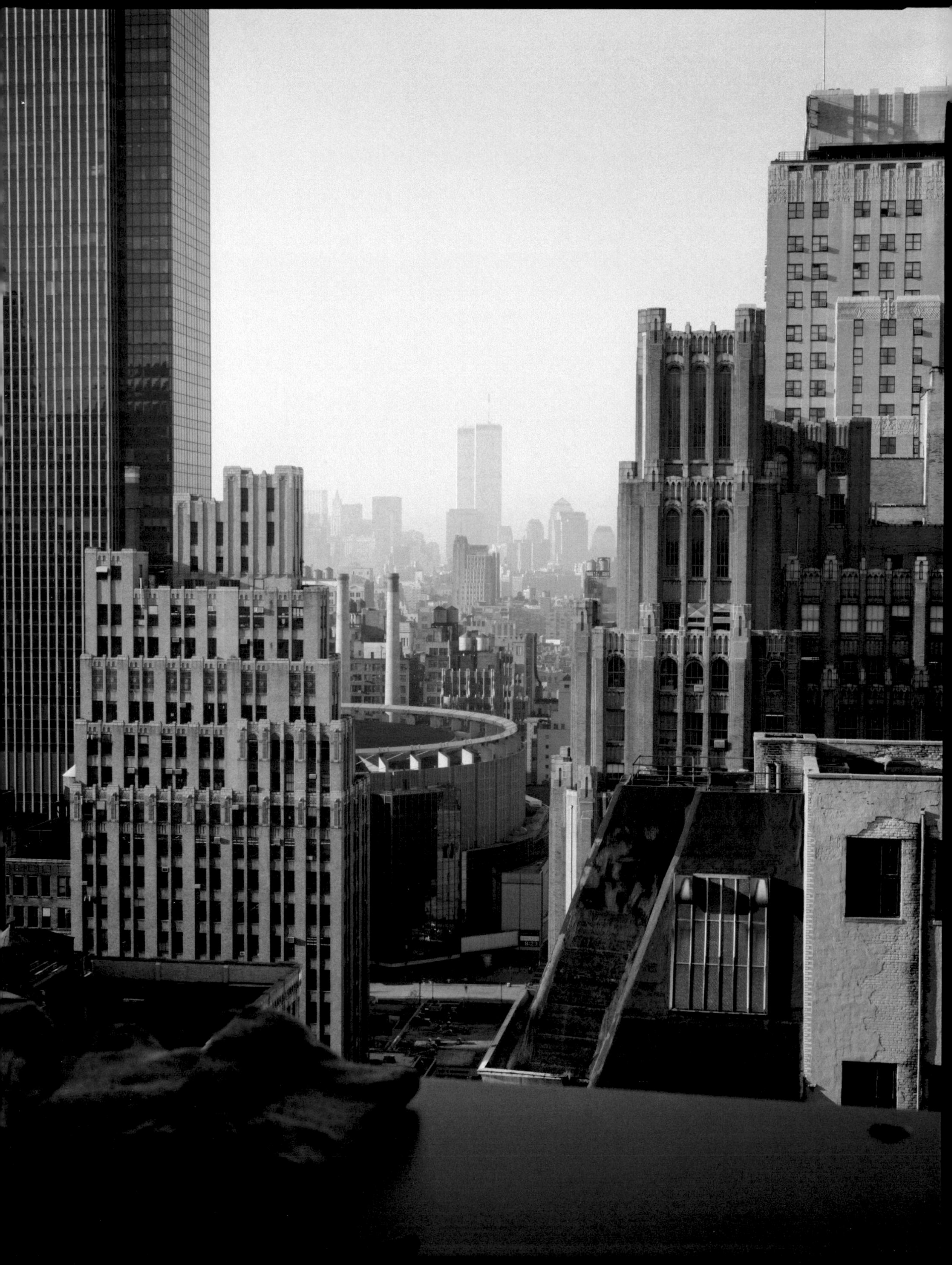

September 1, 1997

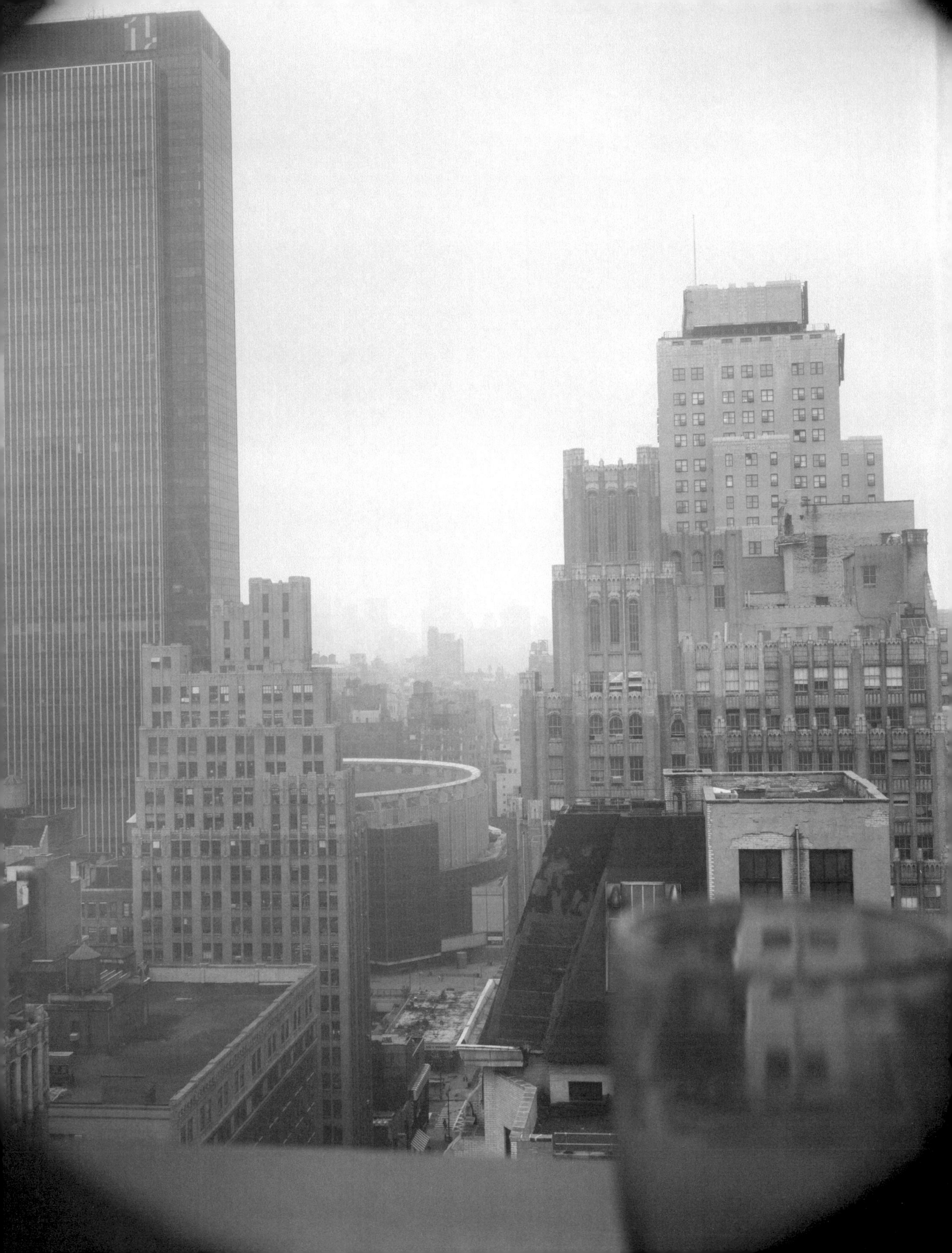

September 2, 1997

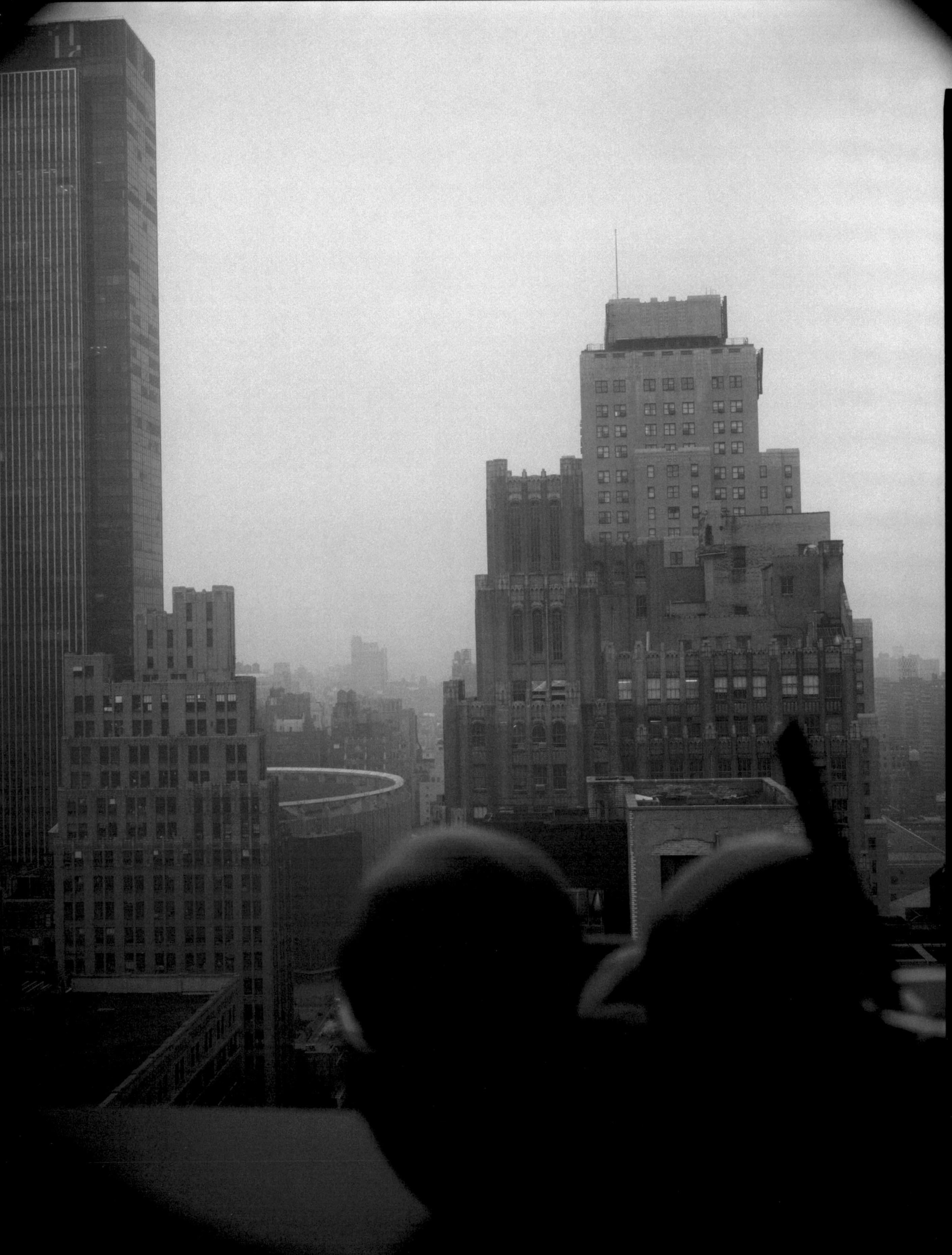

September 3, 1997

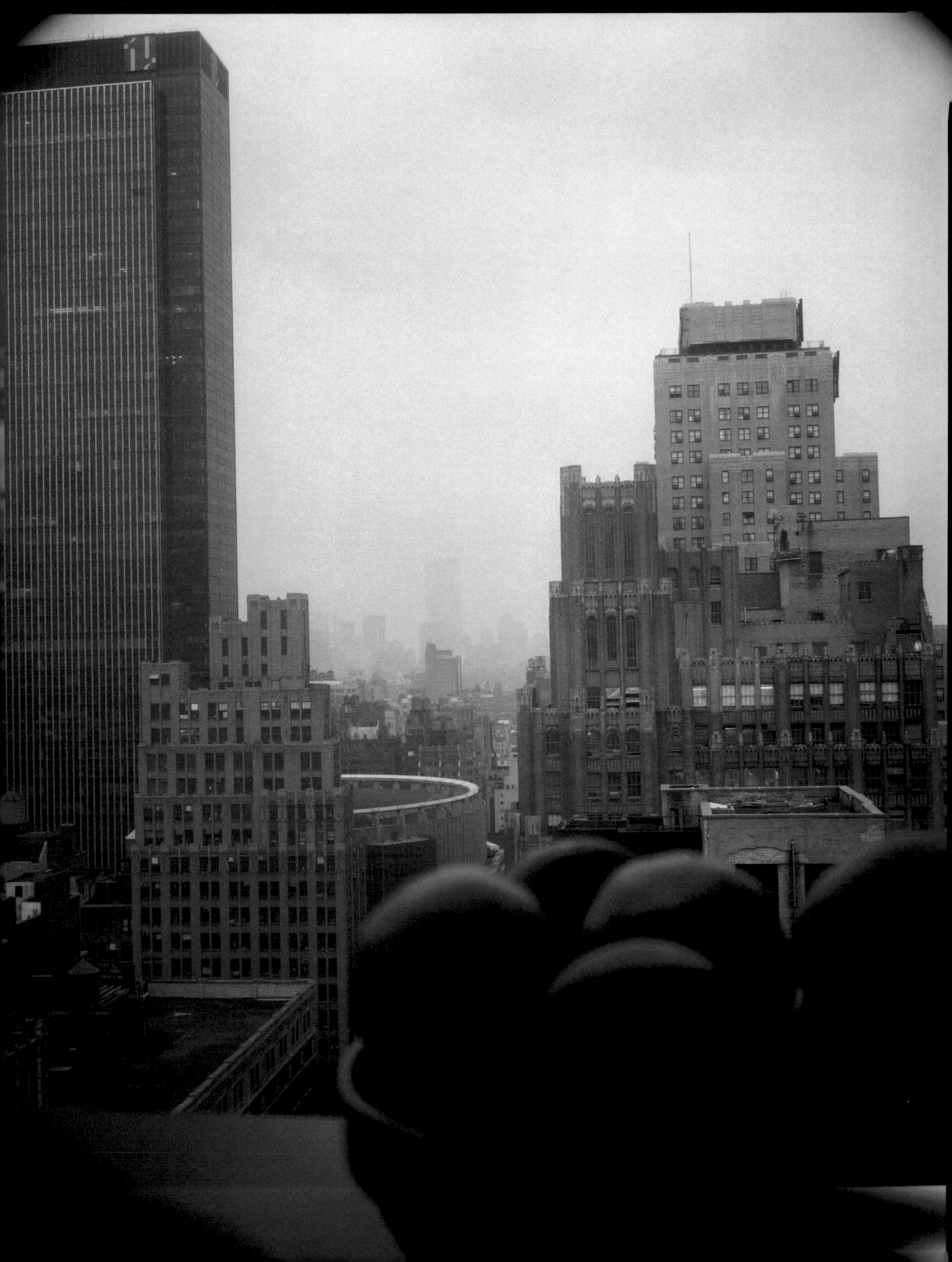

September 4, 1997

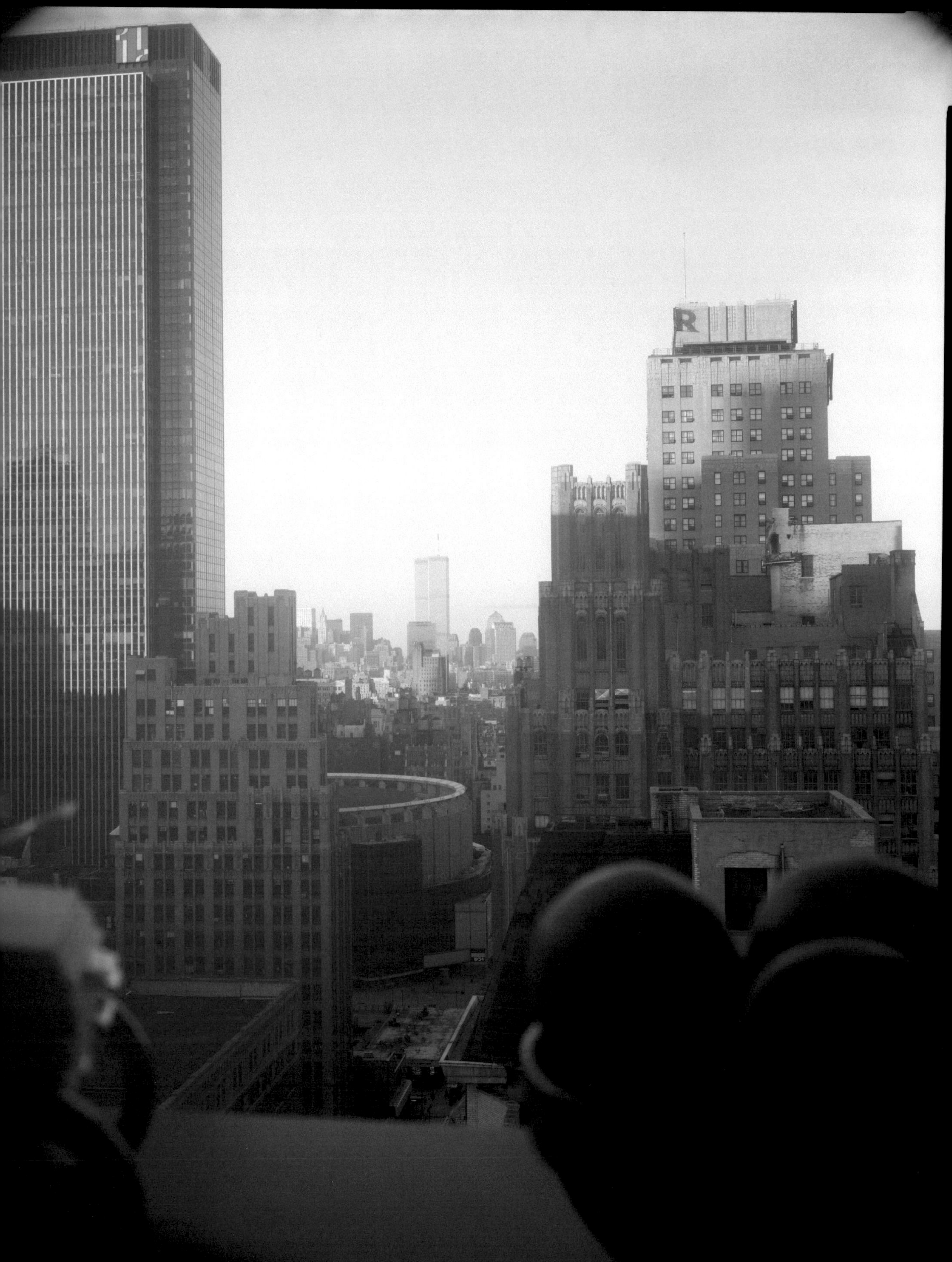

September 5, 1997

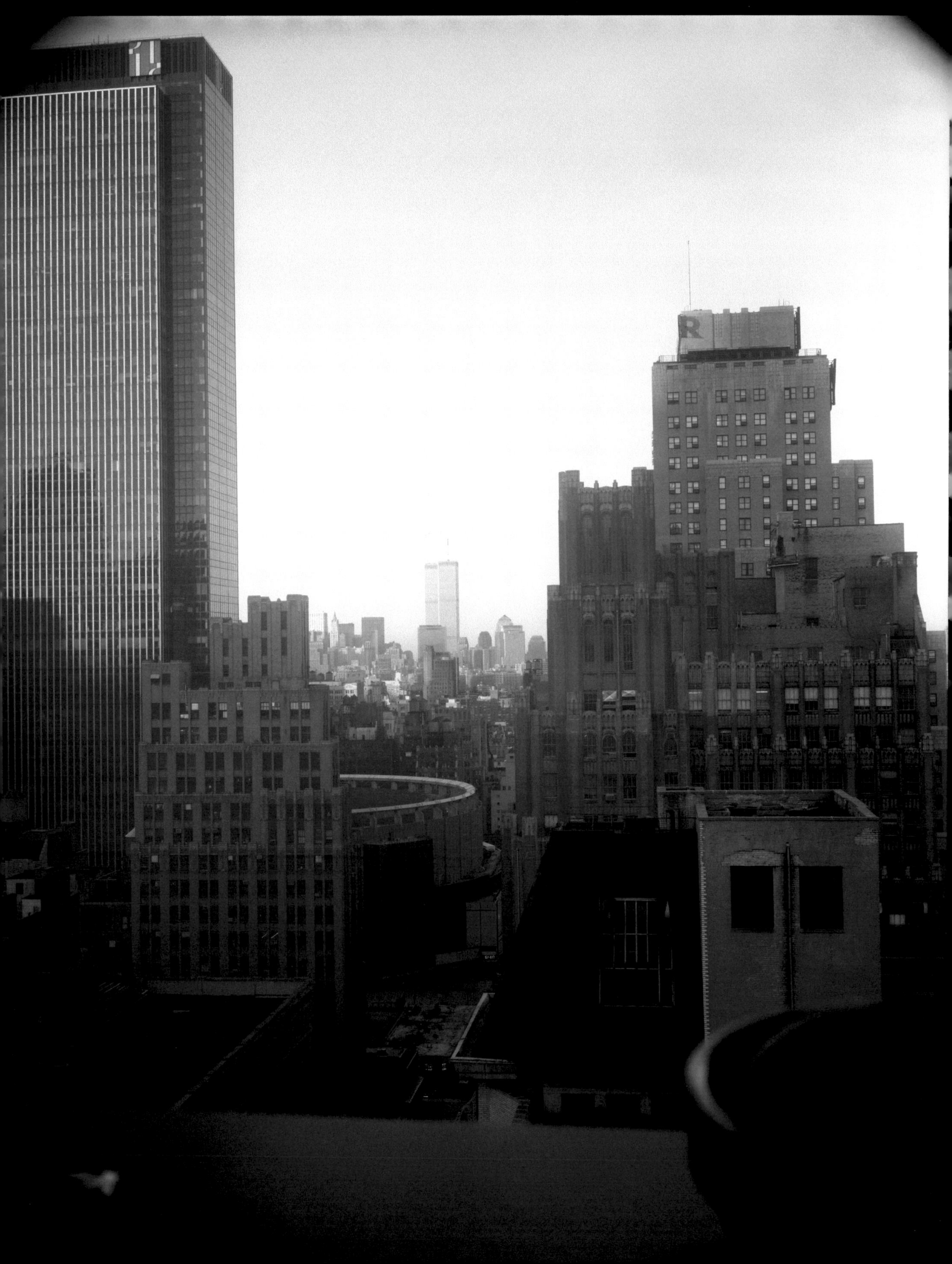

September 6, 1997

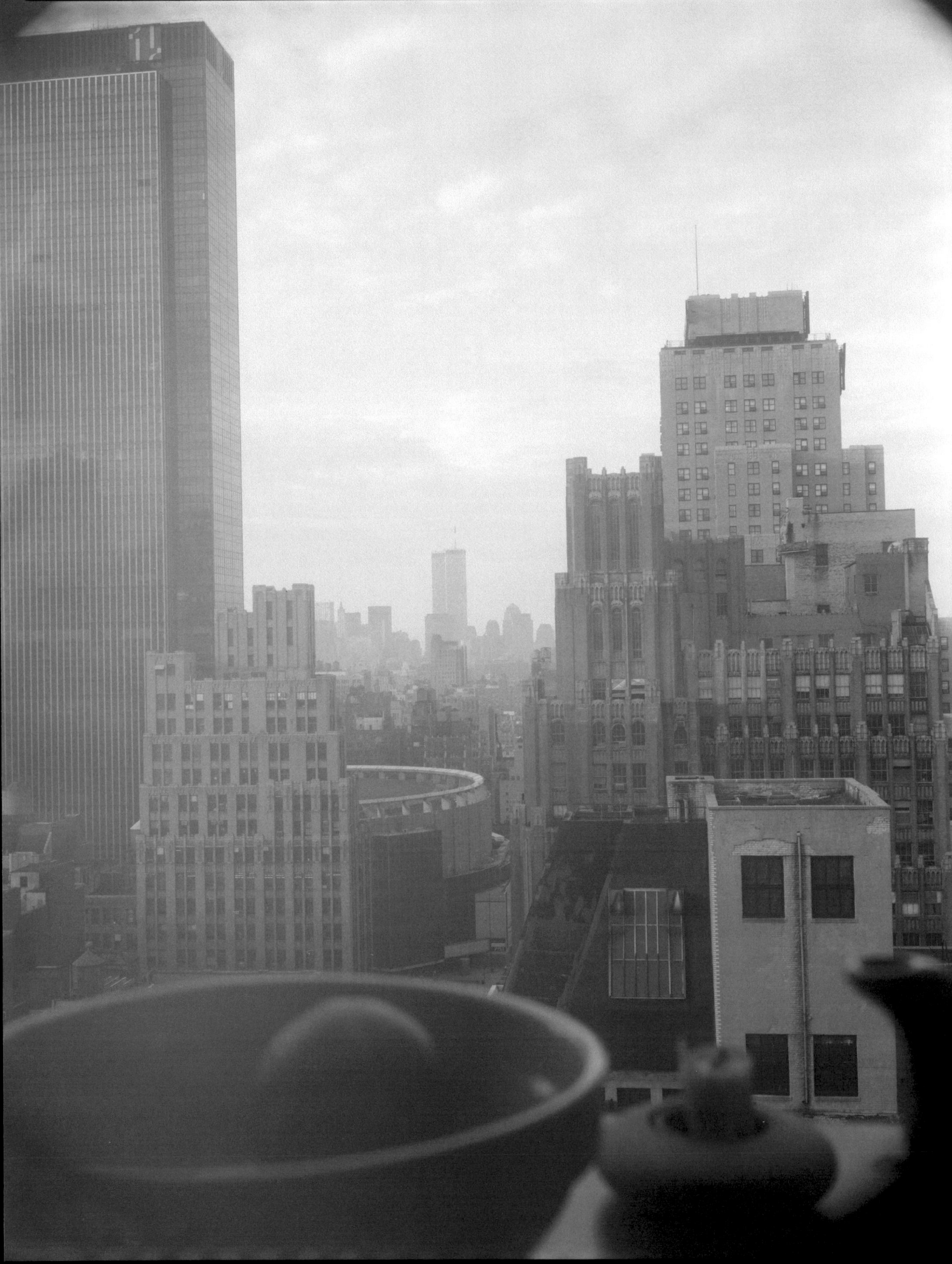

September 7, 1997

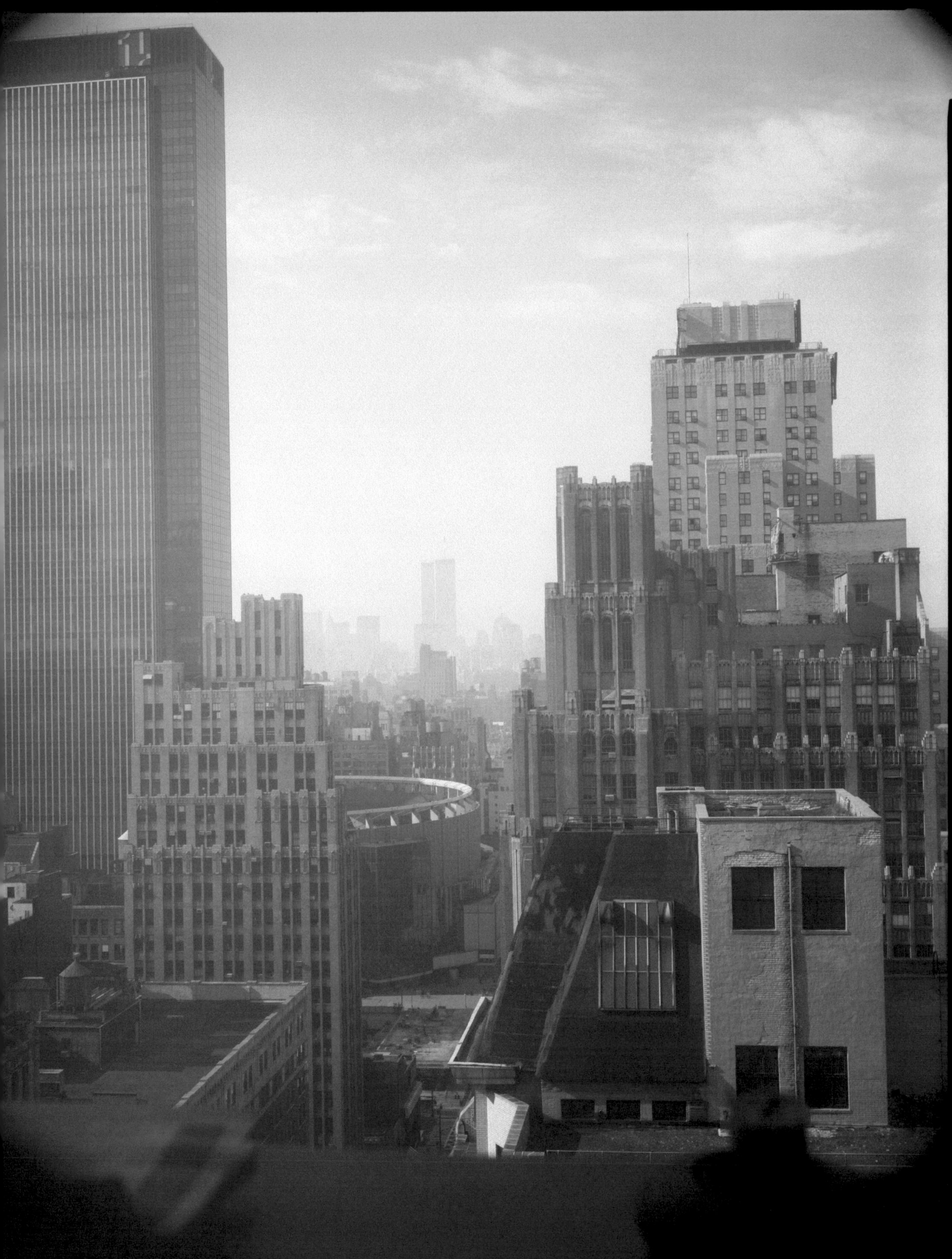

September 8, 1997

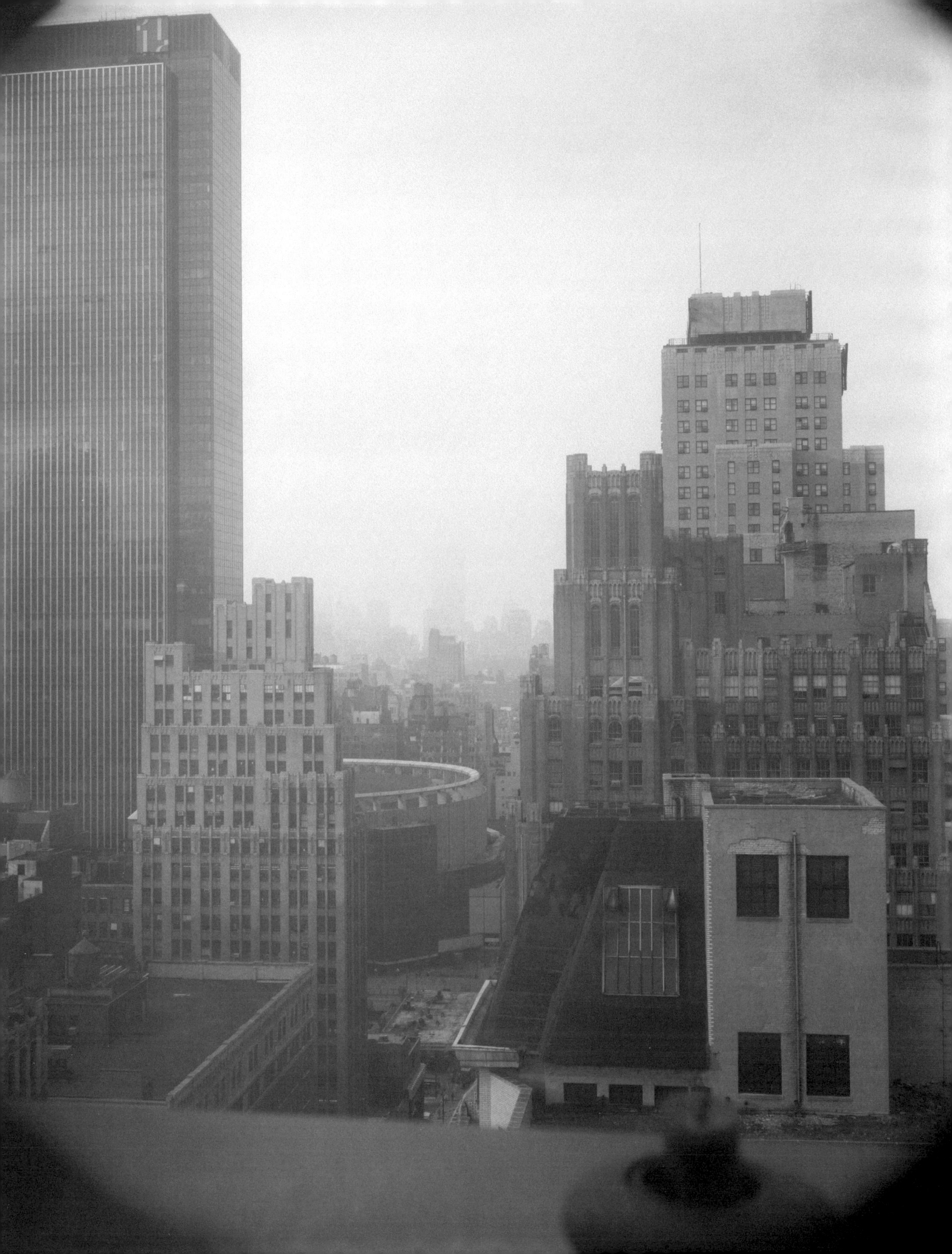

September 9, 1997

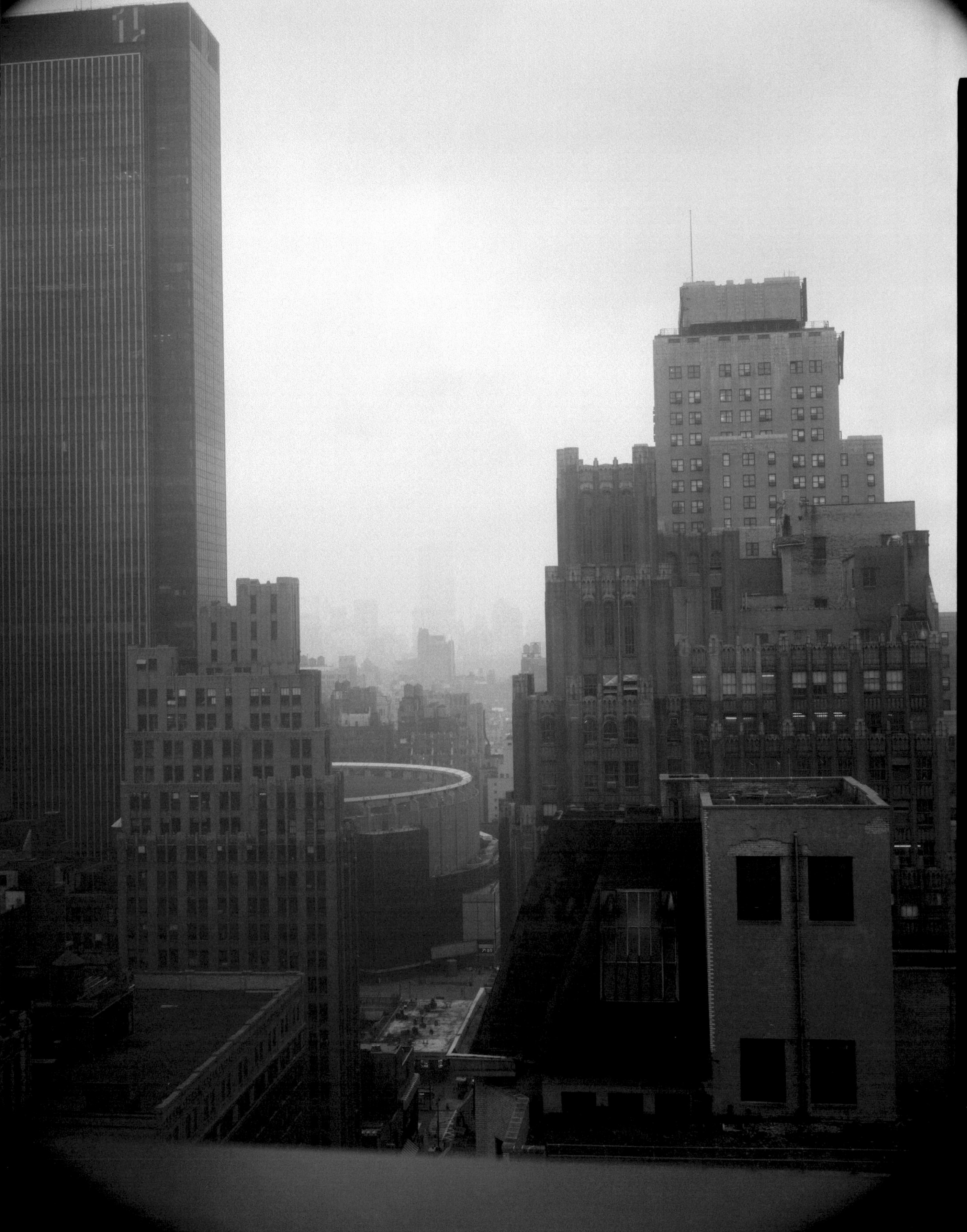

September 10, 1997

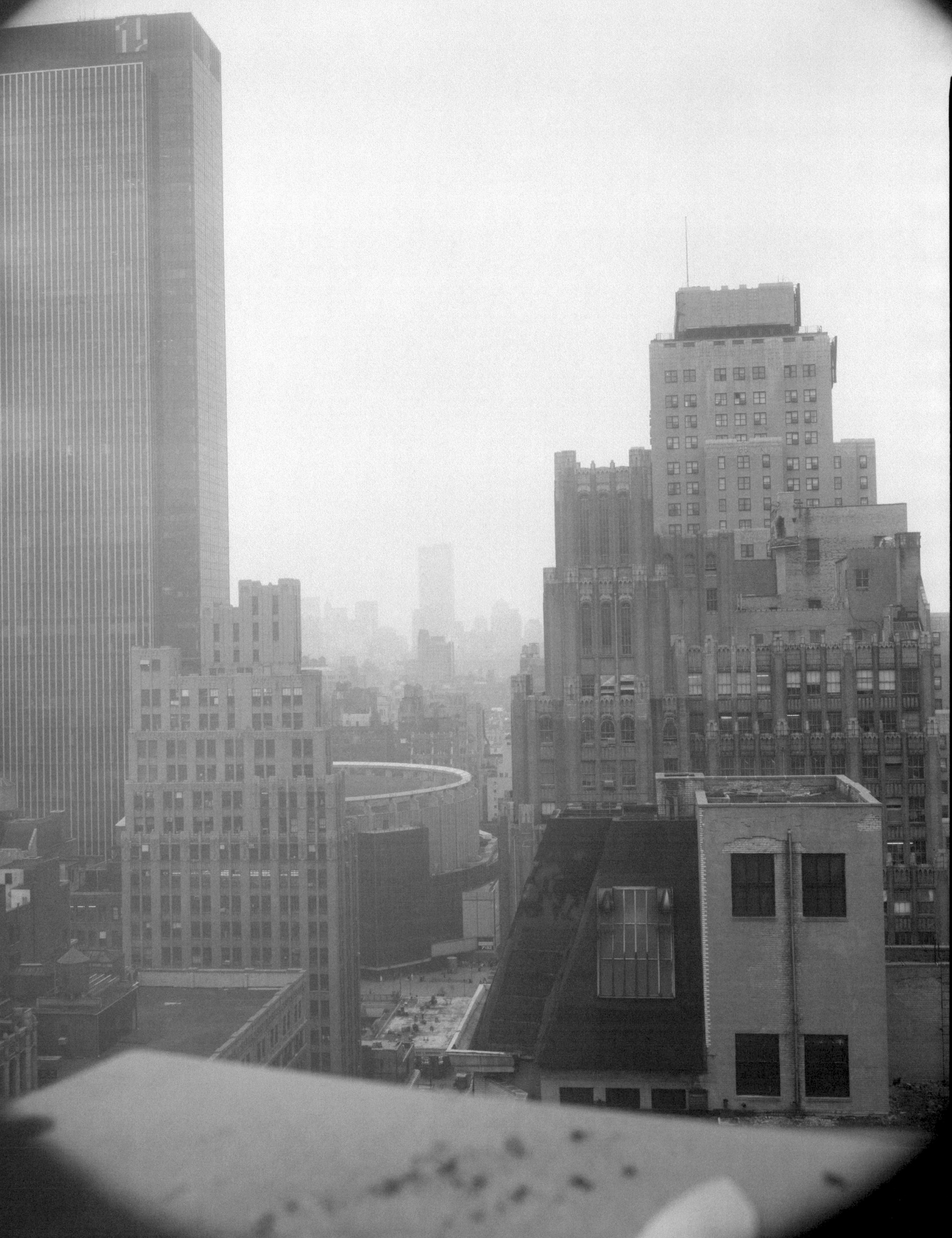

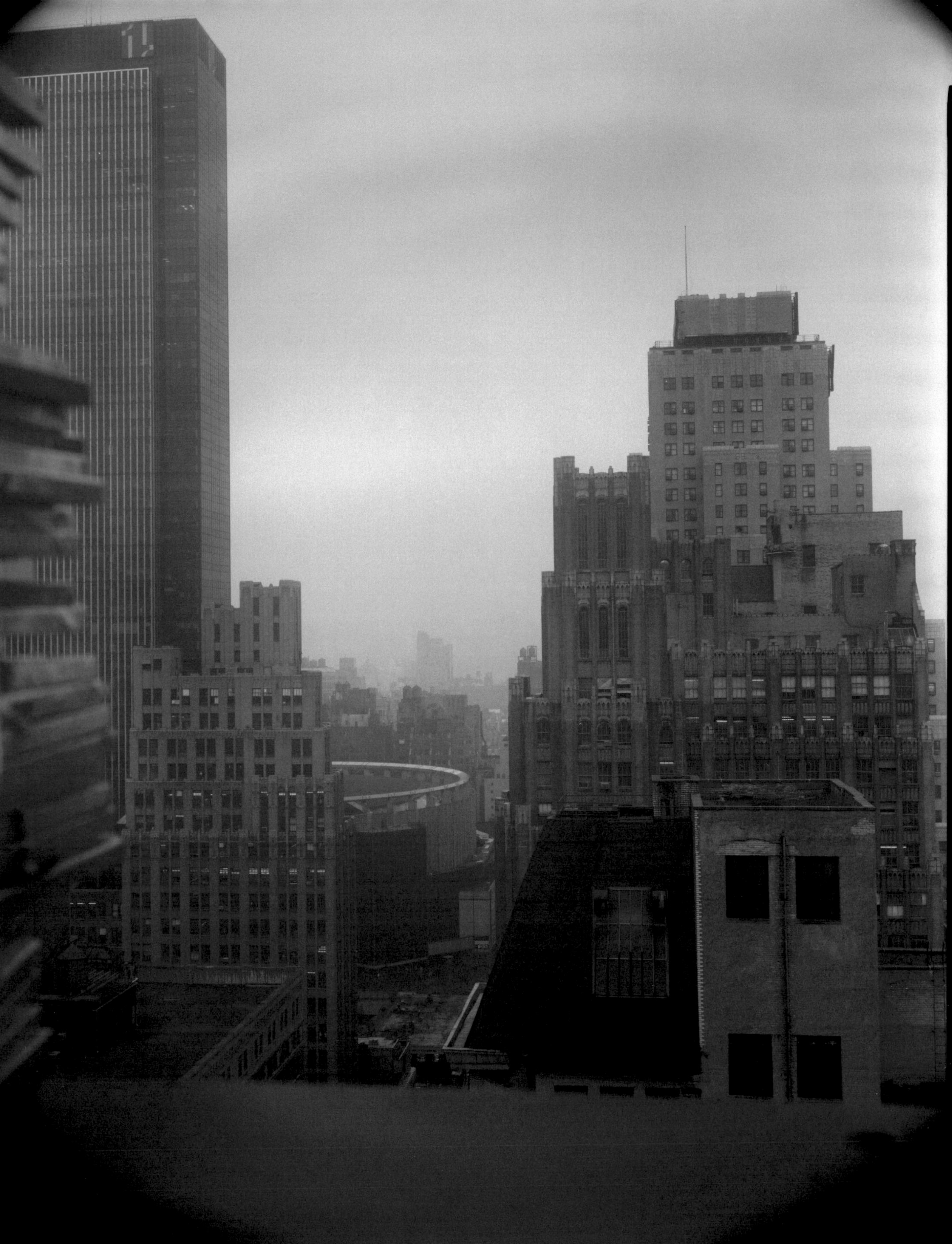

September 12, 1997

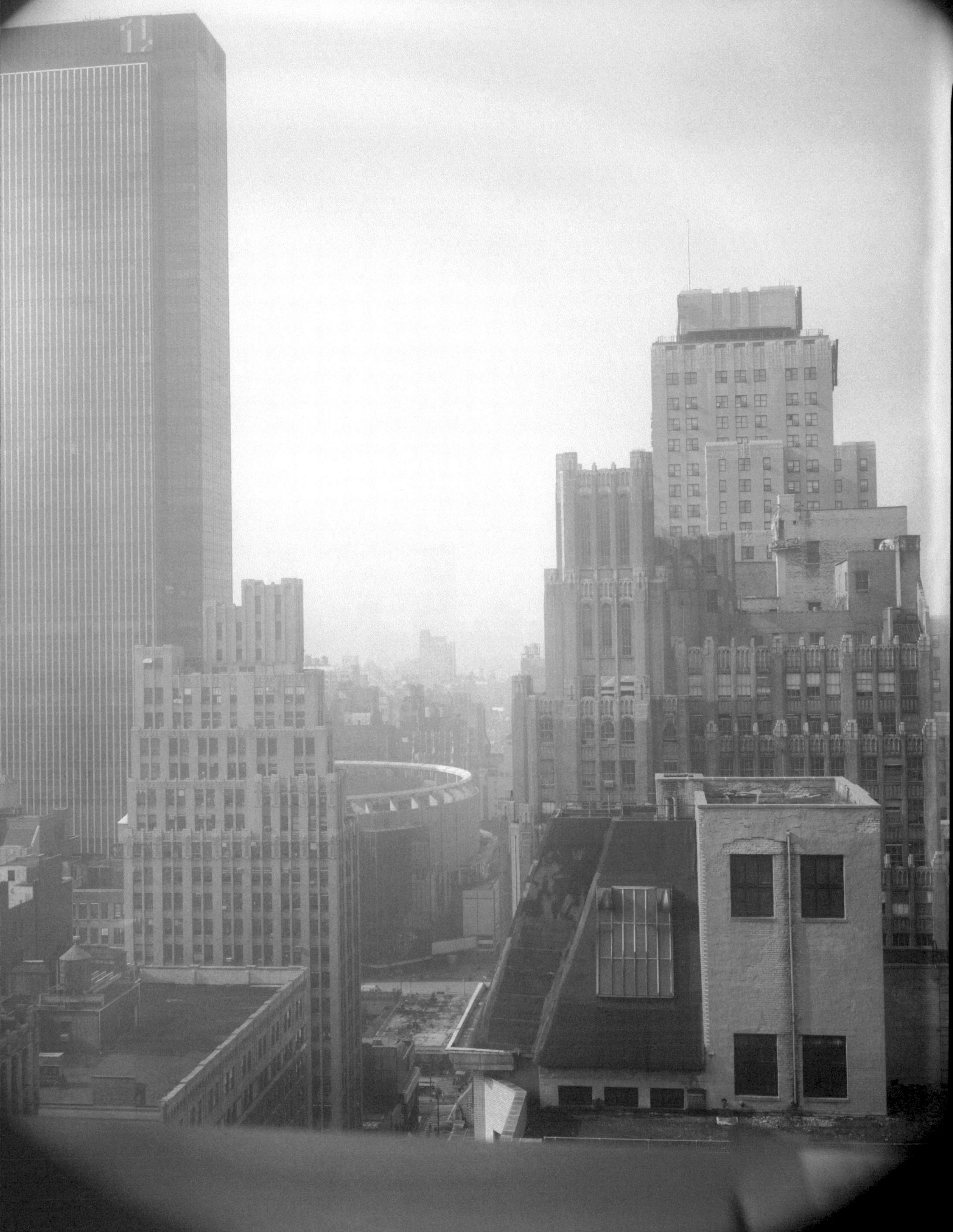

September 13, 1997

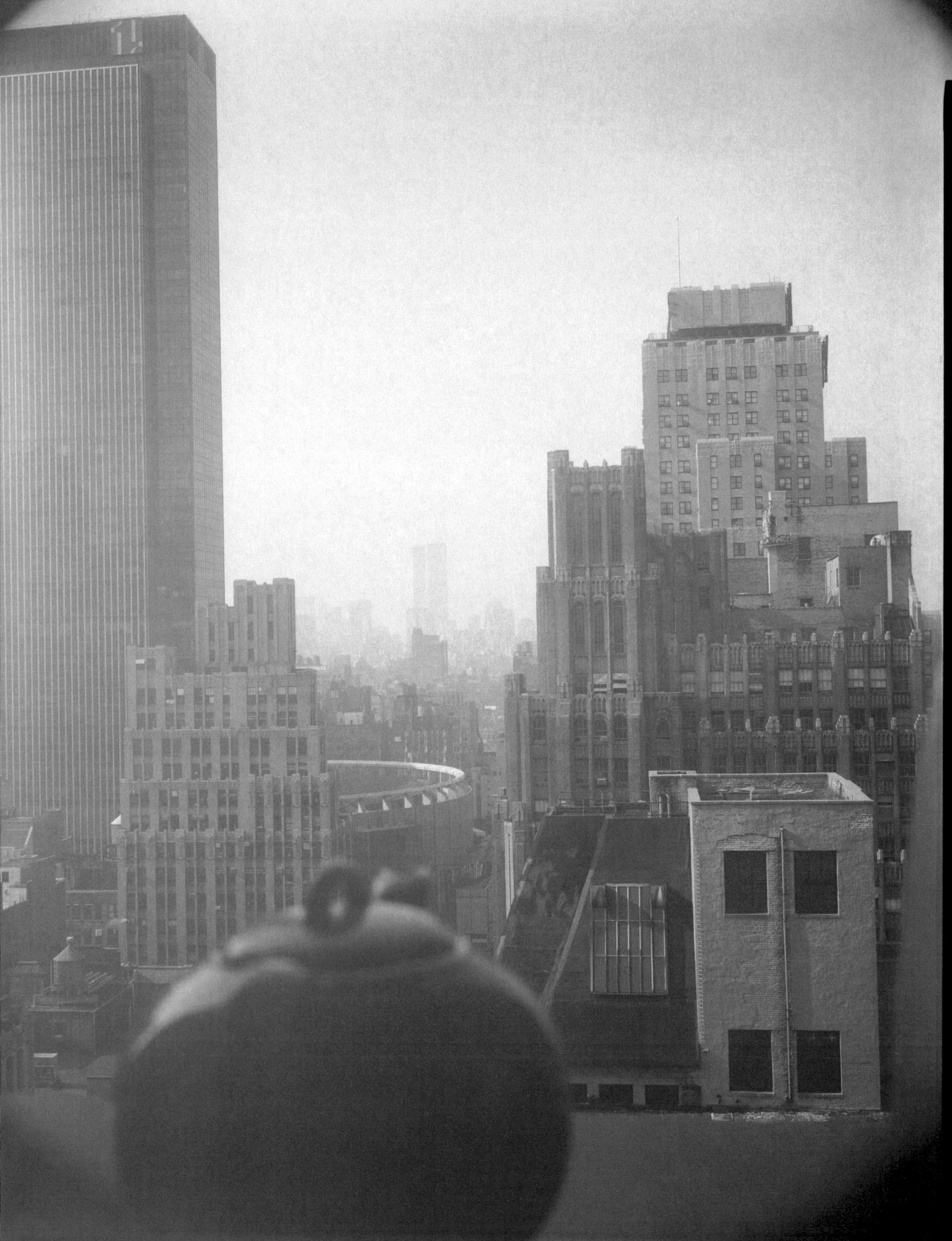

September 14, 1997

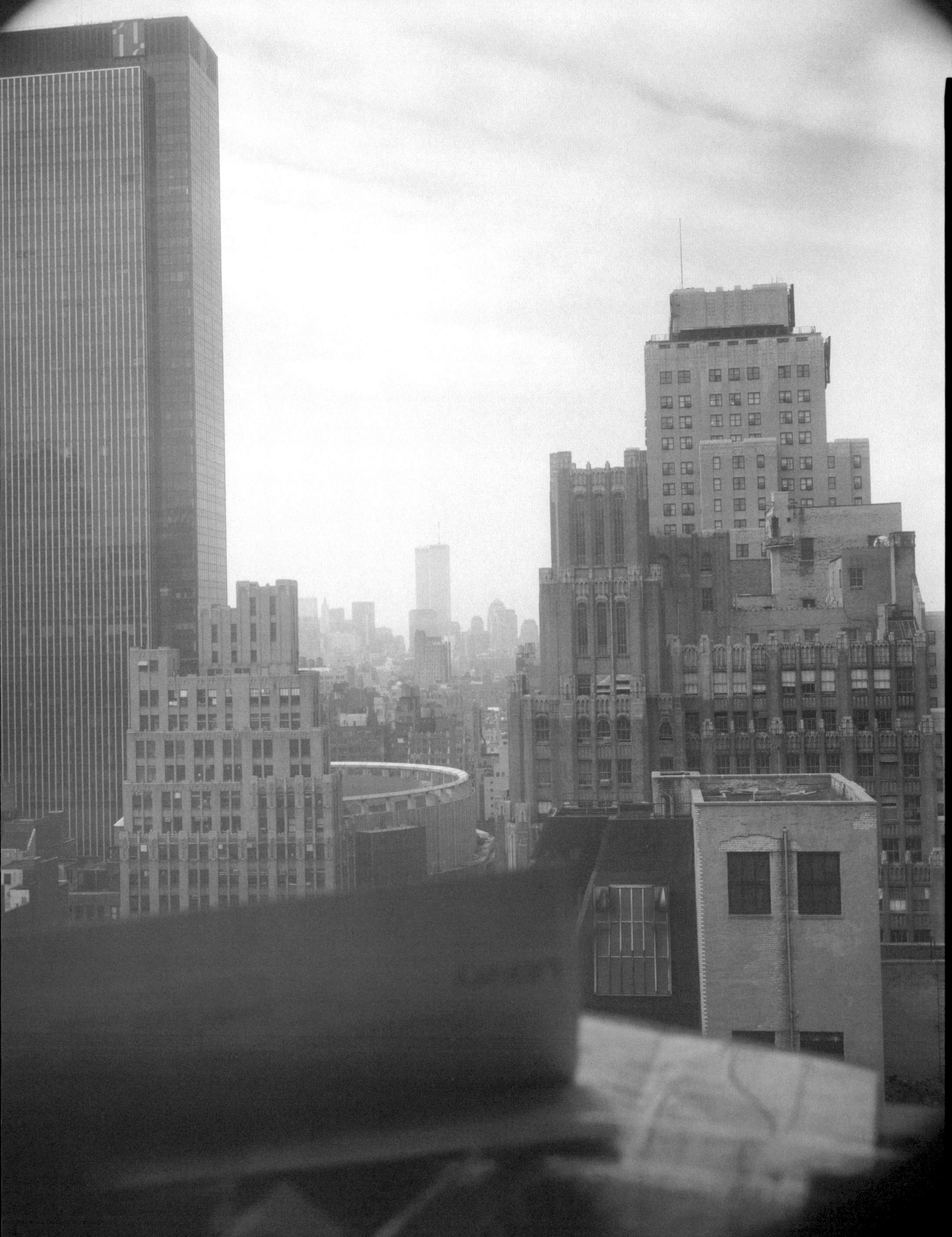

September 15, 1997

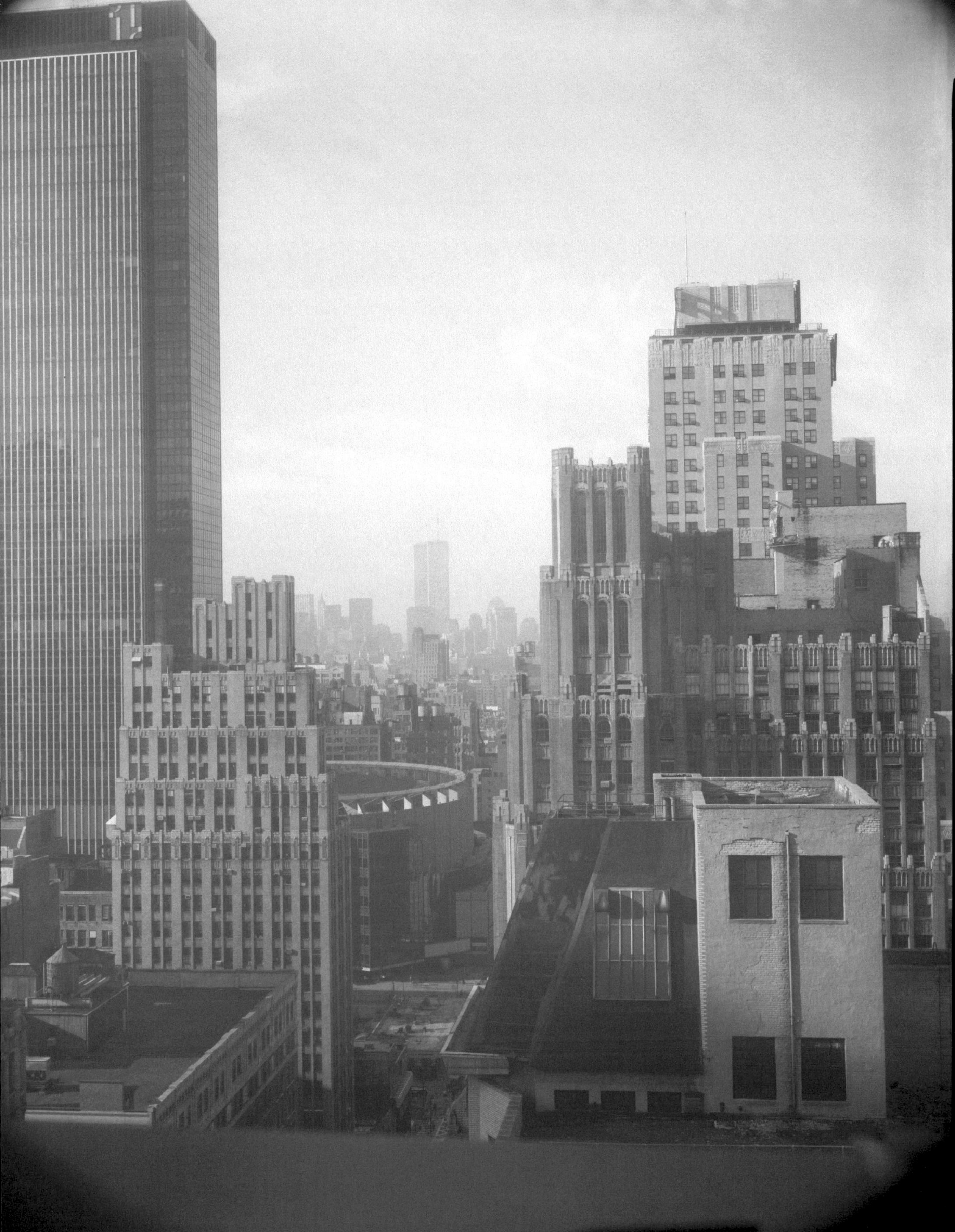

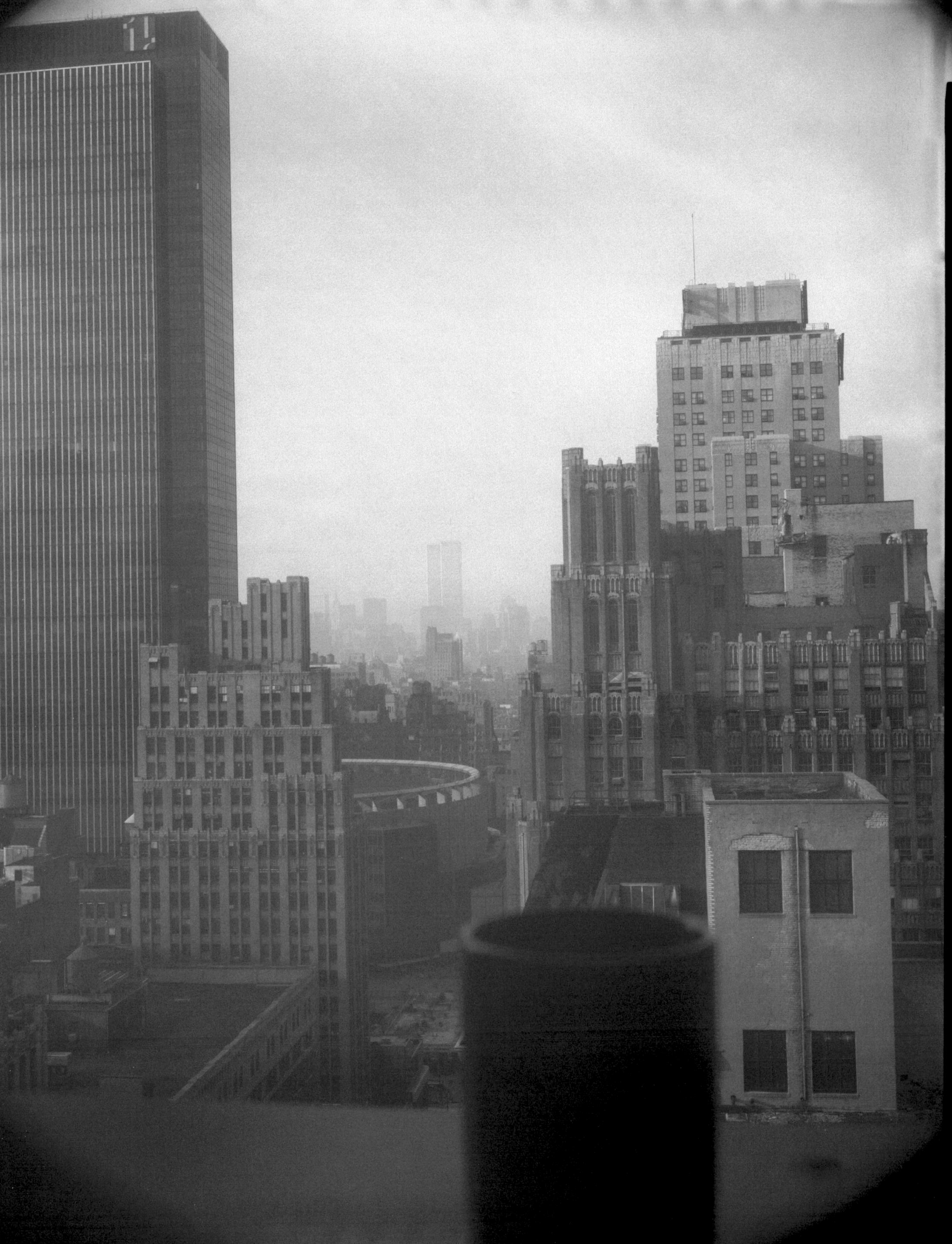

September 17, 1997

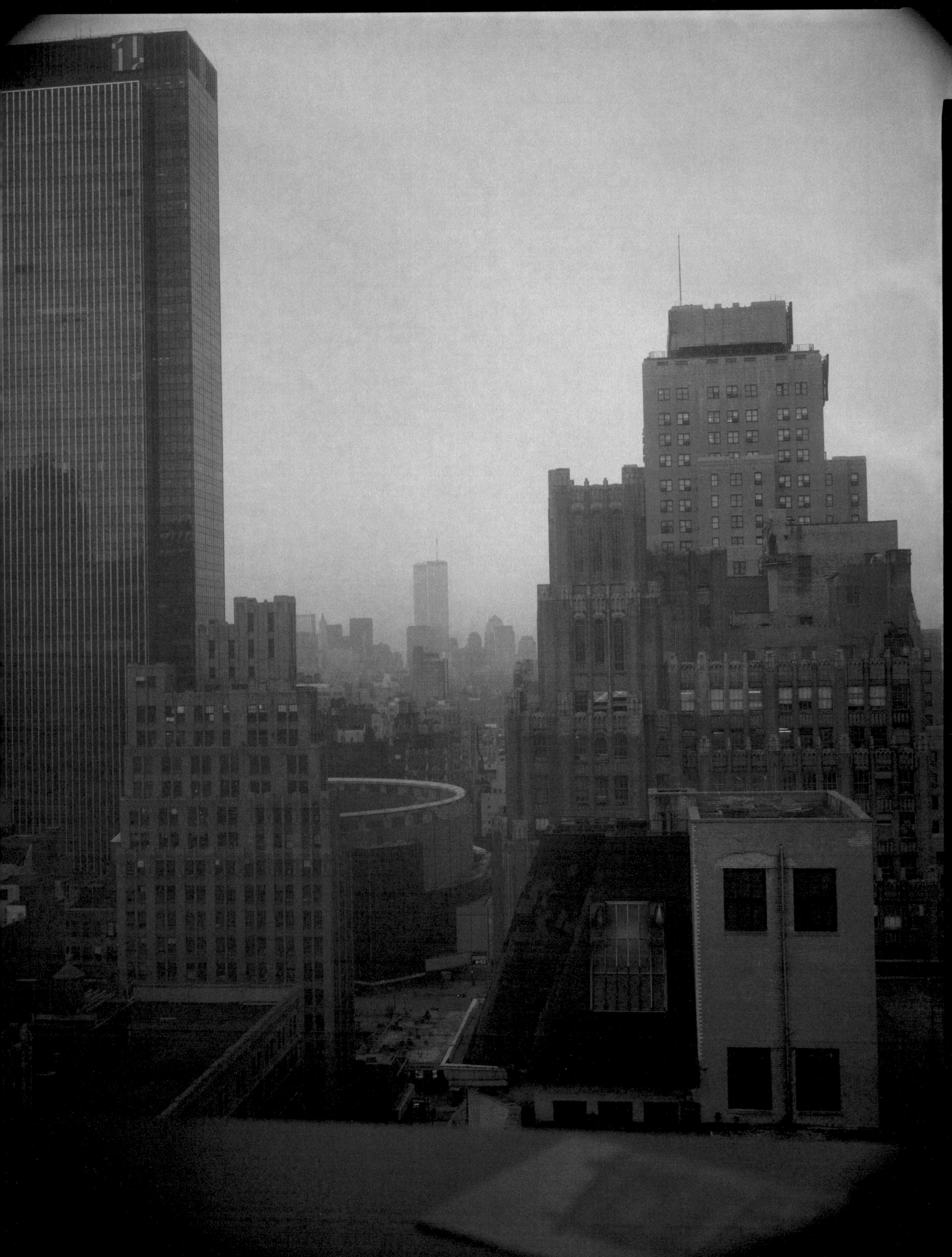

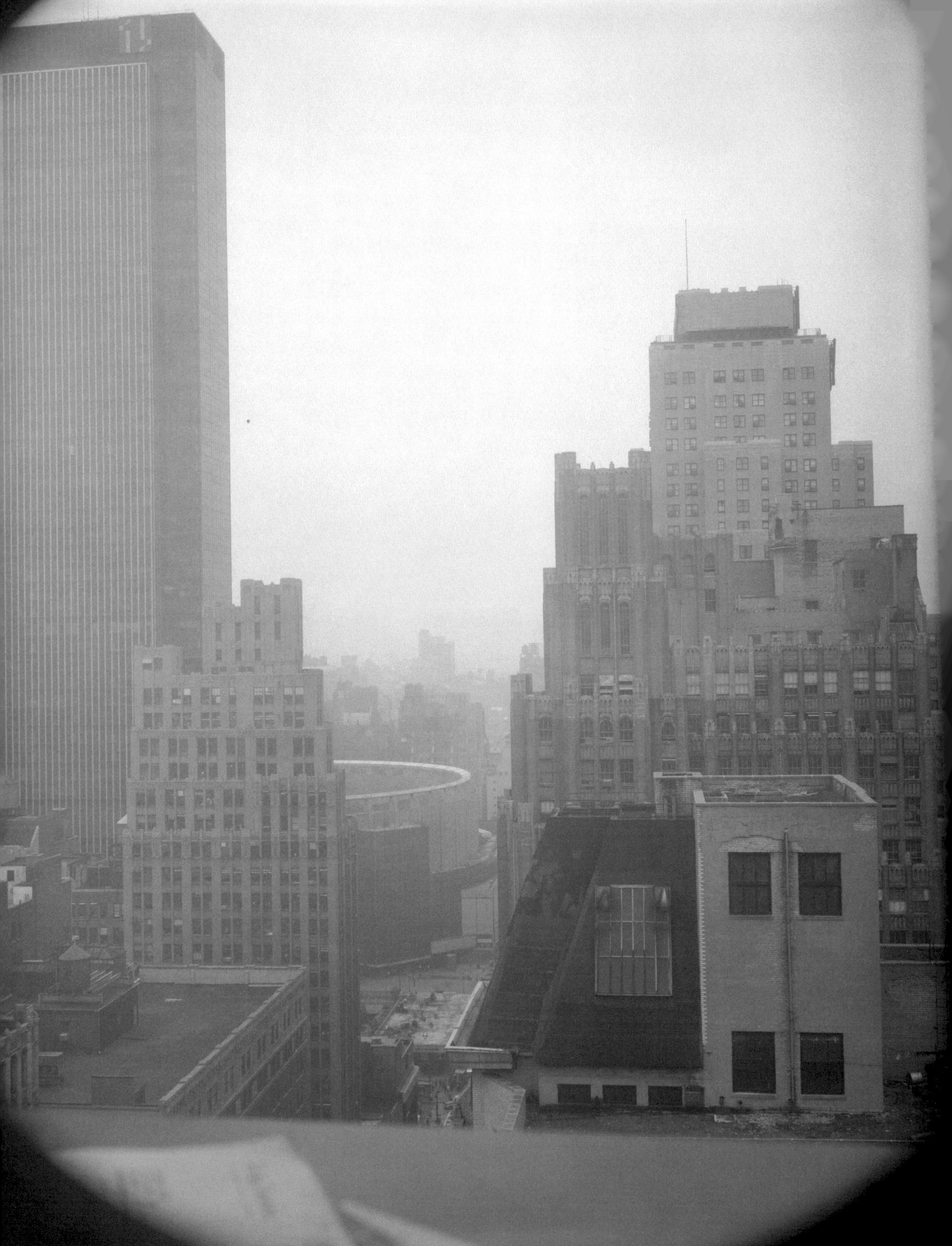

September 19, 1997

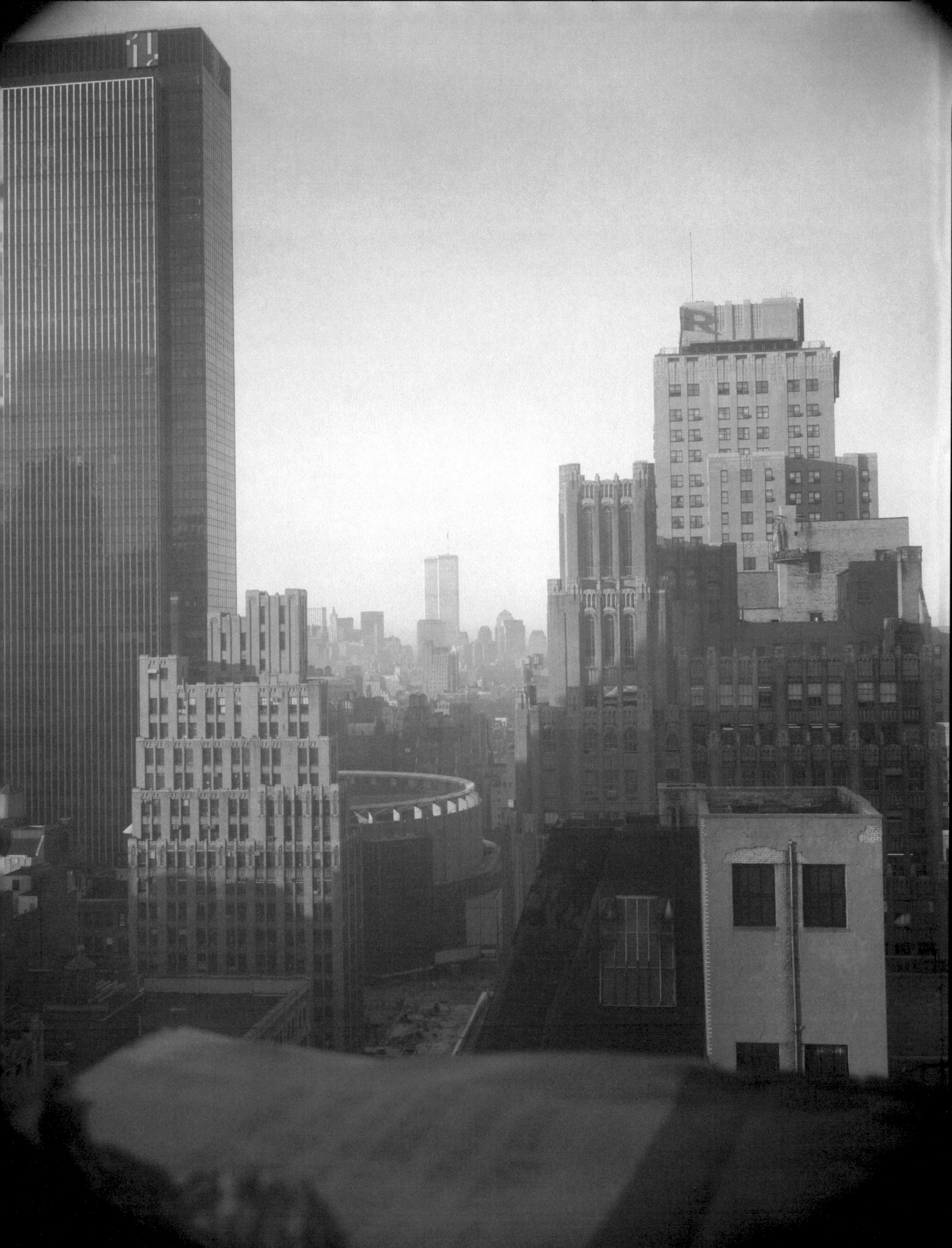

September 20, 1997

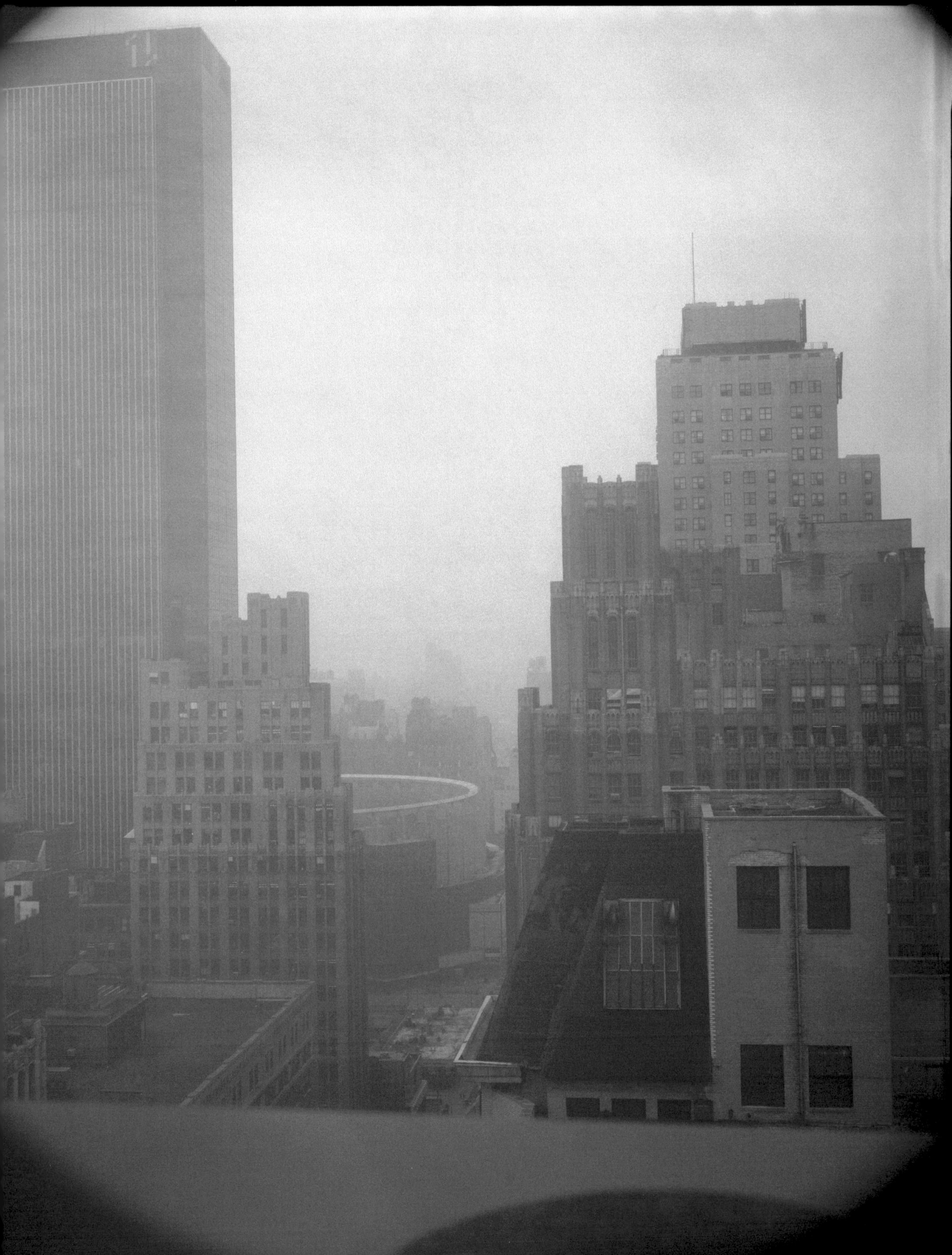

September 21, 1997

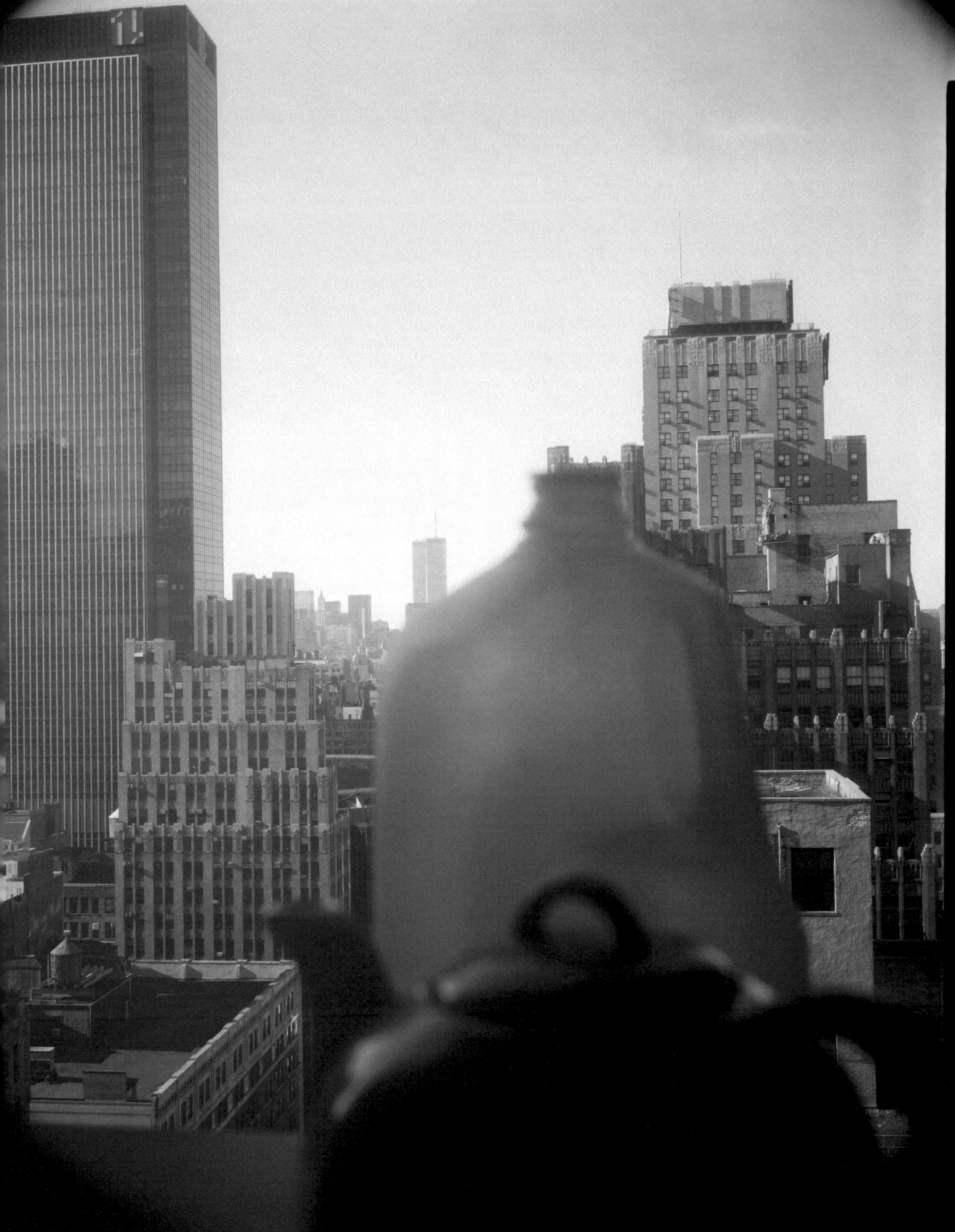

September 22, 1997

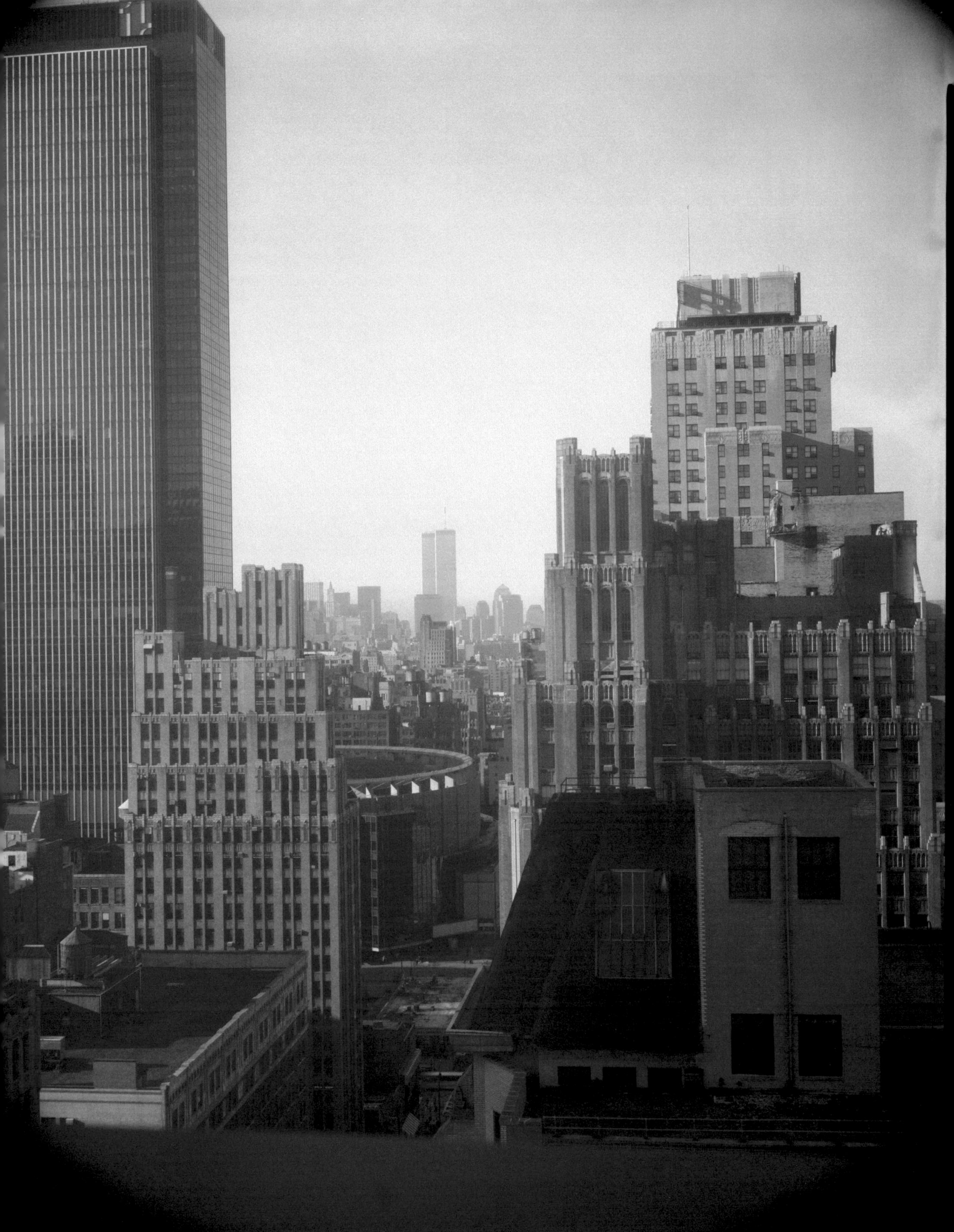

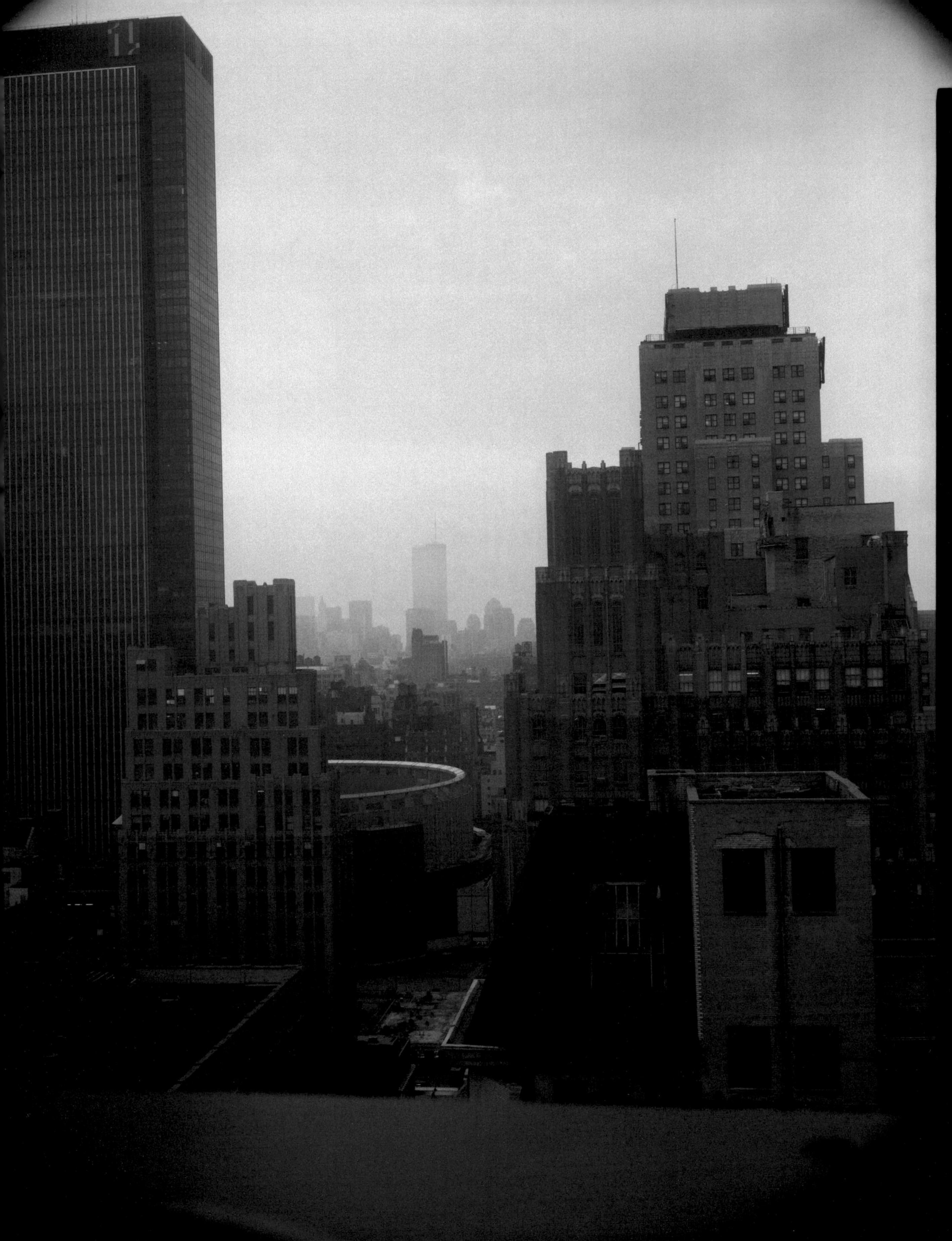

September 24, 1997

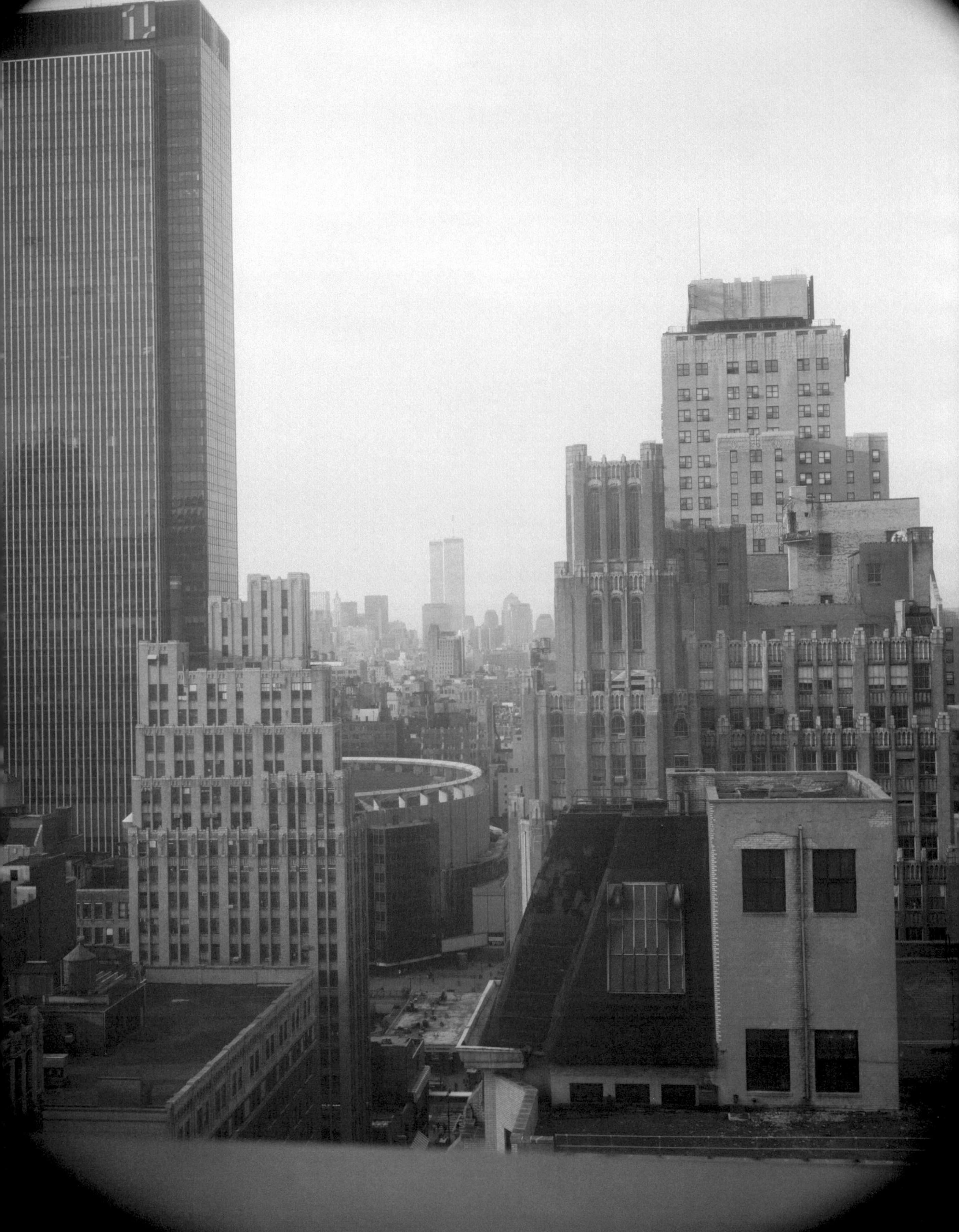

September 25, 1997

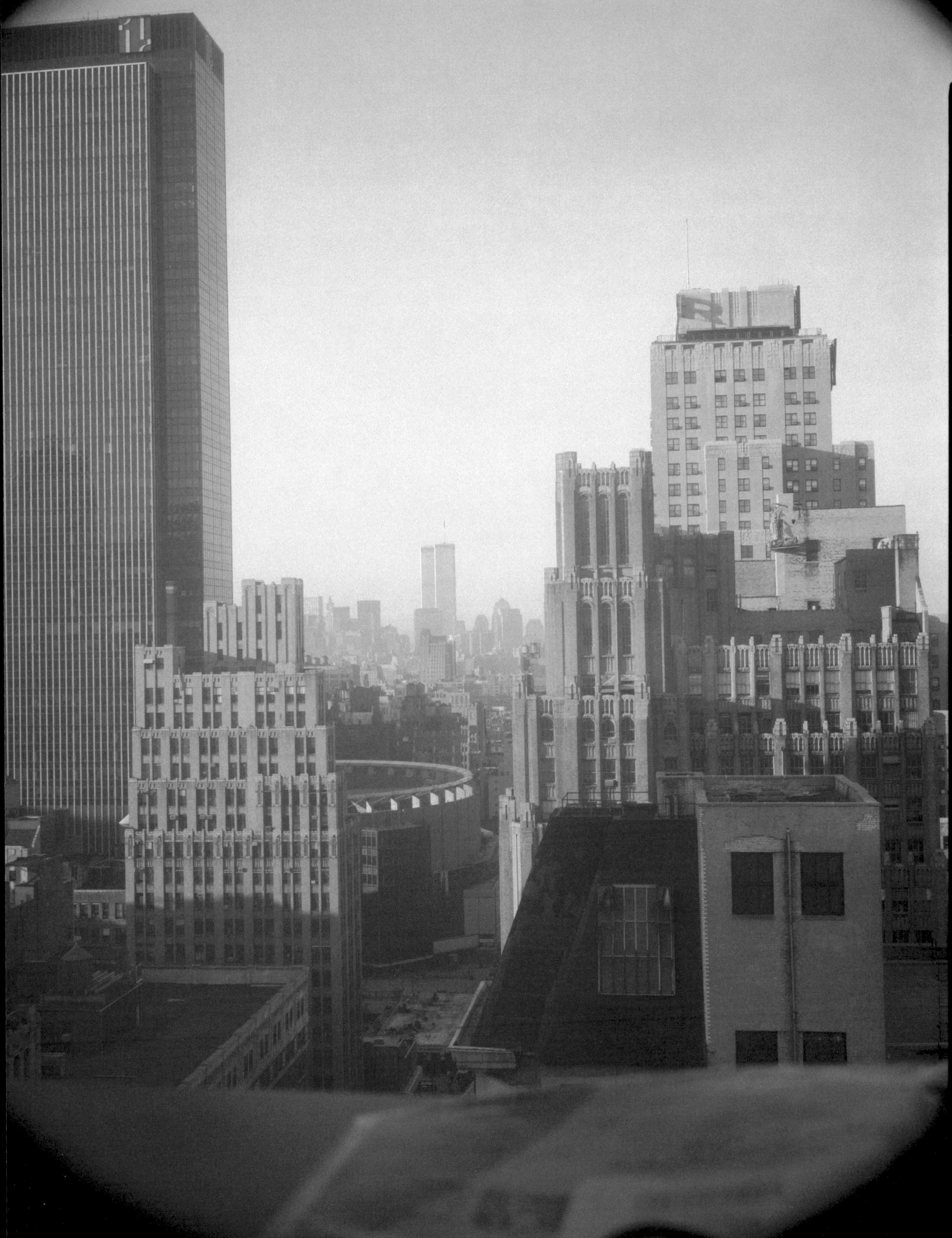

September 26, 1997

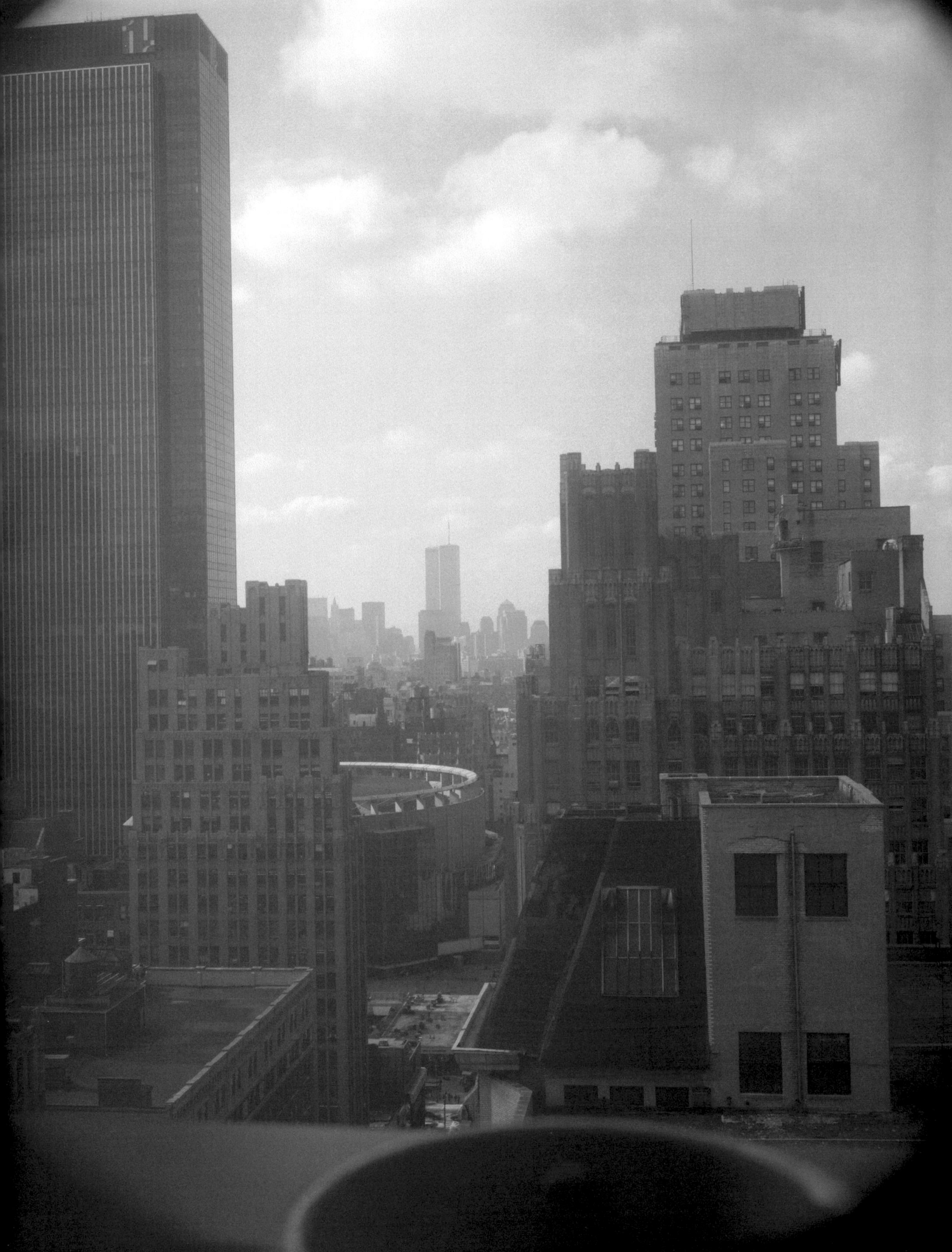

September 27, 1997

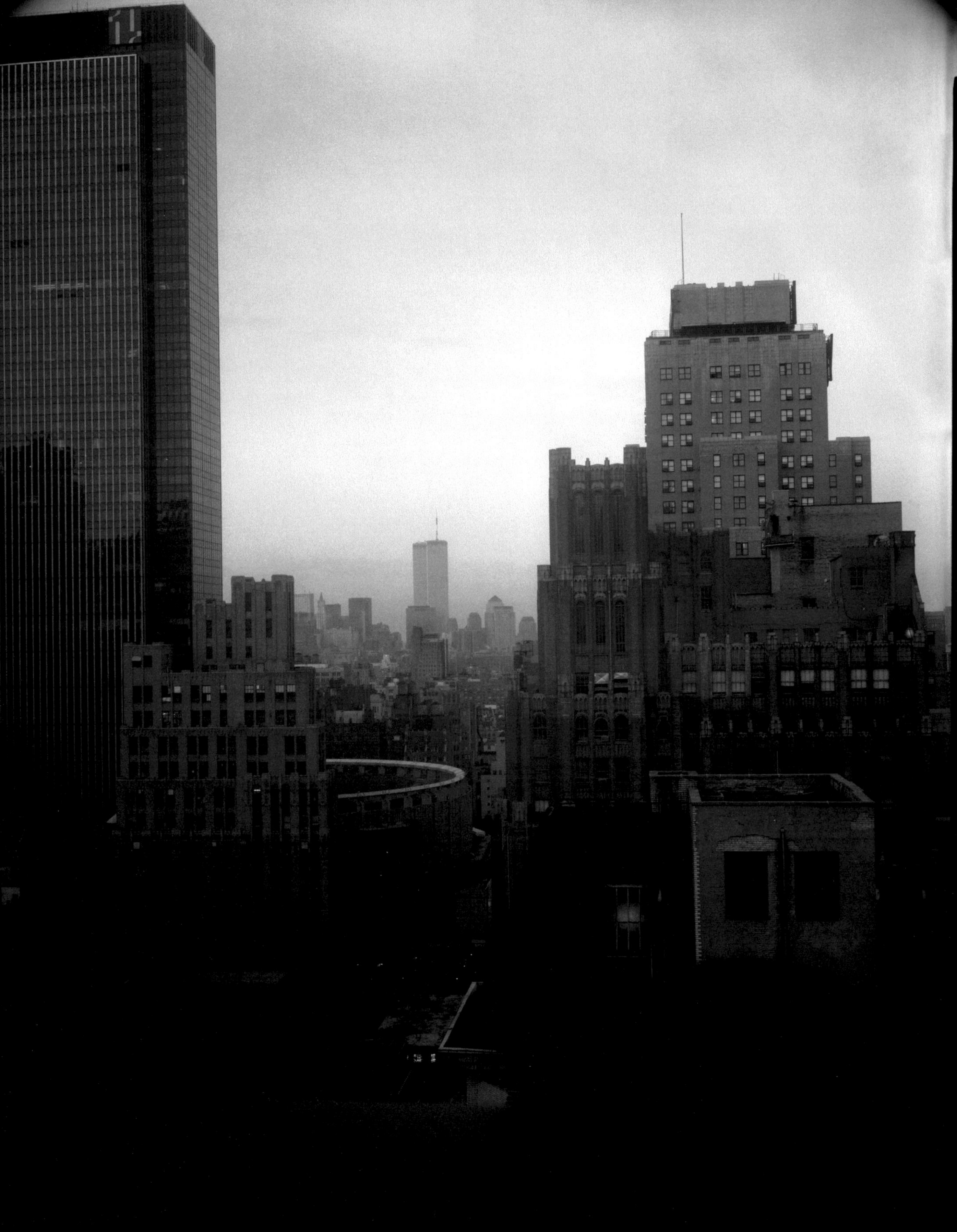

September 28, 1997

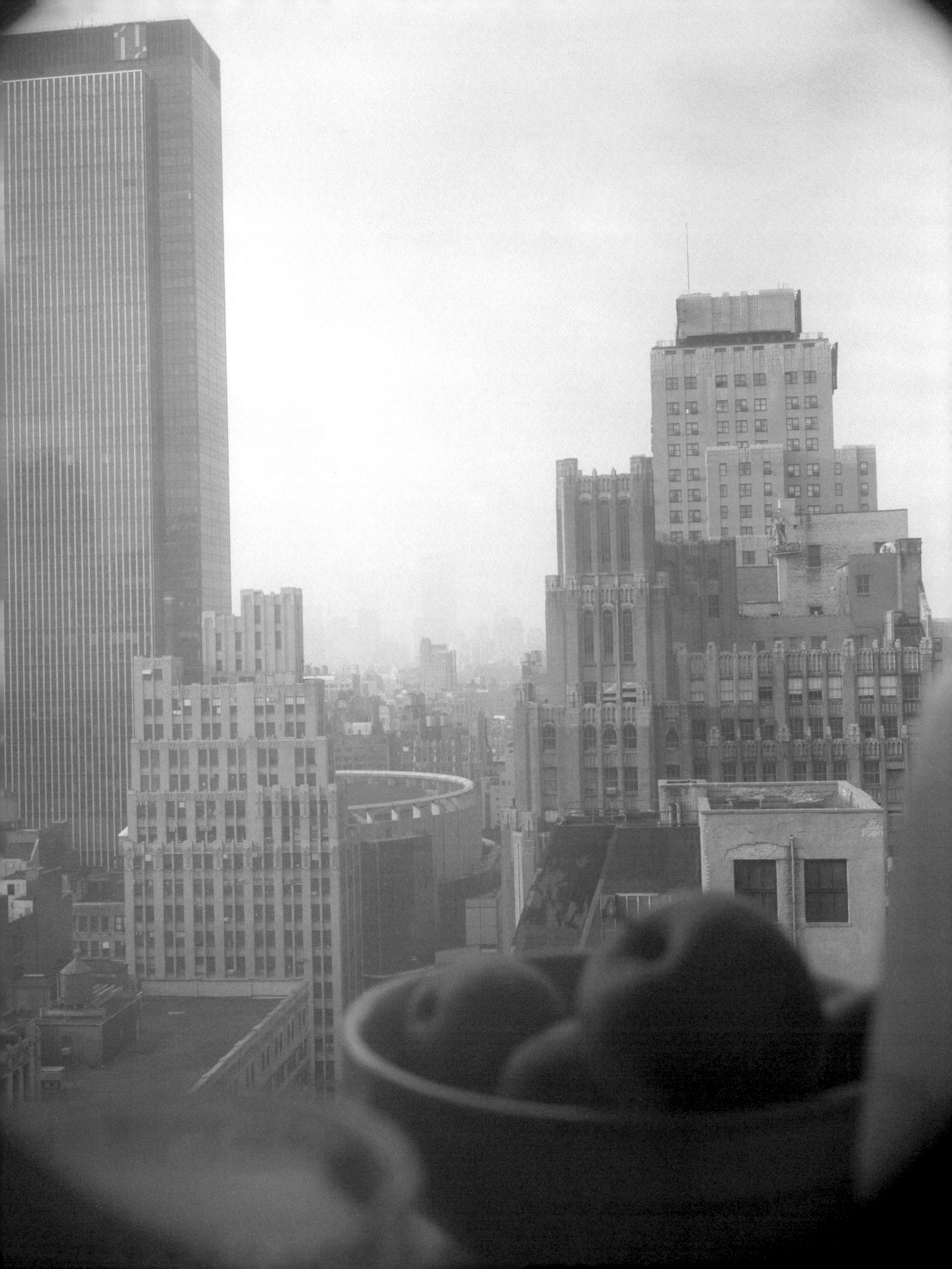

September 29, 1997

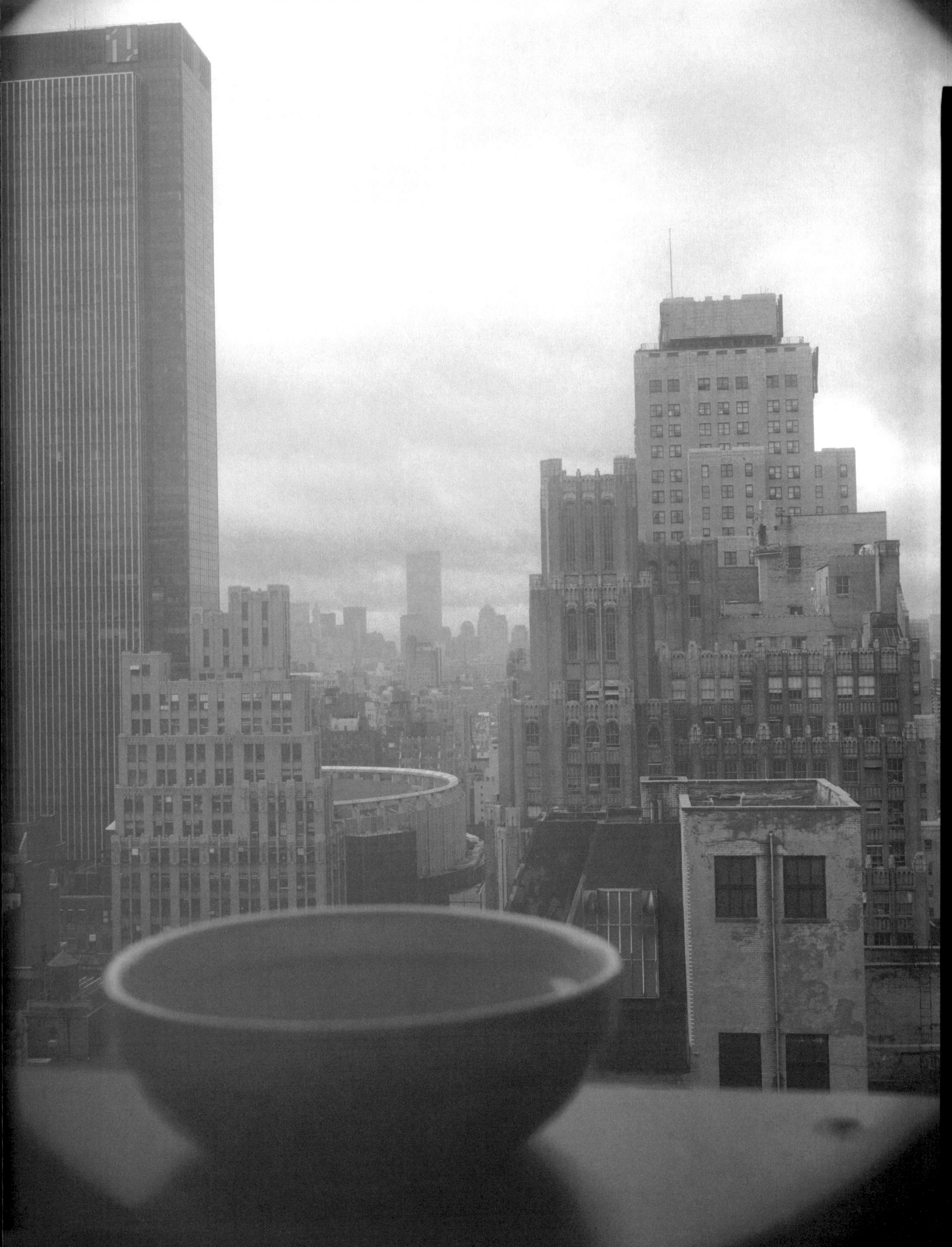

September 1, 1998

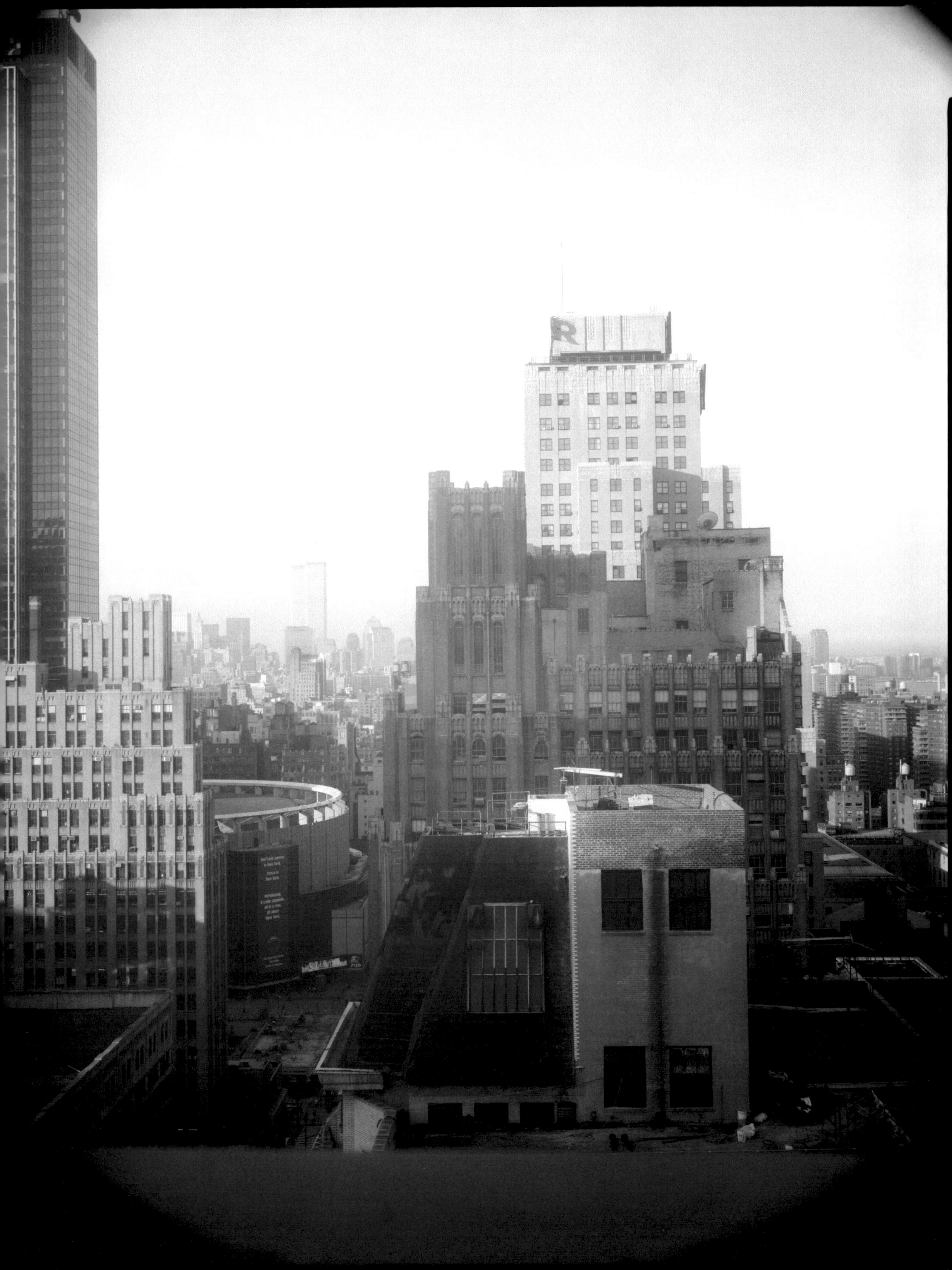

September 2, 1998

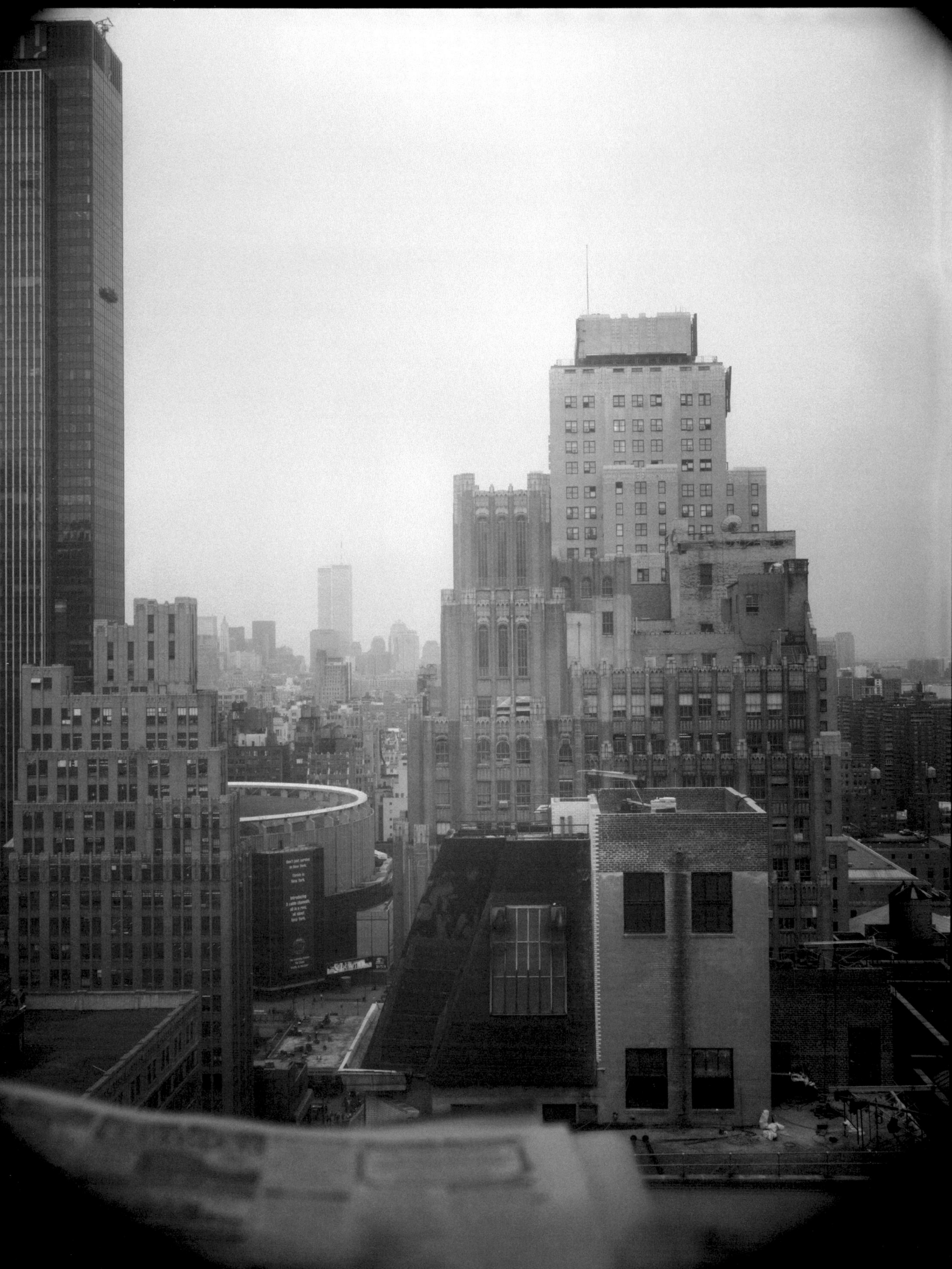

September 3, 1998

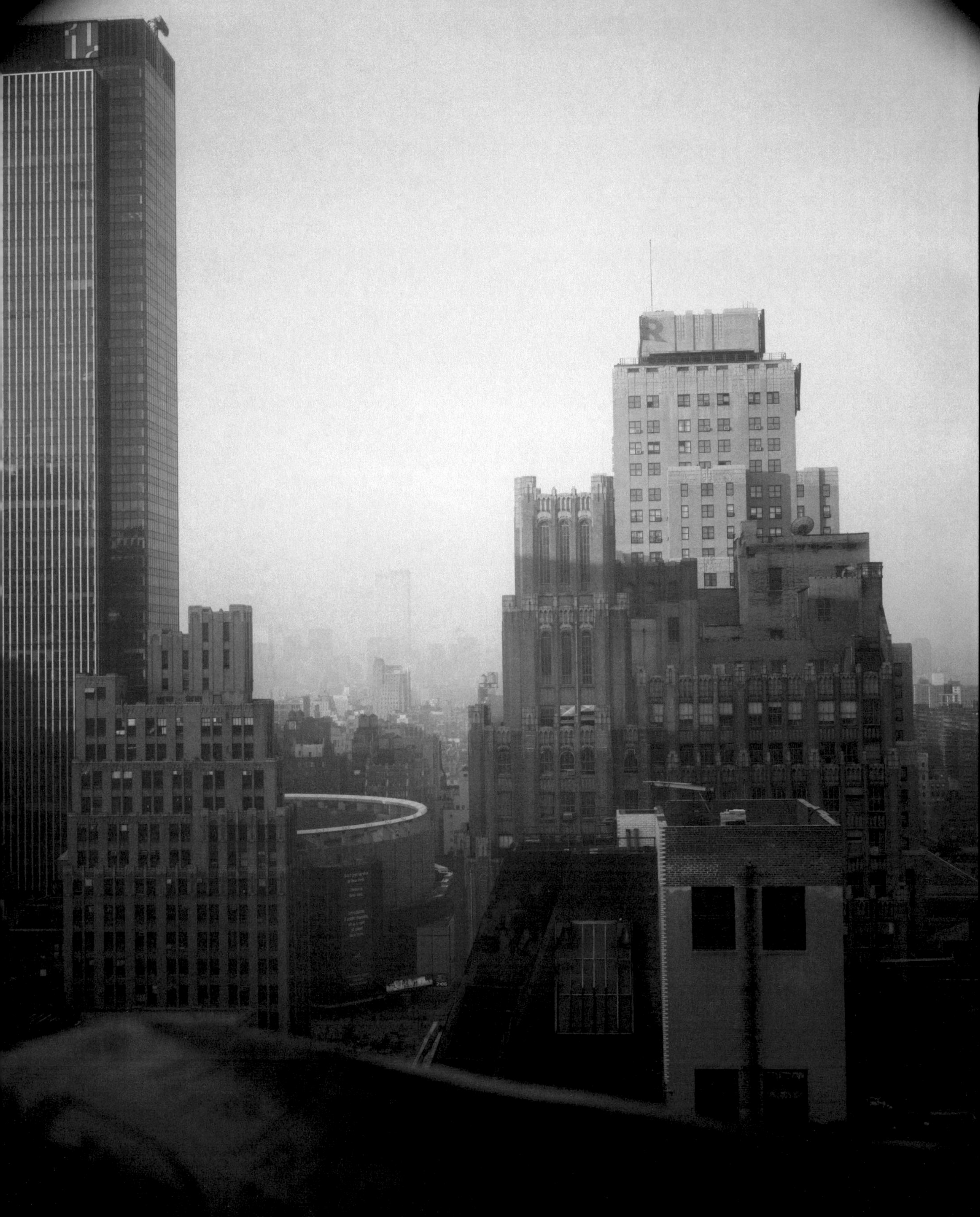

September 4, 1998

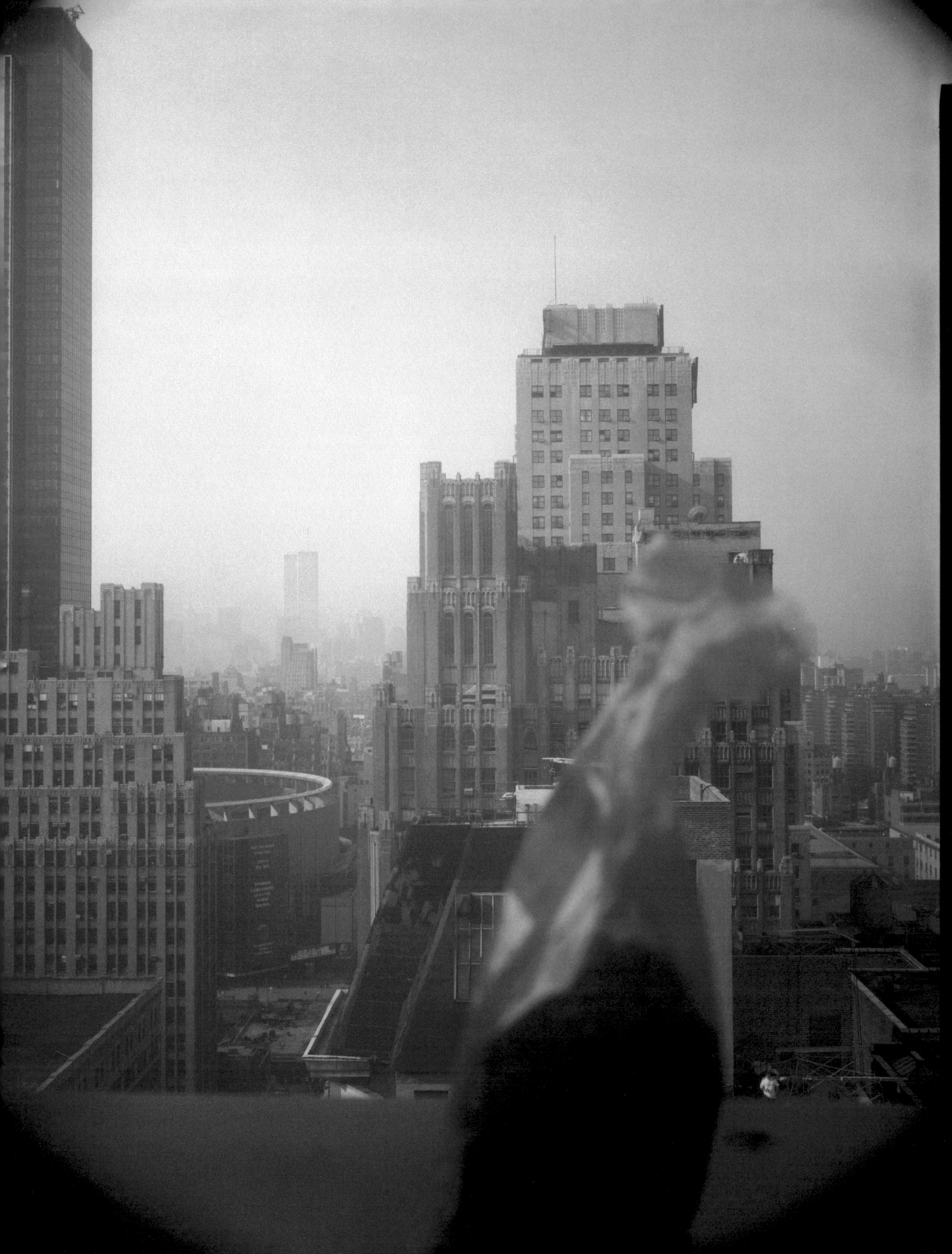

September 5, 1998

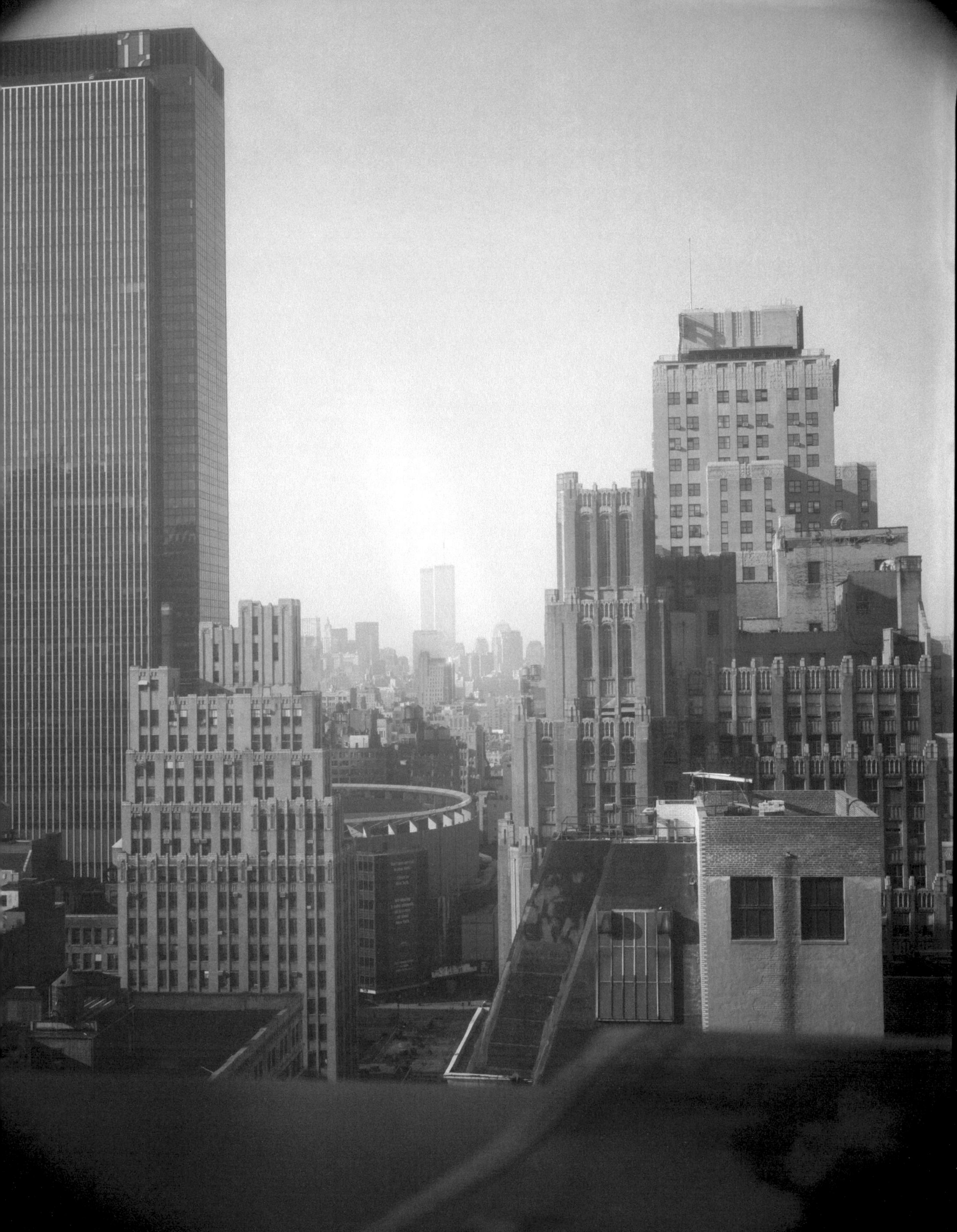

September 6, 1998

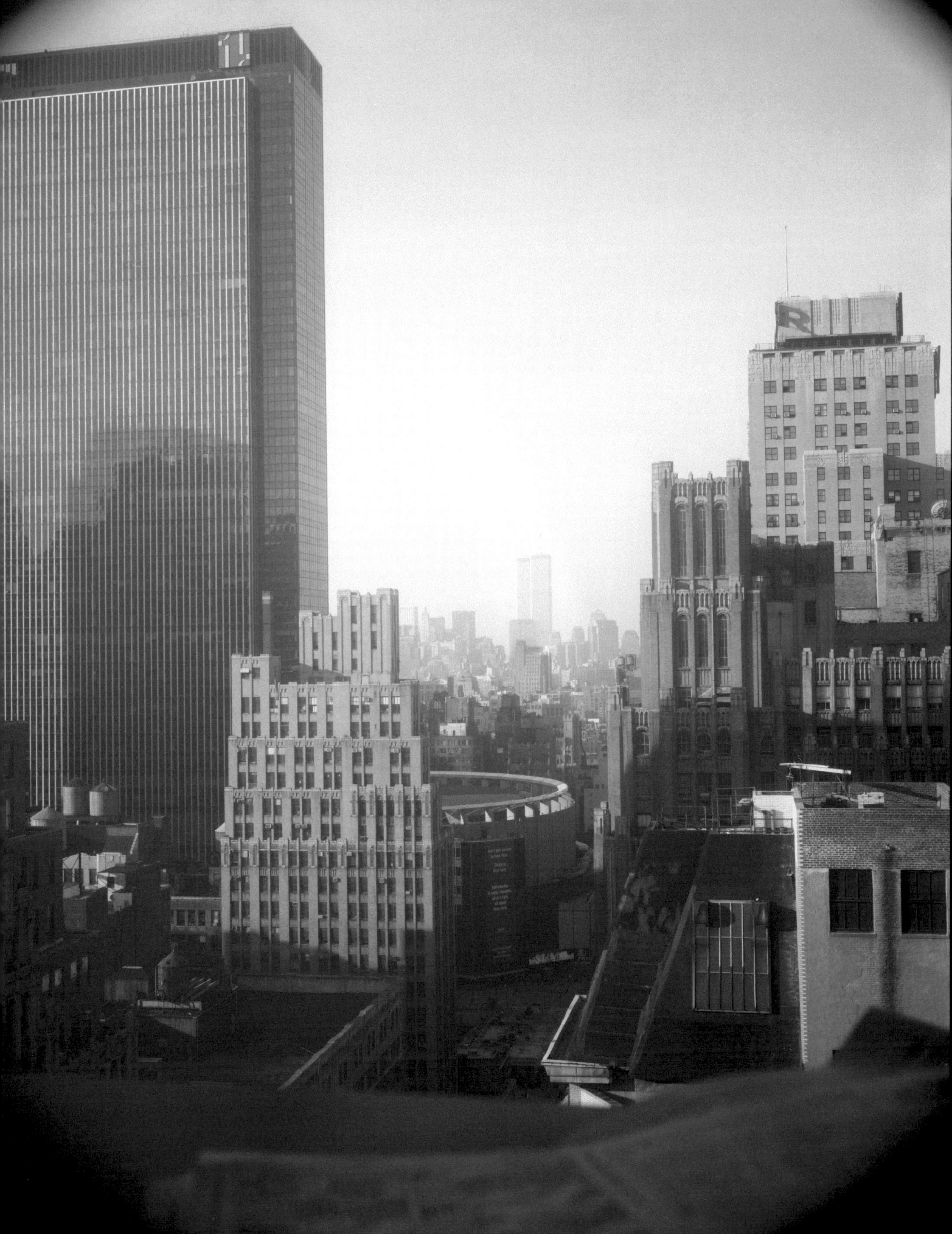

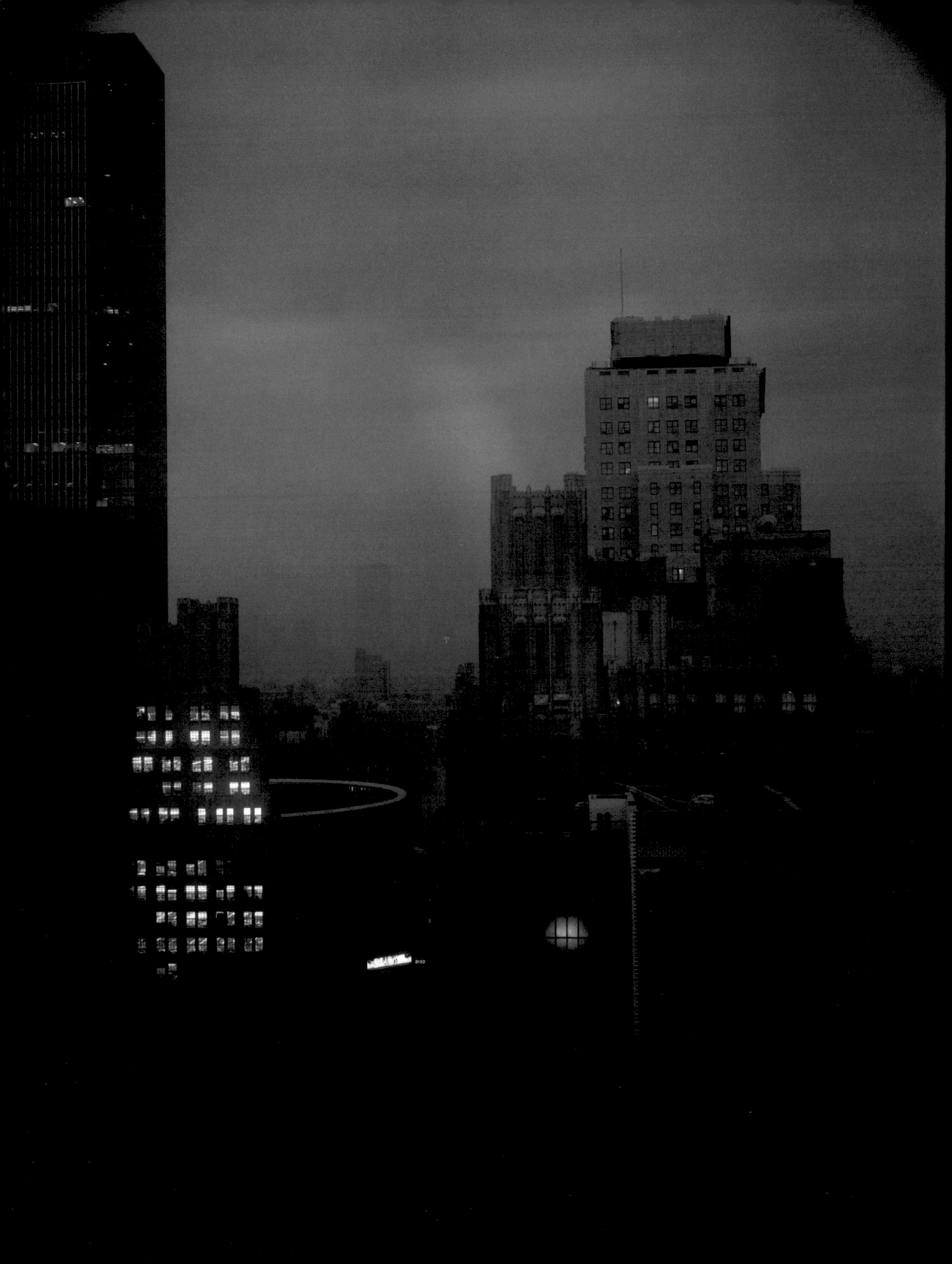

September 8, 1998

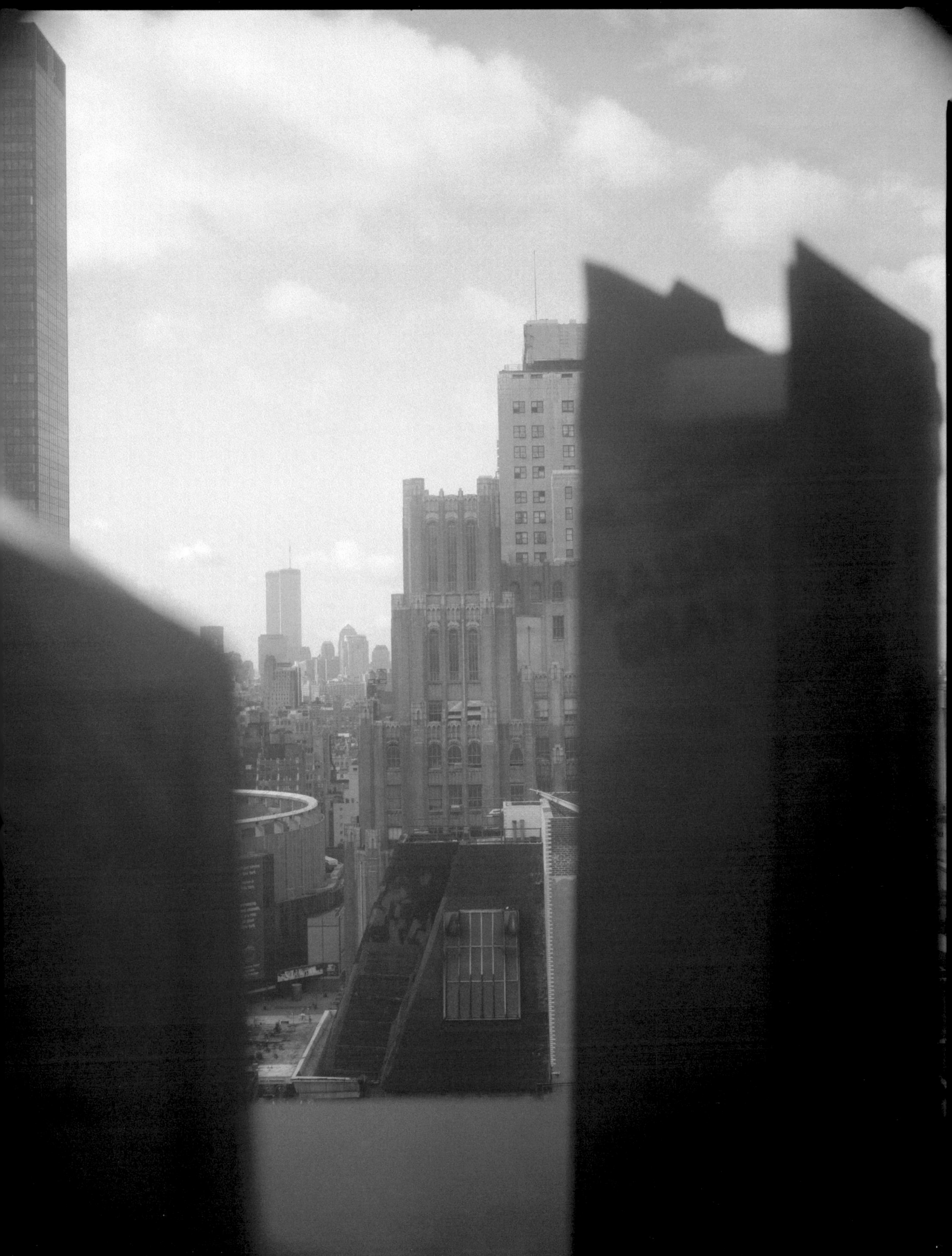

September 9, 1998

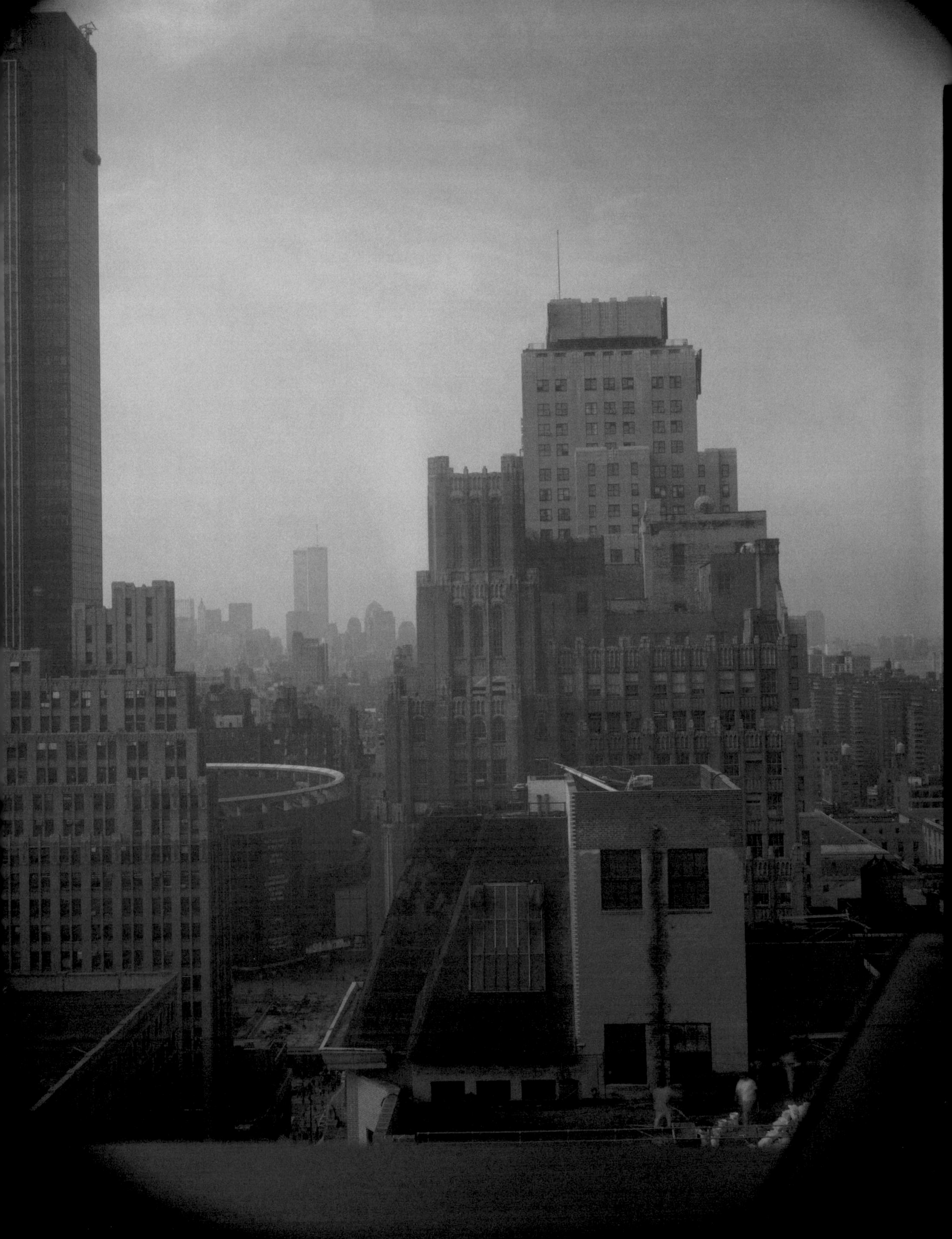

September 10, 1998

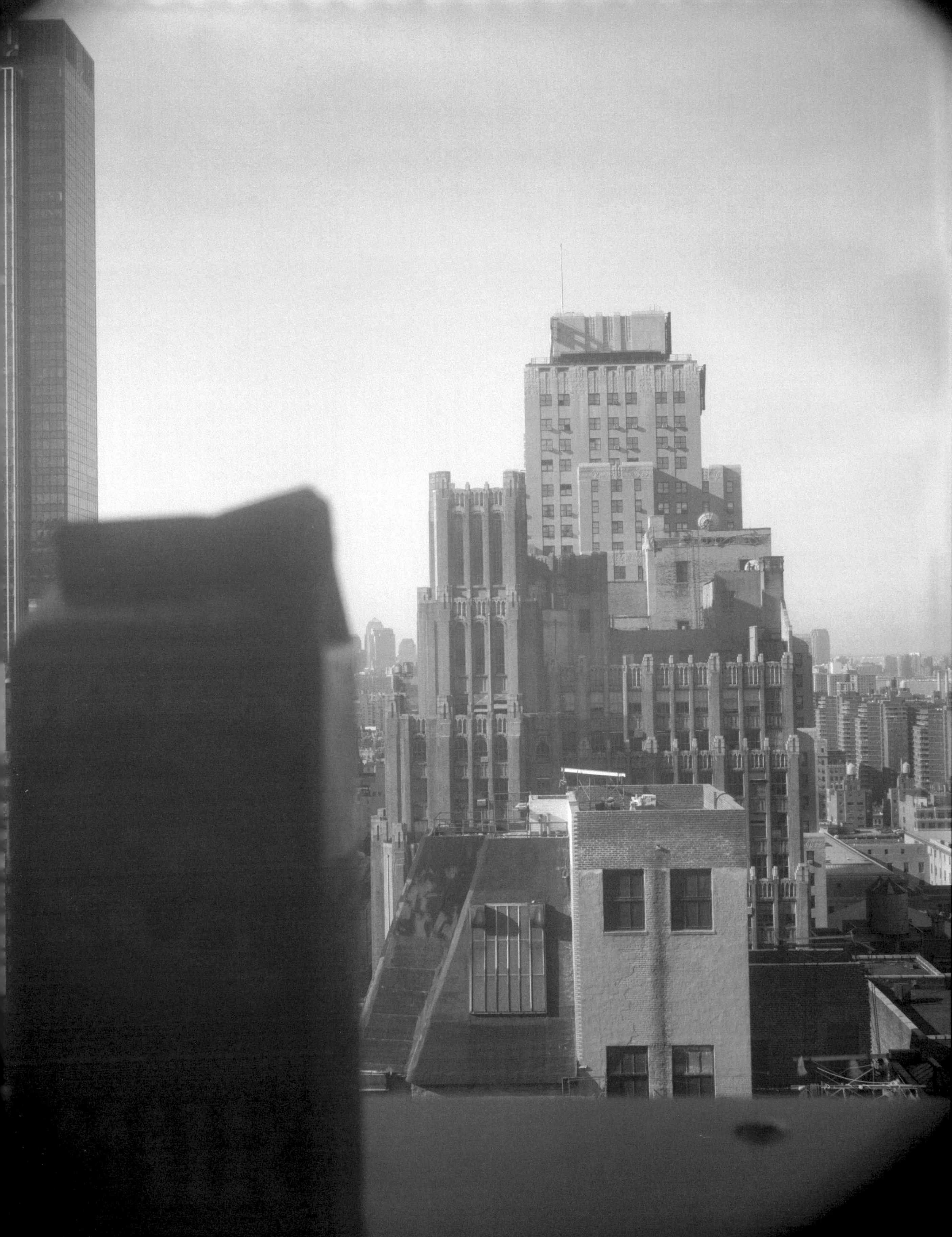

September 11, 1998

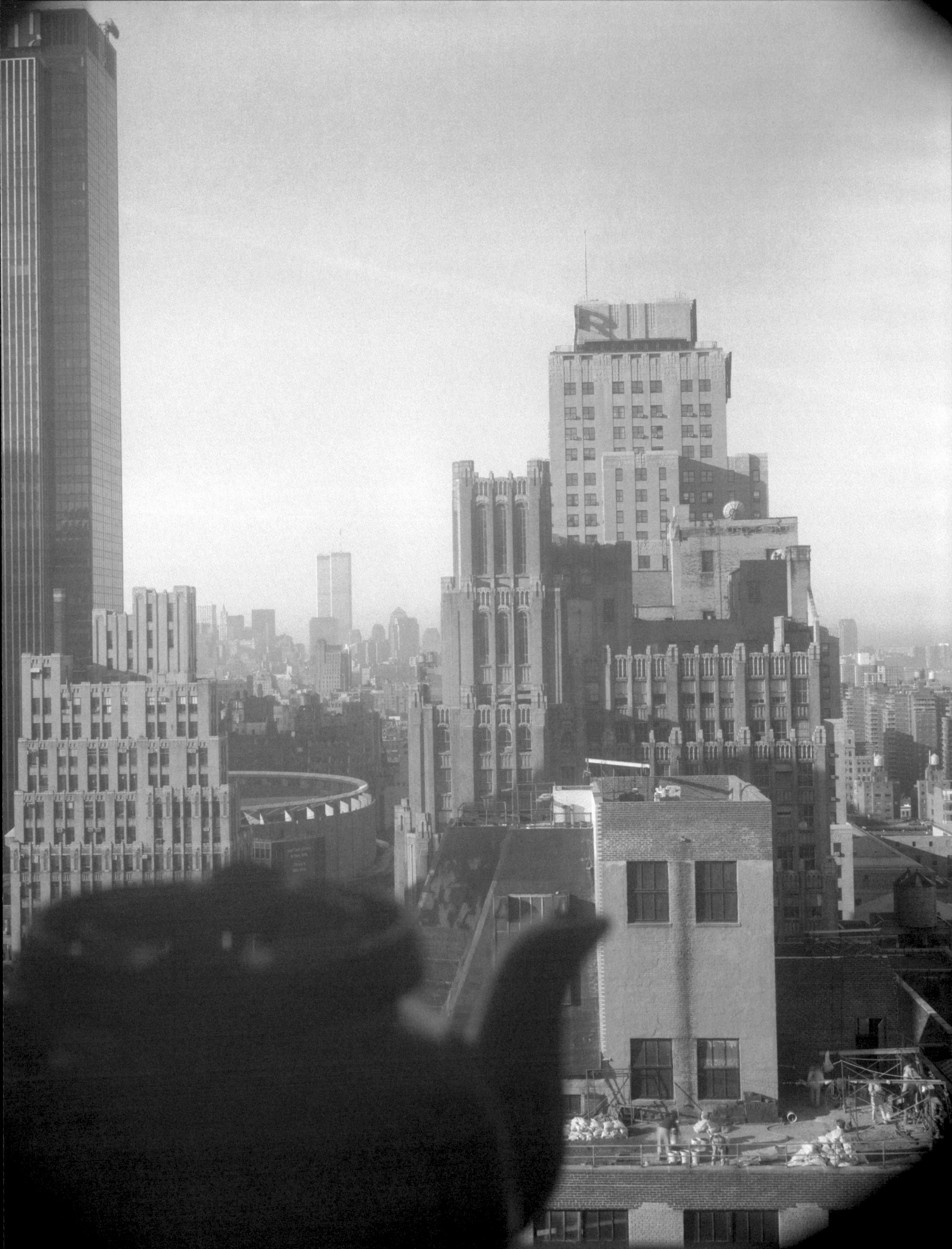

September 12, 1998

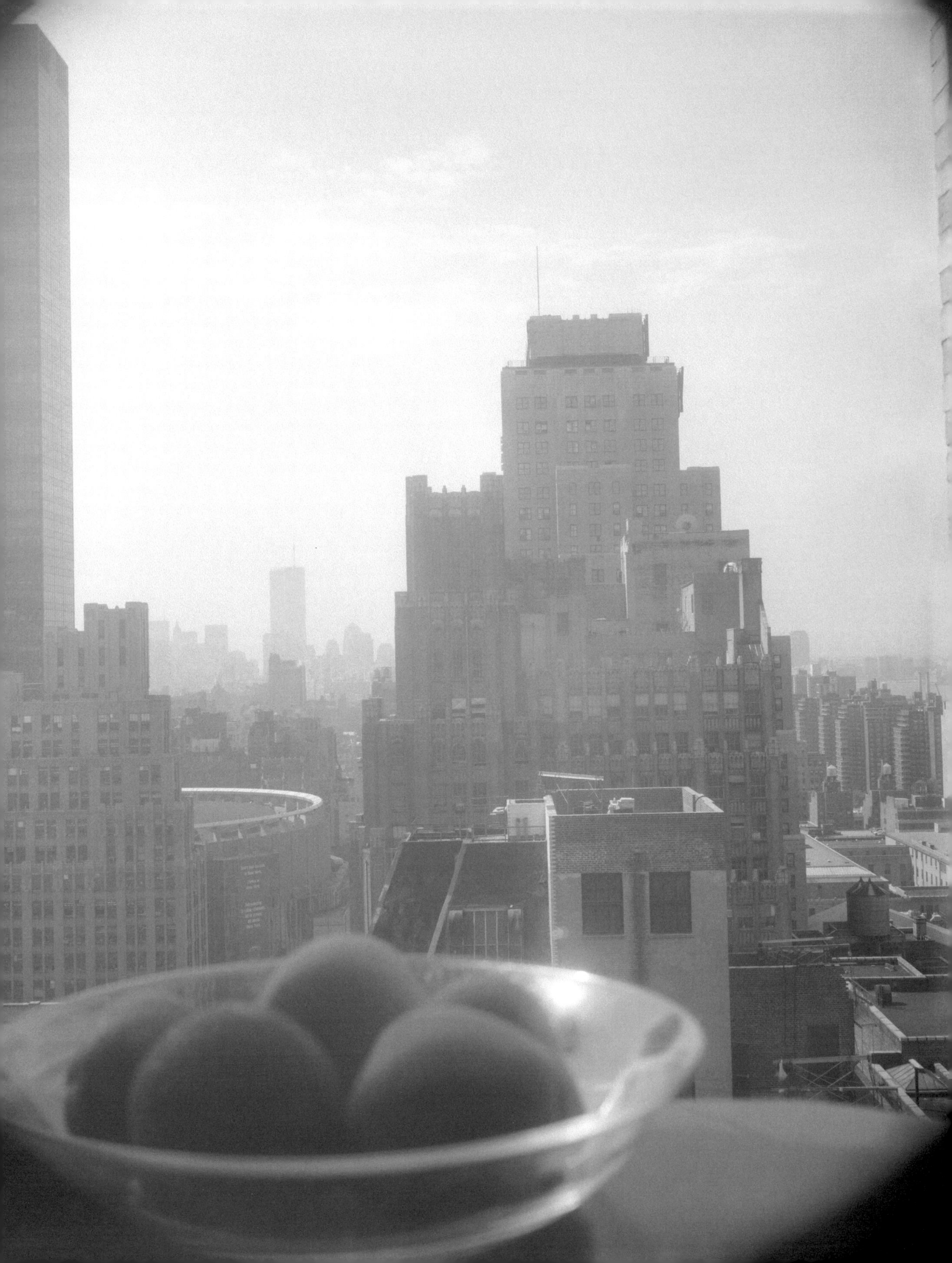

September 13, 1998

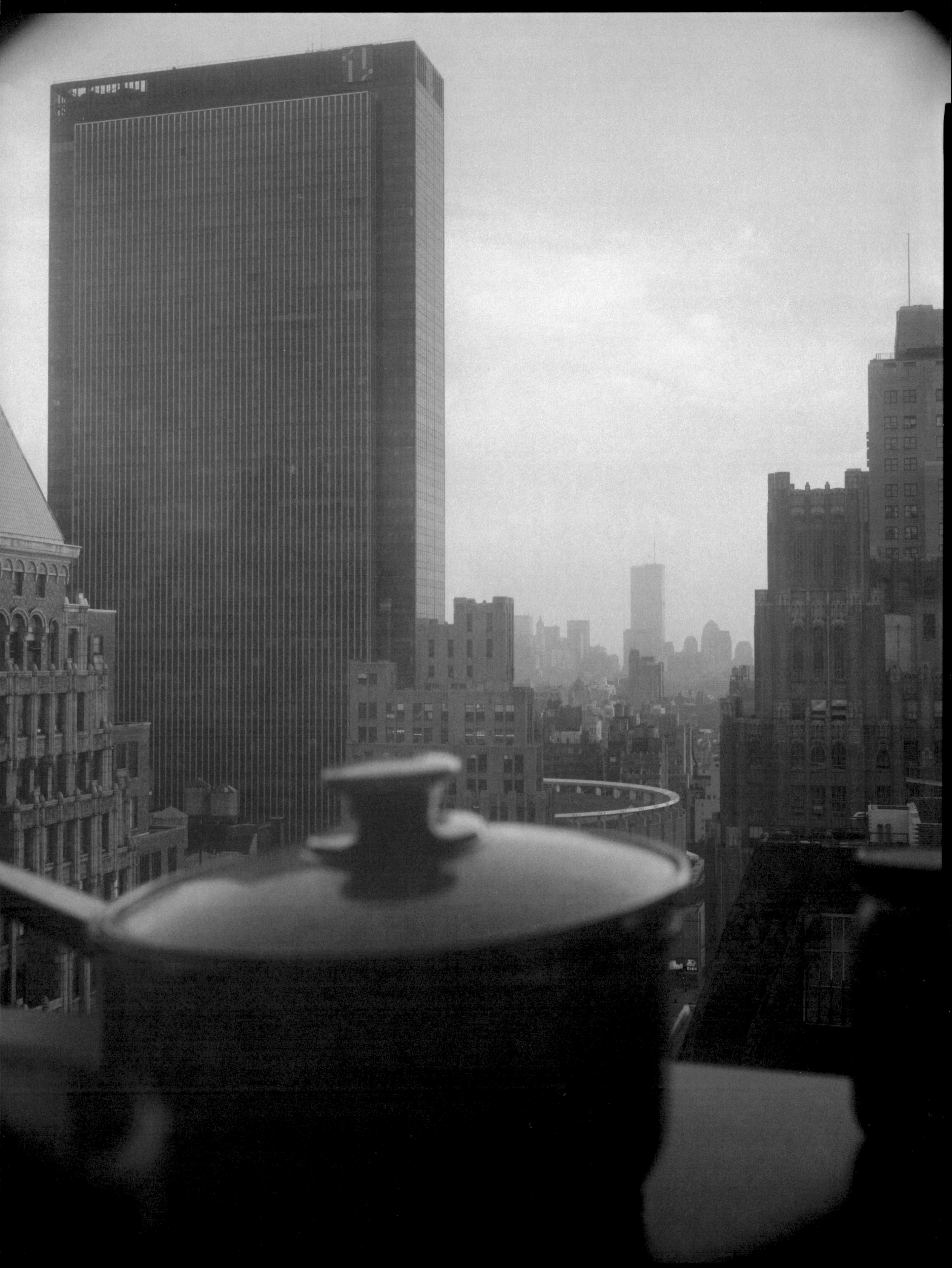

September 14, 1998

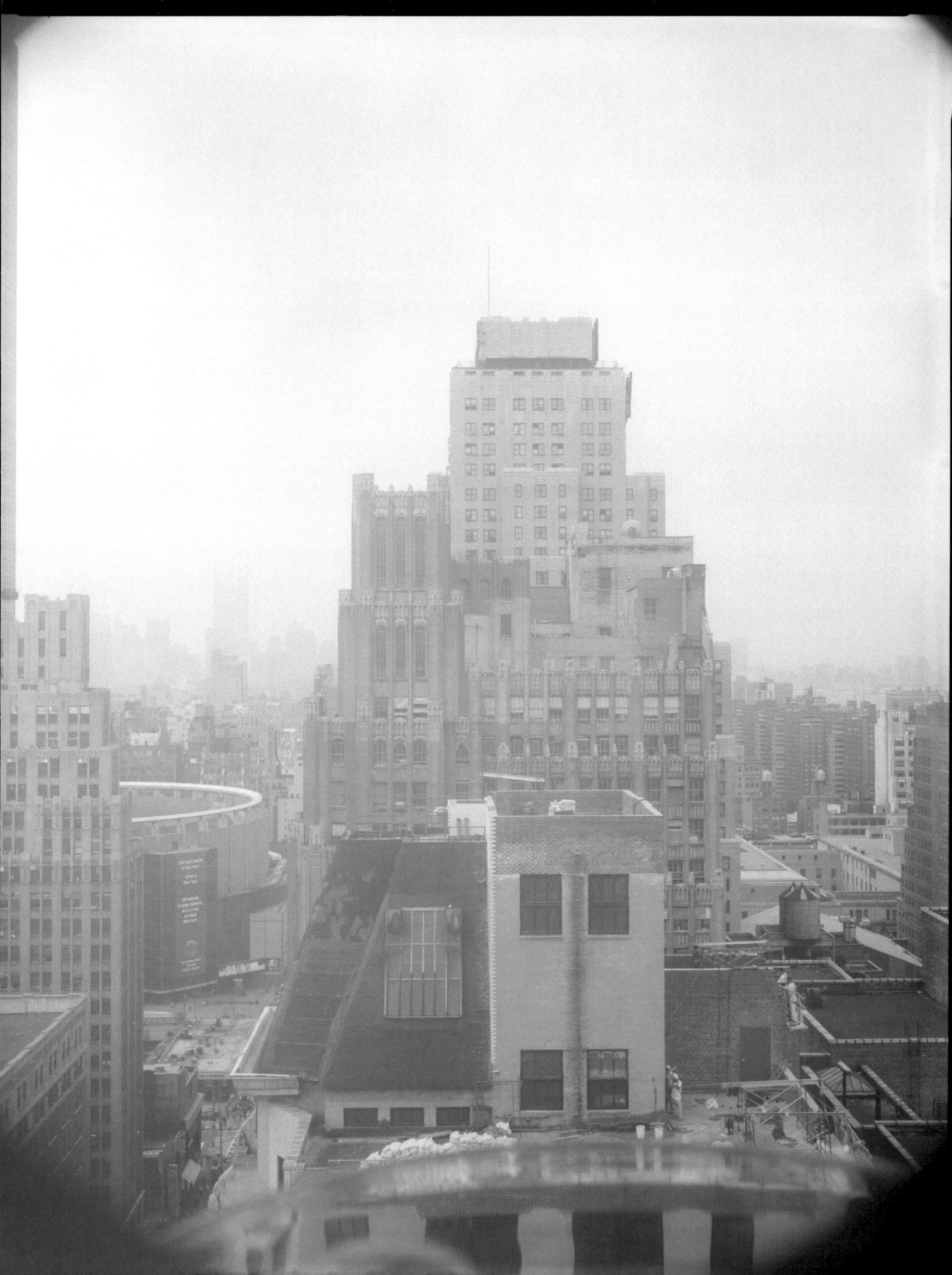

September 15, 1998

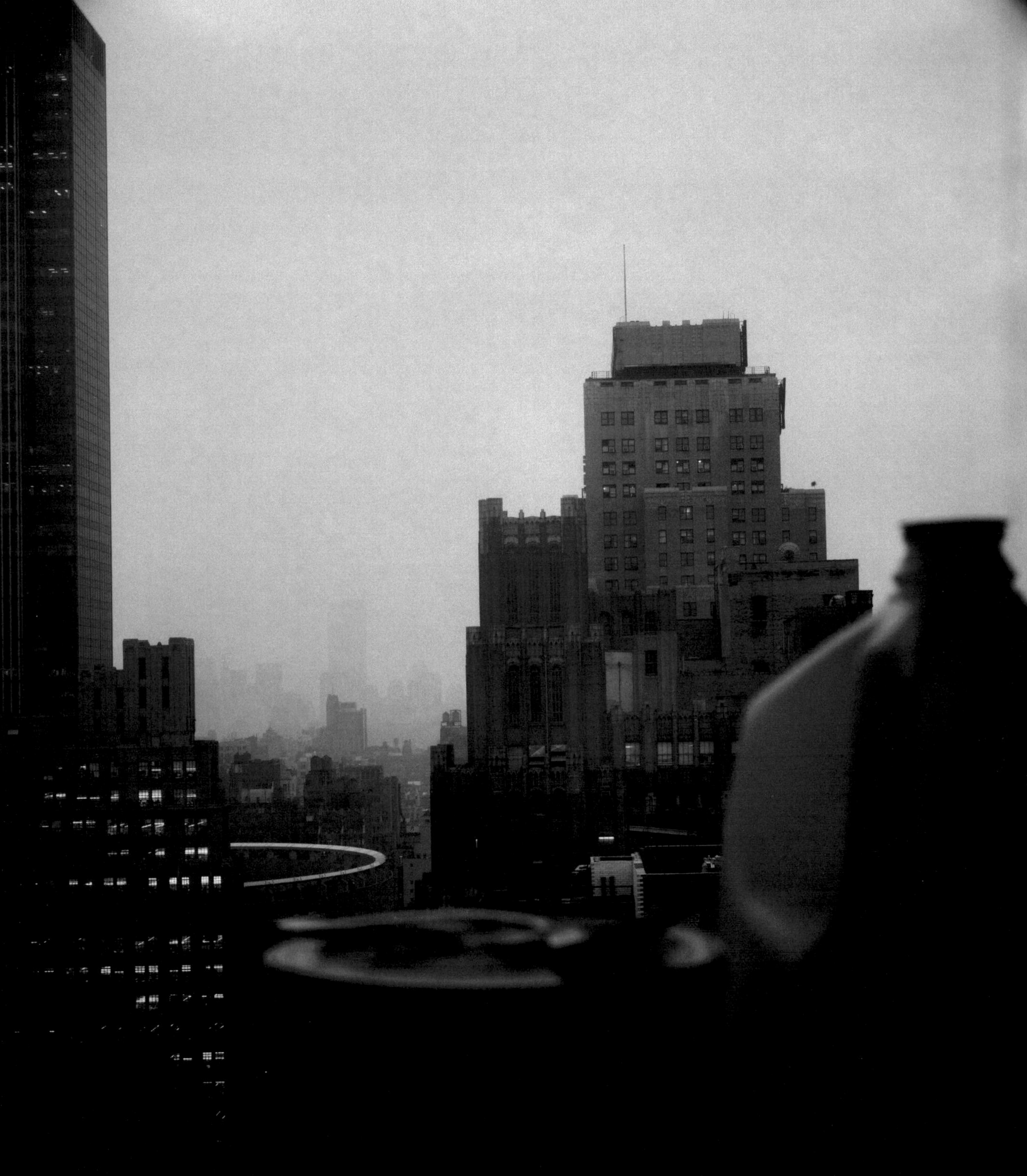

September 16, 1998

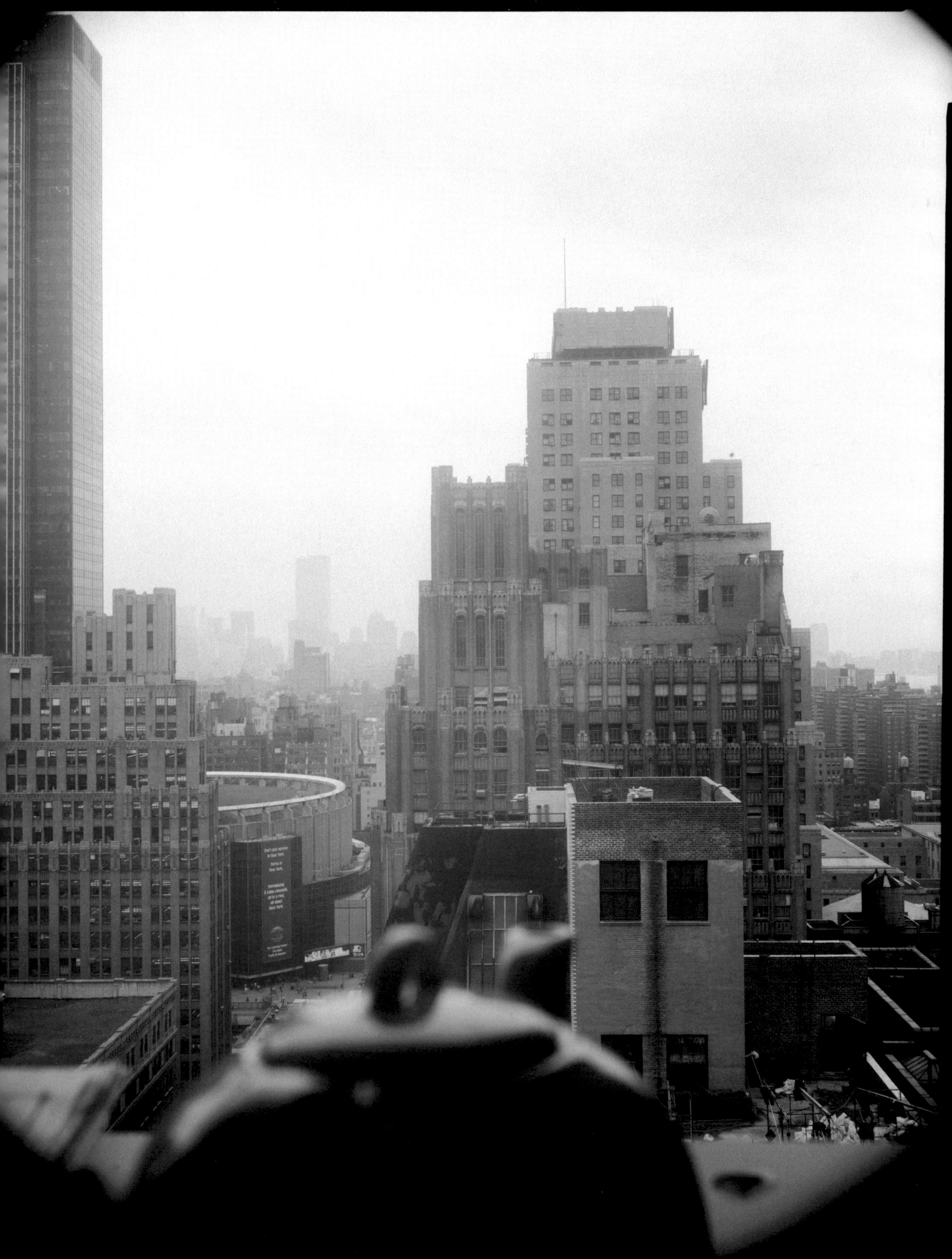

September 17, 1998

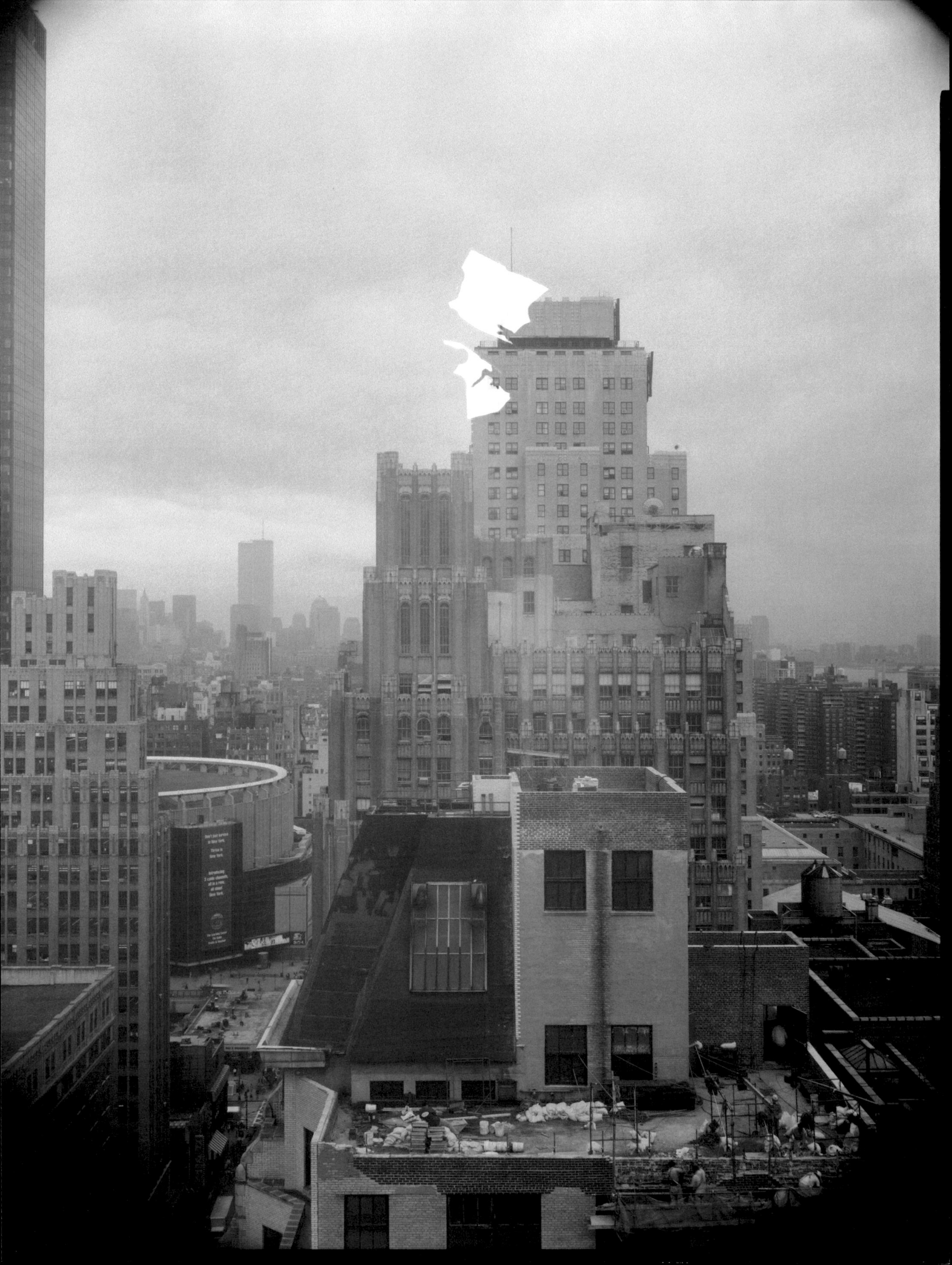

September 18, 1998

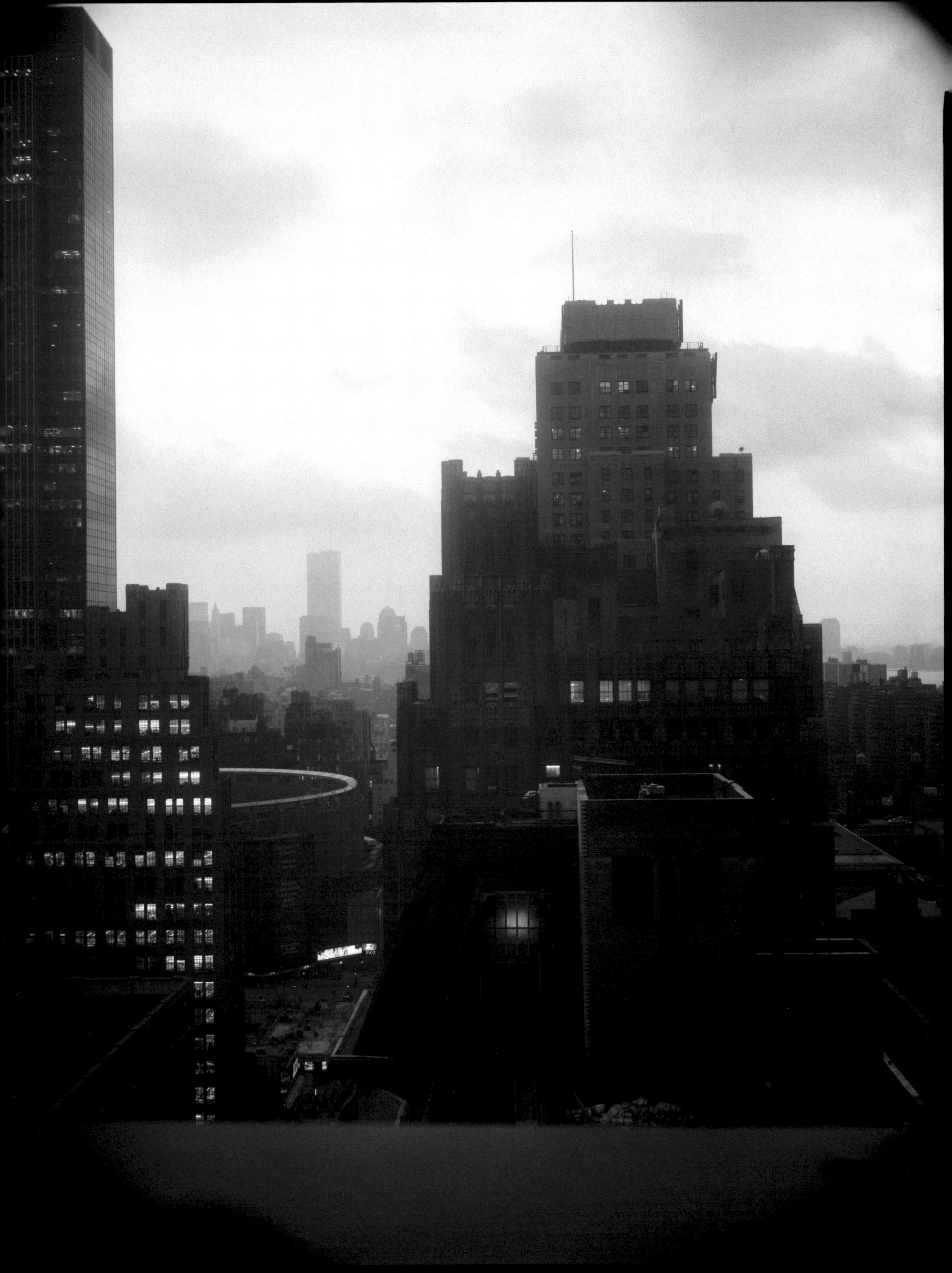

September 19, 1998

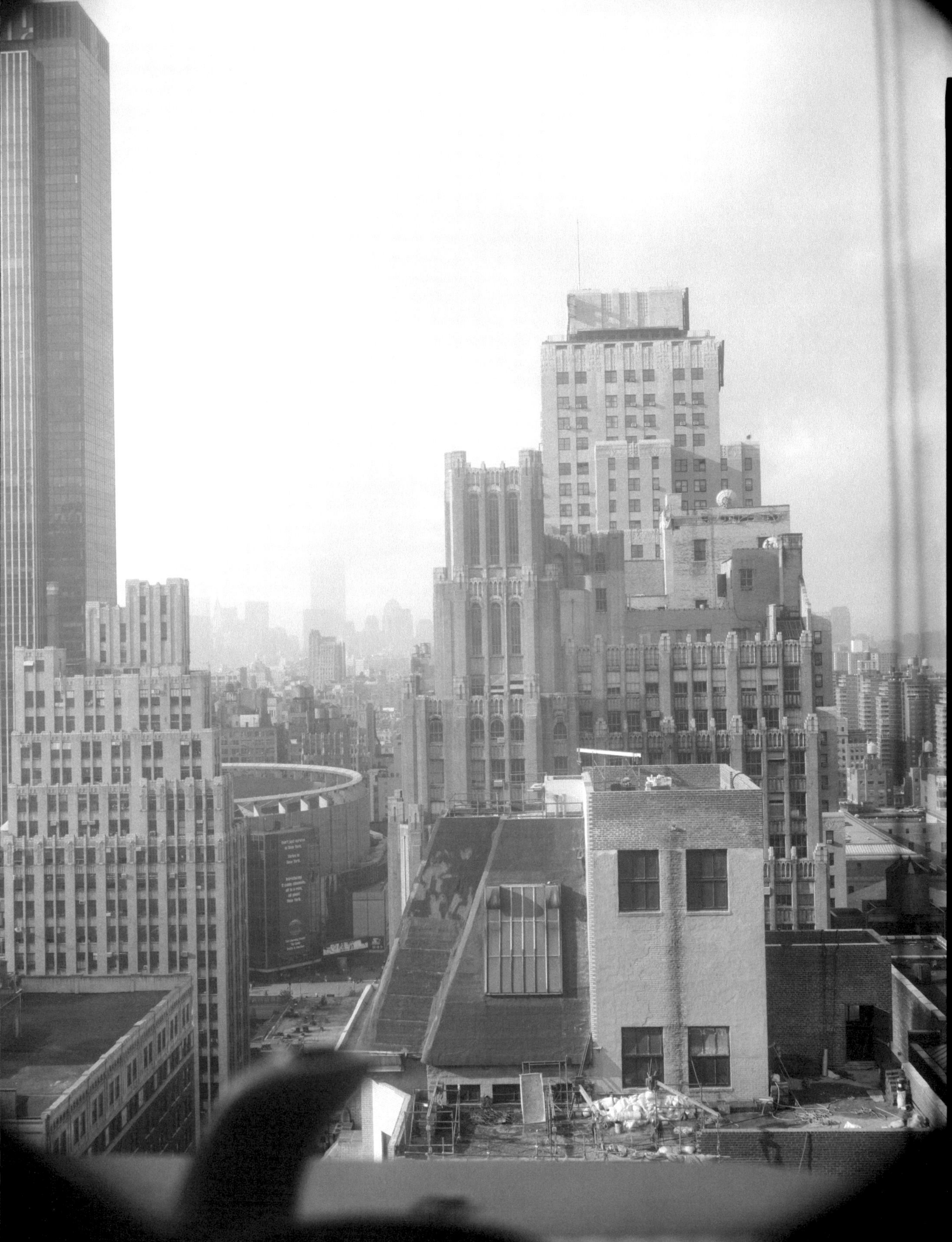

September 20, 1998

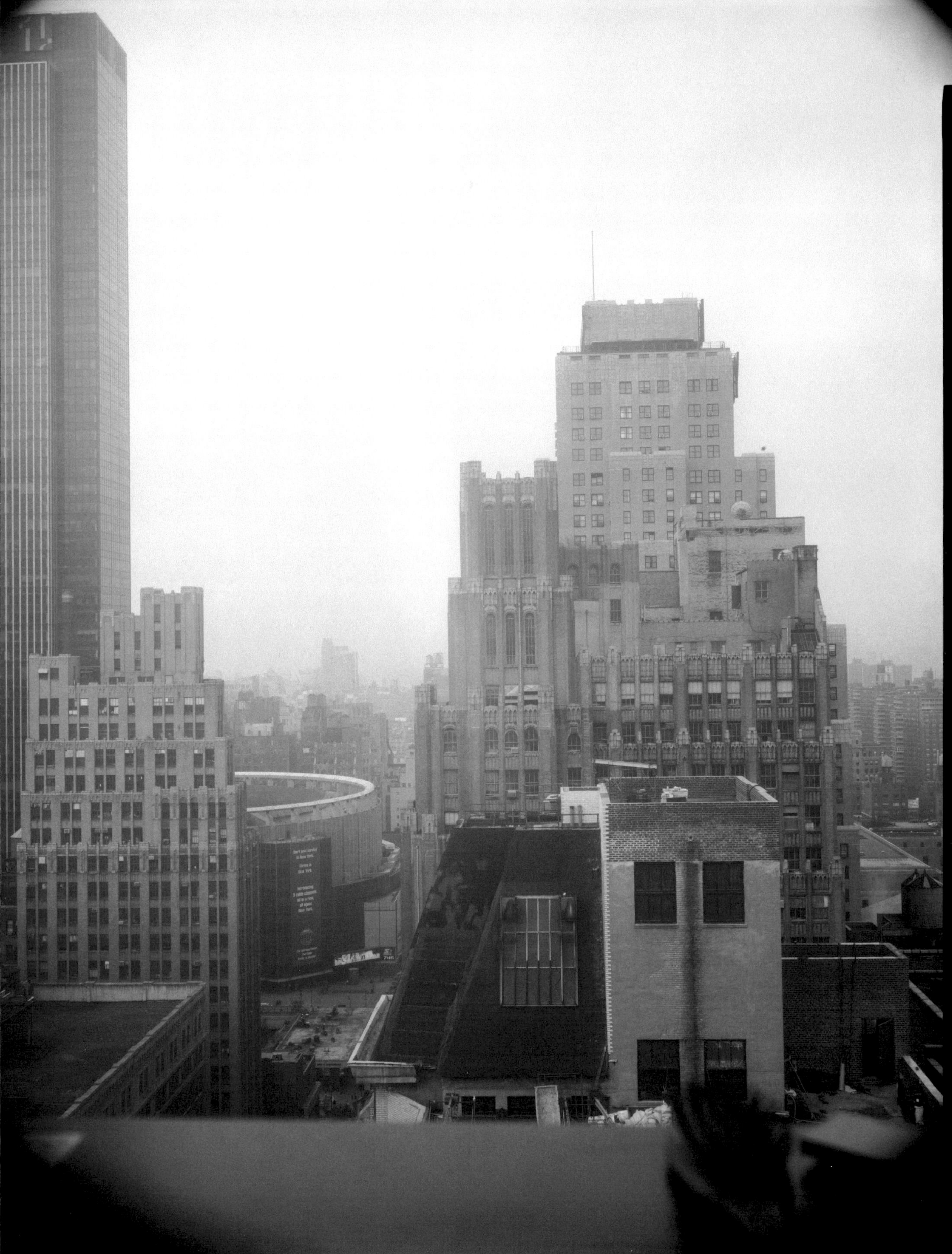

September 21, 1998

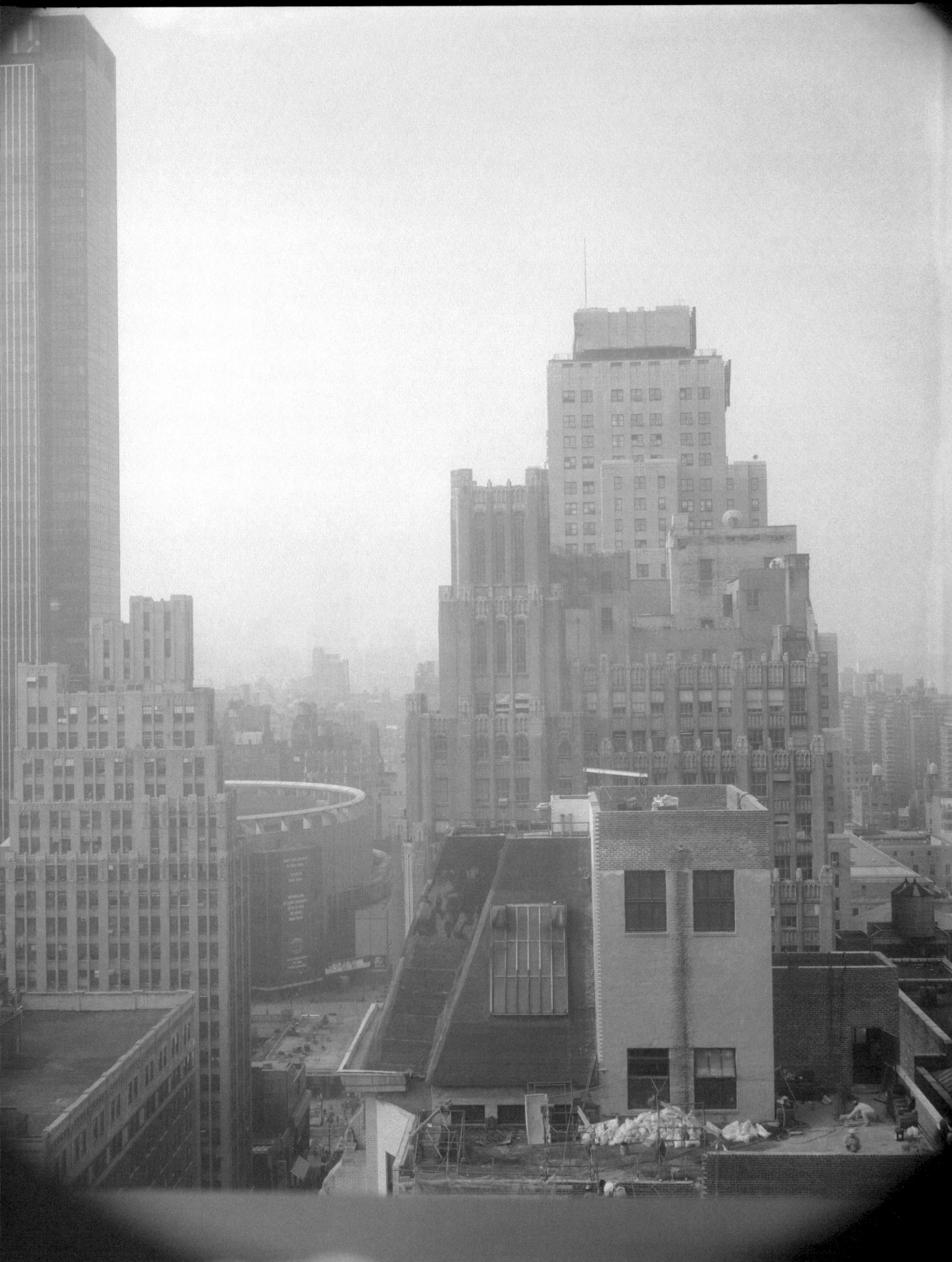

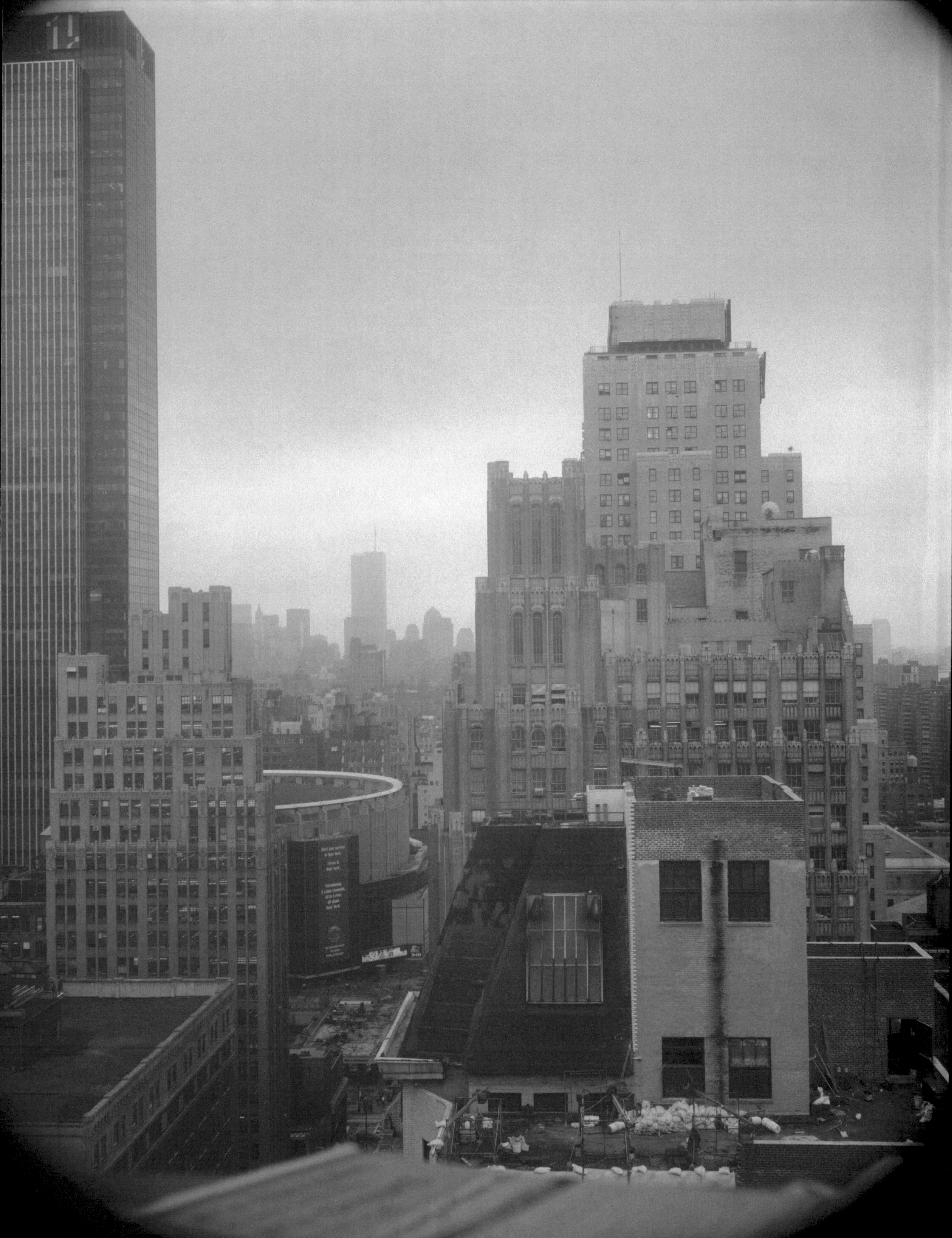

September 23, 1998

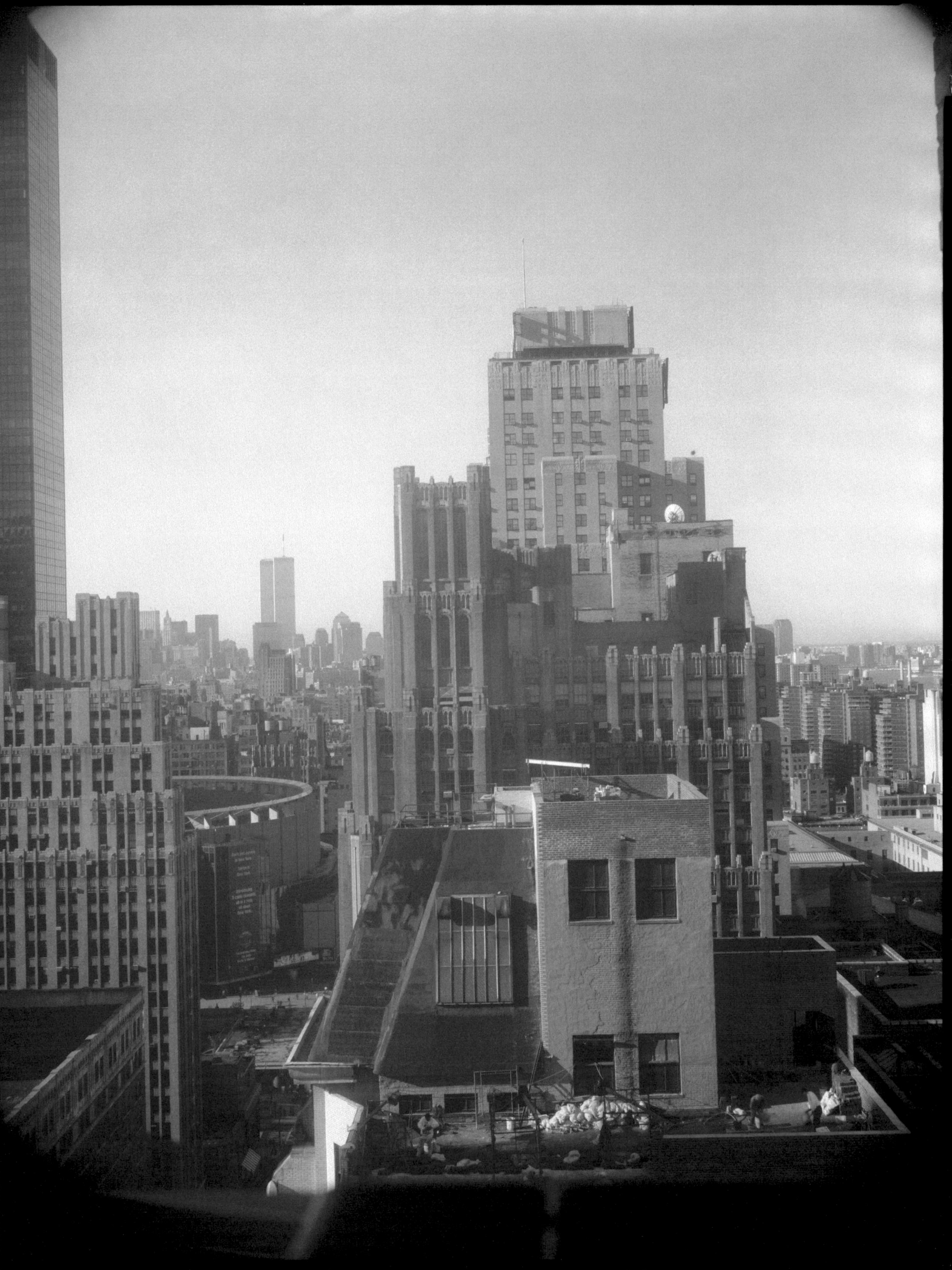

September 24, 1998

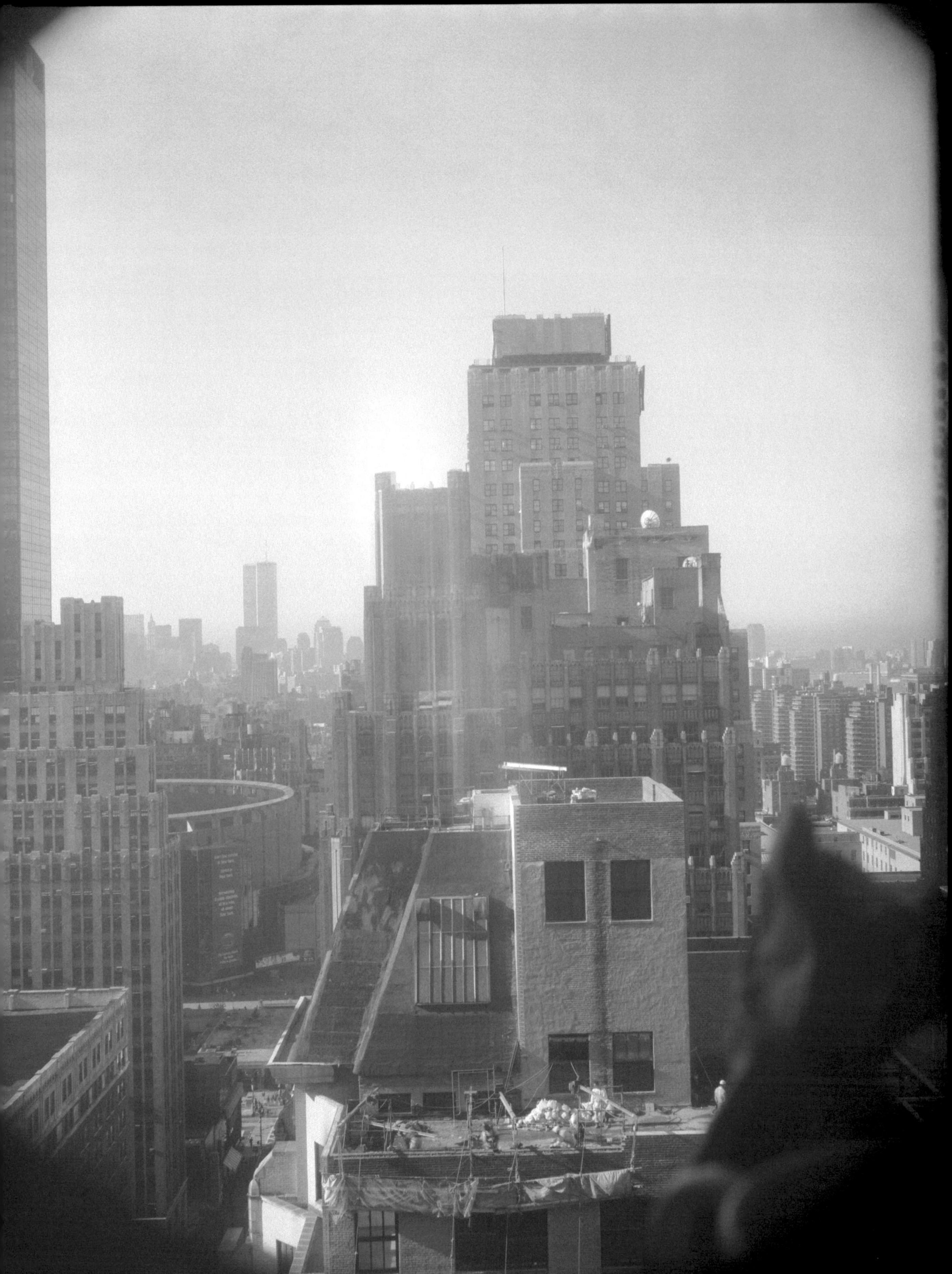

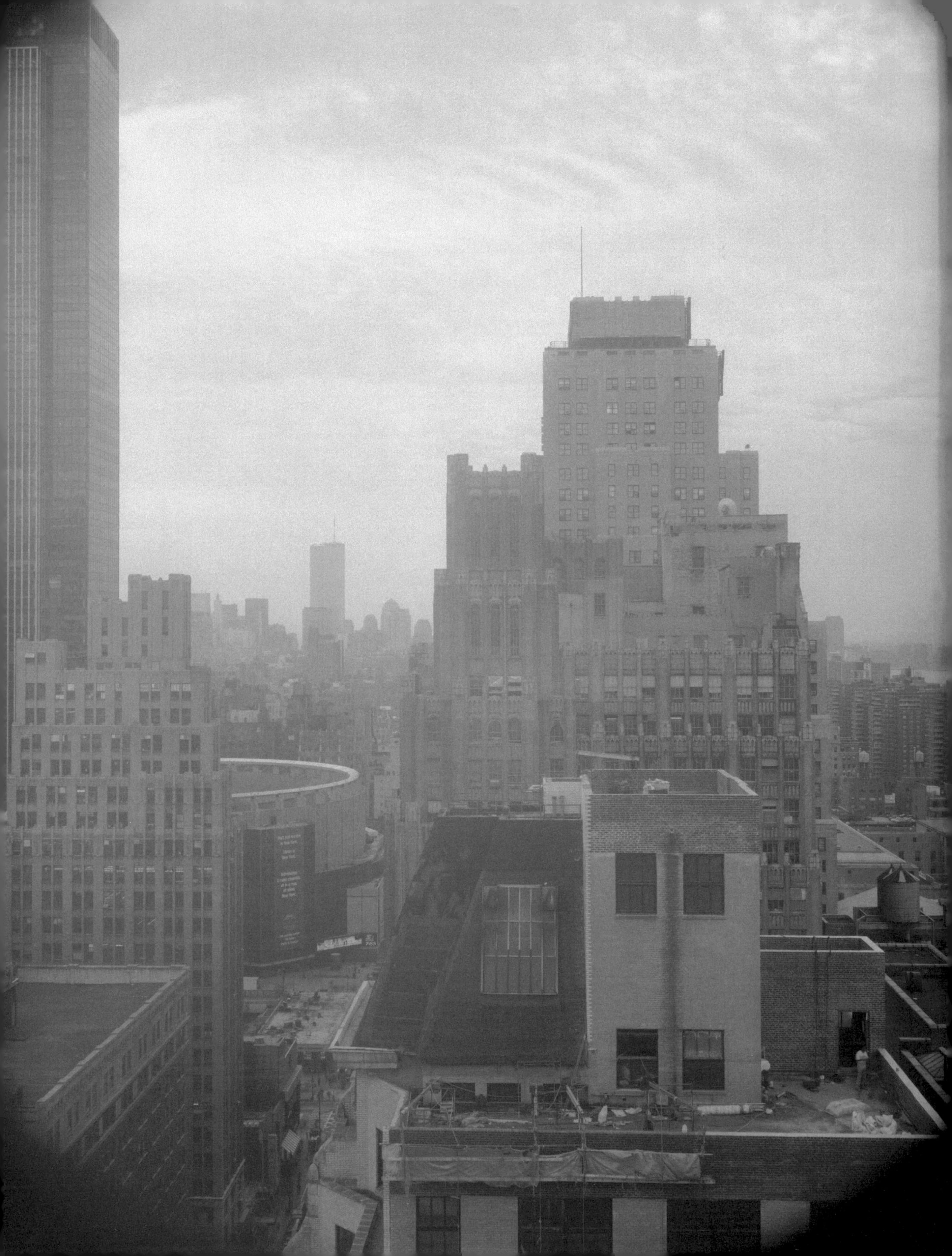

September 26, 1998

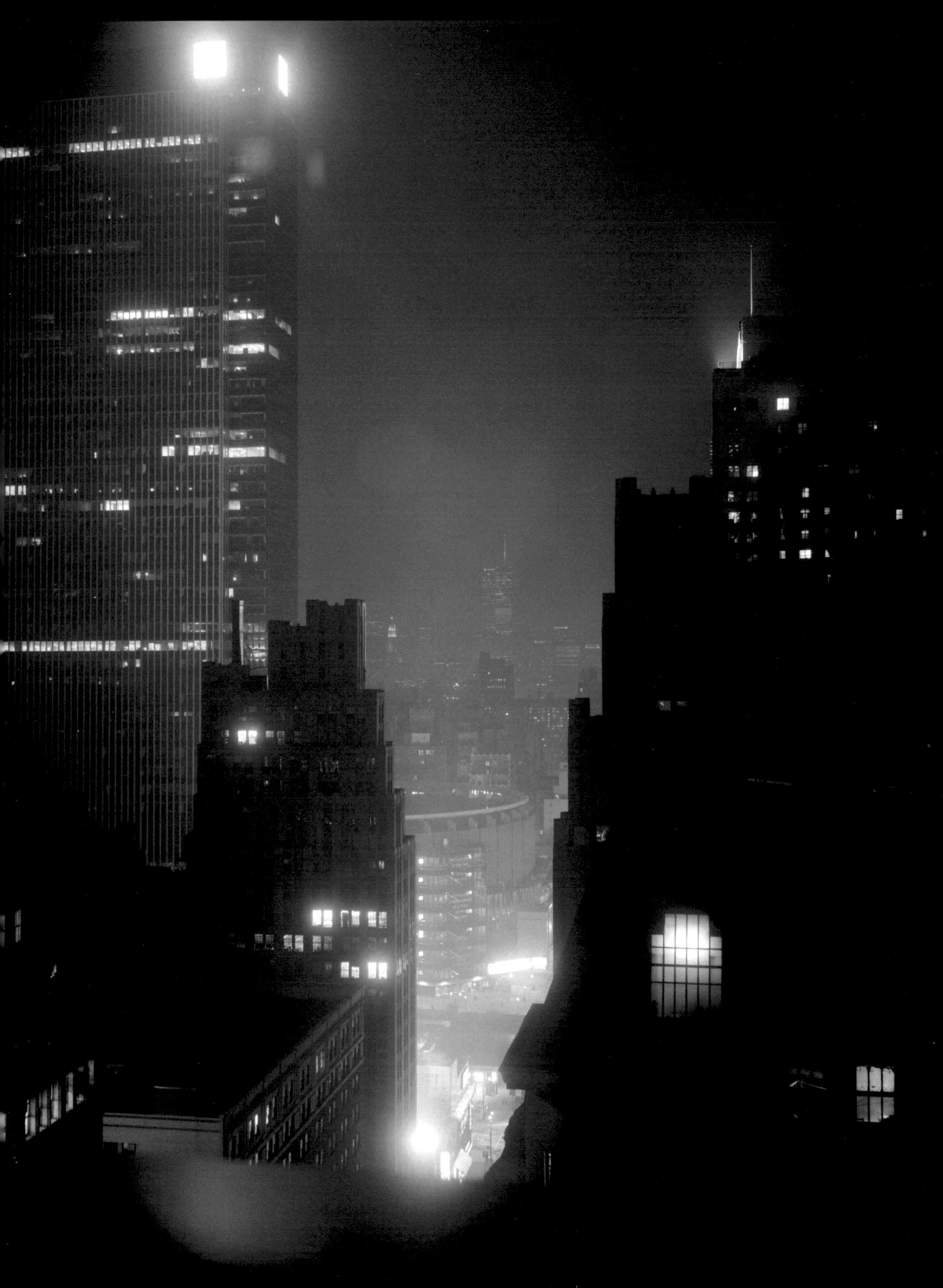

September 27, 1998

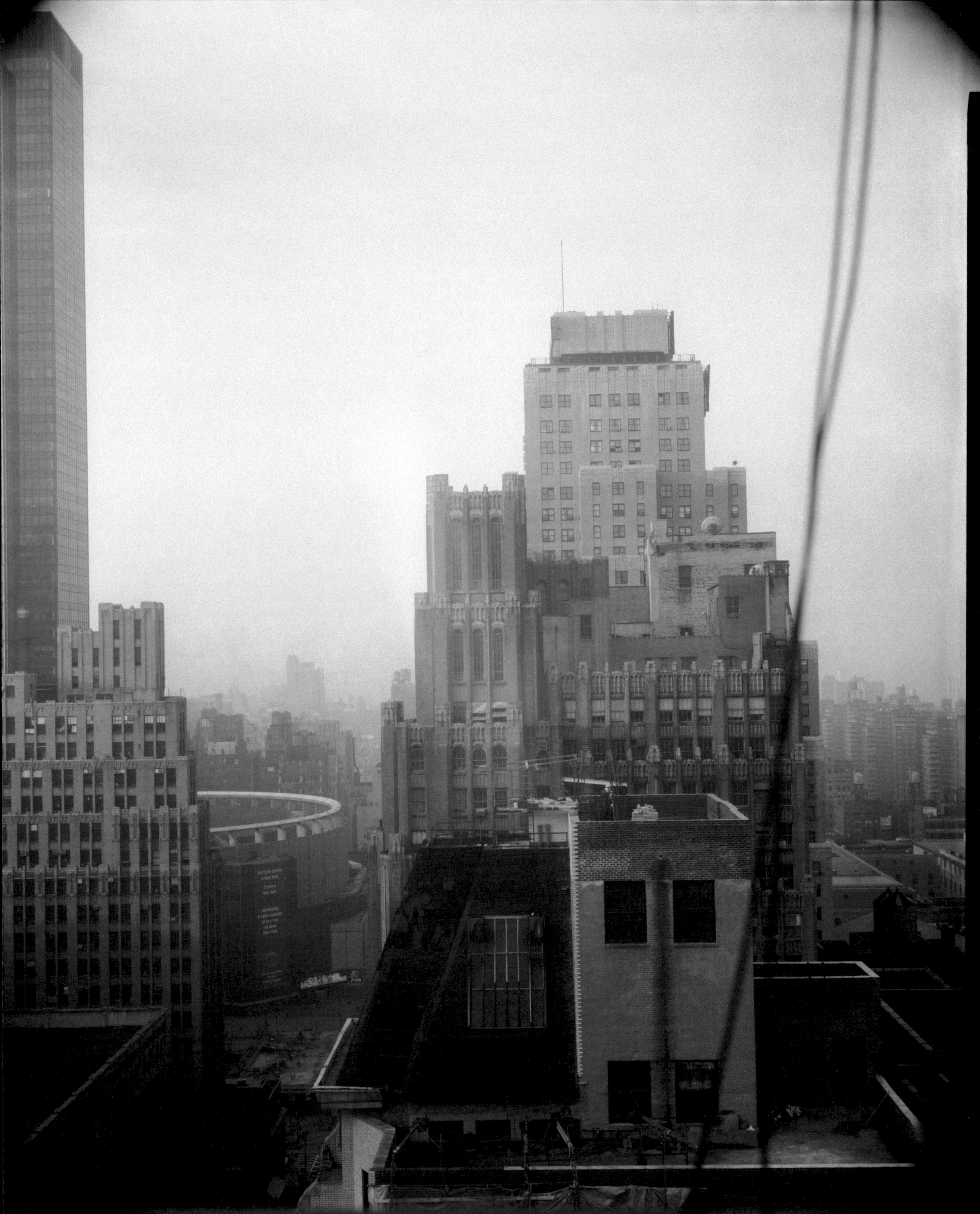

September 28, 1998

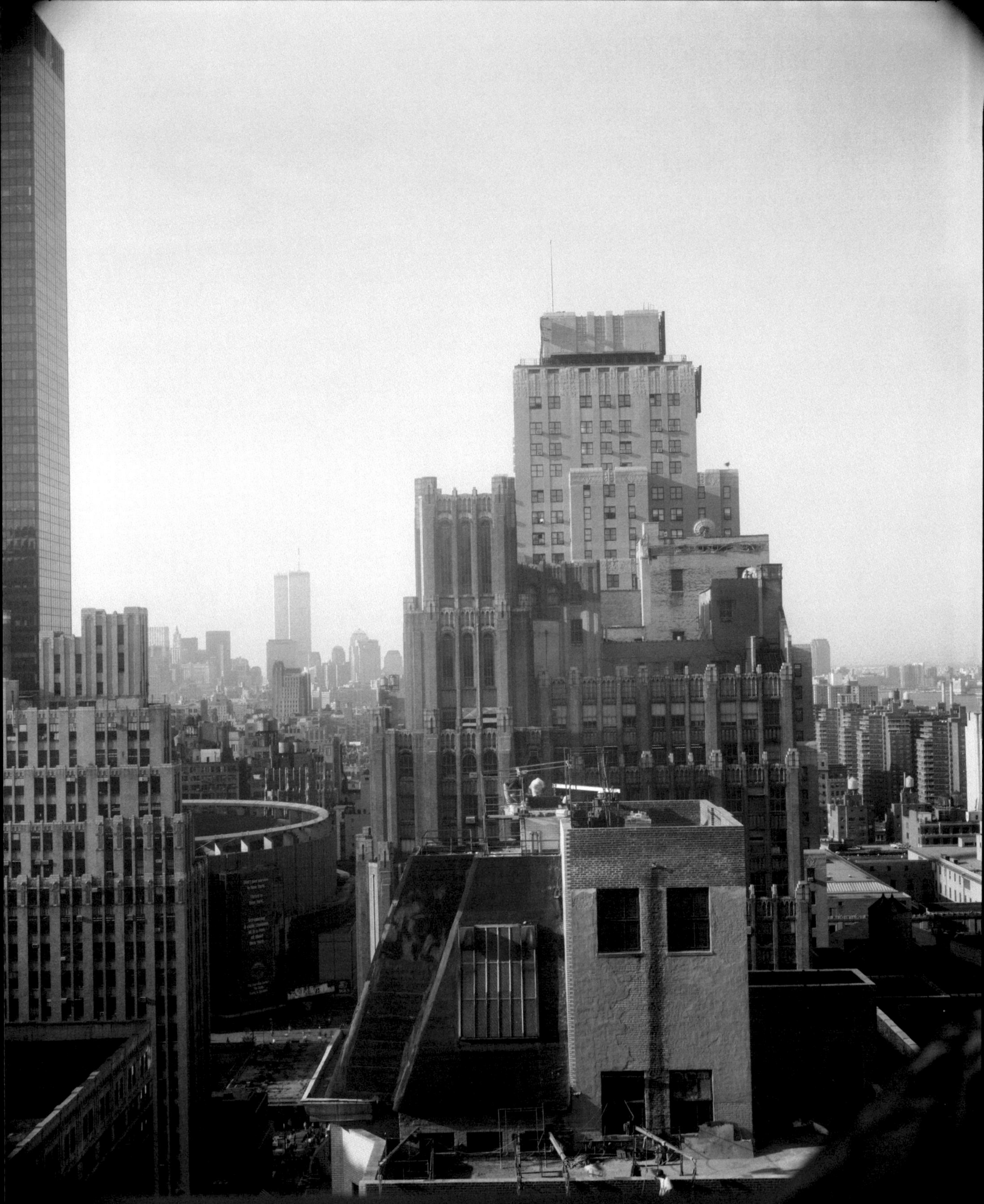

September 29, 1998

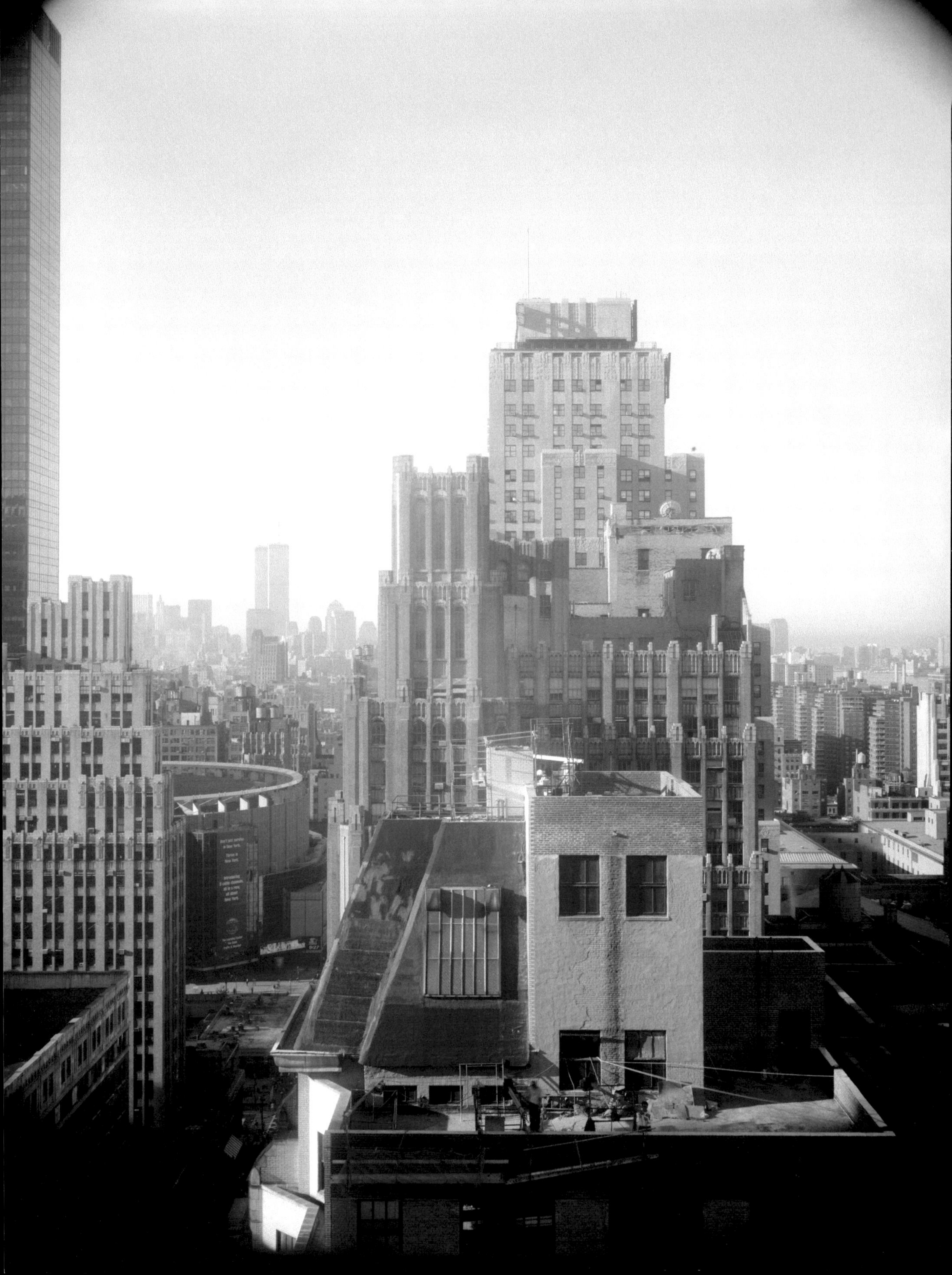

September 30, 1998

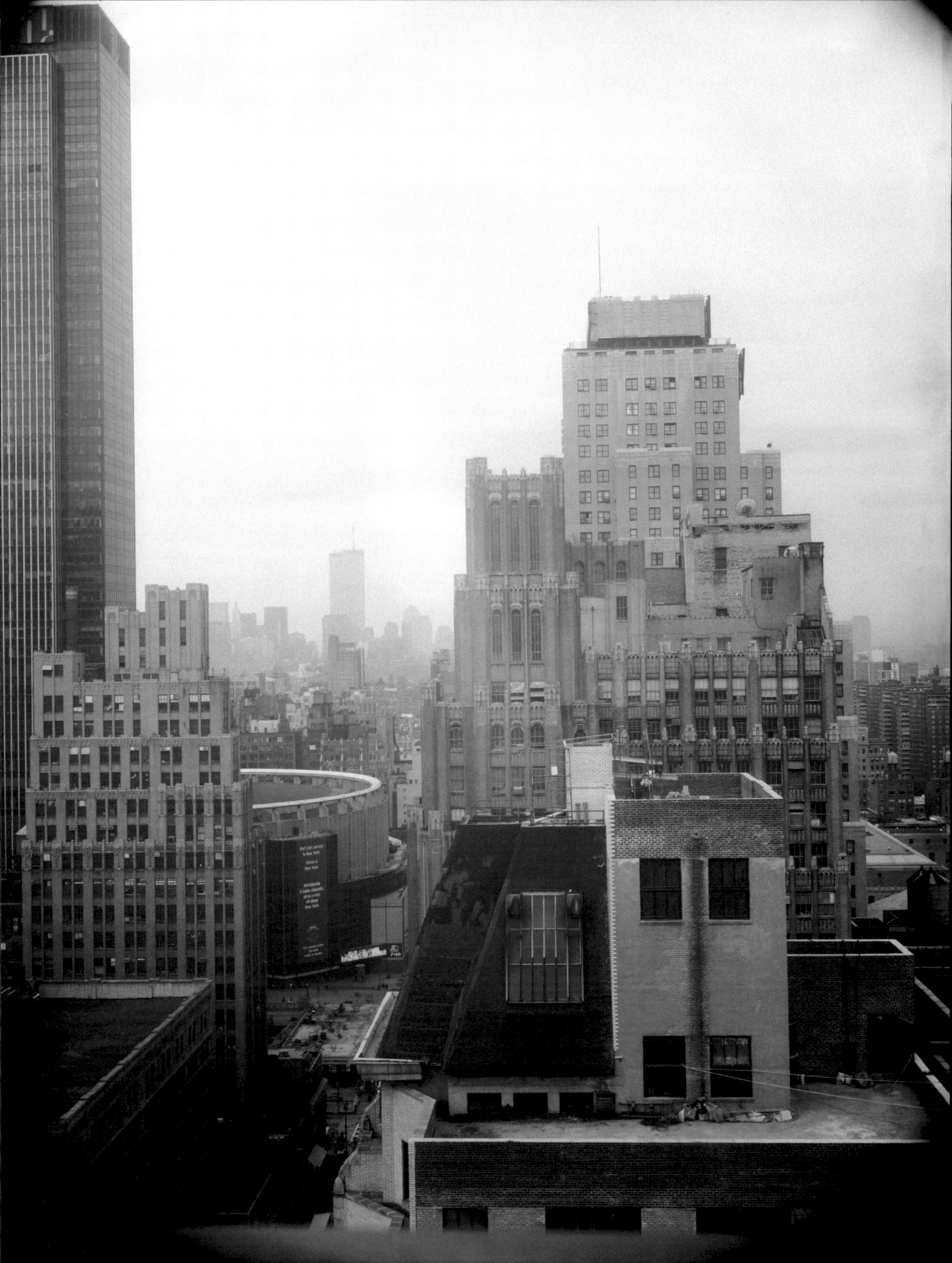

September 1, 1999

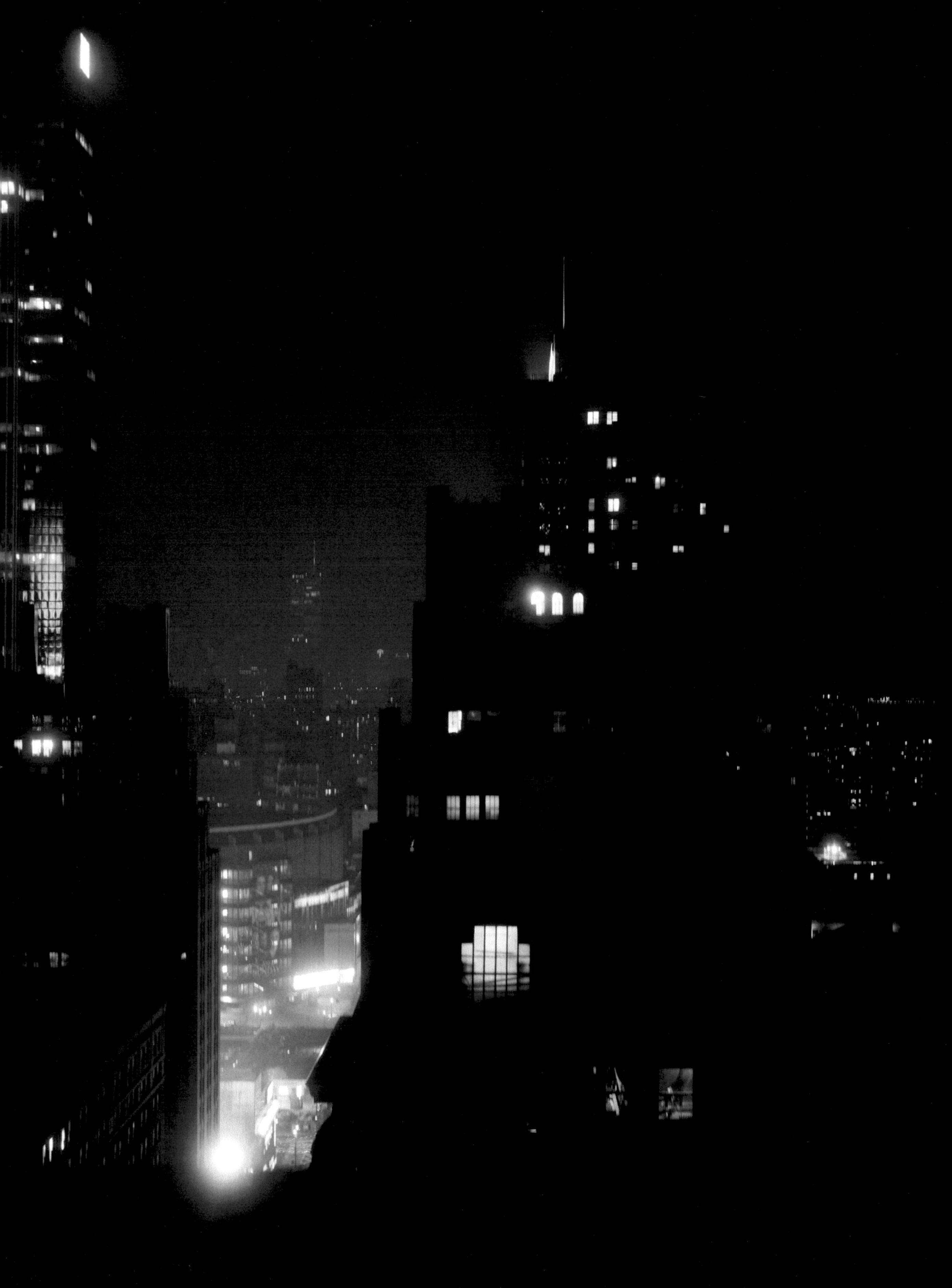

September 2, 1999

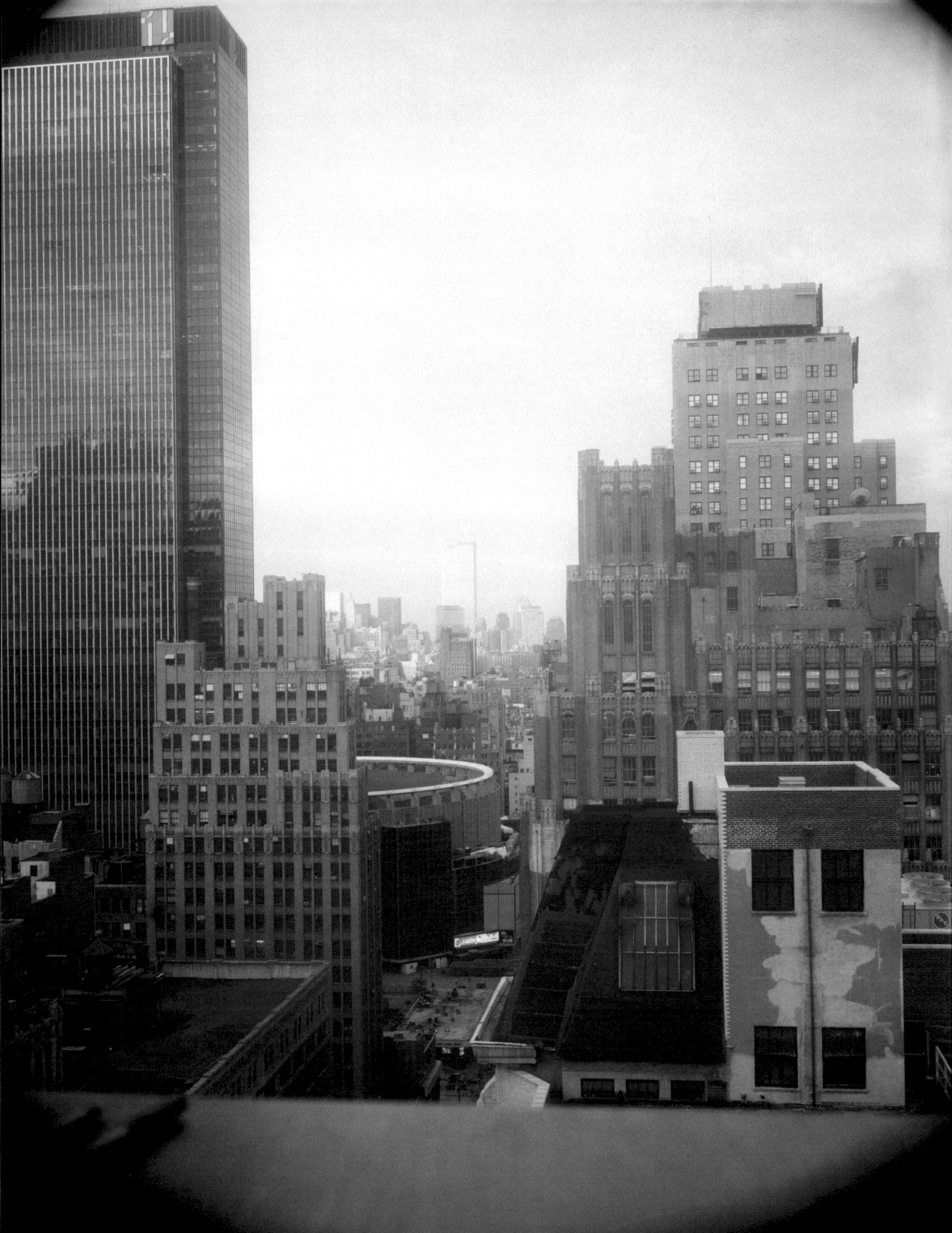

September 3, 1999

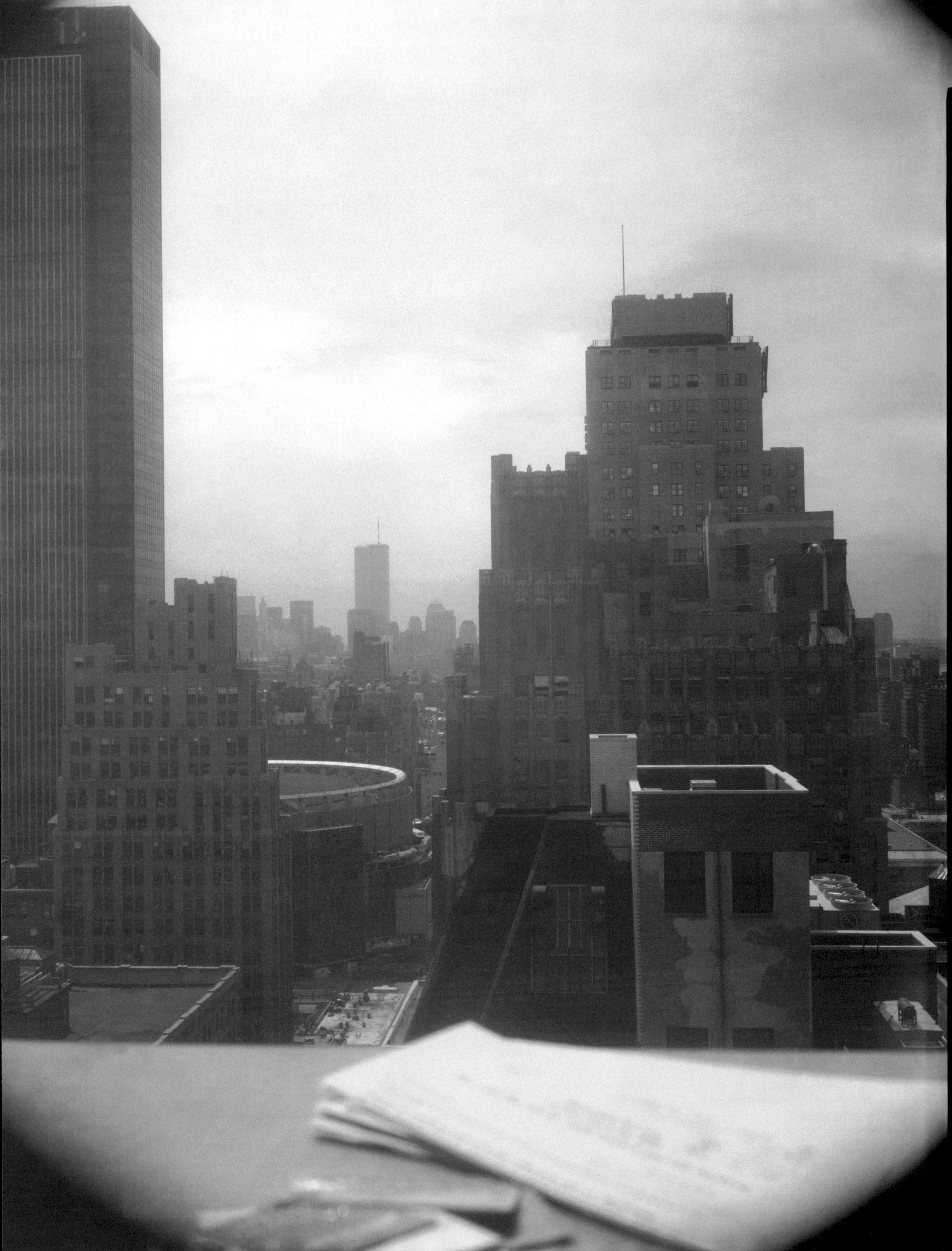

September 24, 1999

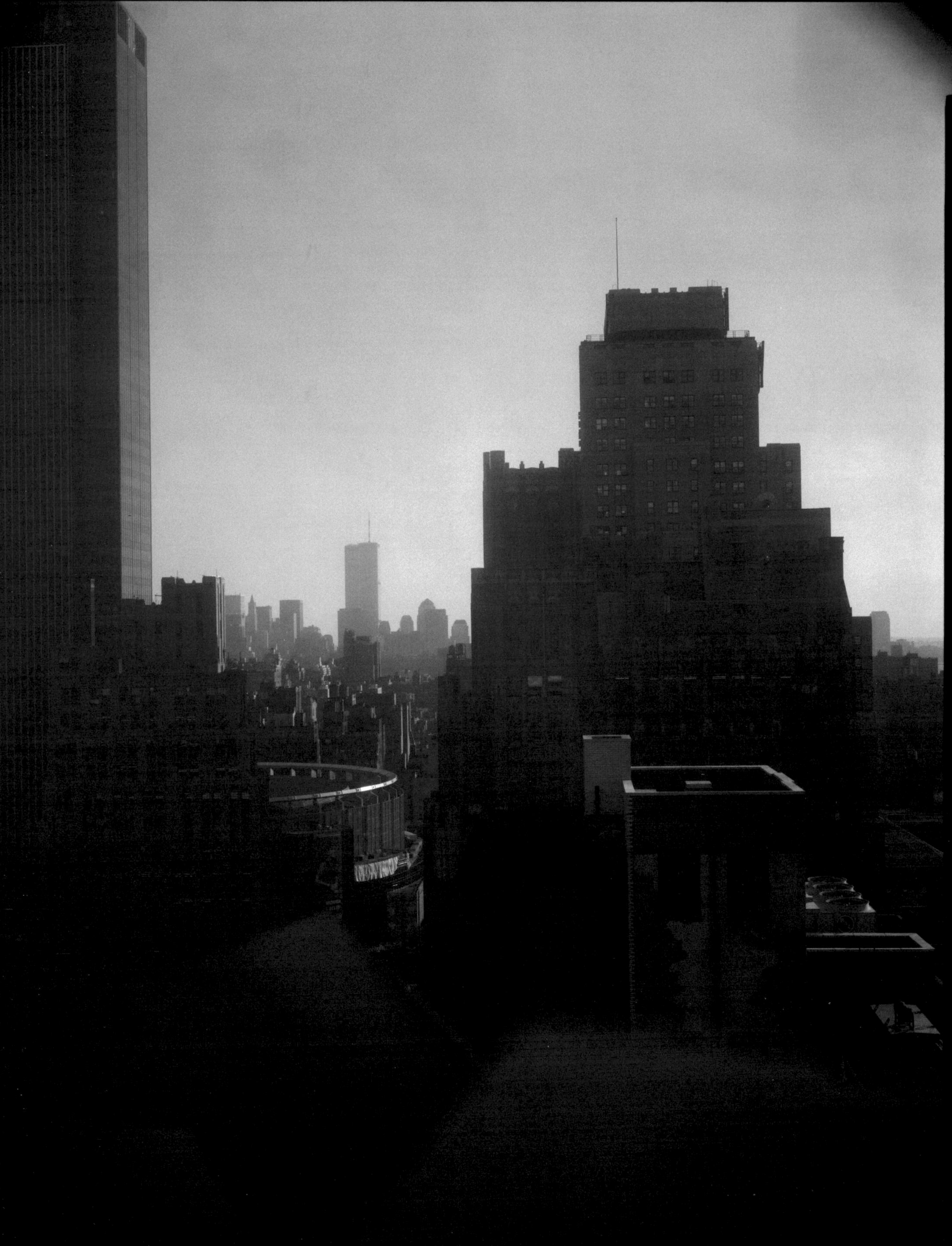

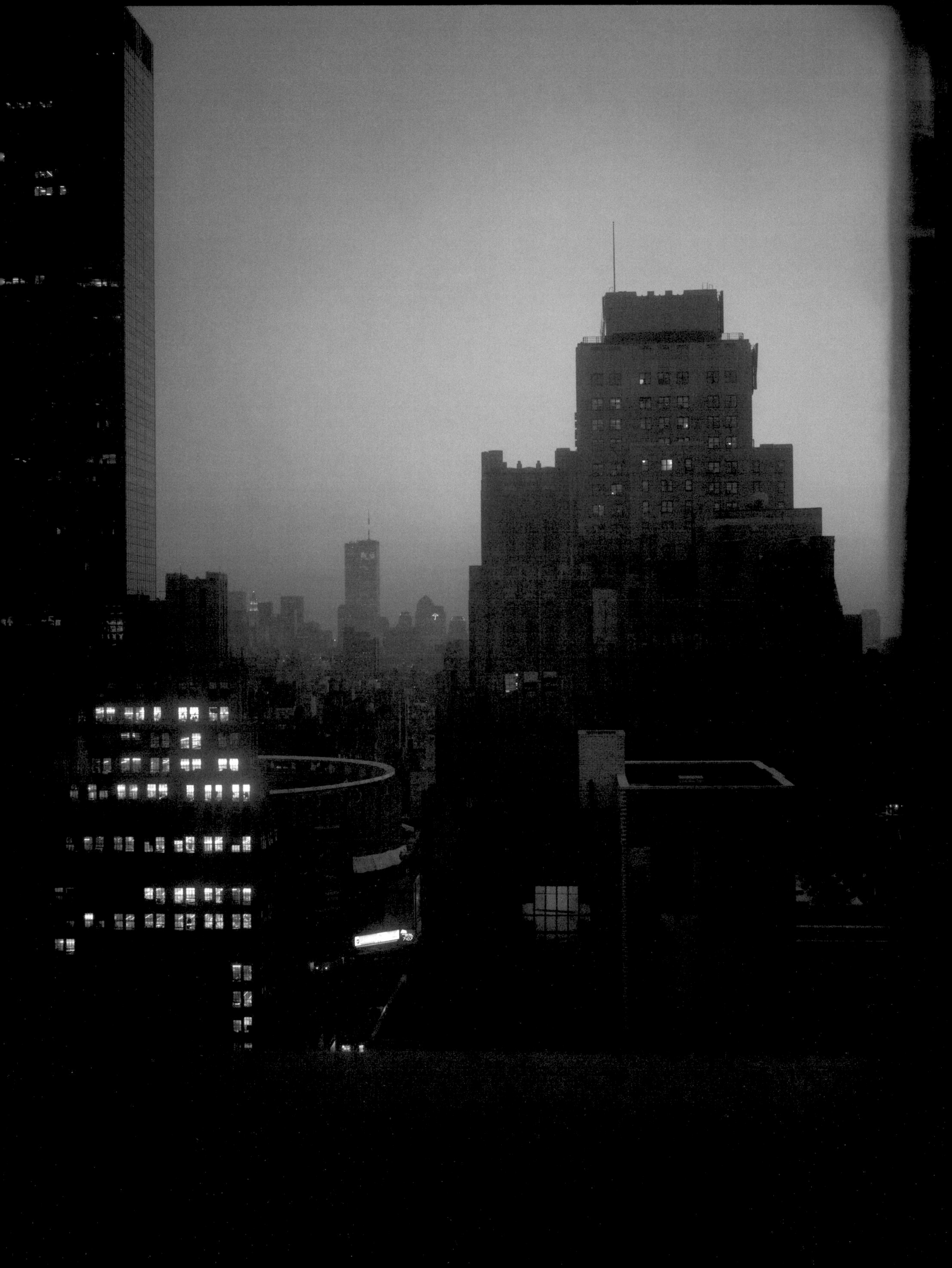

September 26, 1999

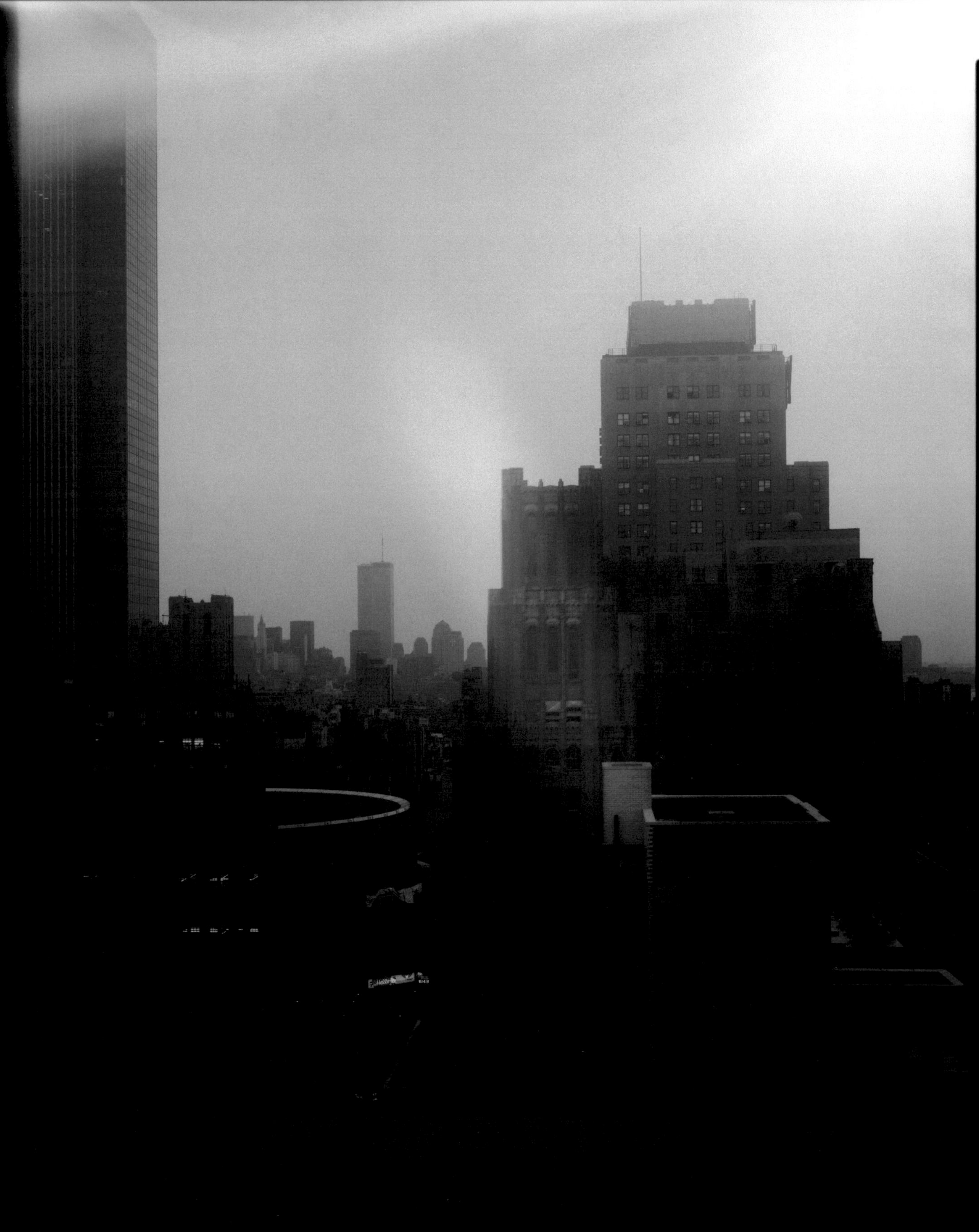

September 27, 1999

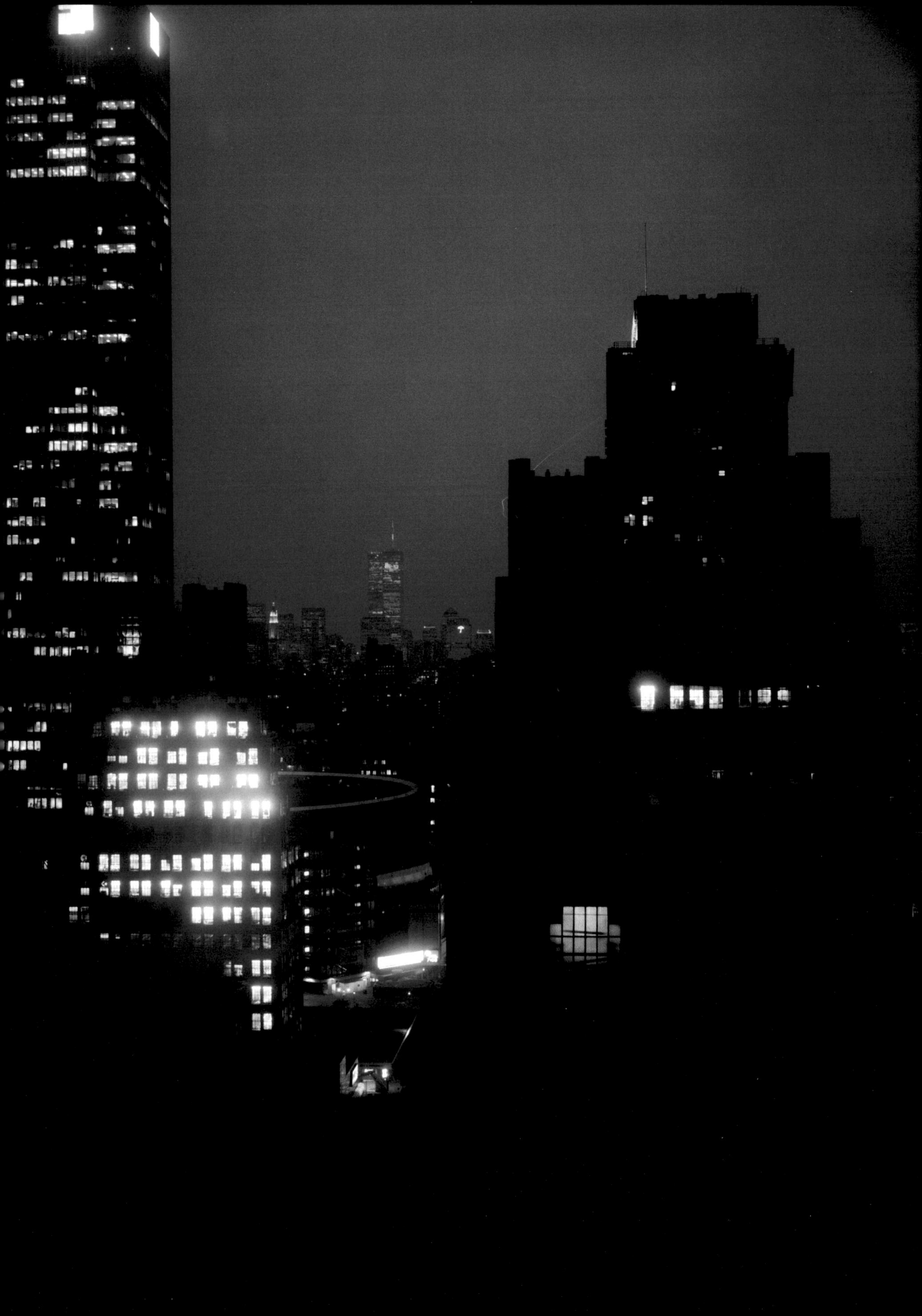

September 28, 1999

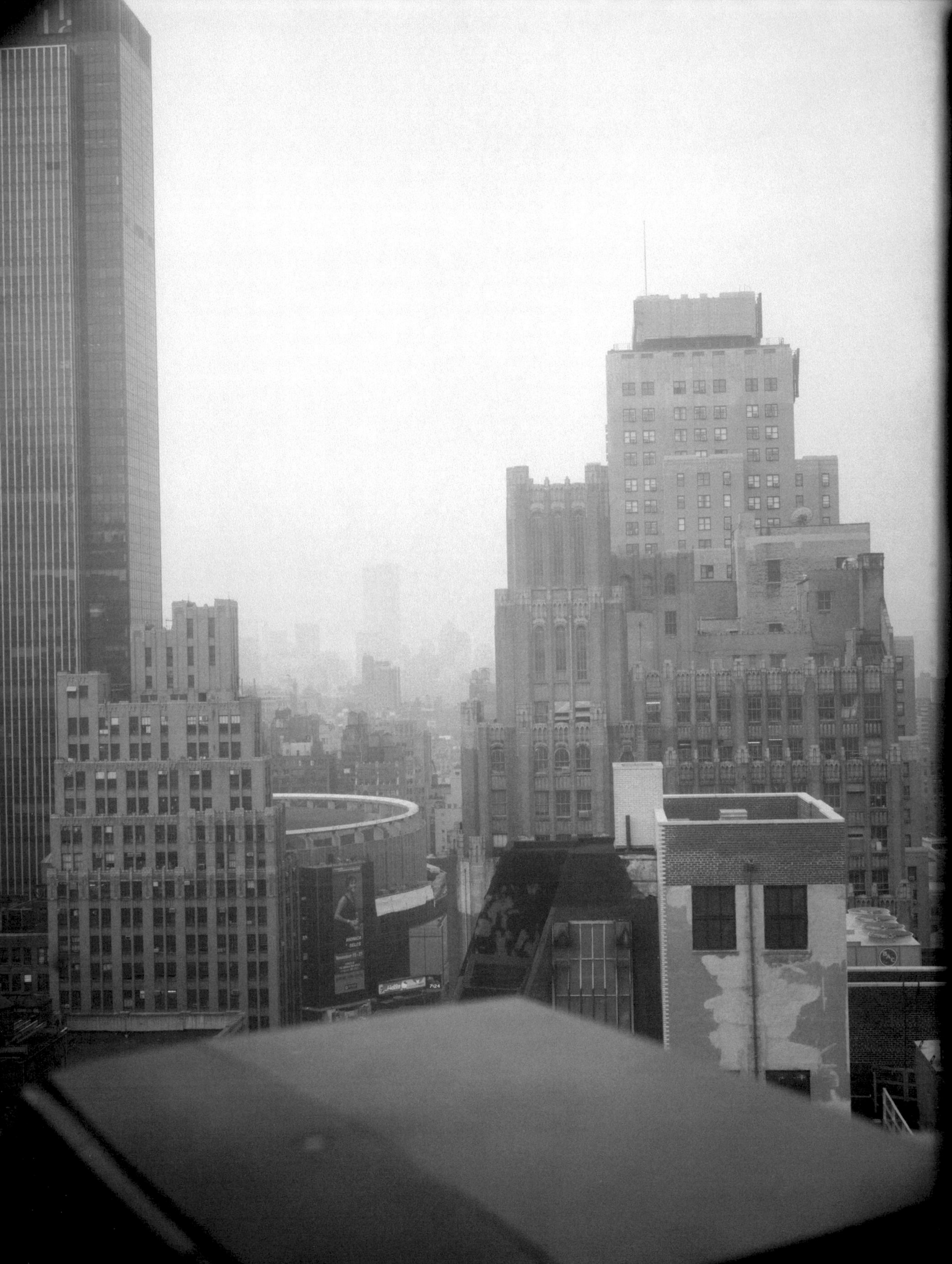

September 29, 1999

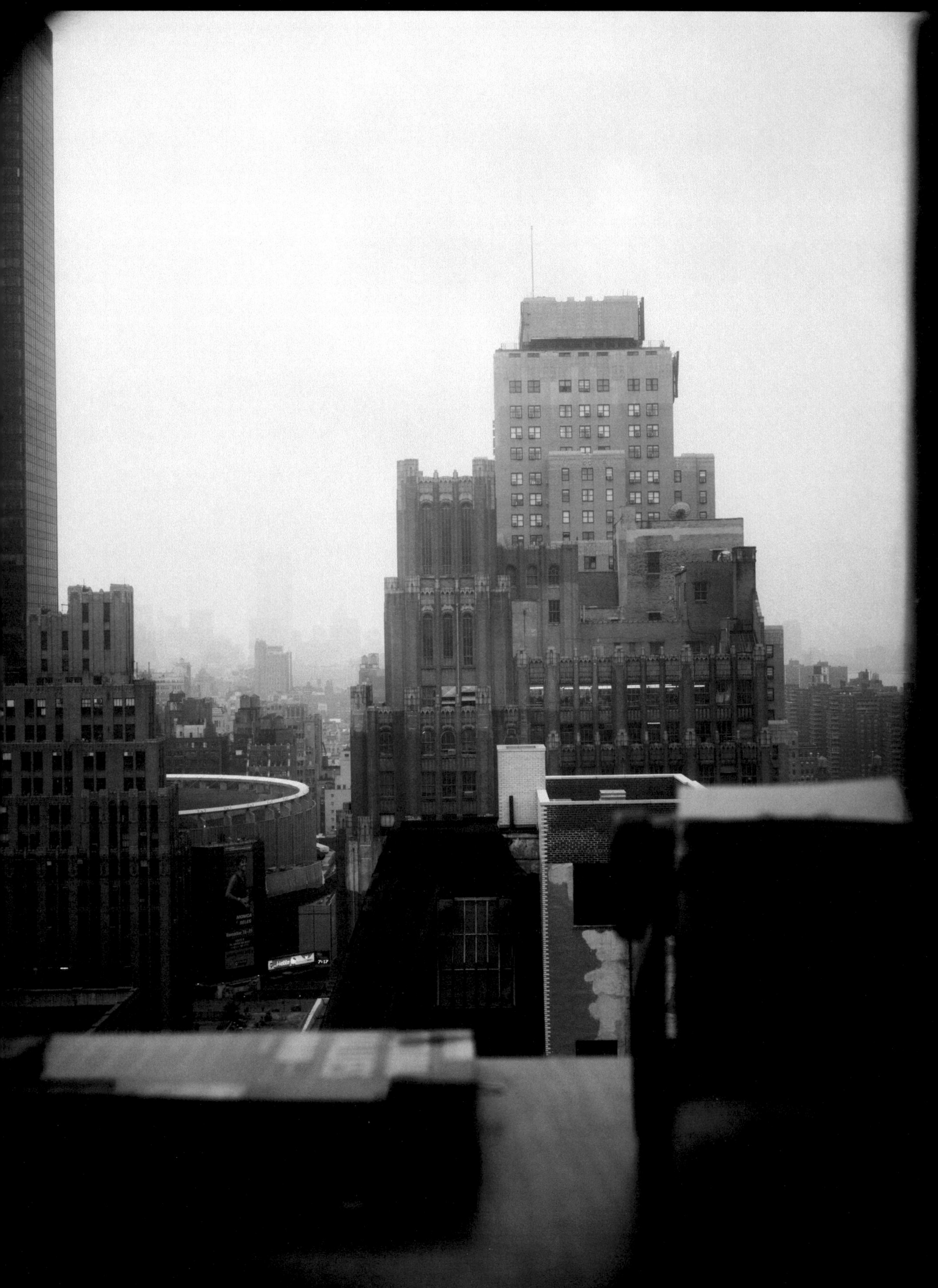

September 30, 1999

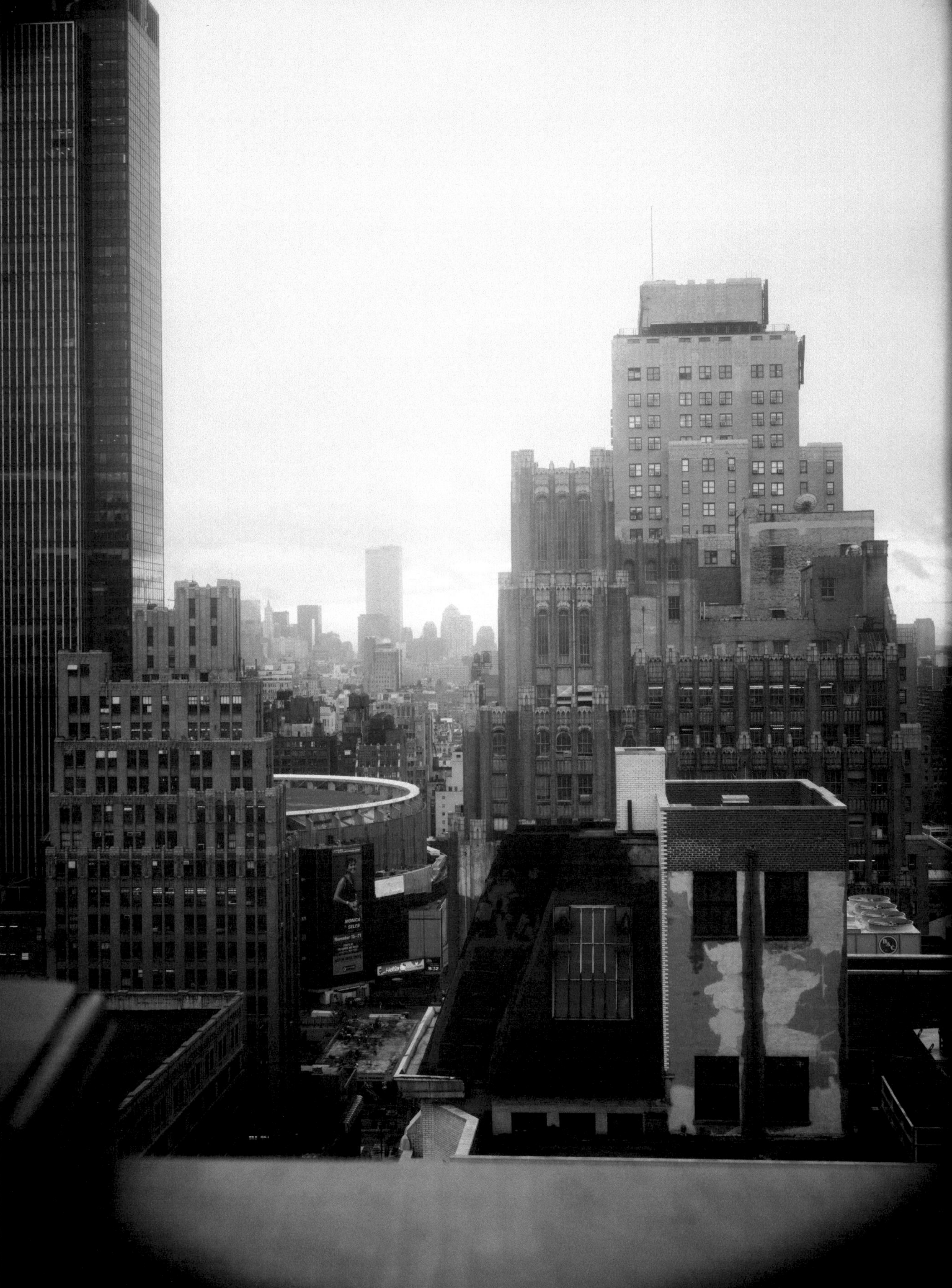

My Art Will Do My Living for Me

Jonathan Santlofer

He has always been a natural foreigner.
A Margaret Mead among the Samoans, a
visual Boswell, taking pictures, making
notes, deciding what is and is not usable.

Like the best method actor he learns
his lines, settles into his temporary
home, and goes about the pretense of
living when his need, purpose you might
say, is about cataloguing and codify-
ing, making something neat and orga-
nized, creating art from the messiness
of existence. A camera replaces normal
vision. He sees in f-stops and aperture
settings, digital imagery to notate
daily routine, hours spent in the near
blackout of a darkroom, paper exposed
to bursts of light, life through a lens
emerging in chemical baths.

Days, weeks, months pass. Stacks of
photographs mount up. A chronicle of
time spent amid, though not quite part
of, the alien culture.

The pictures become a book. A color is
chosen: *This place must be blue.* A for-
mal decision or one meant to convey
emotional resonance? The answer is
unclear, but blue it will be, cool and
slightly unreal, the natural exchanged
for something imposed and artificial.
The book is bound, location checked off
the list, Cape Town, South Africa,
blue. What he wanted here, complete.
The place exhausted, he packs the
equipment, time to go.

He reads a story, "One Out of Many," by
V.S. Naipaul. In it, a character who
has left his native Bombay suggests the
following observation: Stay away long
enough, and you belong nowhere.

He worries: *Is that me?* Perhaps it is
time to put down roots. His idea: plant
his feet in the middle of a highway,
documenting a scene in micro-seconds,
camera winking in slow motion.

Later, when he prints and reviews these
360-degree panoramas, they offer a sur-
prisingly agitated, anxious abstraction
of time and place, nothing the human
eye could ever recall, impressionistic
whirs, blurs, and streaks—a Whistler
nocturne or Turner storm—the physical
made temporal, oddly beautiful, and
slightly disturbing.

Like everything in his life this
becomes an obsession, what criminal
profilers call a "ritual," a set of
rules and needs that must be met: go
here, stand there, watch, wait. San
Marco Square, a Hong Kong intersection,
an Arizona river. Position the camera.
Count off seconds and minutes. Ignore
time while recording it. Forget the
cappuccino, Szechuan noodles, Indian fry
bread. *My art will do my living for me.*

A flare is sent up and he responds,
loads his camera and takes off across
the United States in search of that
most elusive of indigenous species, the
American. Park rangers, old burlesque
queens, prison wardens, housewives,
artists, writers, all tell him their
stories. He asks each for a photo—something from their past—and photographs
them now, a way to bracket their lives.
His America is a series of snapshots
and anecdotes seen backwards and for-
wards, famous politicos once awkward
boys, former beauty queens restored to
their finest hour. It is a country
represented without its strip malls,
slums, riots, old-age homes, fast-food
vendors, or disaffected youth, nothing
sensational for the nightly news or the
morning paper. His vision is closer to
still life, *nature morte*. He takes what
he wants and puts it under glass.

He moves to New York, the most anonymous of cities, and finds an apartment,
a bizarre aerie, something out of Fritz
Lang or Alfred Hitchcock, hidden behind
an elevator's housing, and thinks: *No
one will know I am here.* Everything
about it is small and he is large; he

folds himself into bed, bends in half to use the sink. But the doll's house comes with something extraordinary, a window on the world, a vertiginous bird's-eye view that sweeps down Eighth Avenue capturing sports arena and rail-road station, post office and skyscrap-ers, delis and cross streets, towering billboards, and a quarter inch of river which suggests something less tangible beyond the concrete and steel: a promise of travel, escape, potential encounters, a future.

He digs out an old camera he bought in South Africa, which looks like a traveling magician's box of tricks, and sets it up by the window. Every day he takes a picture. And an odd thing happens. He stays.

Weeks stretch into months. Months into years. Eleven years of documenting clouds and sky, days and nights, build-ings erected and razed, a Warholian audition tape, this particular strip of city his very own "superstar," a fanatic's chronicle that will cause him to bolt in mid-conversation to record yet another moment in the dawn-to-dusk cycle. It is a meticulous diary that he has come to depend upon, and quite pos-sibly this slice of architecture and city life depends on him, too. Consider a painter and his model, the deal that is struck: If you let me paint you I will make you immortal.

Each summer he leaves the city, abandons his model, camera left sitting by the window.

One day he hears the news and watches it on television, a barely comprehensible, horrific abstraction of planes crashing into buildings, towers falling, again and again and again. And he has missed it. He will have no pictures of the explosions and implosions, the black funnels of smoke.

He returns within the week, the ash still settling. He looks out the window and sees that his model has changed her pose.

He is filled with regret. But to think of pictures, of art, now? Unspeakable.

Of course he is wrong: Art is his speech, his sound, his taste, his sight. It is his proper response.

He looks again and notes that the anonymous landscape has been charged by omission, the past reinvented by the present.

He builds light-boxes to display each day of every year he has witnessed and photographed. For the days he has missed he creates something at once tangible and elusive, blank sheets of film that act like minimal paintings filled with narrative poignancy, reminders that his attention was else-where, his back turned.

He goes to Vietnam and photographs twins; he visits Japan and takes pic-tures of men and women, boys and girls, with and without smiles, everything in duplicate, as if he needs the insurance. Those 360-degree panoramas that converted reality into abstraction—a nowhere man's gorgeous idea of time and place—are set aside for the physical and factual. He considers a second volume of Americans, logging more stories on paper, printing more pictures, creating more books. *Does loss become bearable if you have the negative in a box or a picture in a frame?*

He goes back to his window, his strip of altered city seemingly unemotional in its posture. He resumes his picture taking, the routine a balm. Summer arrives and once again he leaves his magician's camera behind, focused on the window. Perhaps this time the lens is watching even while he is not.

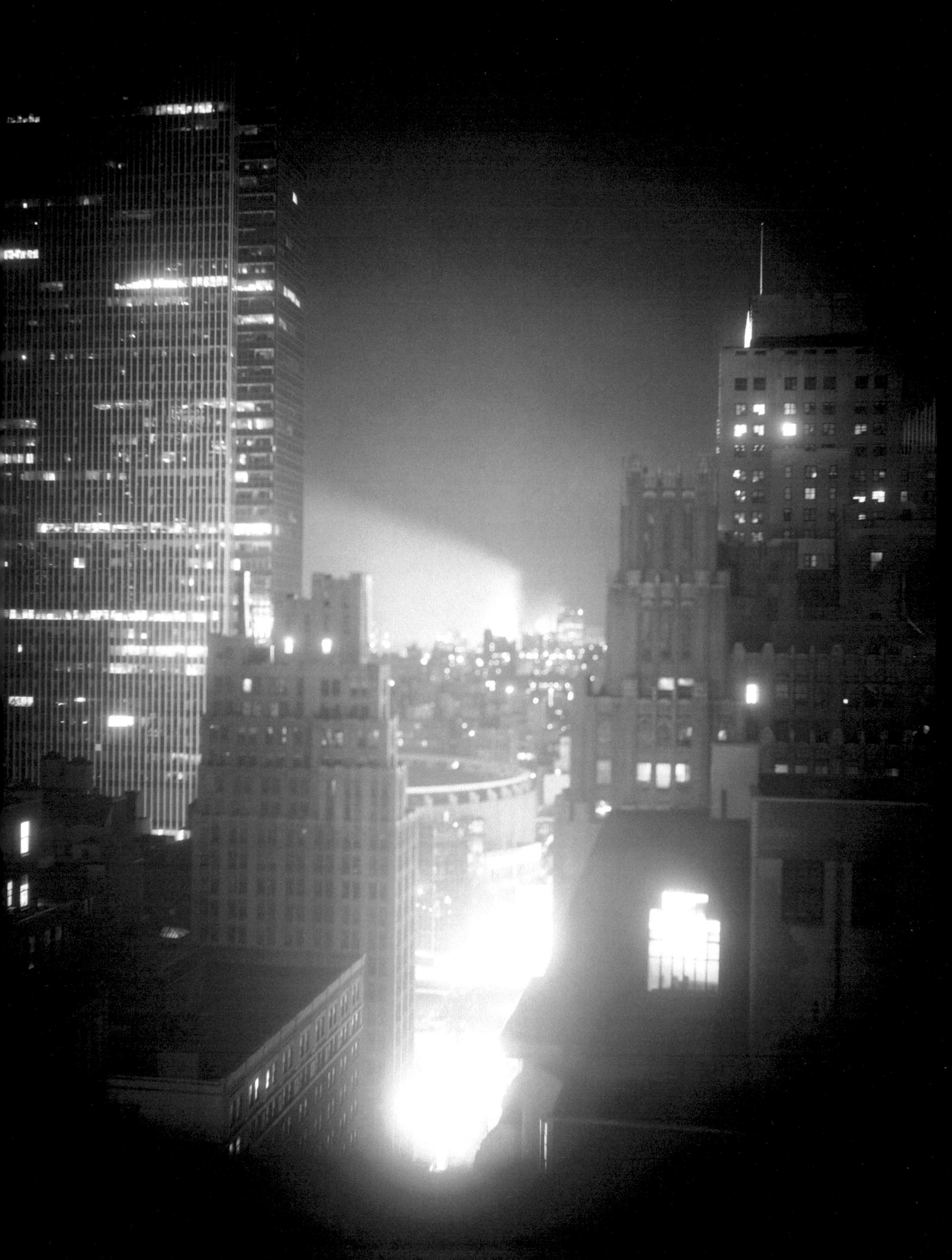

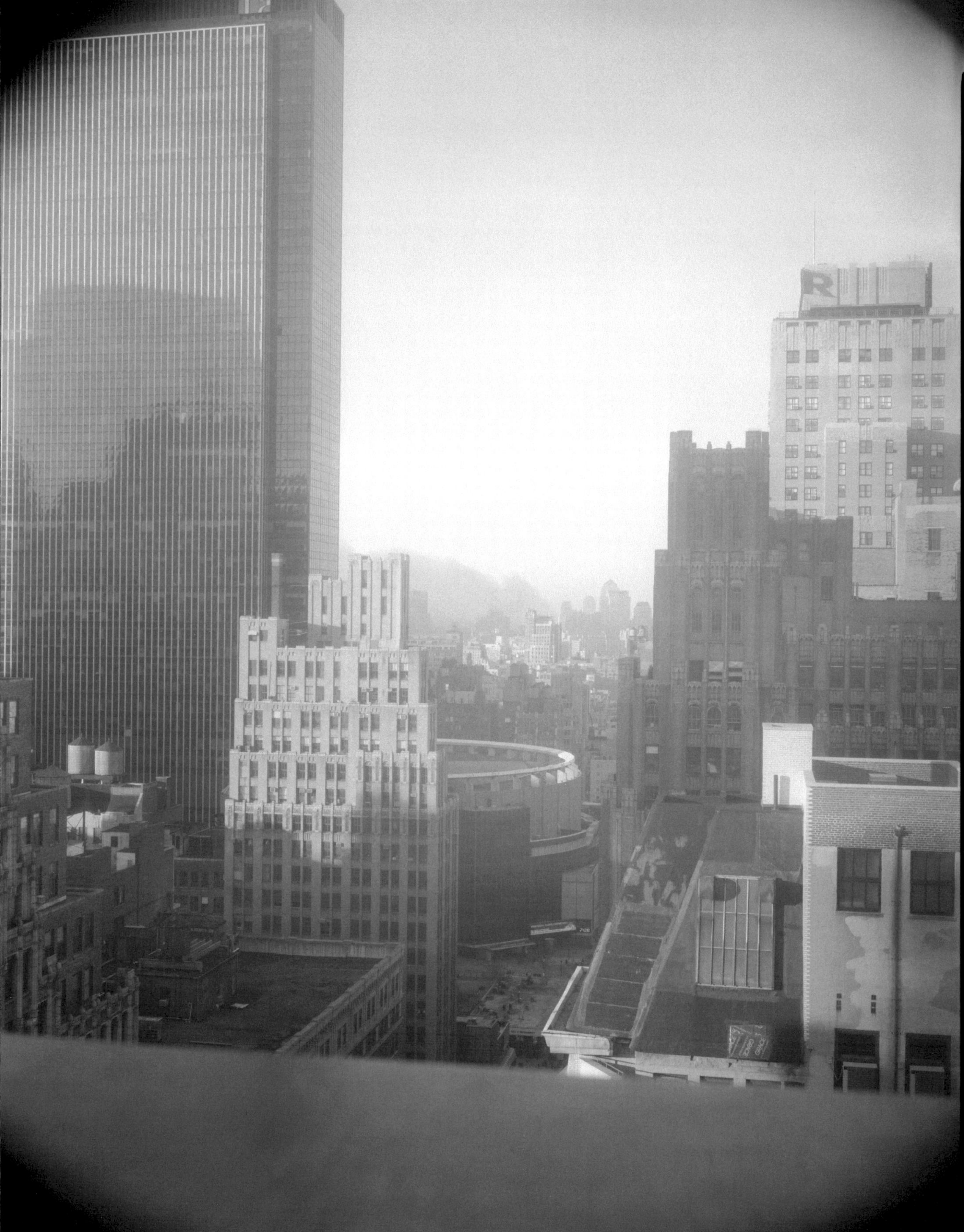

September 14, 2001

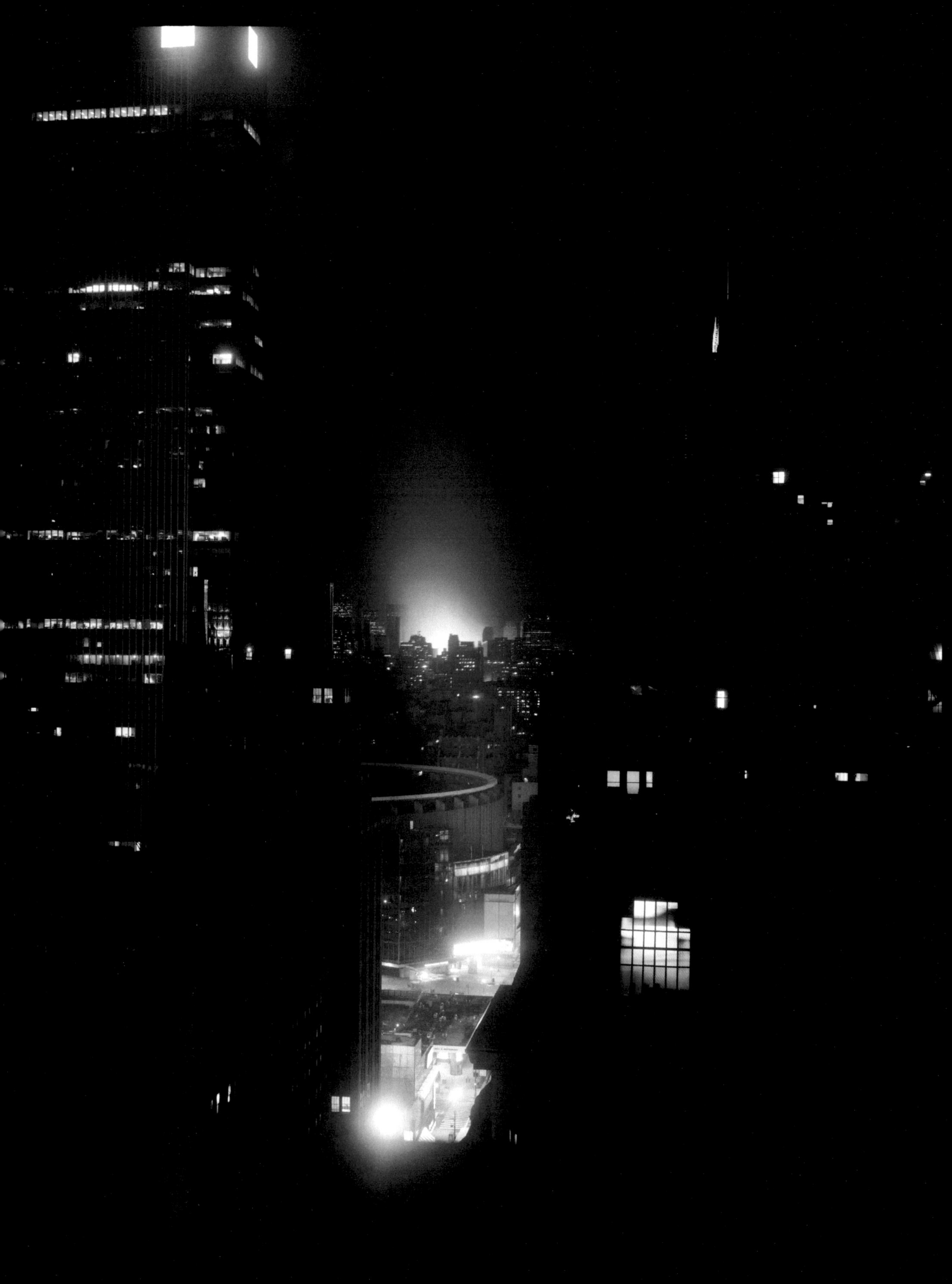

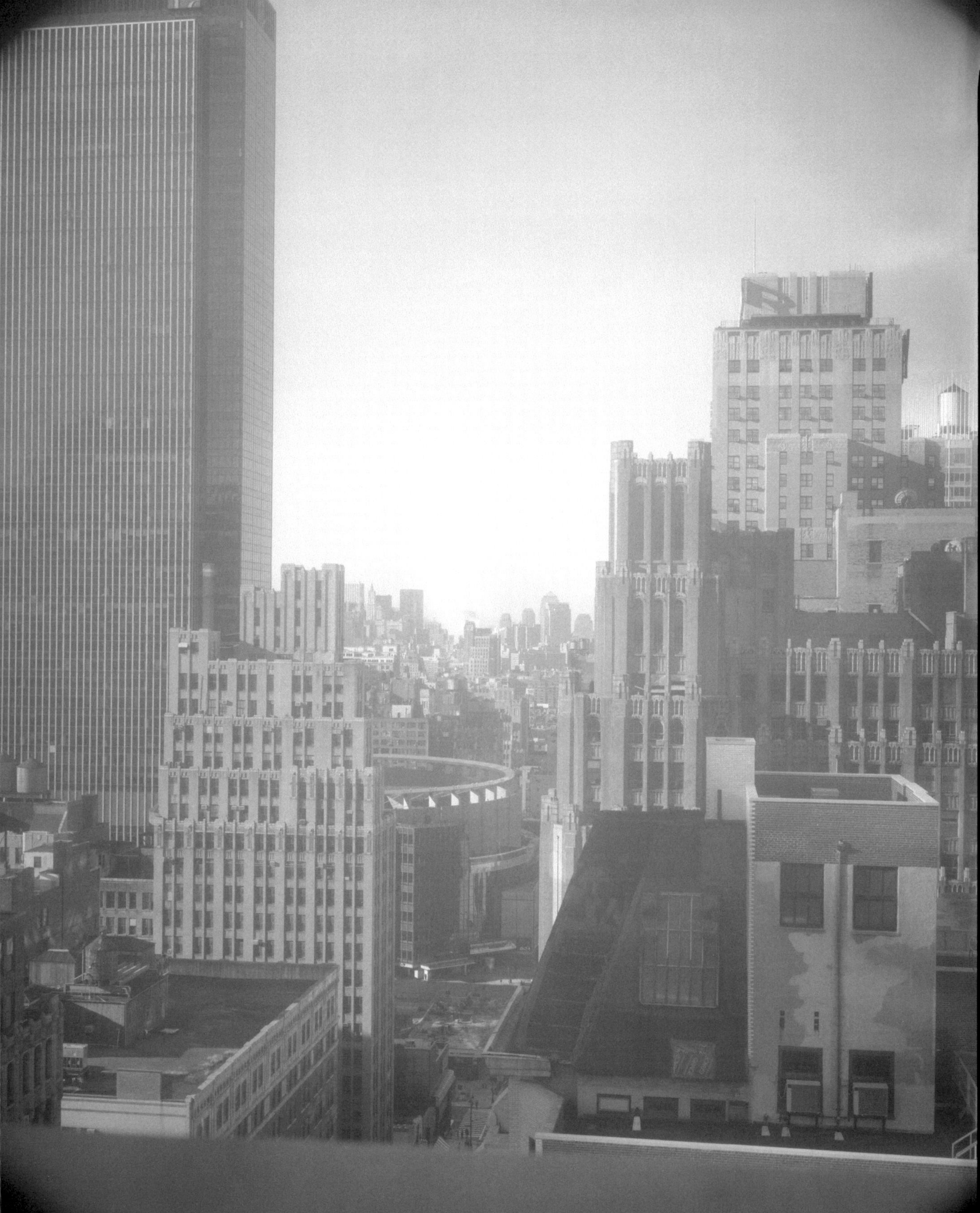

September 16, 2001

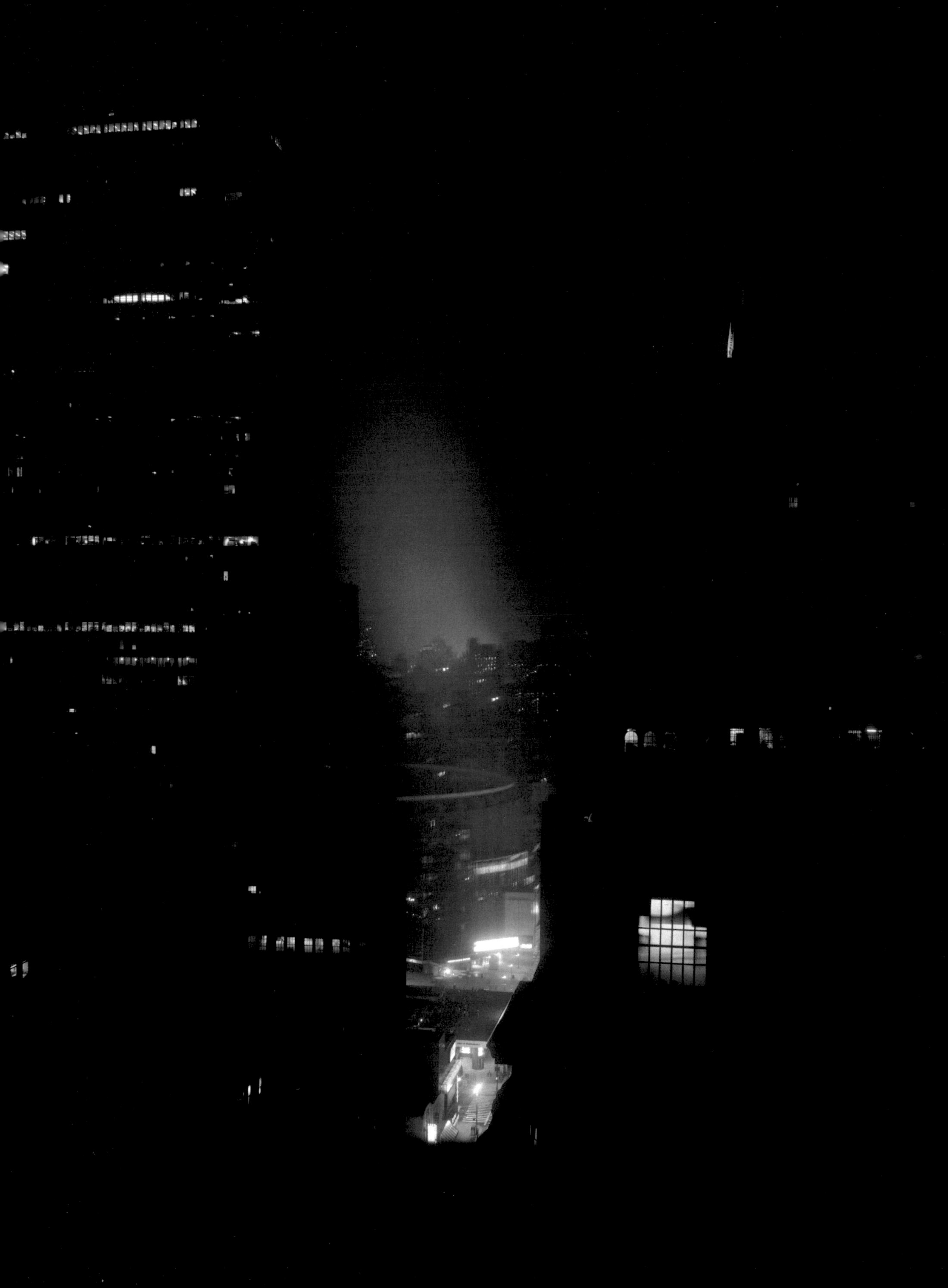

September 17, 2001

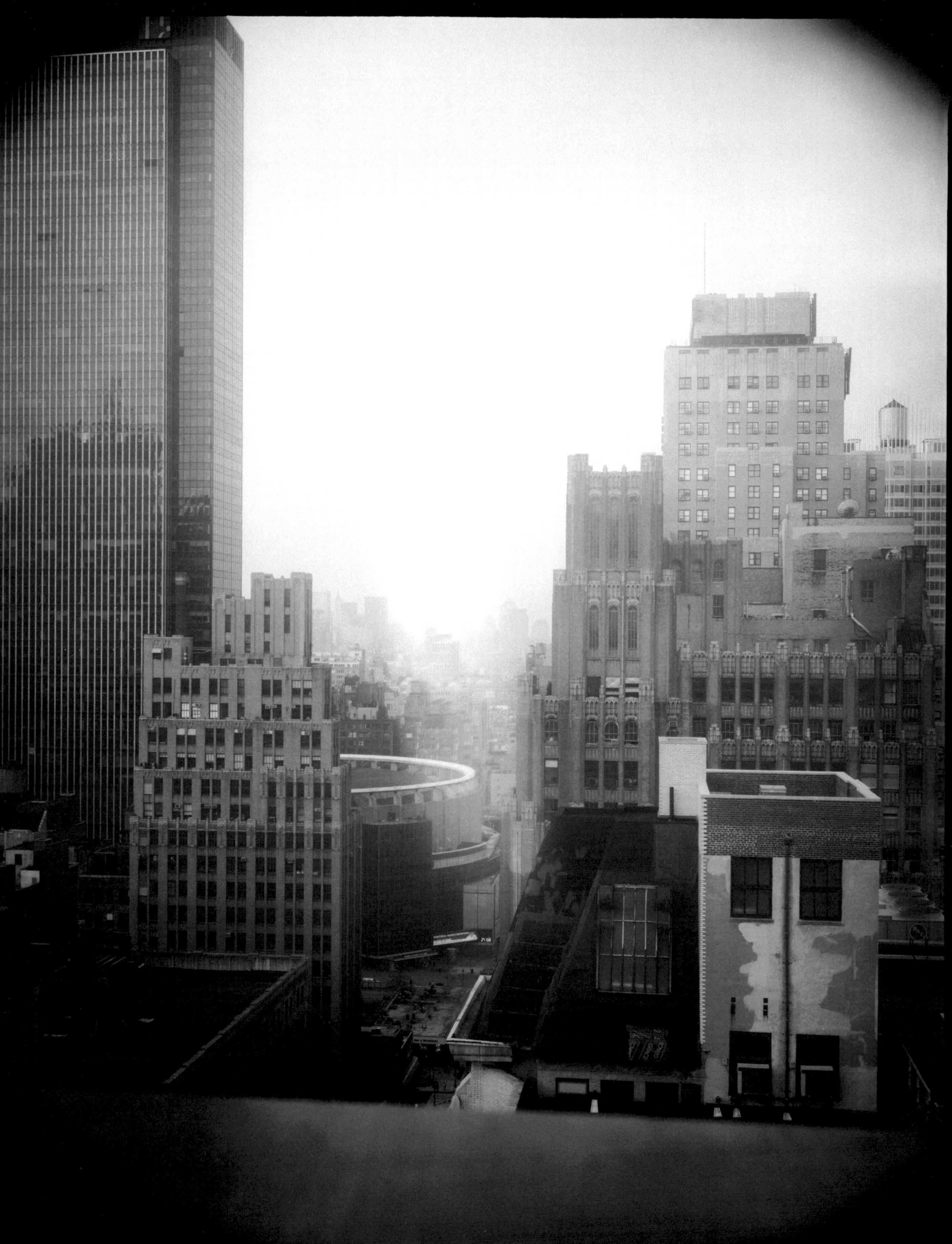

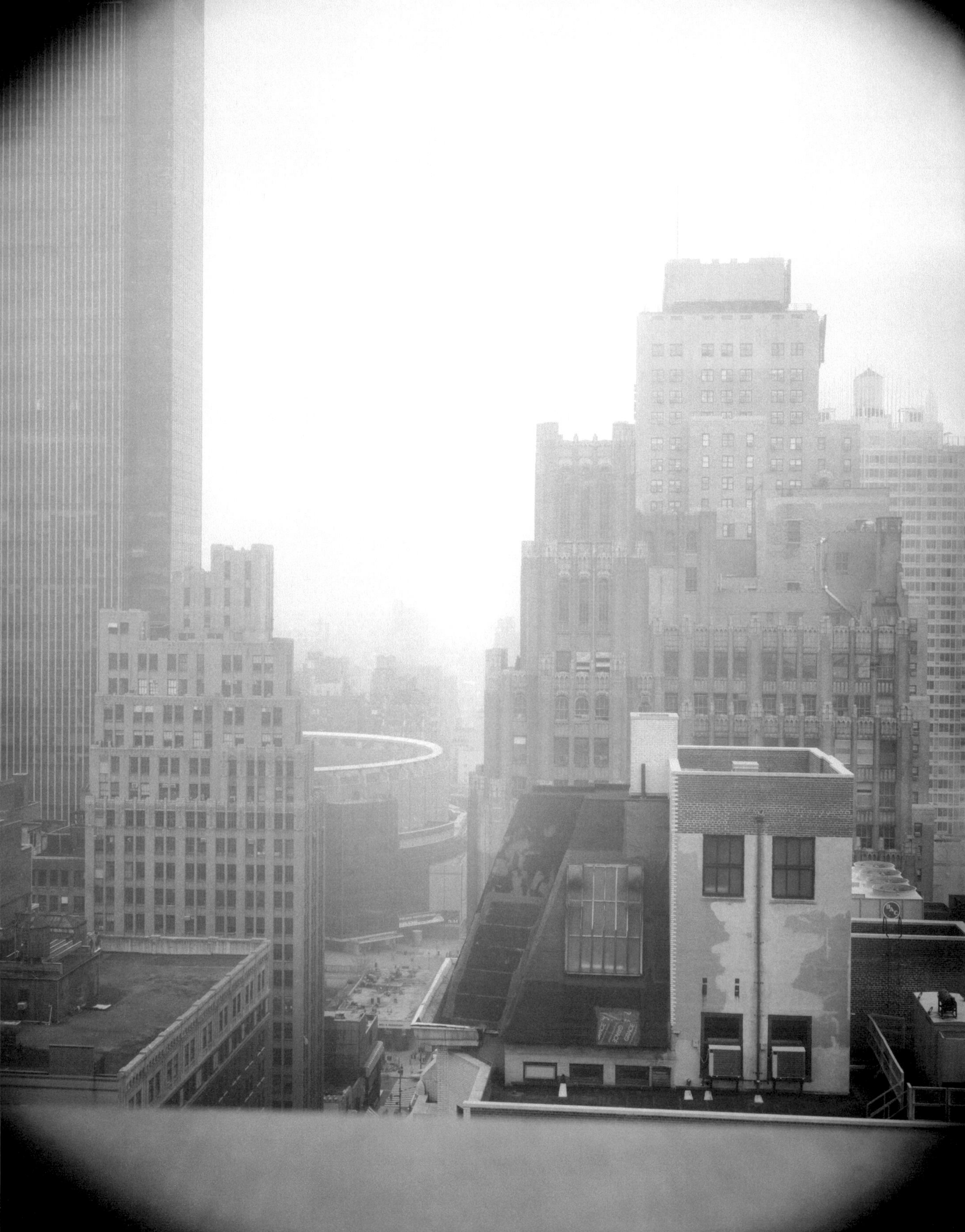

September 19, 2001

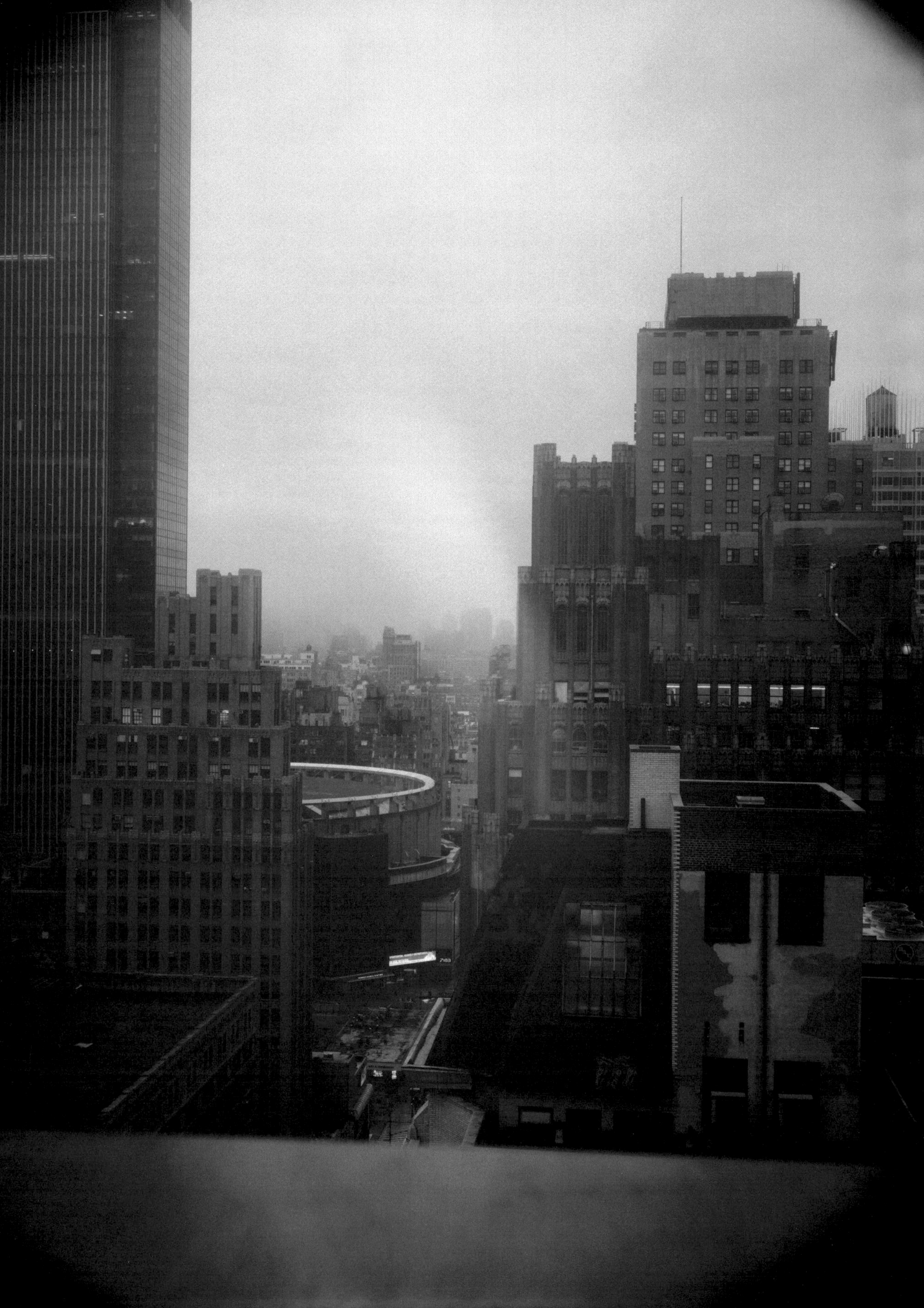

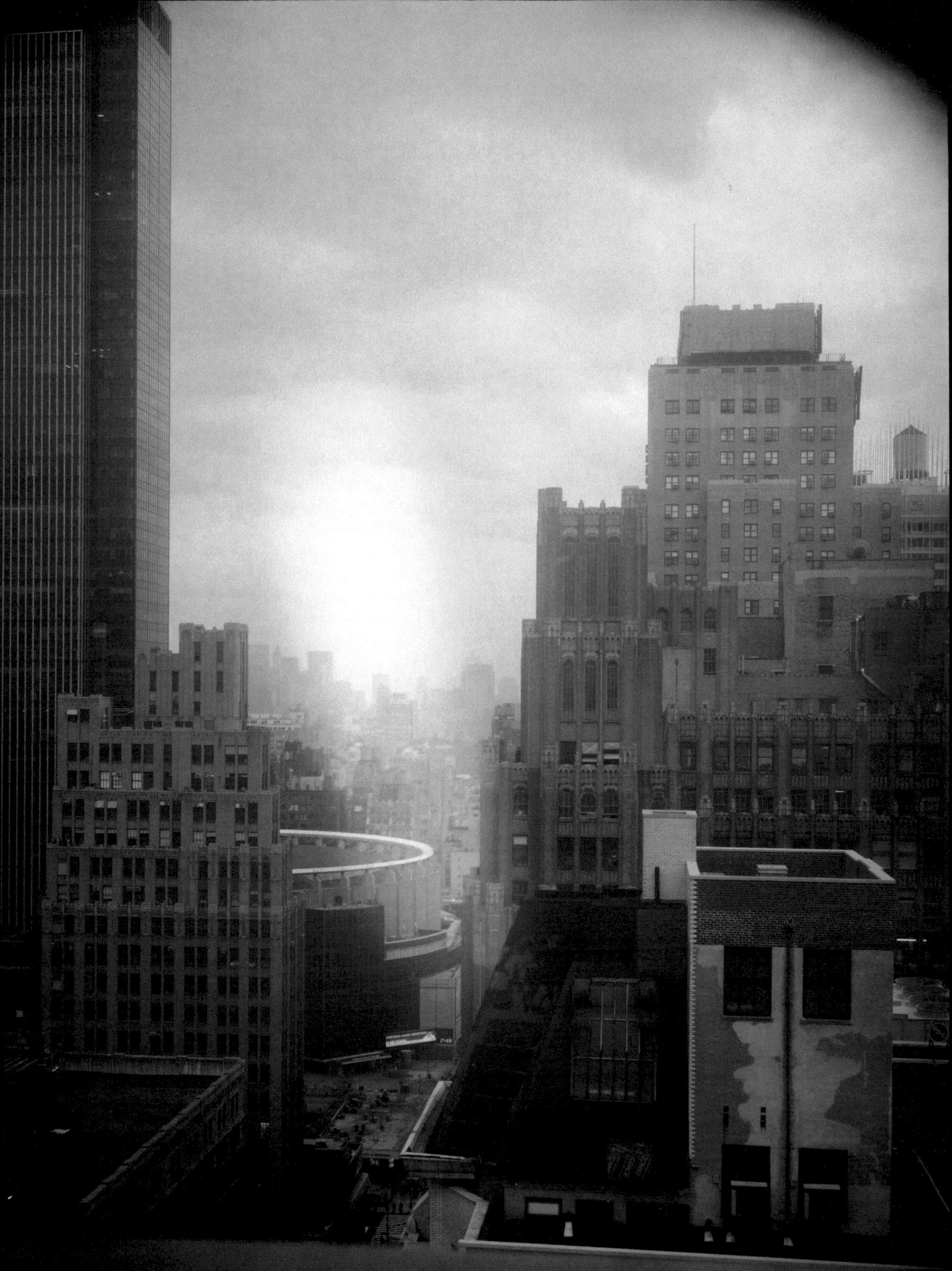

September 21, 2001

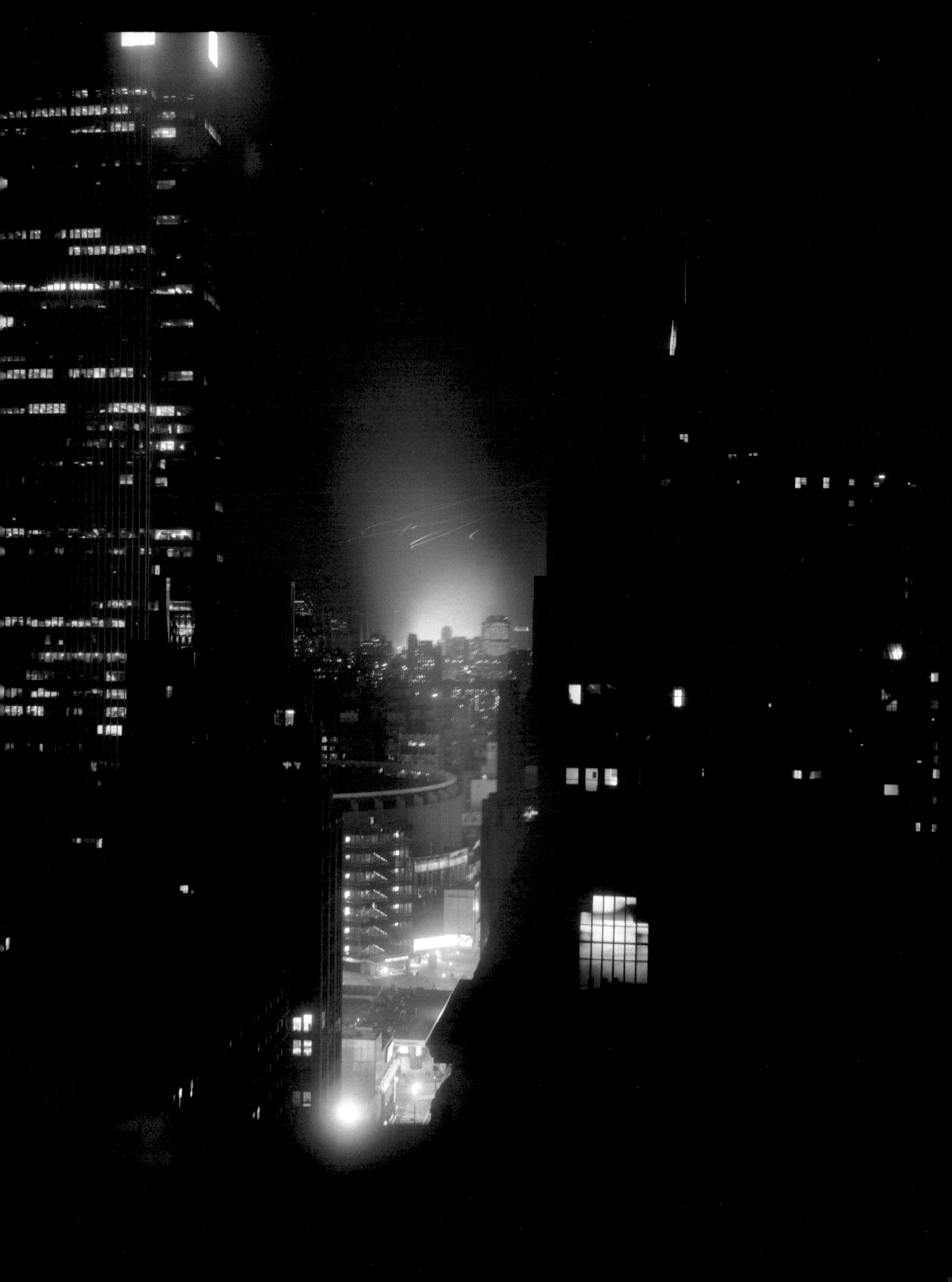

September 22, 2001

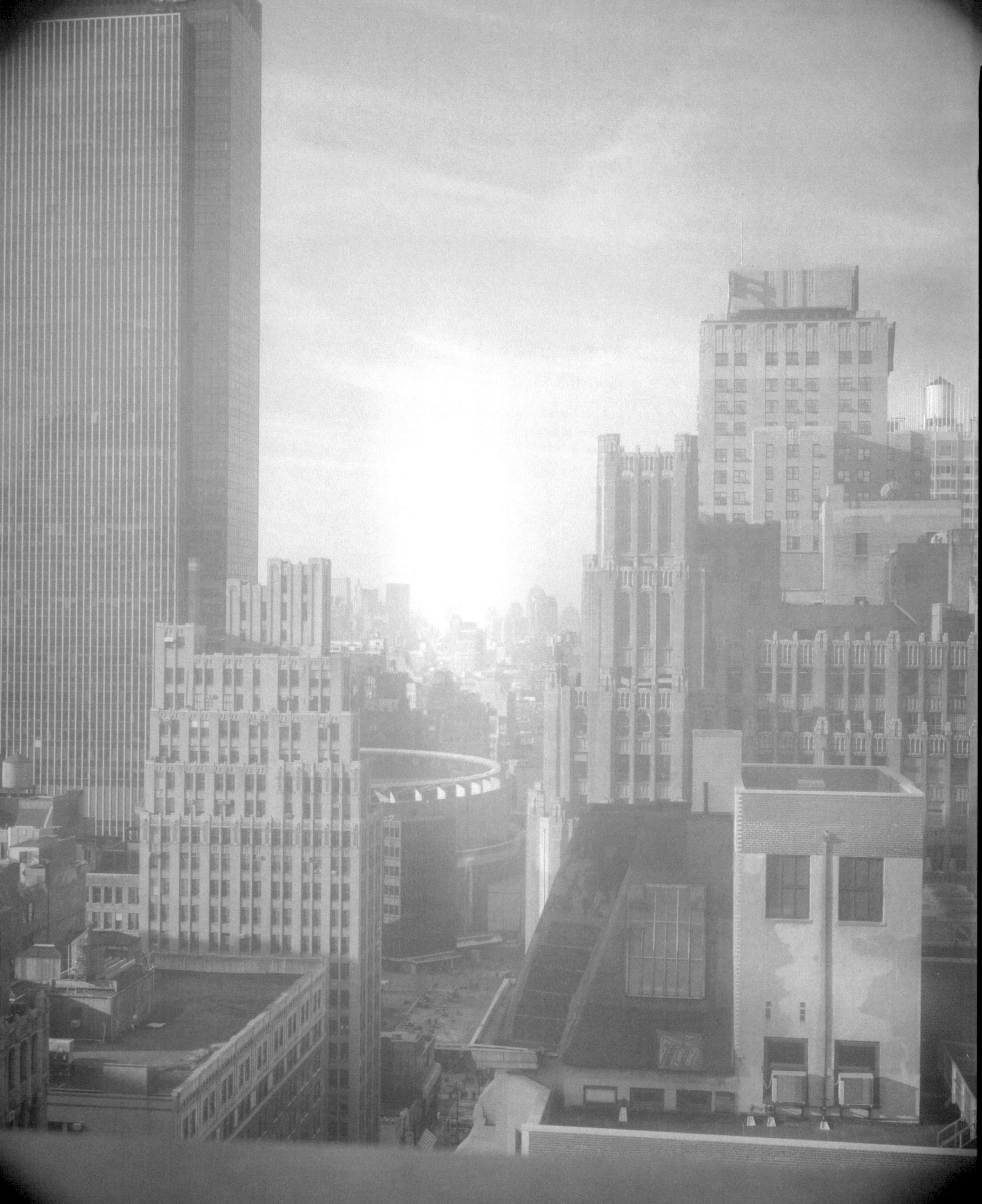

September 23, 2001

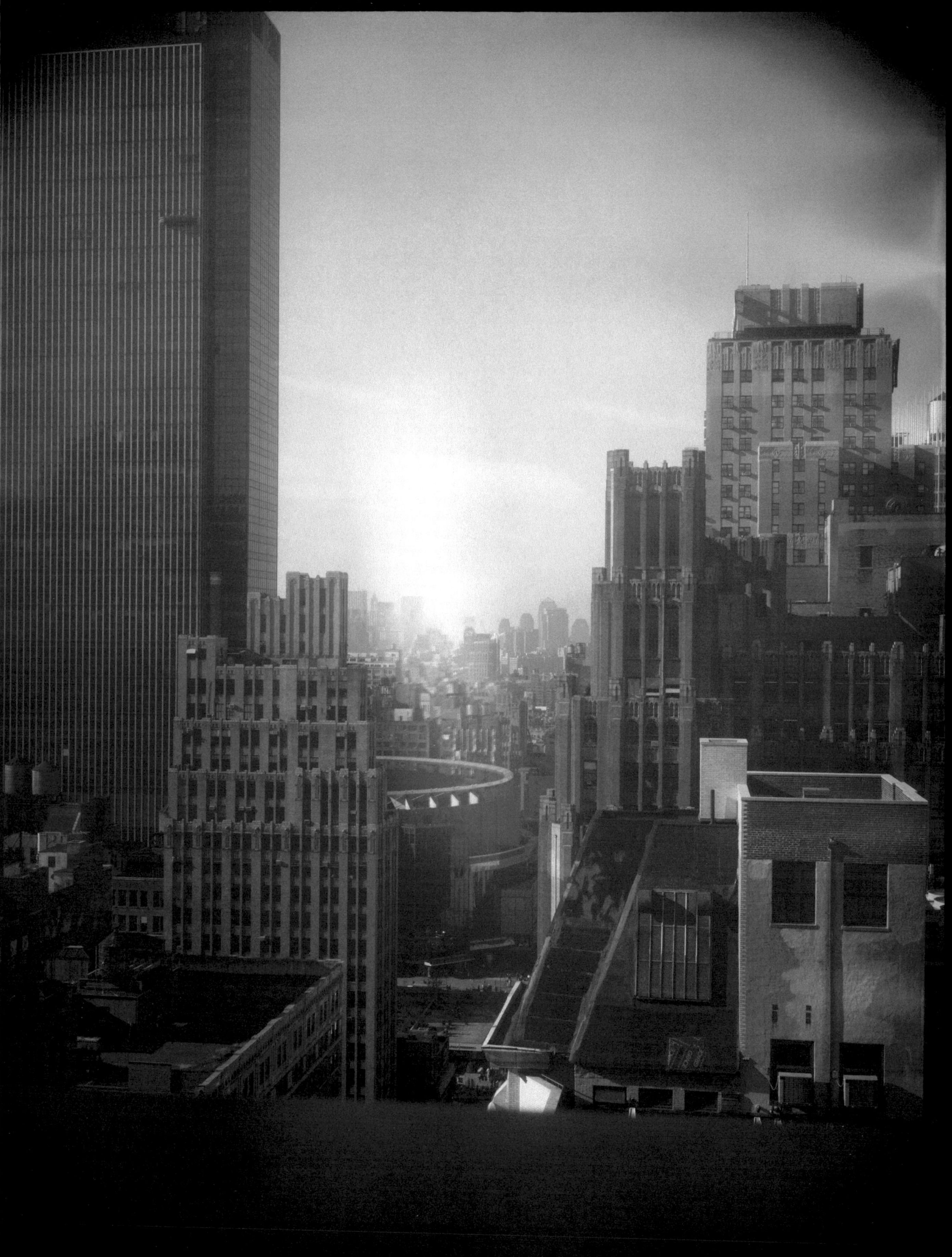

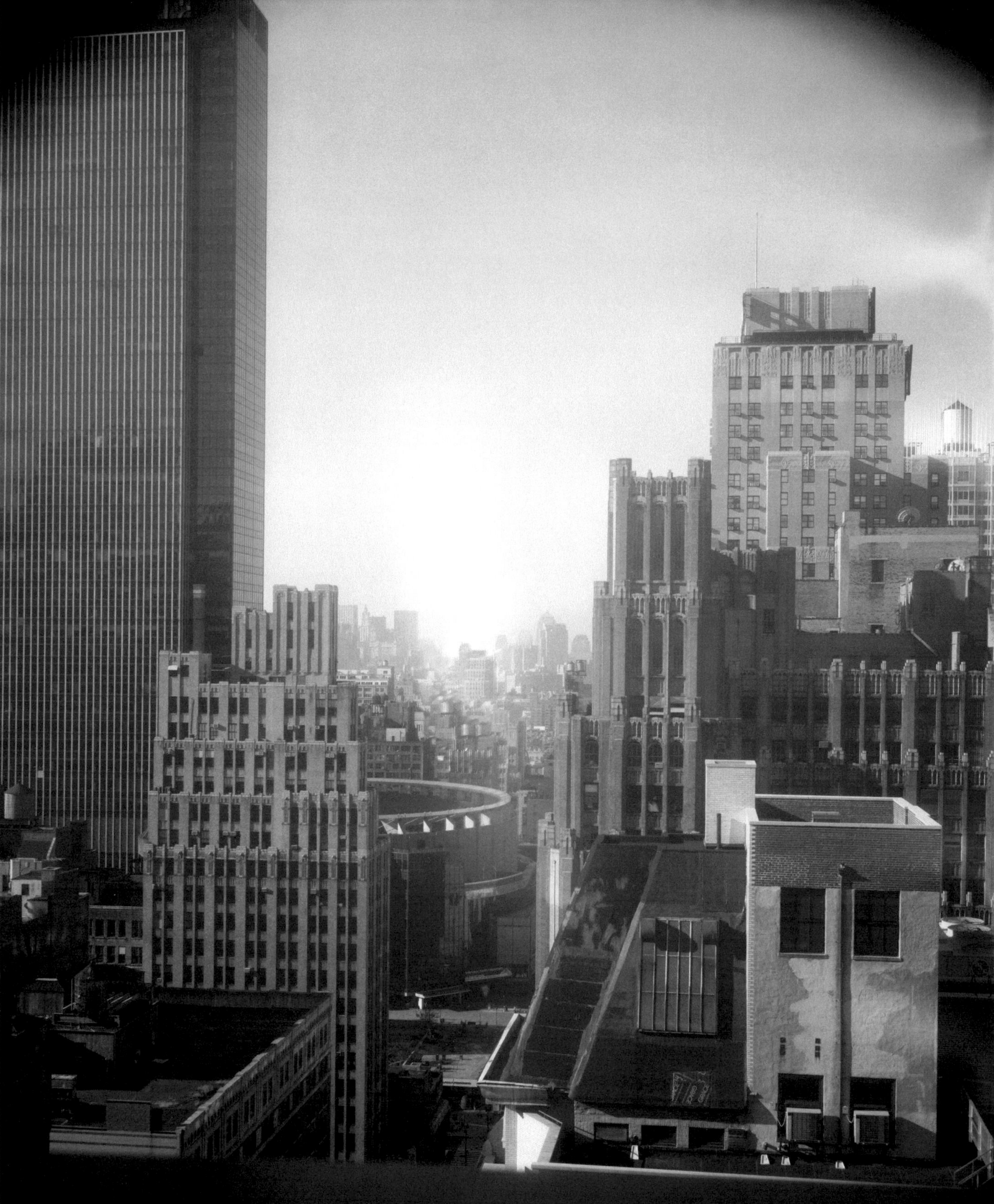

September 25, 2001

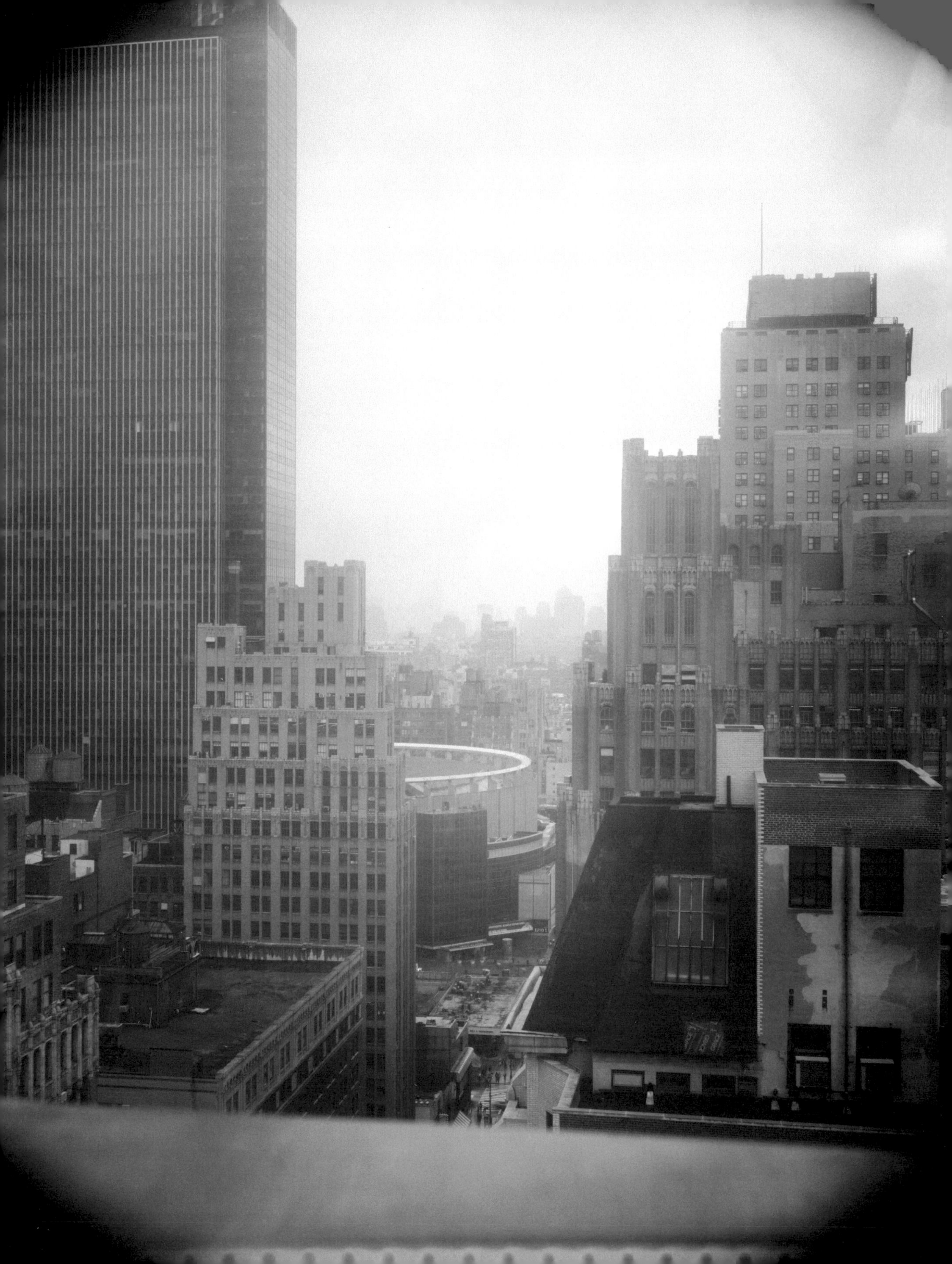

September 26, 2001

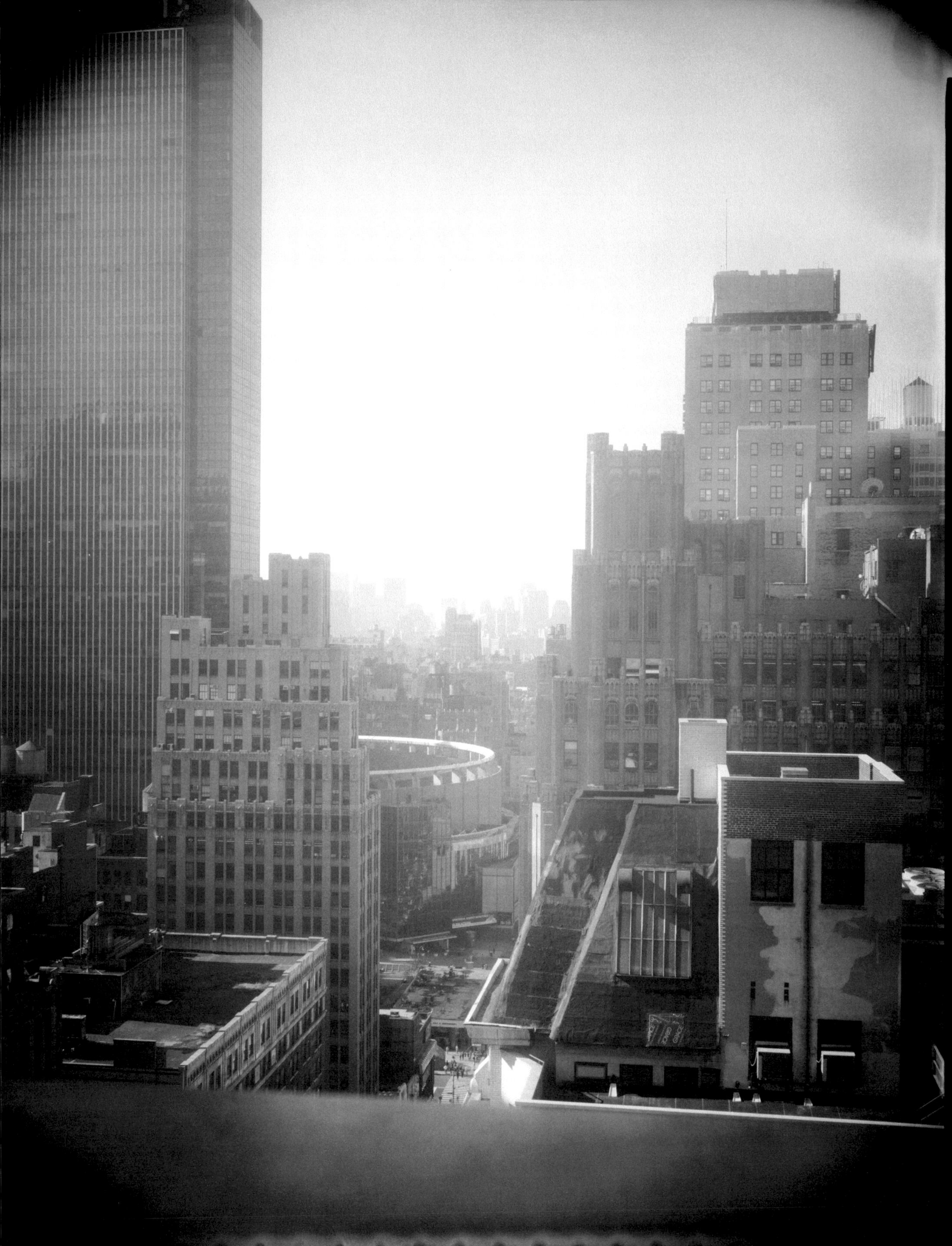

September 27, 2001

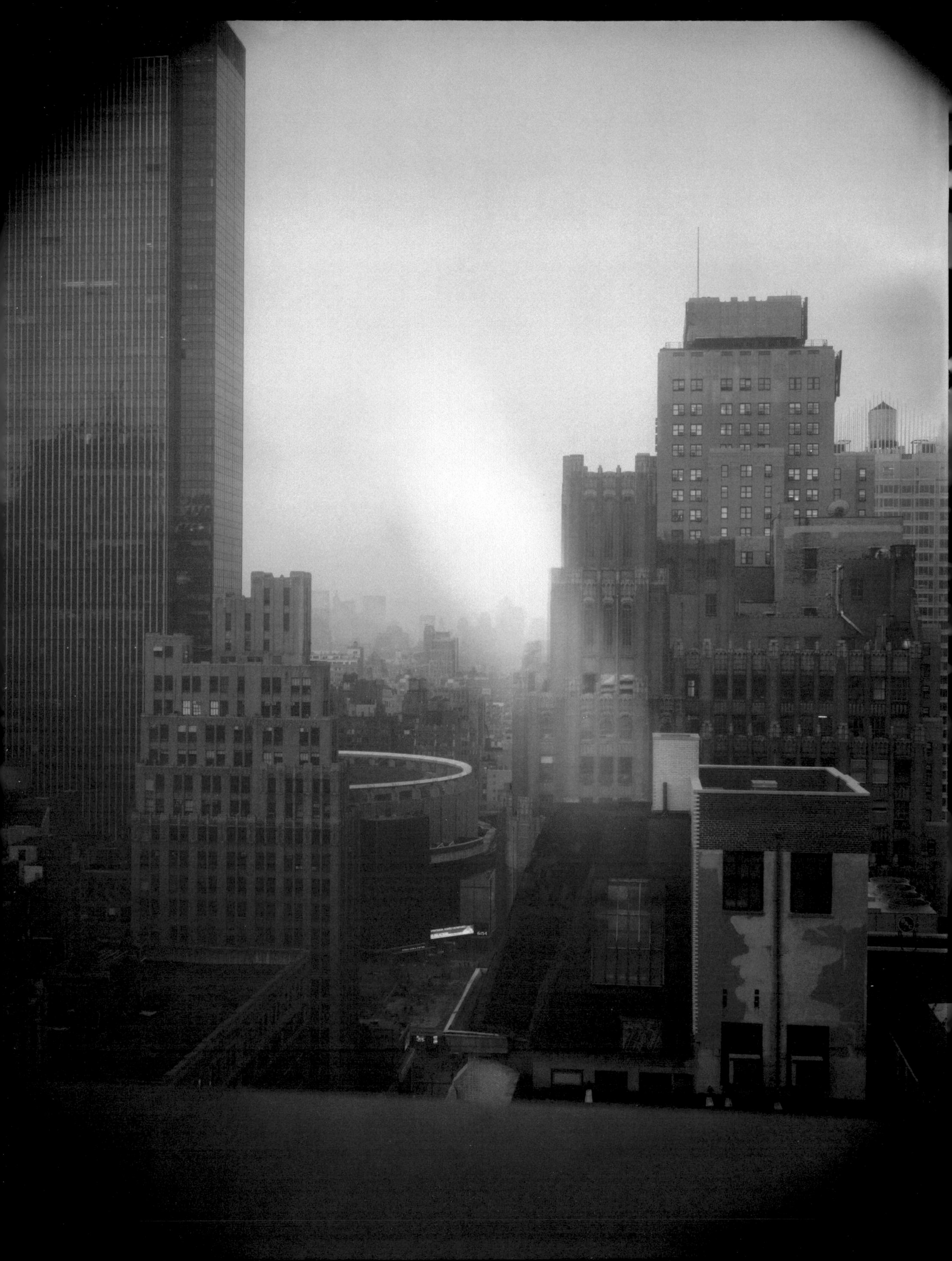

September 28, 2001

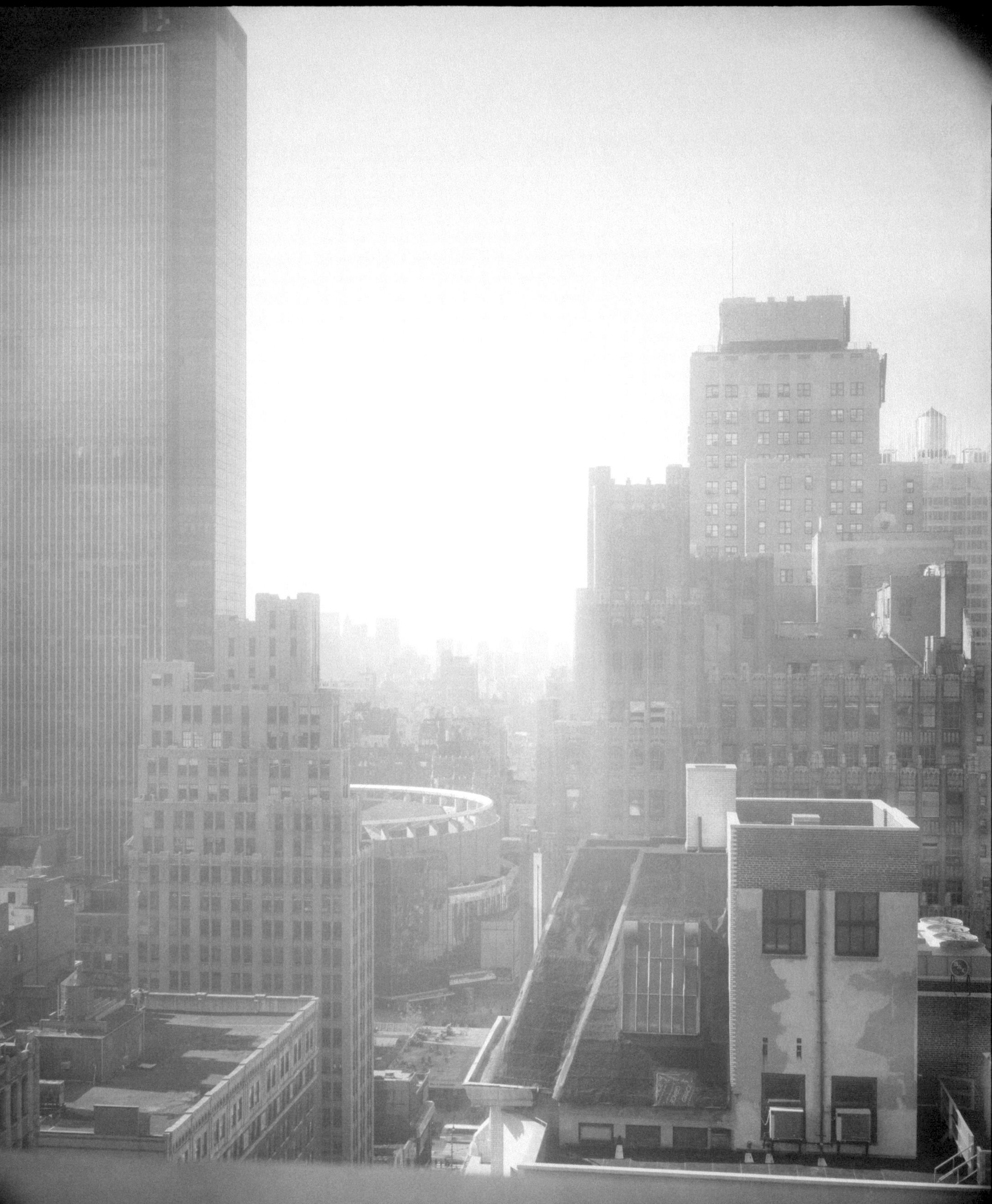

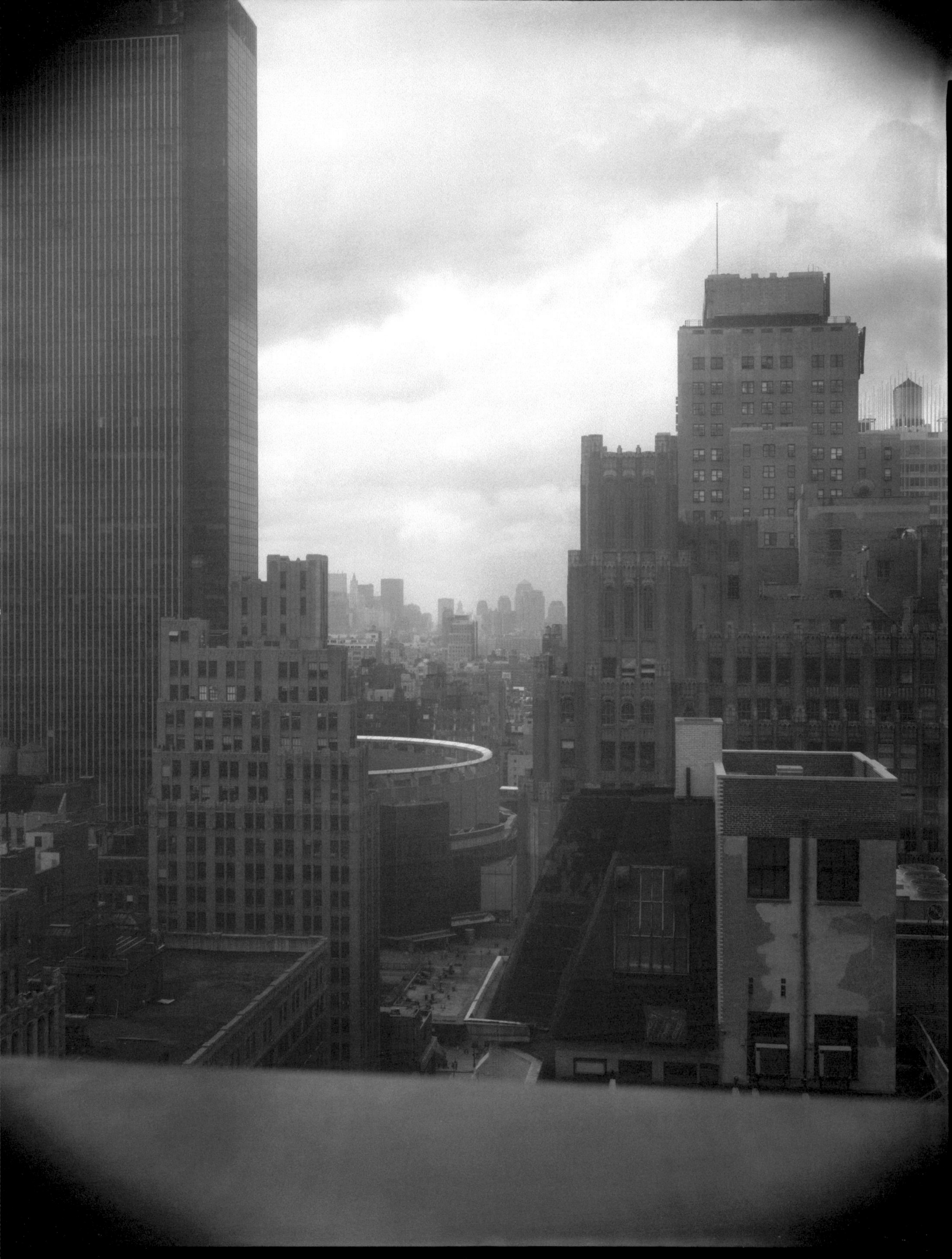

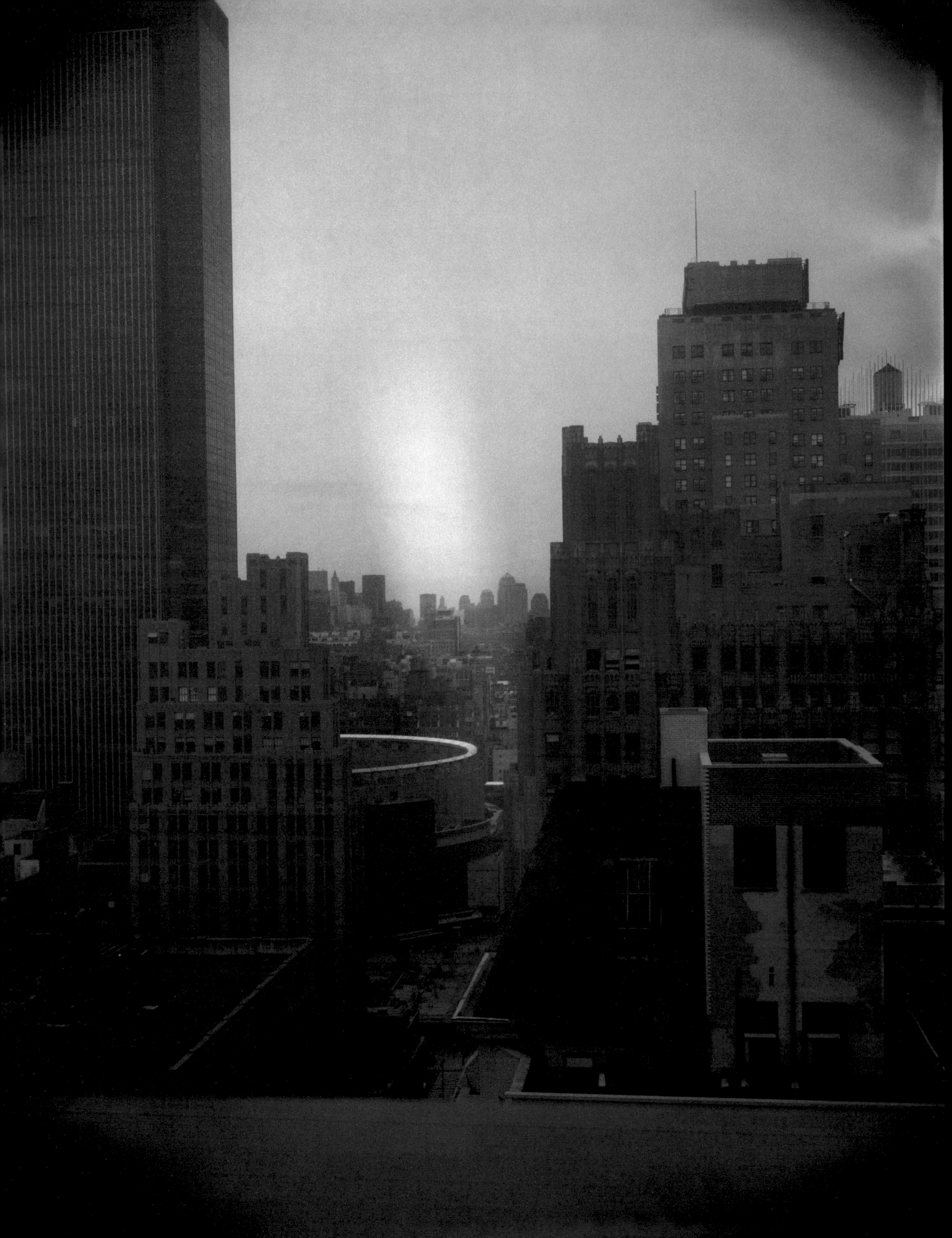

September 4, 2002

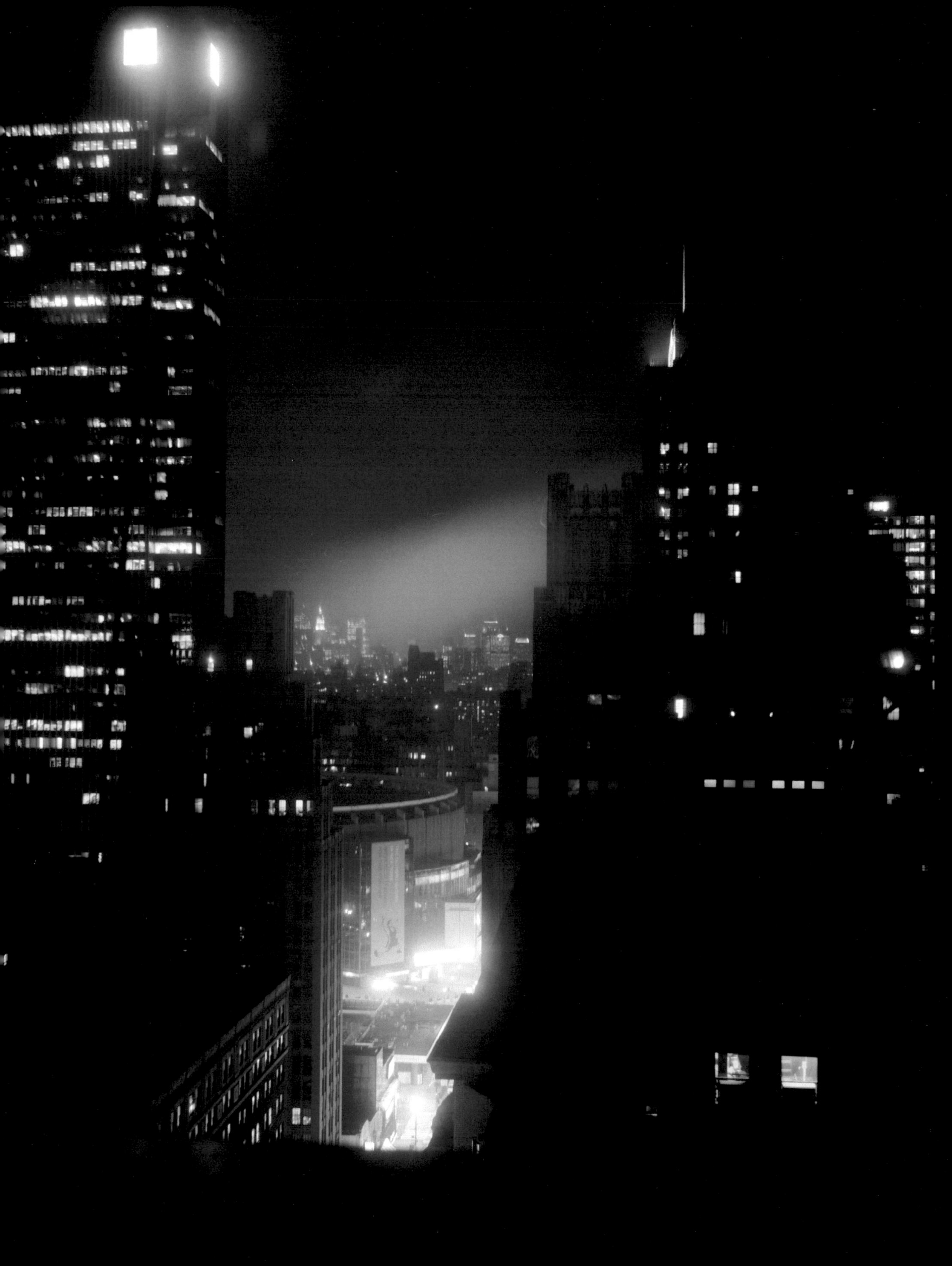

September 5, 2002

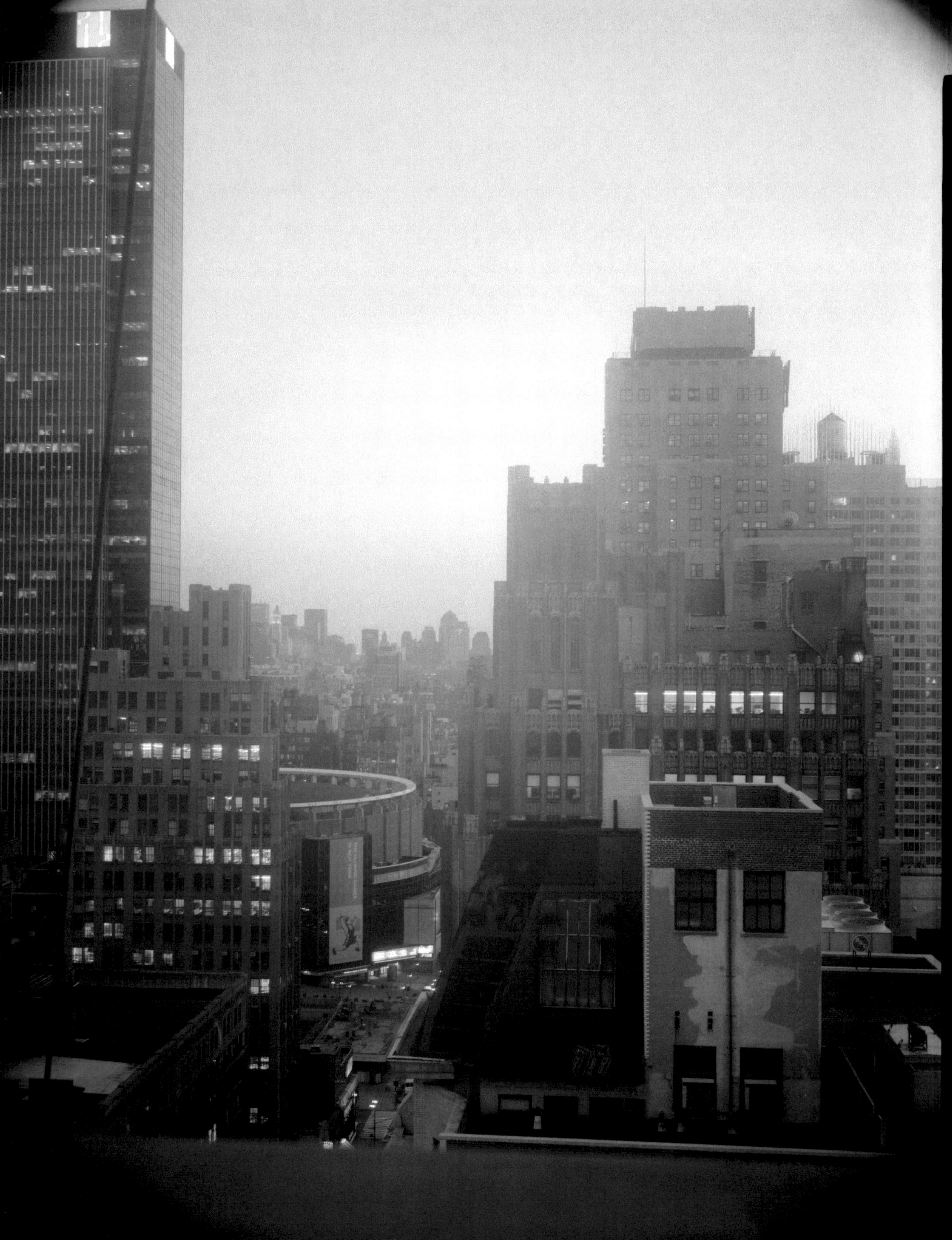

September 6, 2002

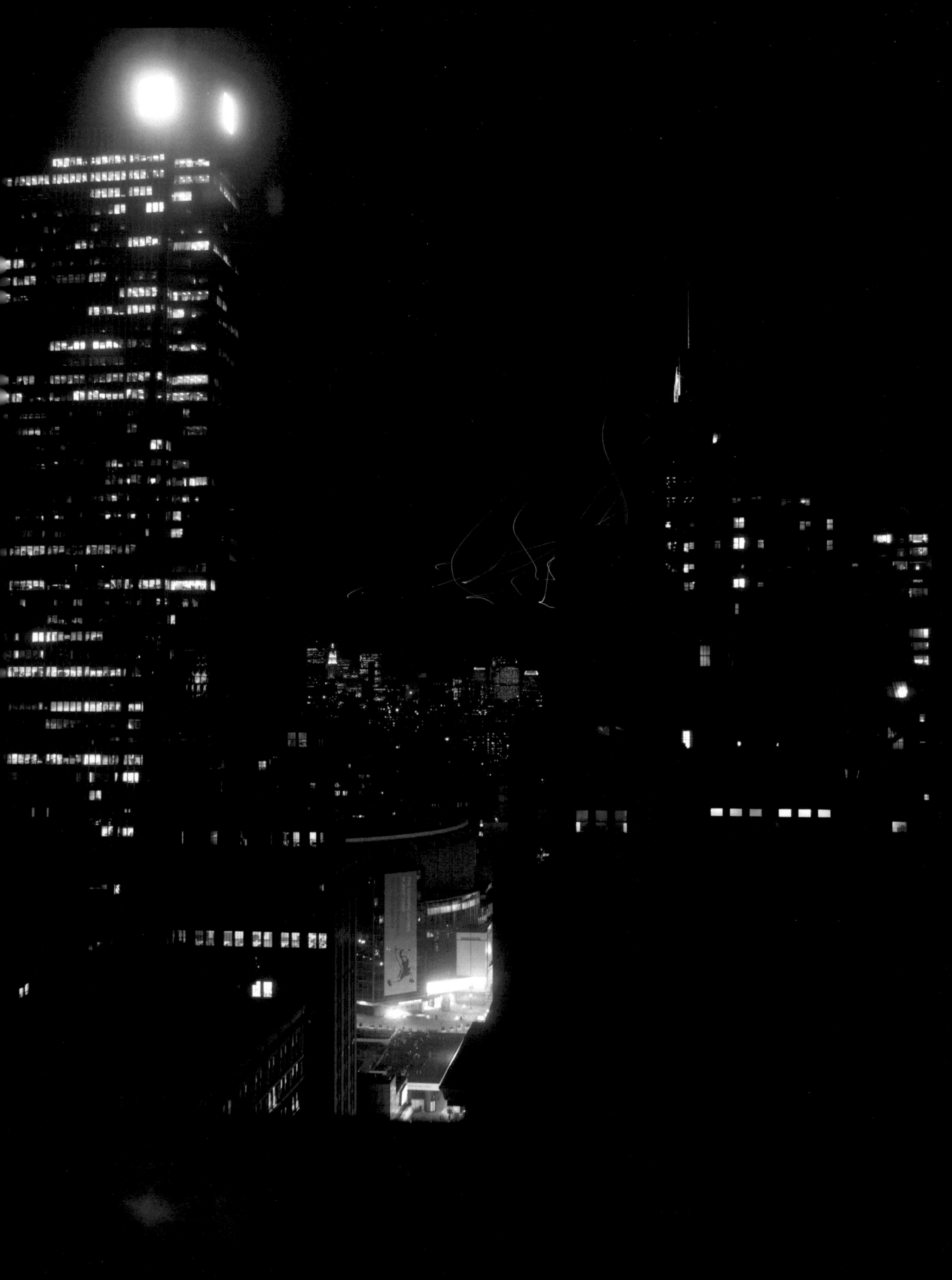

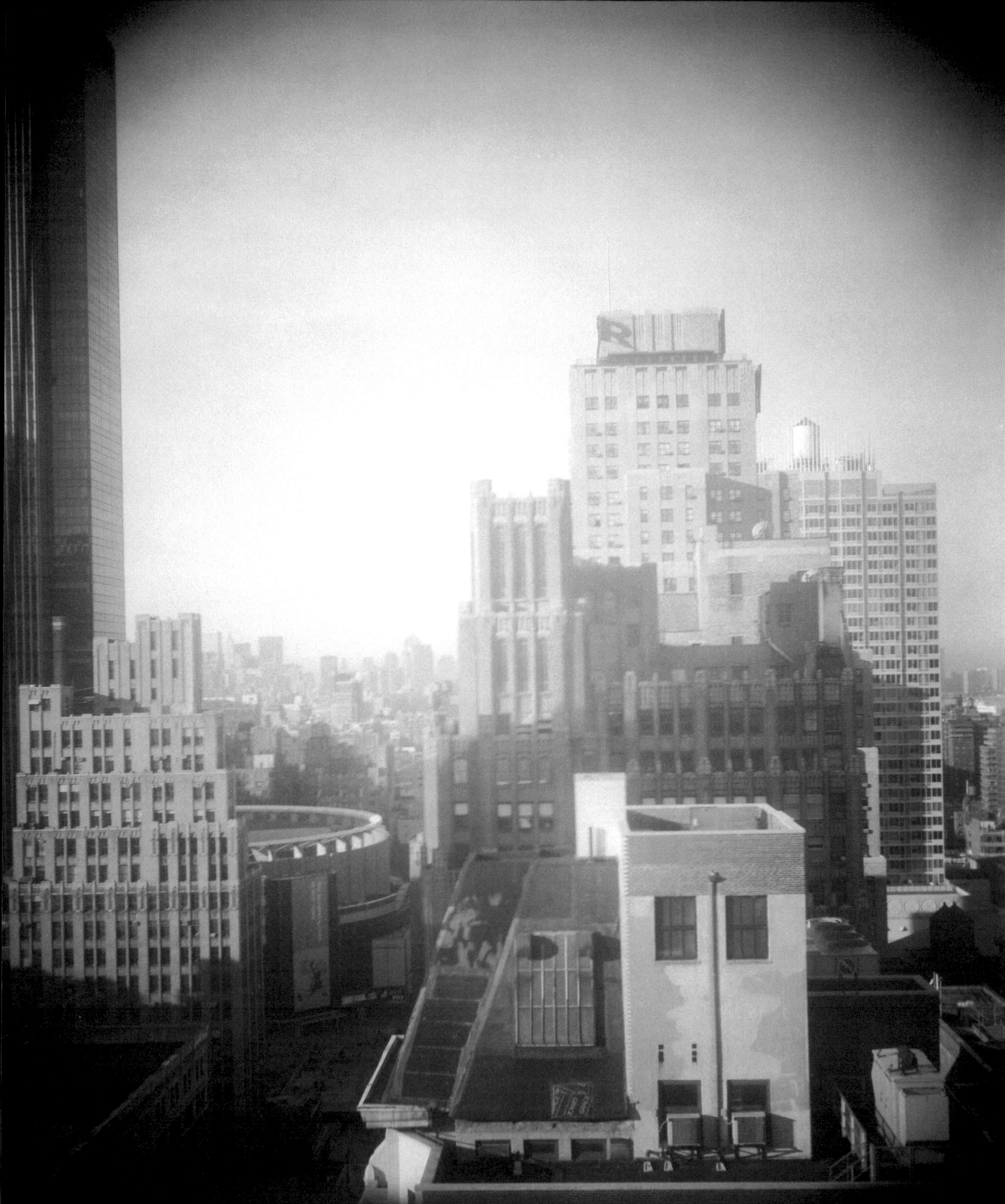

September 8, 2002

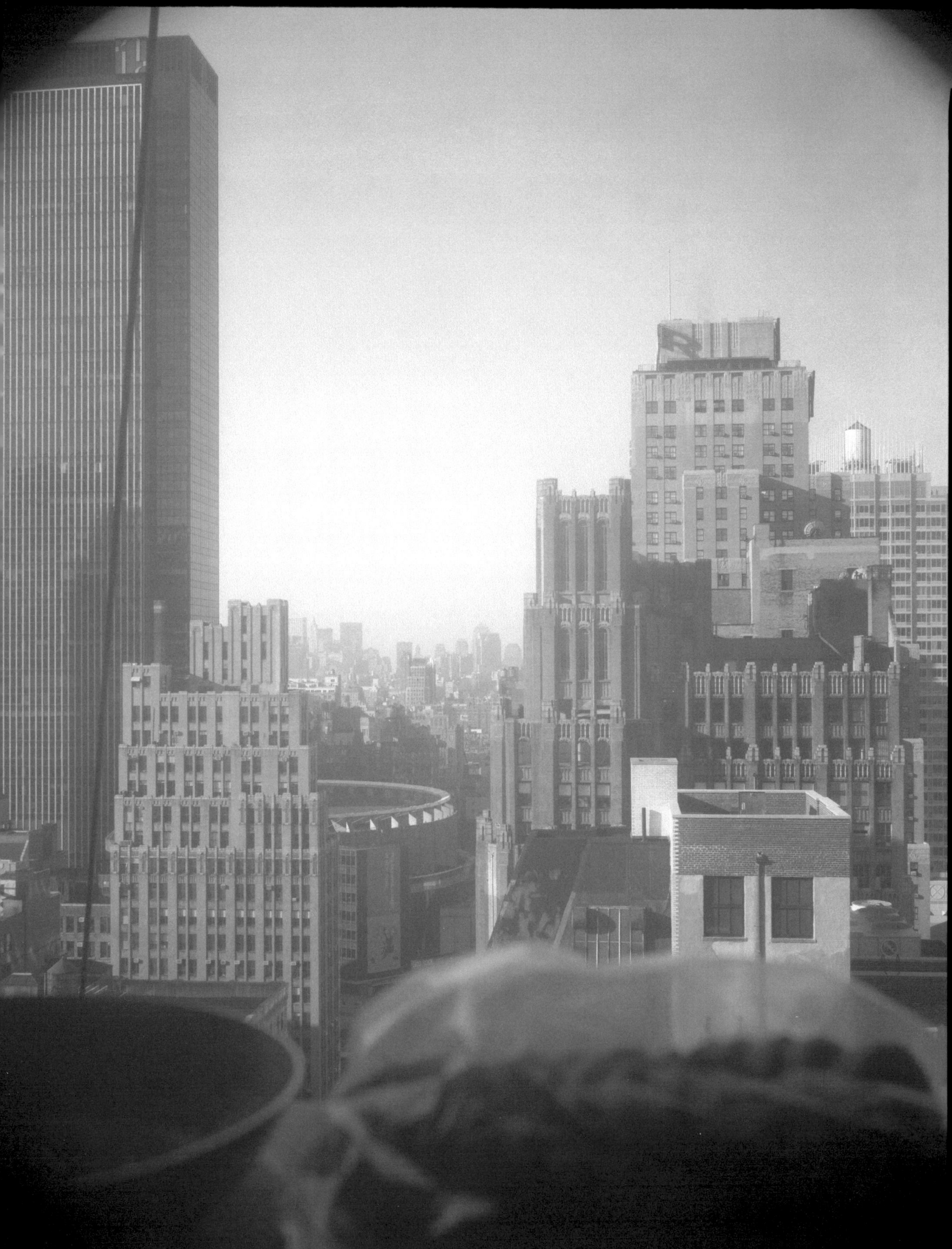

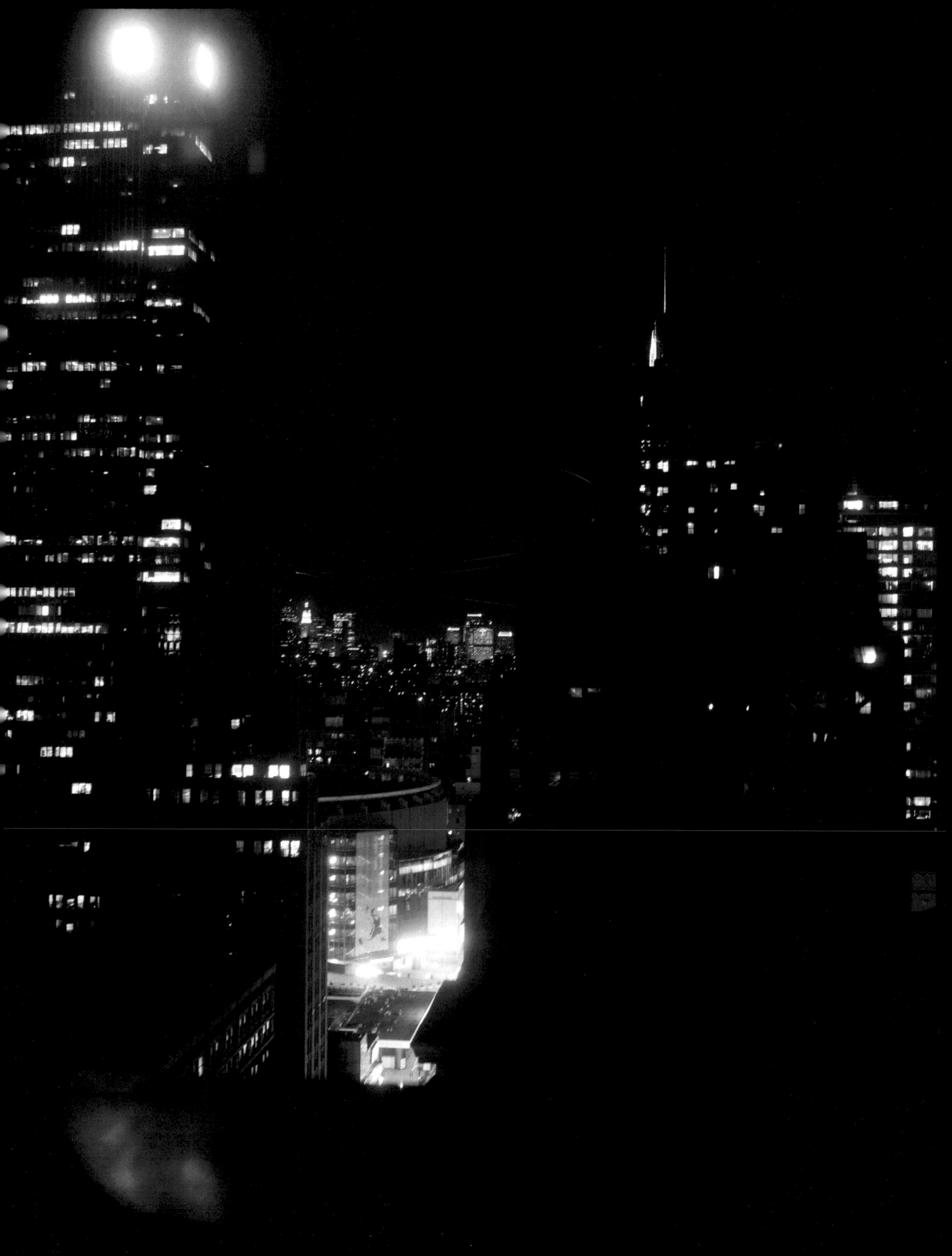

September 12, 2002

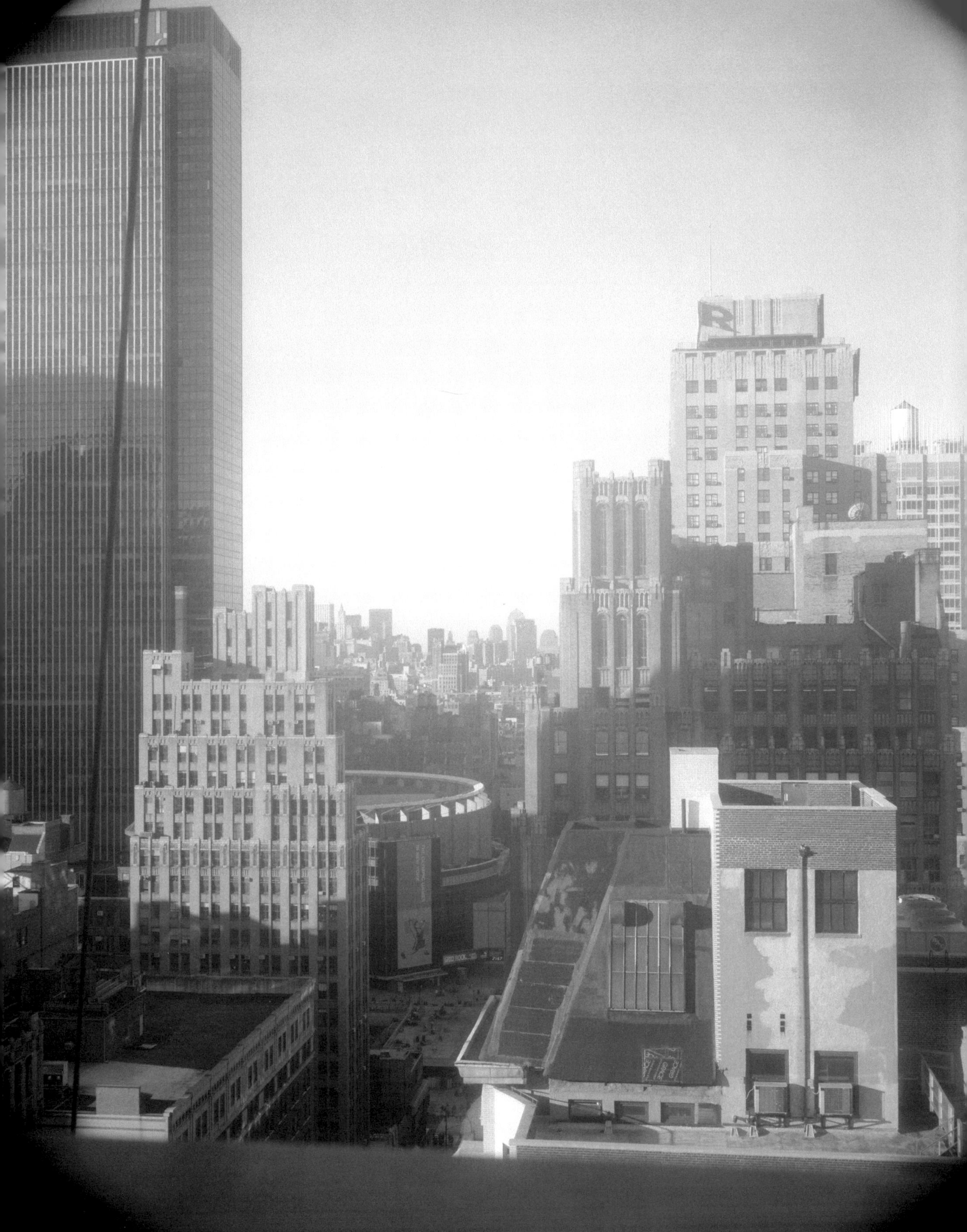

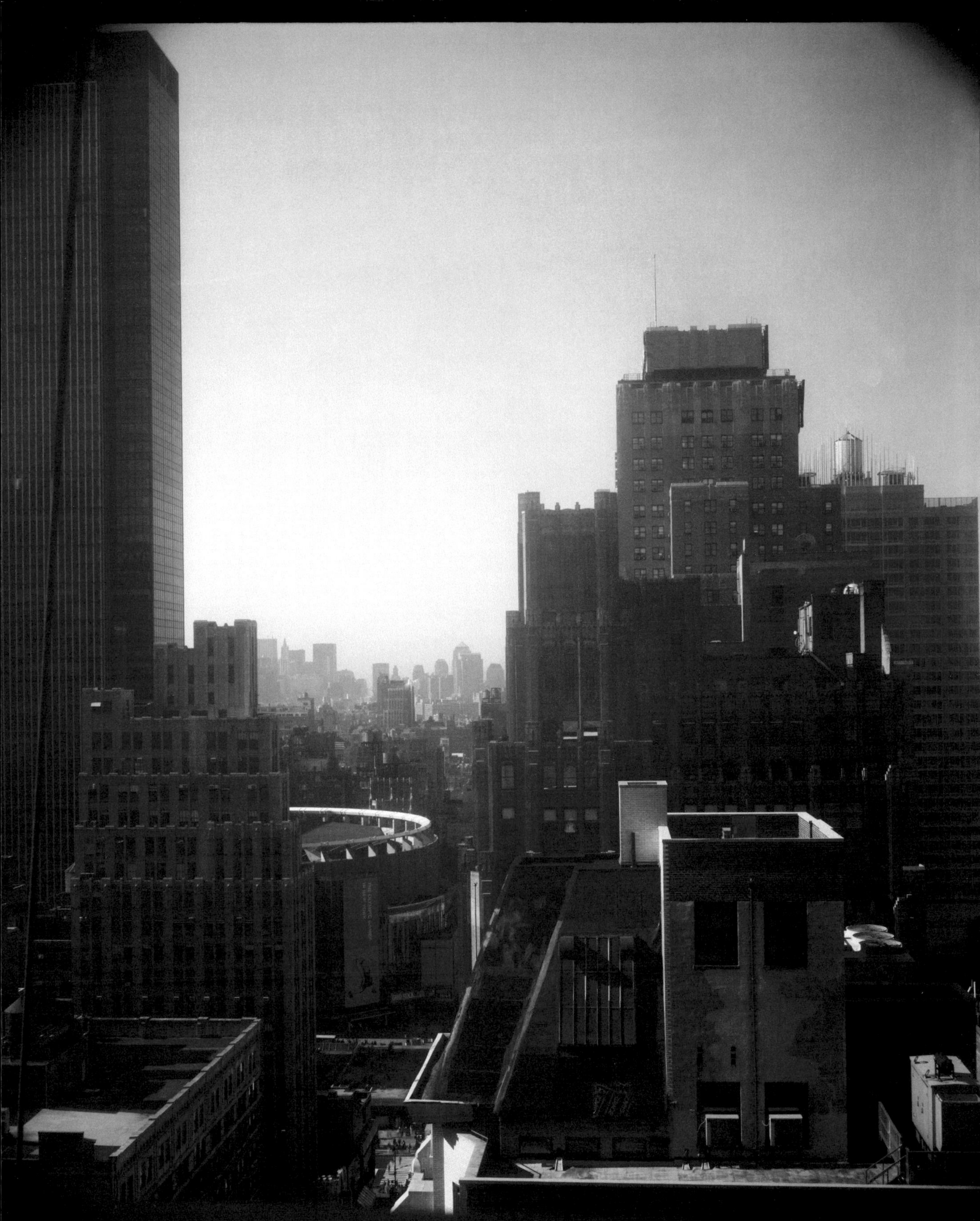

September 14, 2002

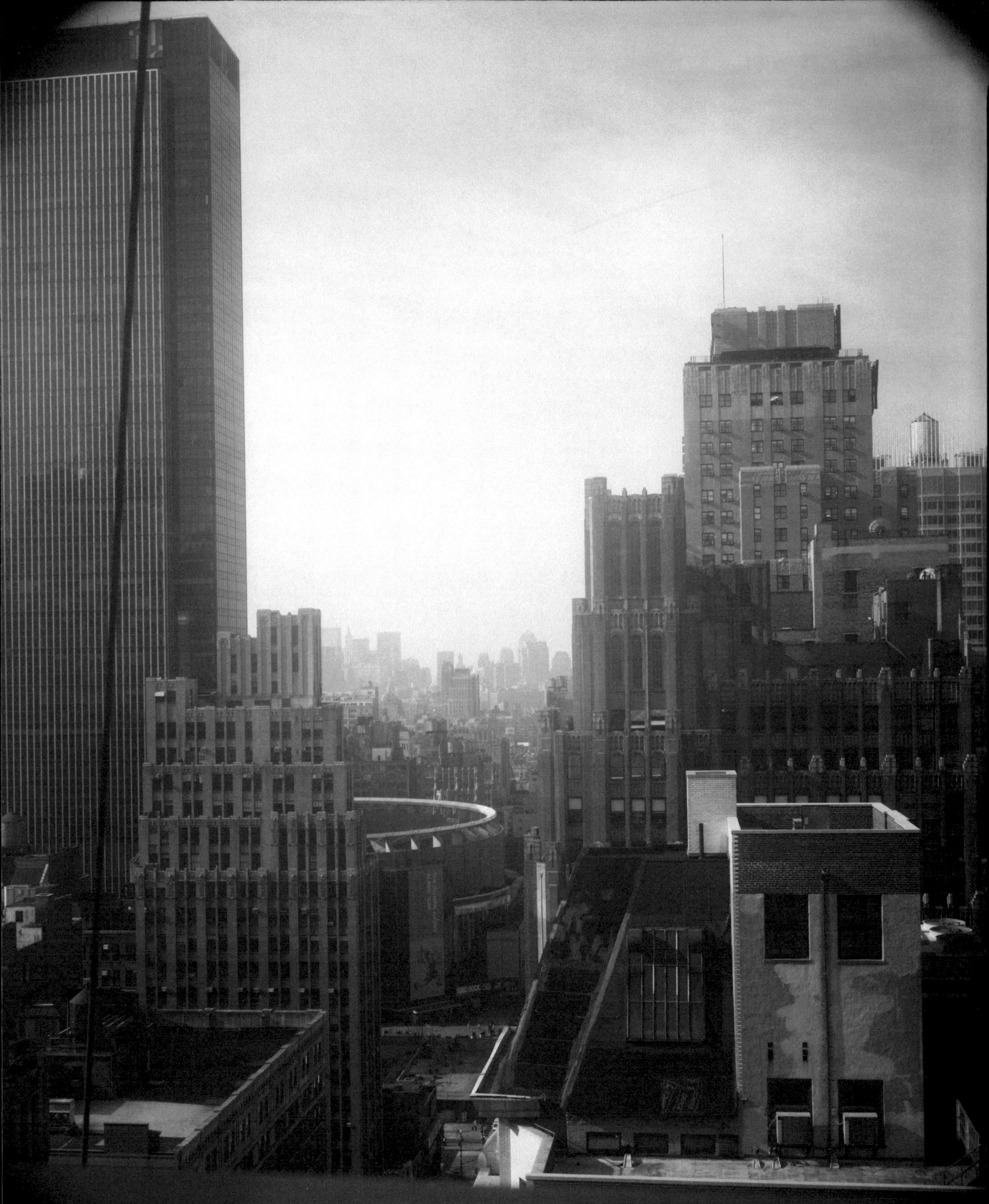

September 15, 2002

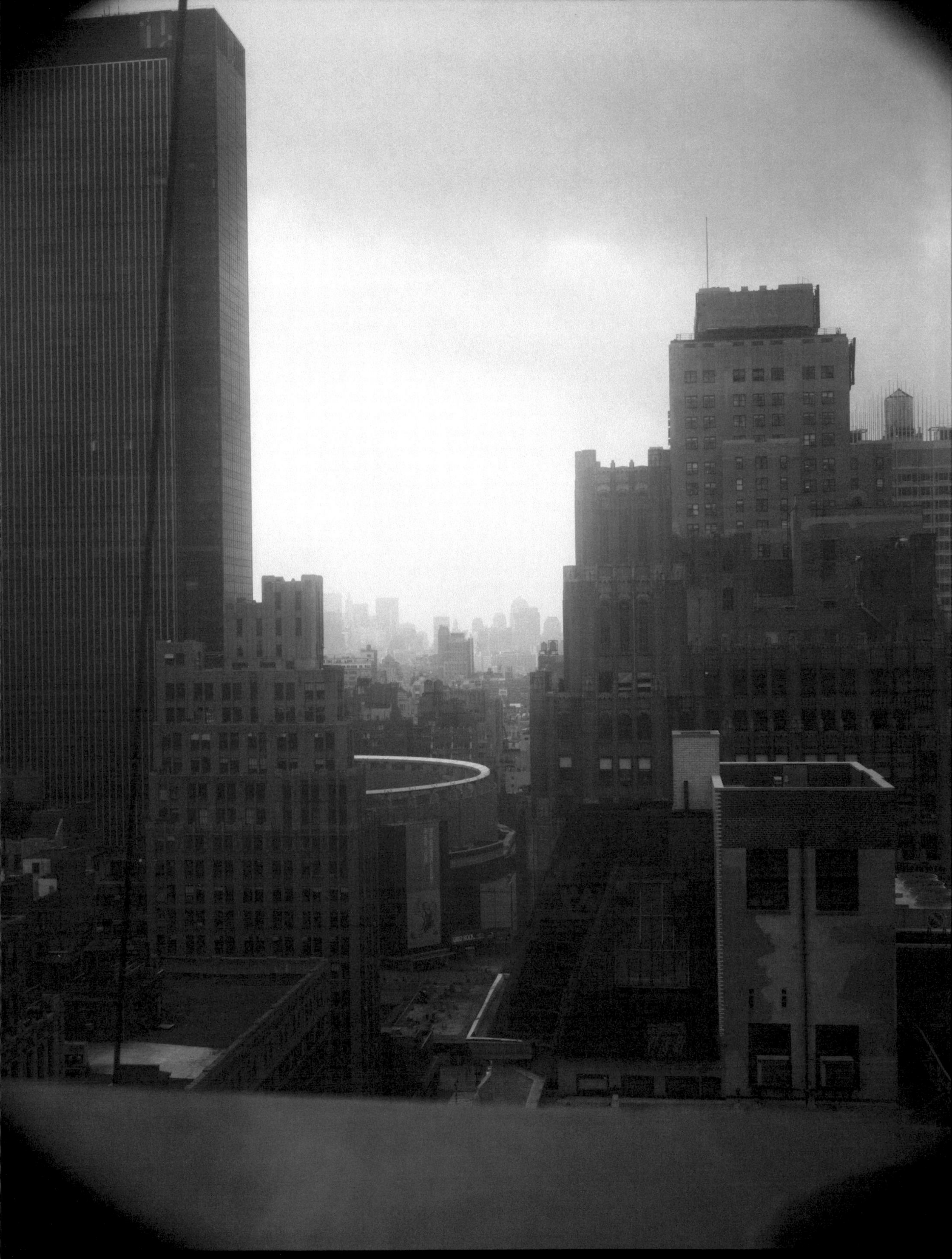

September 20, 2002

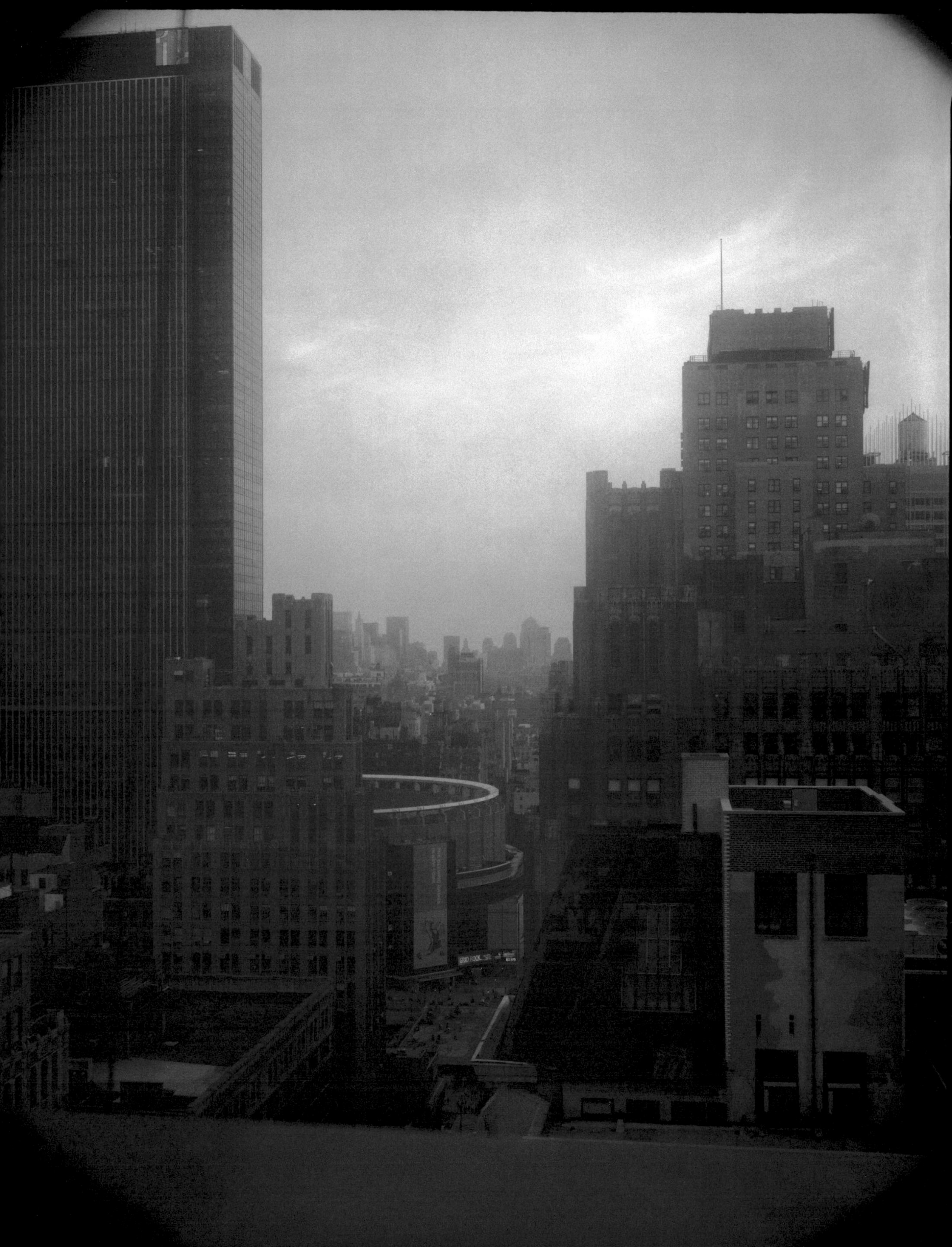

September 21, 2002

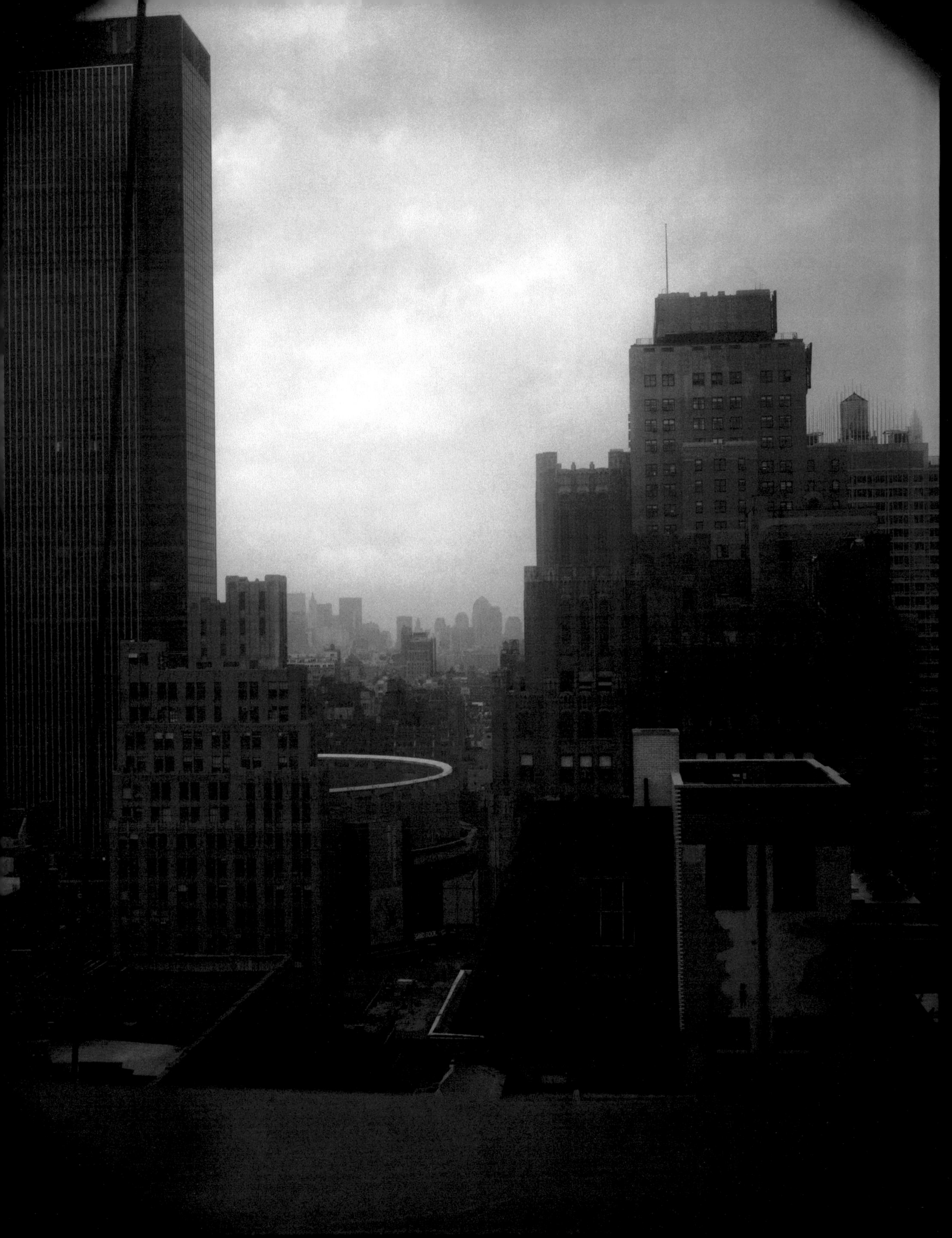

September 22, 2002

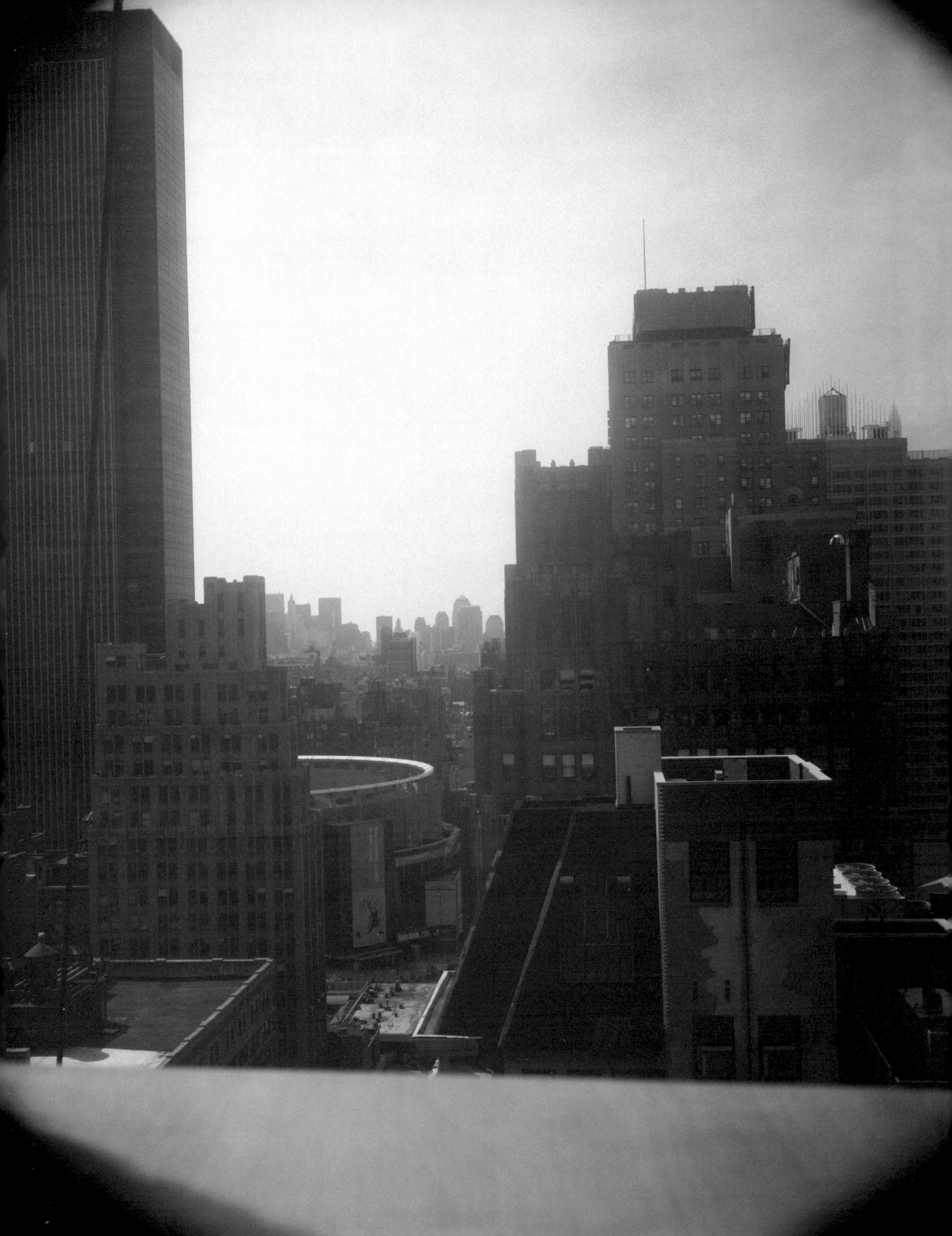

September 23, 2002

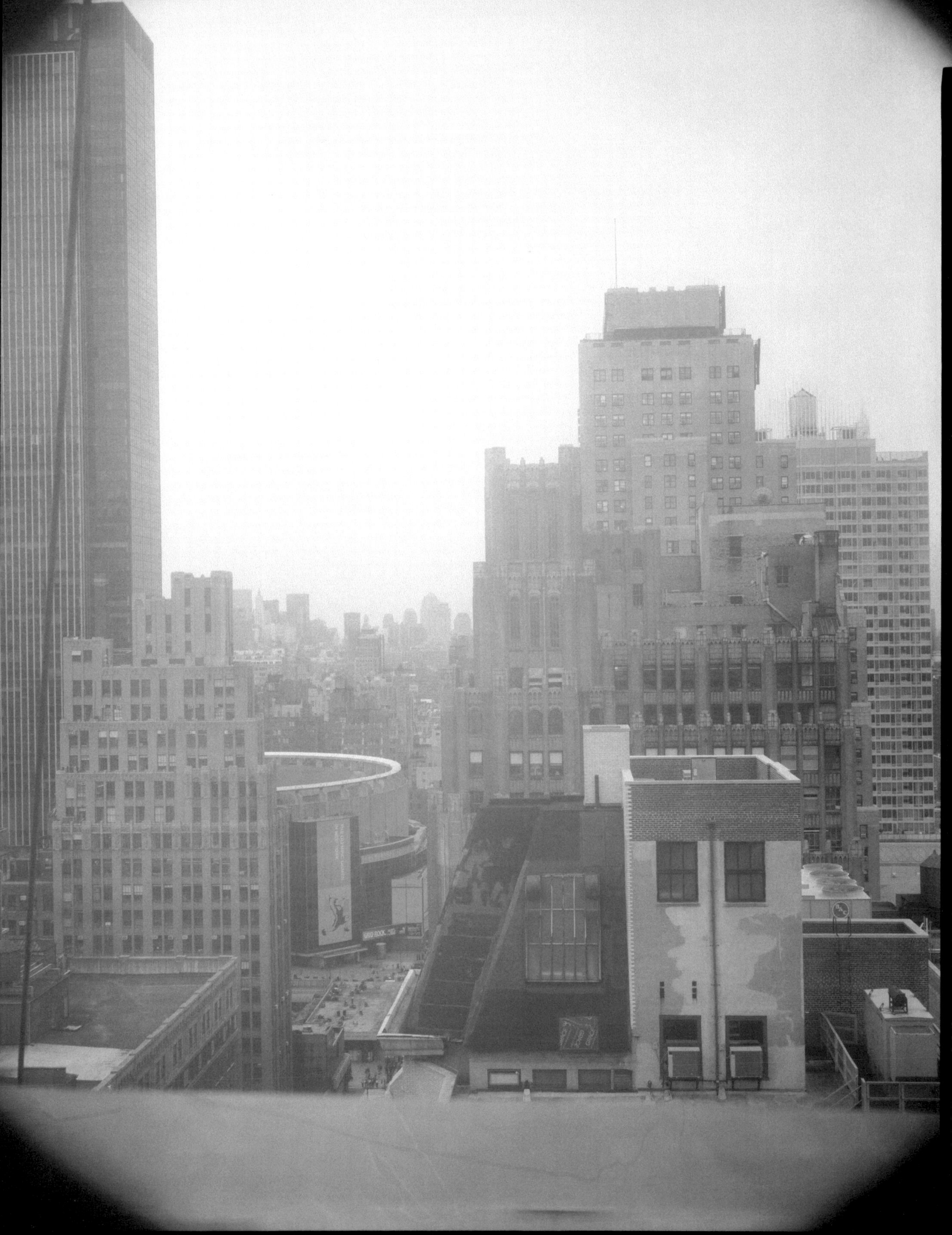

September 1, 2003

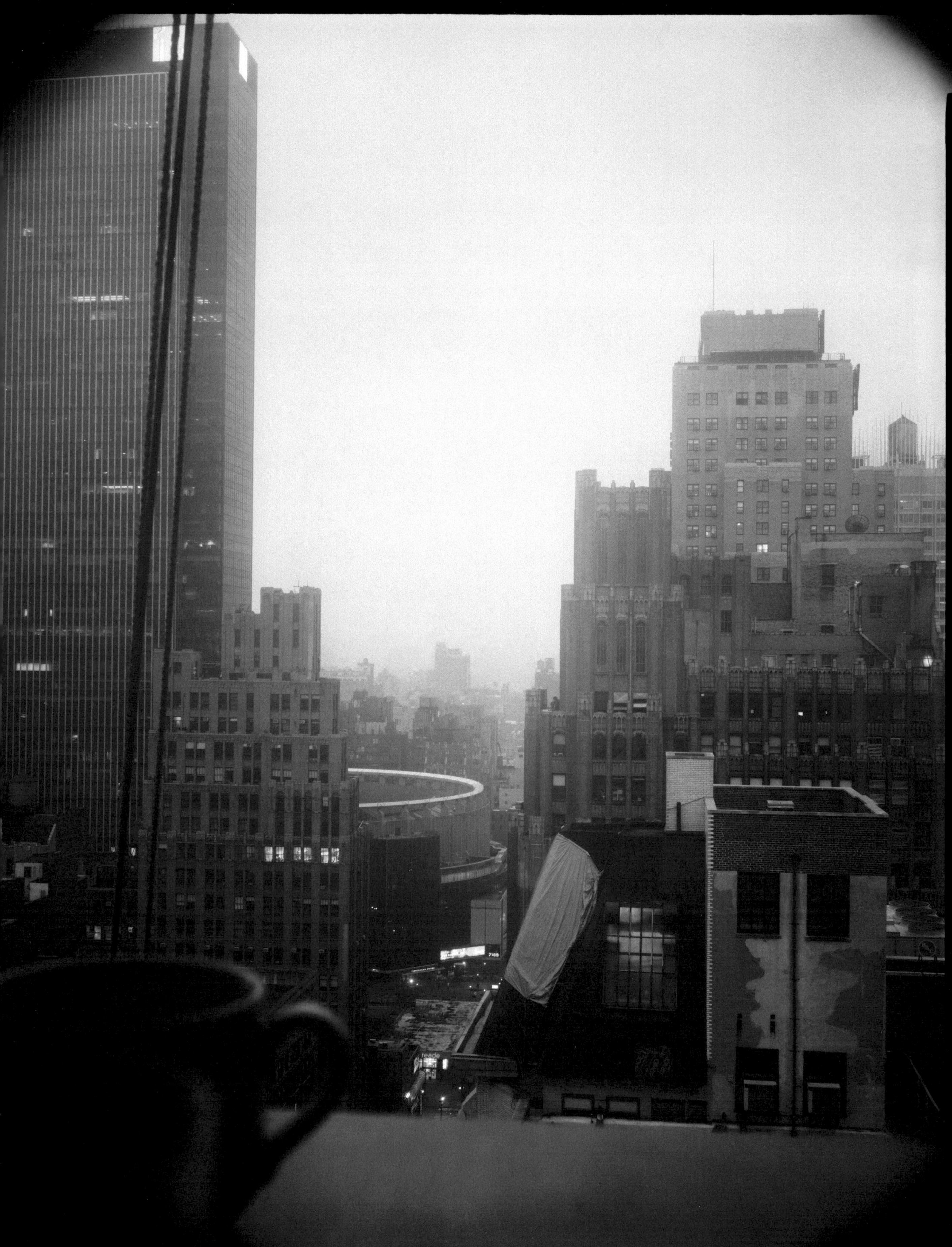

September 2, 2003

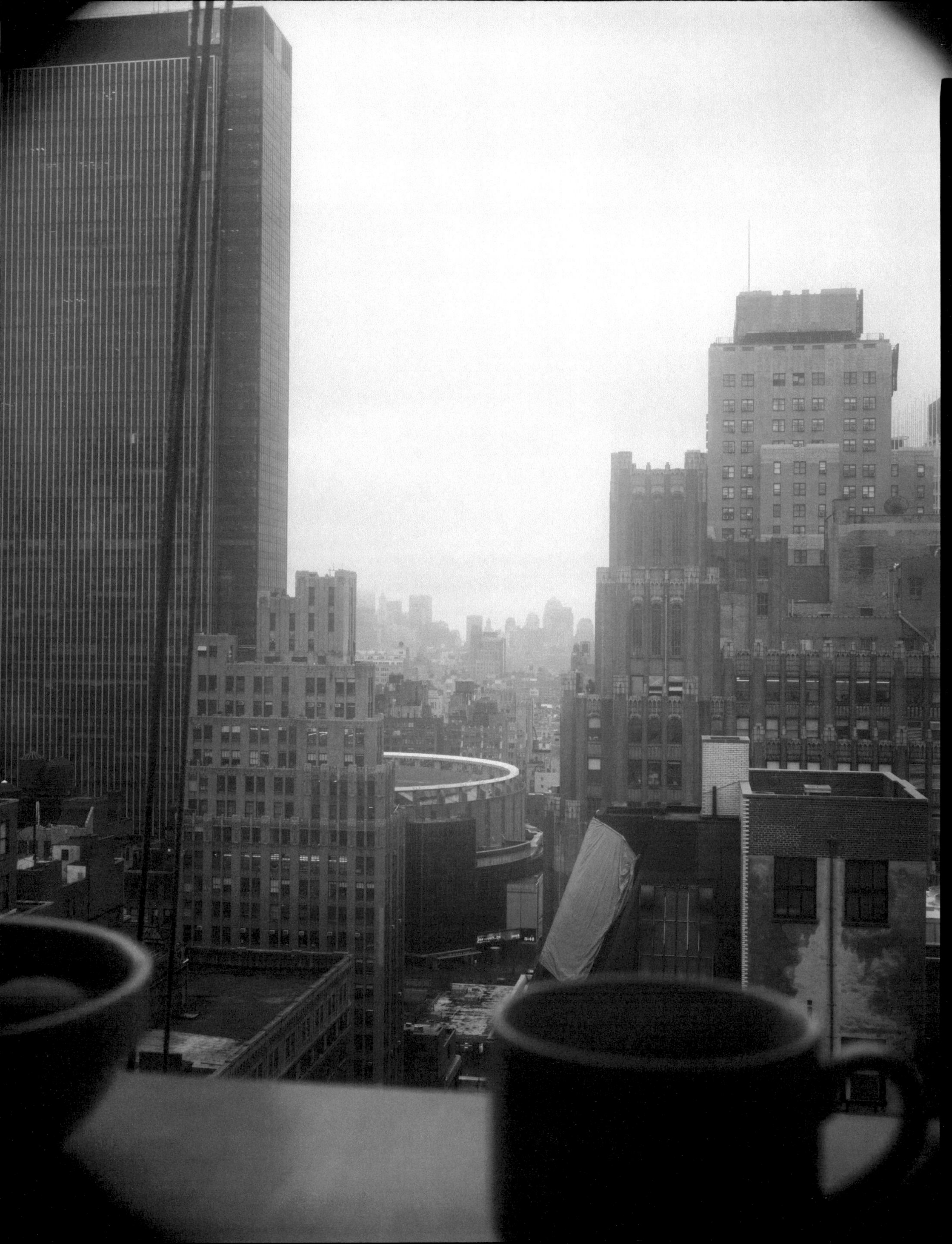

September 3, 2003

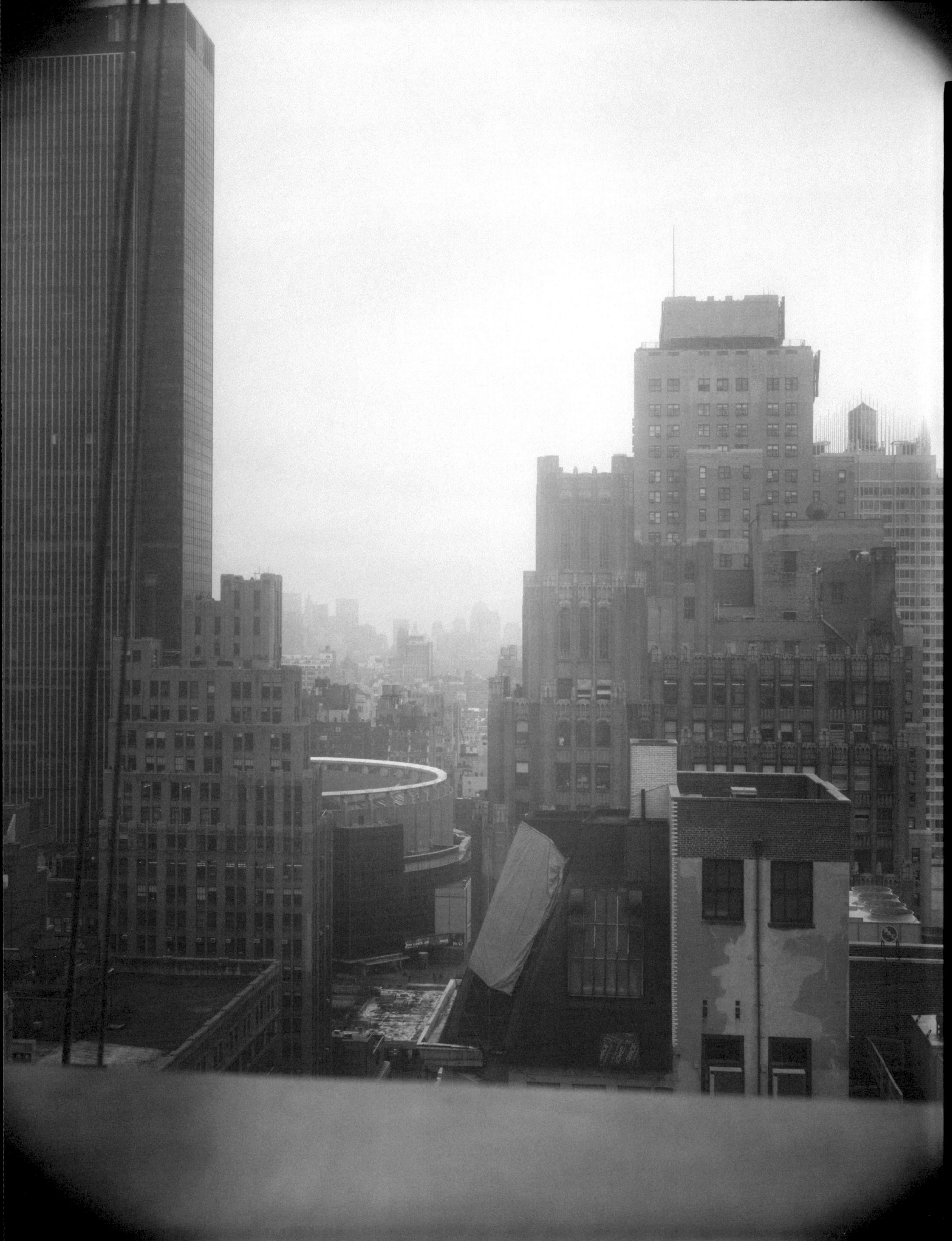

September 4, 2003

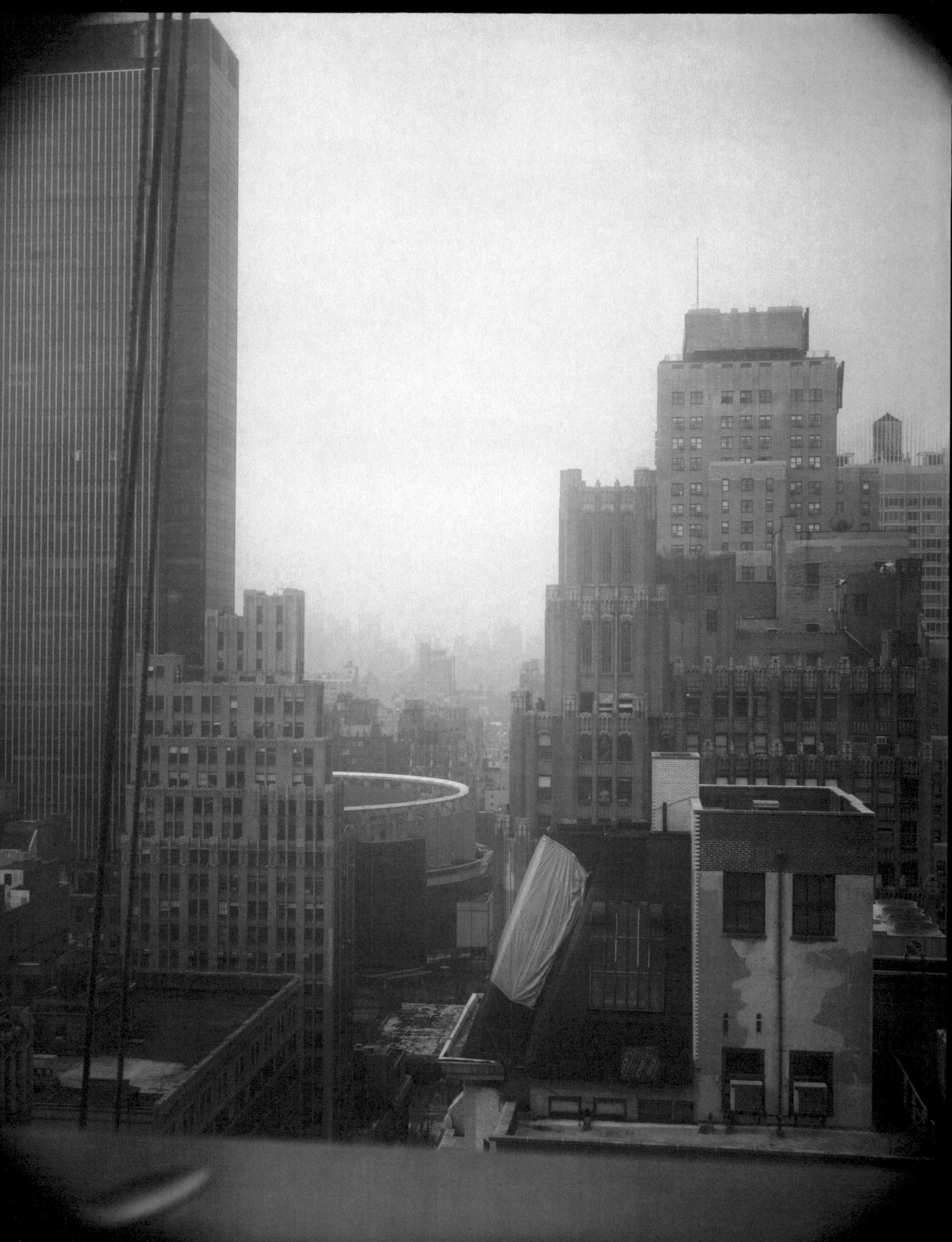

September 5, 2003

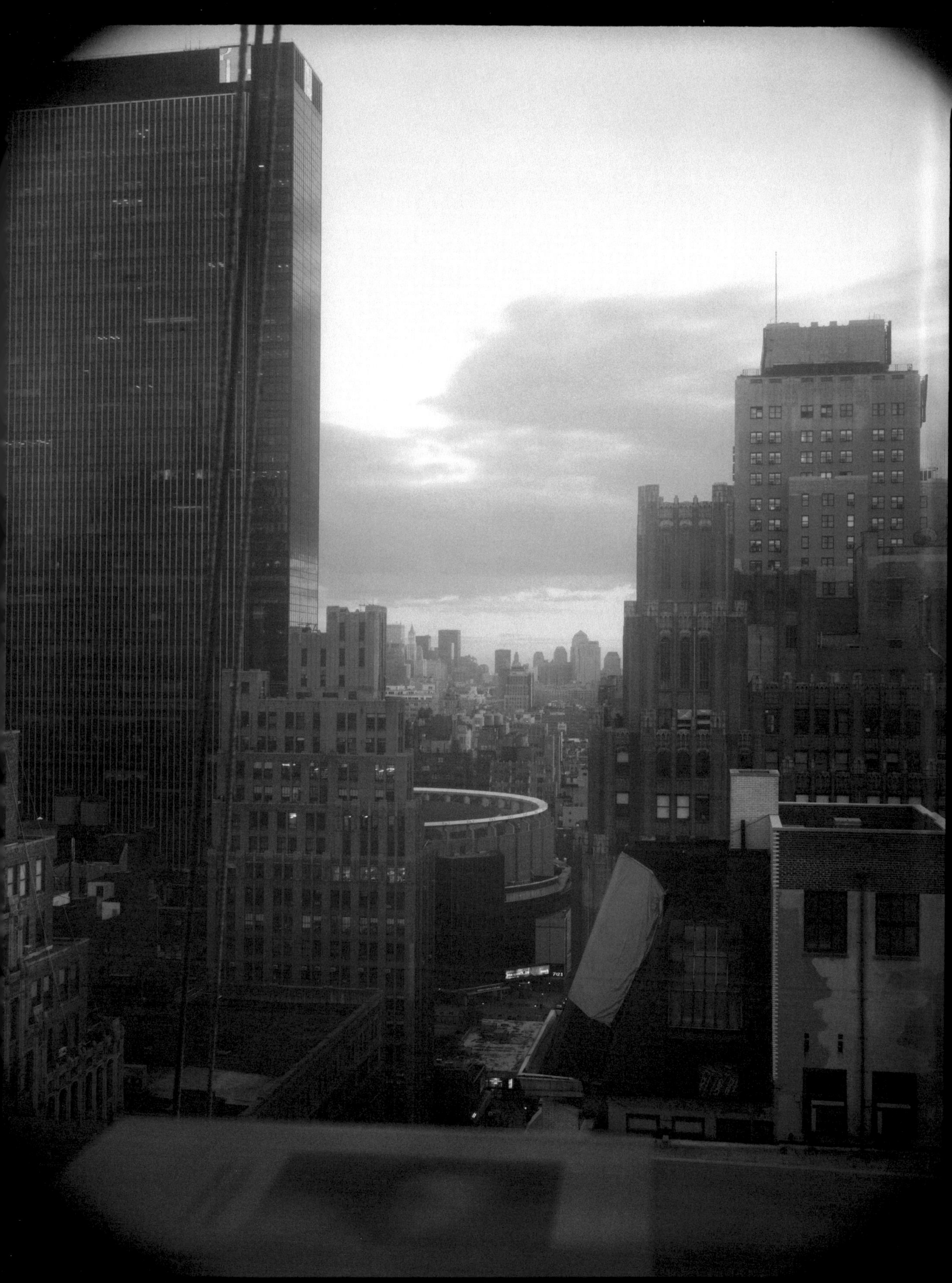

September 6, 2003

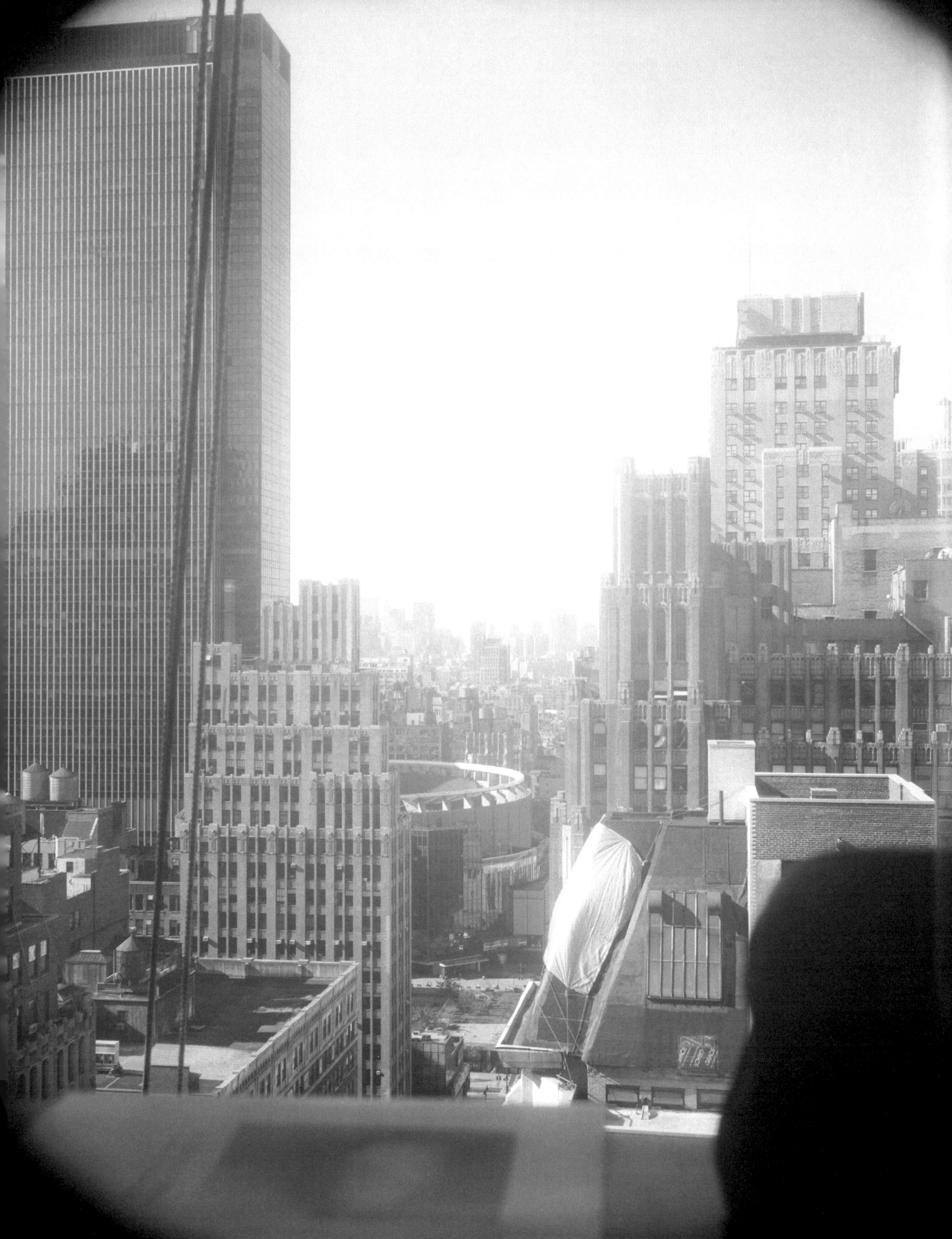

September 7, 2003

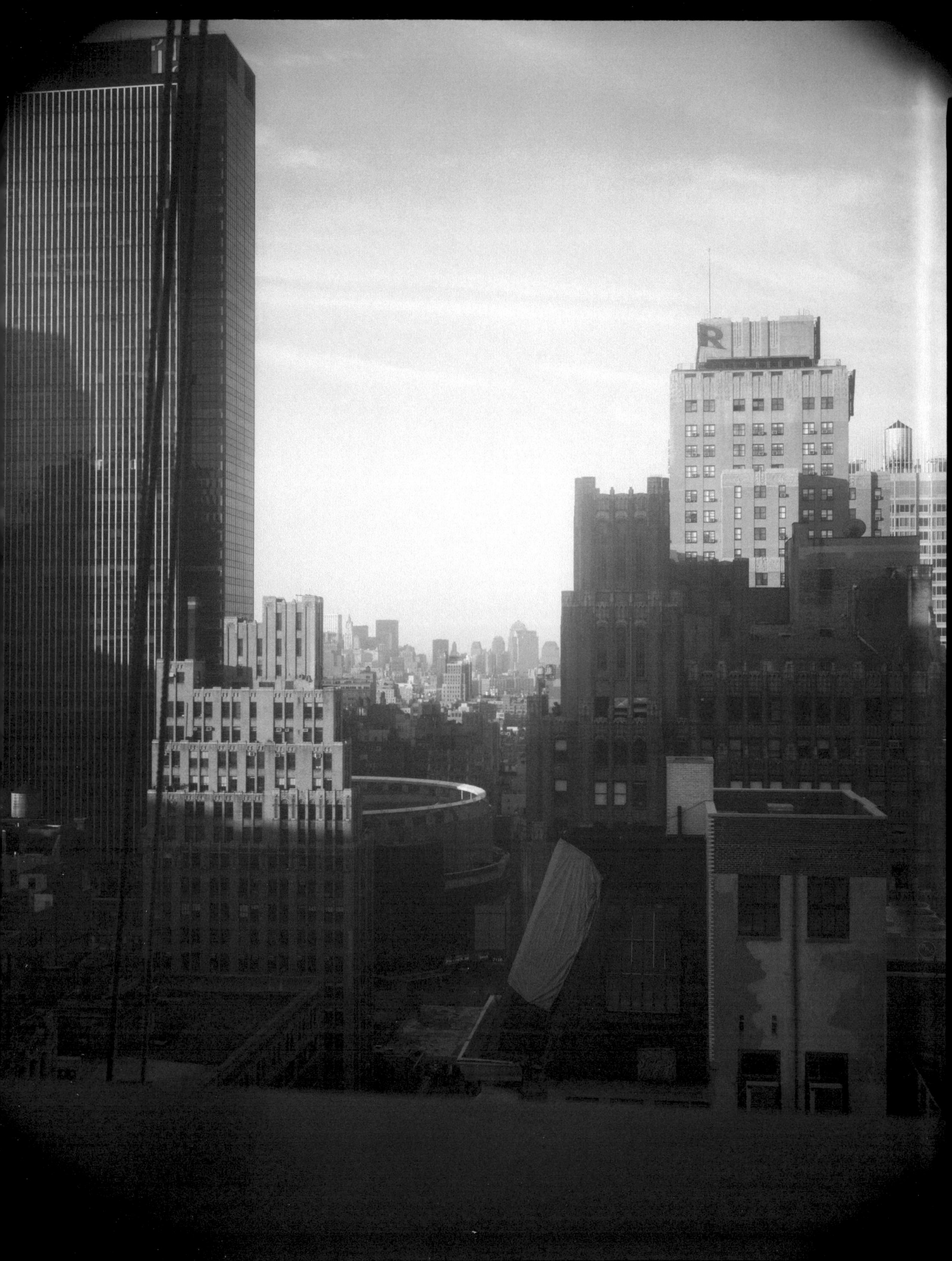

September 8, 2003

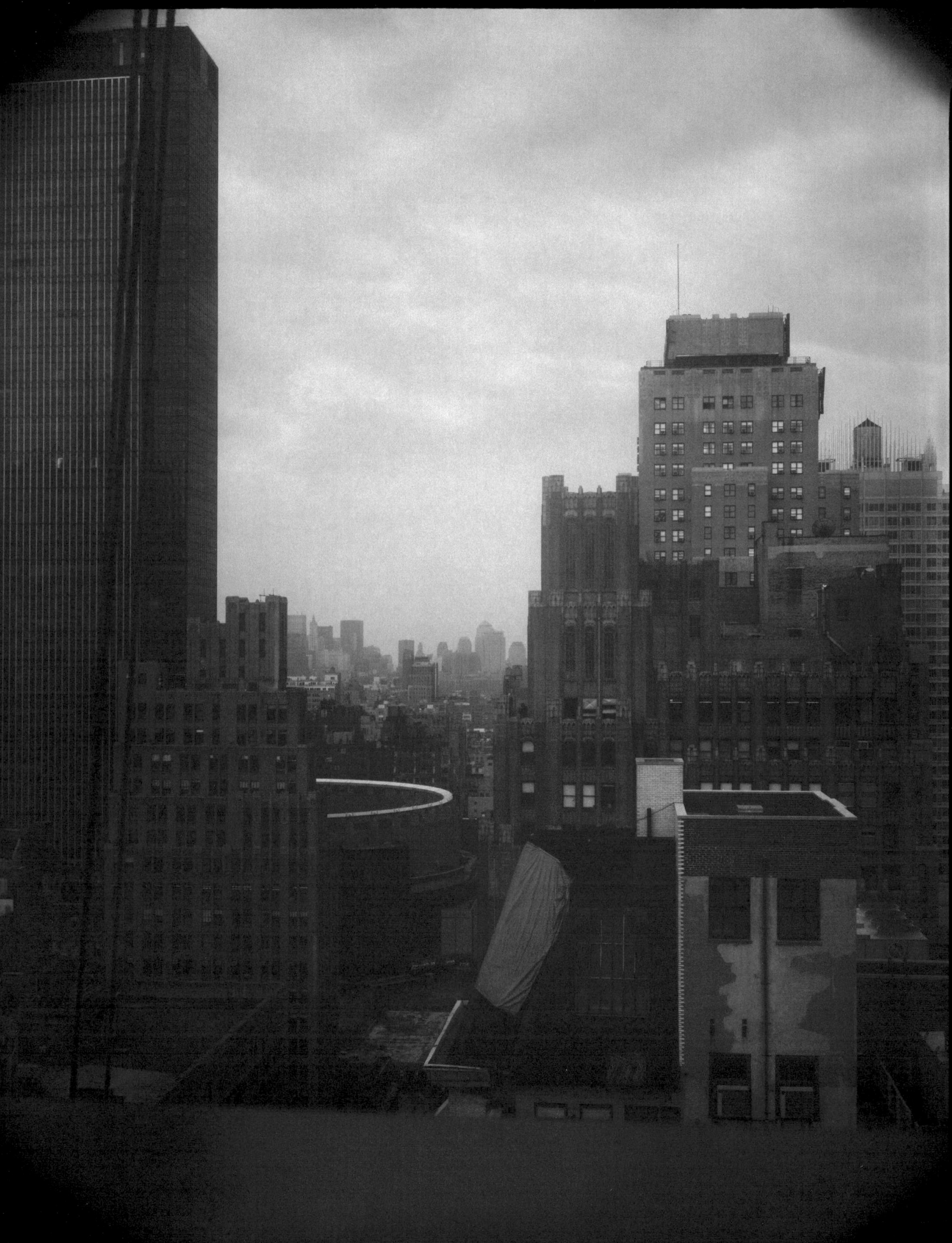

September 9, 2003

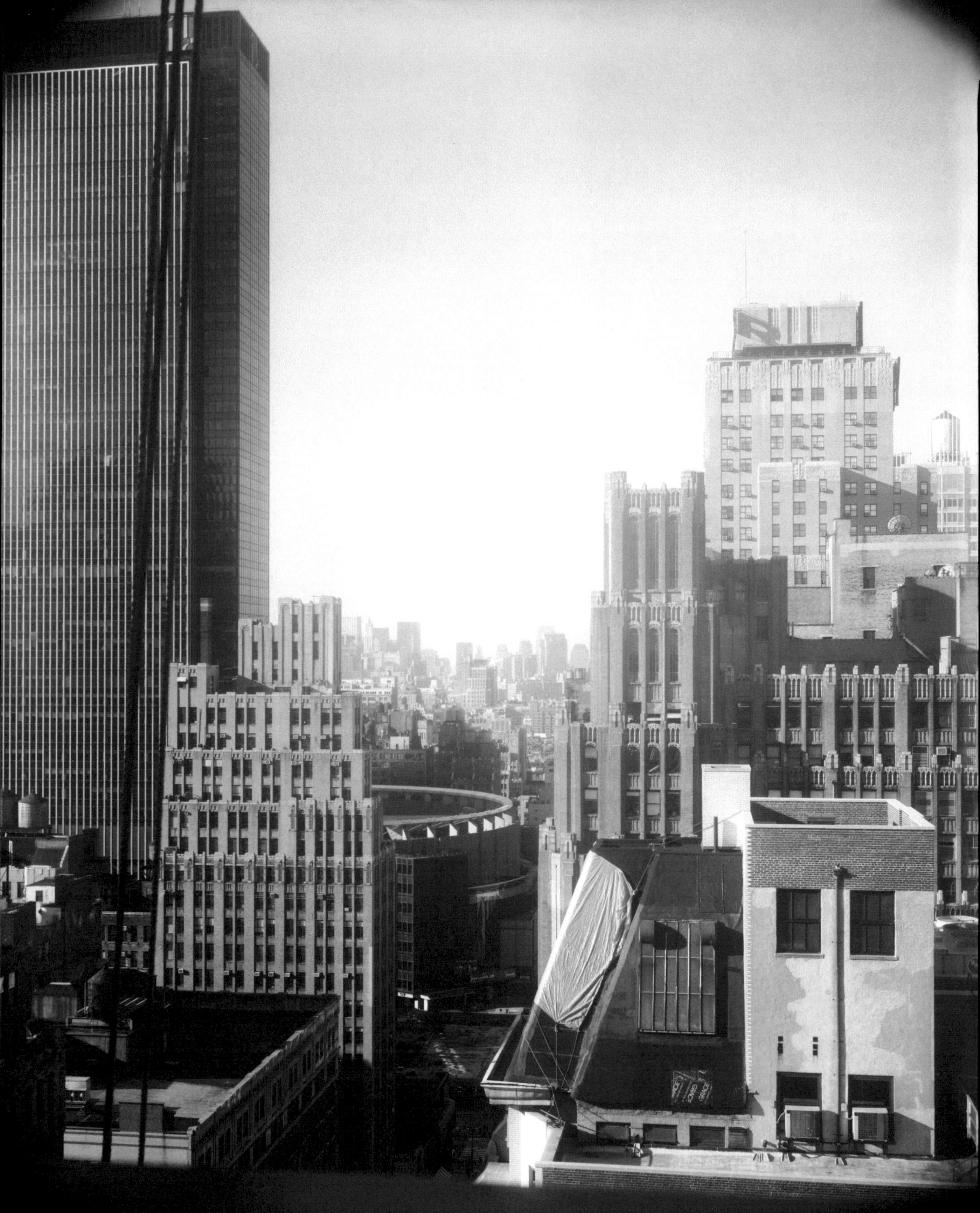

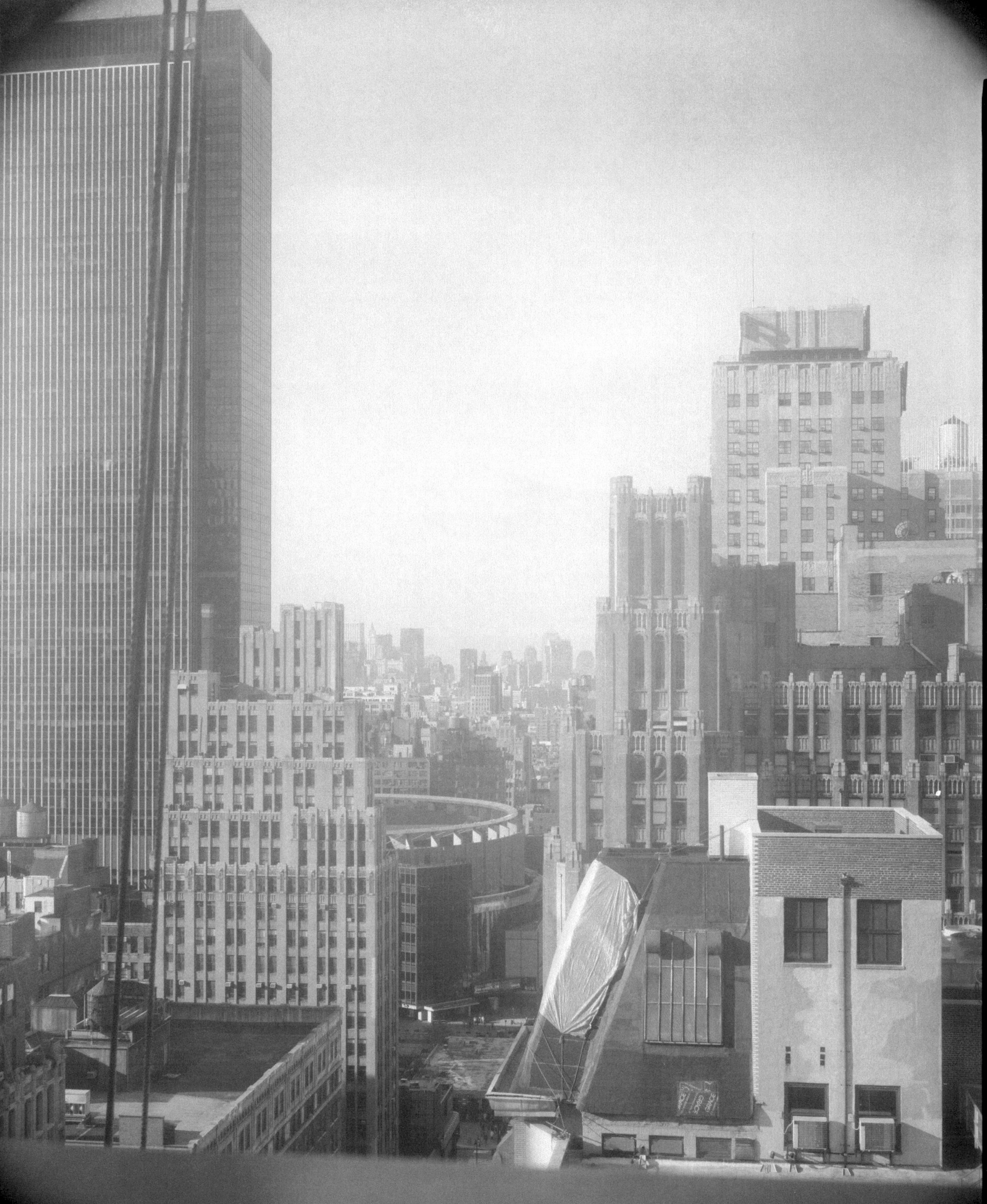

September 11, 2003

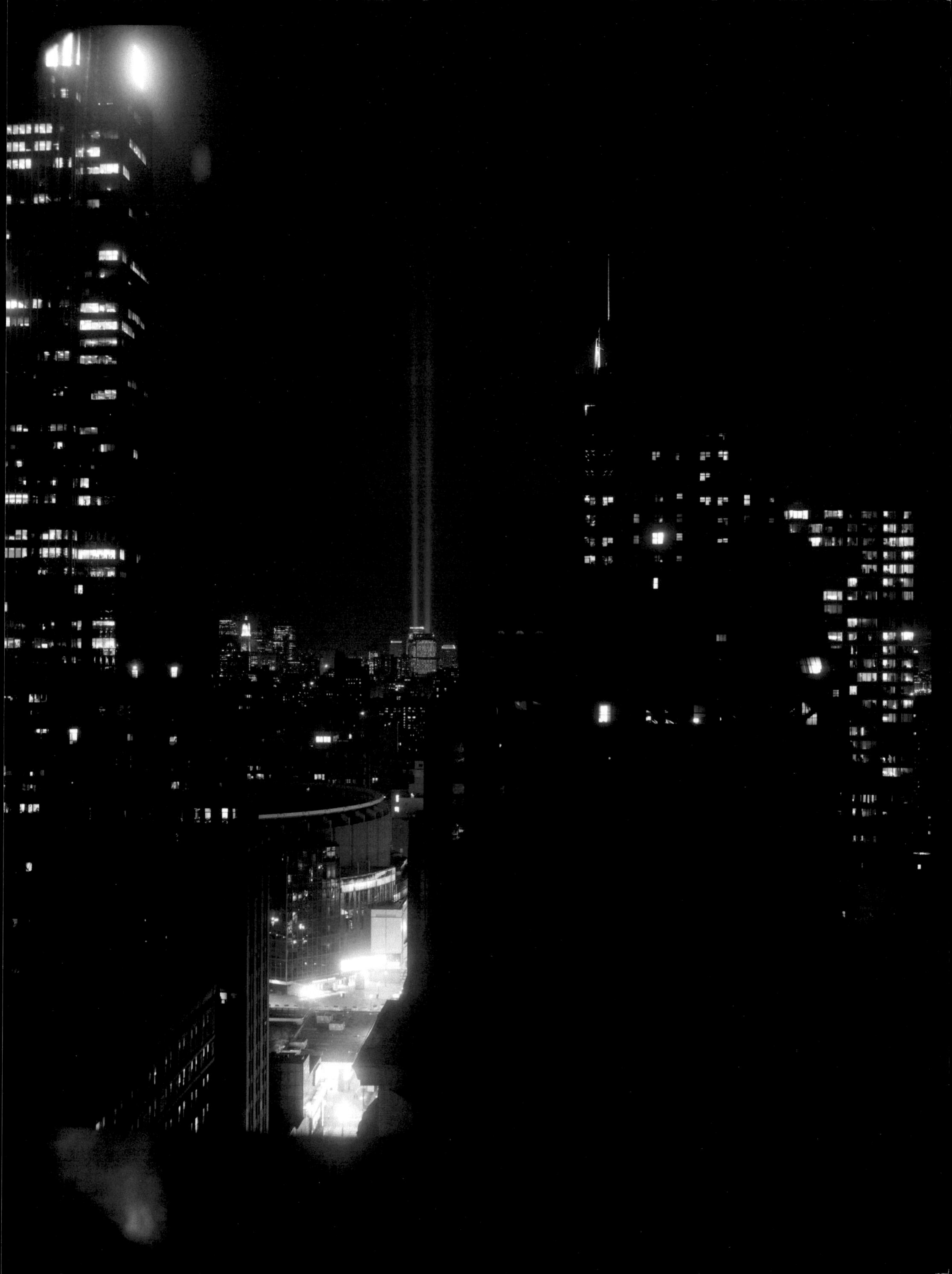

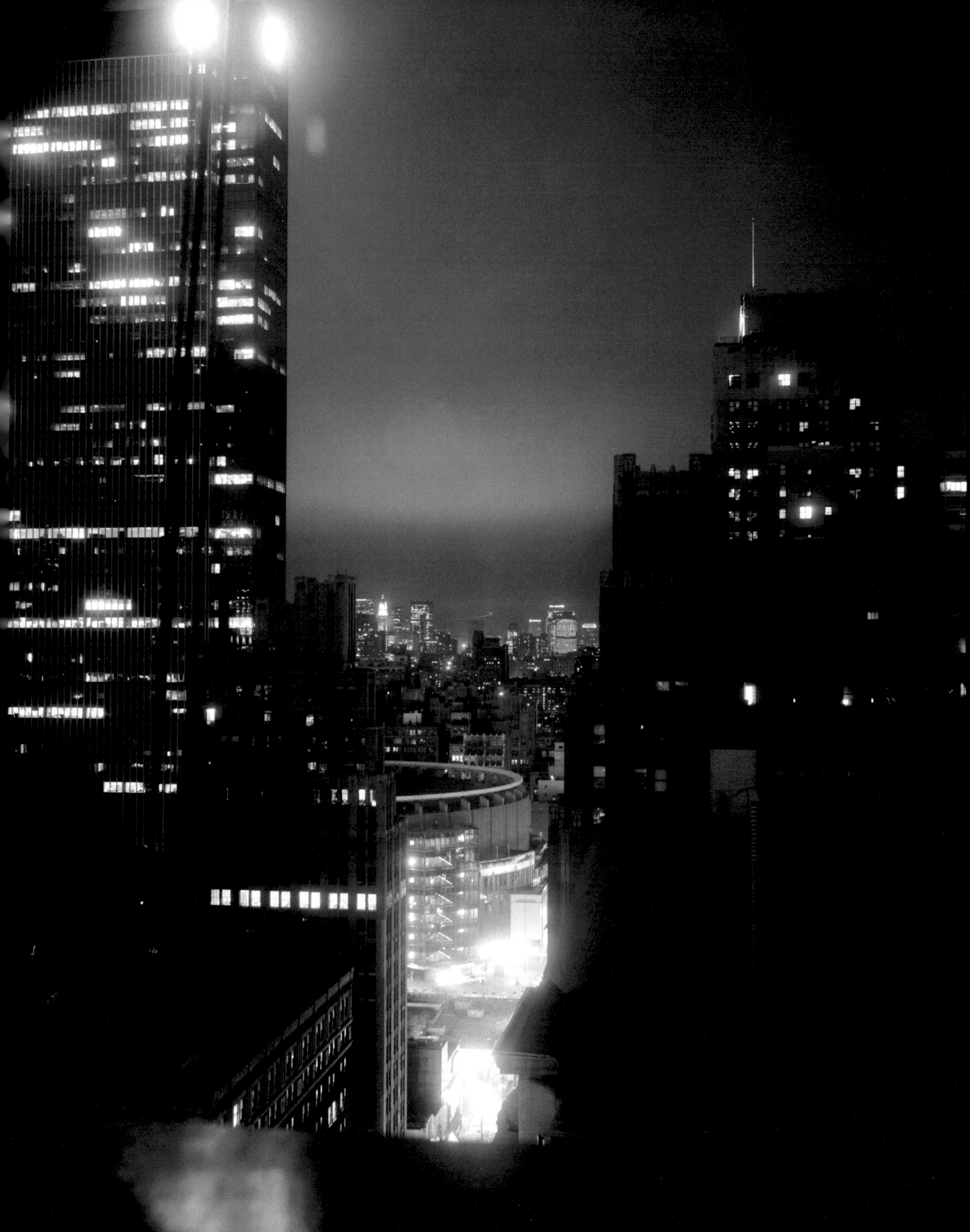

September 13, 2003

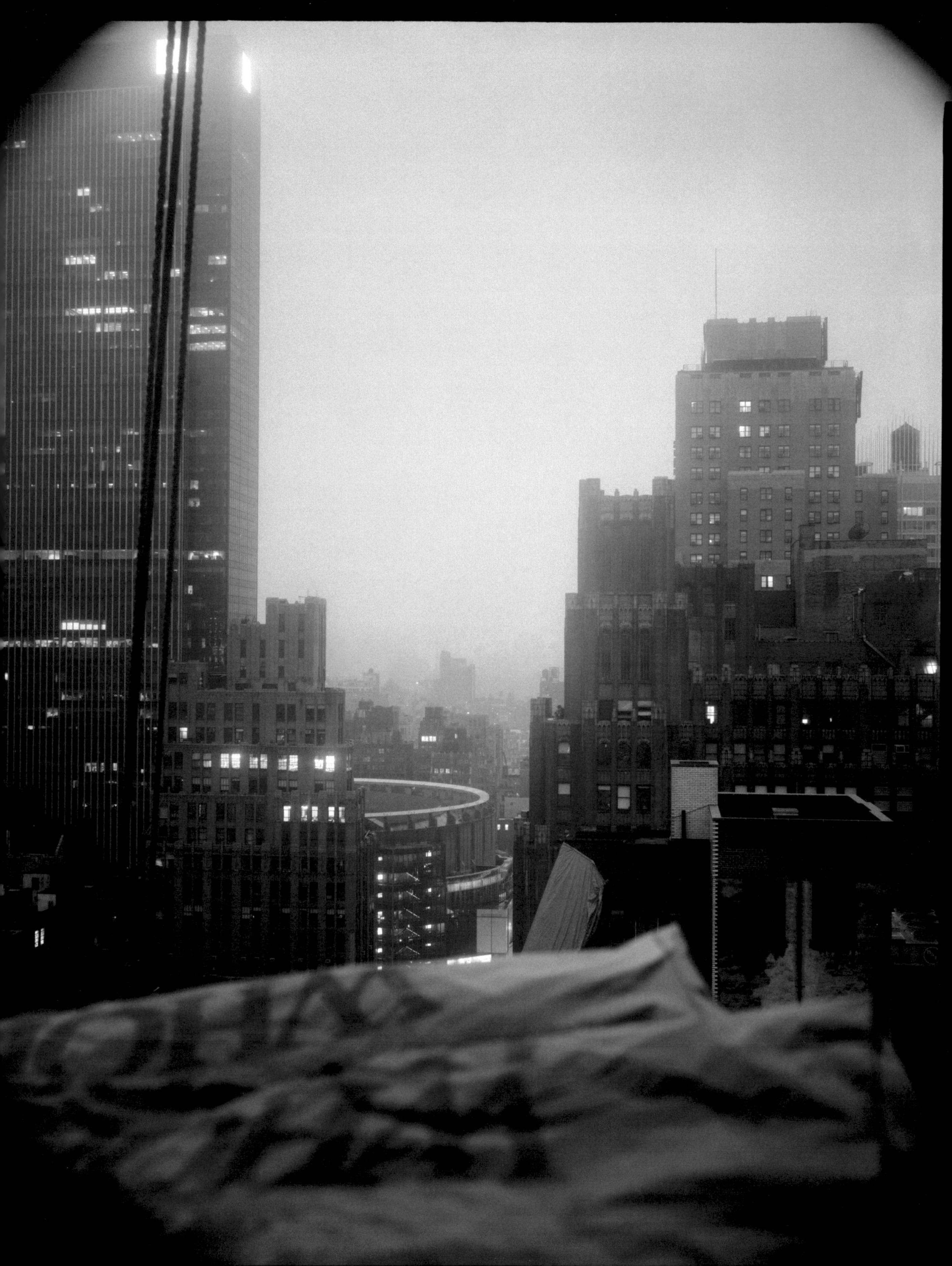

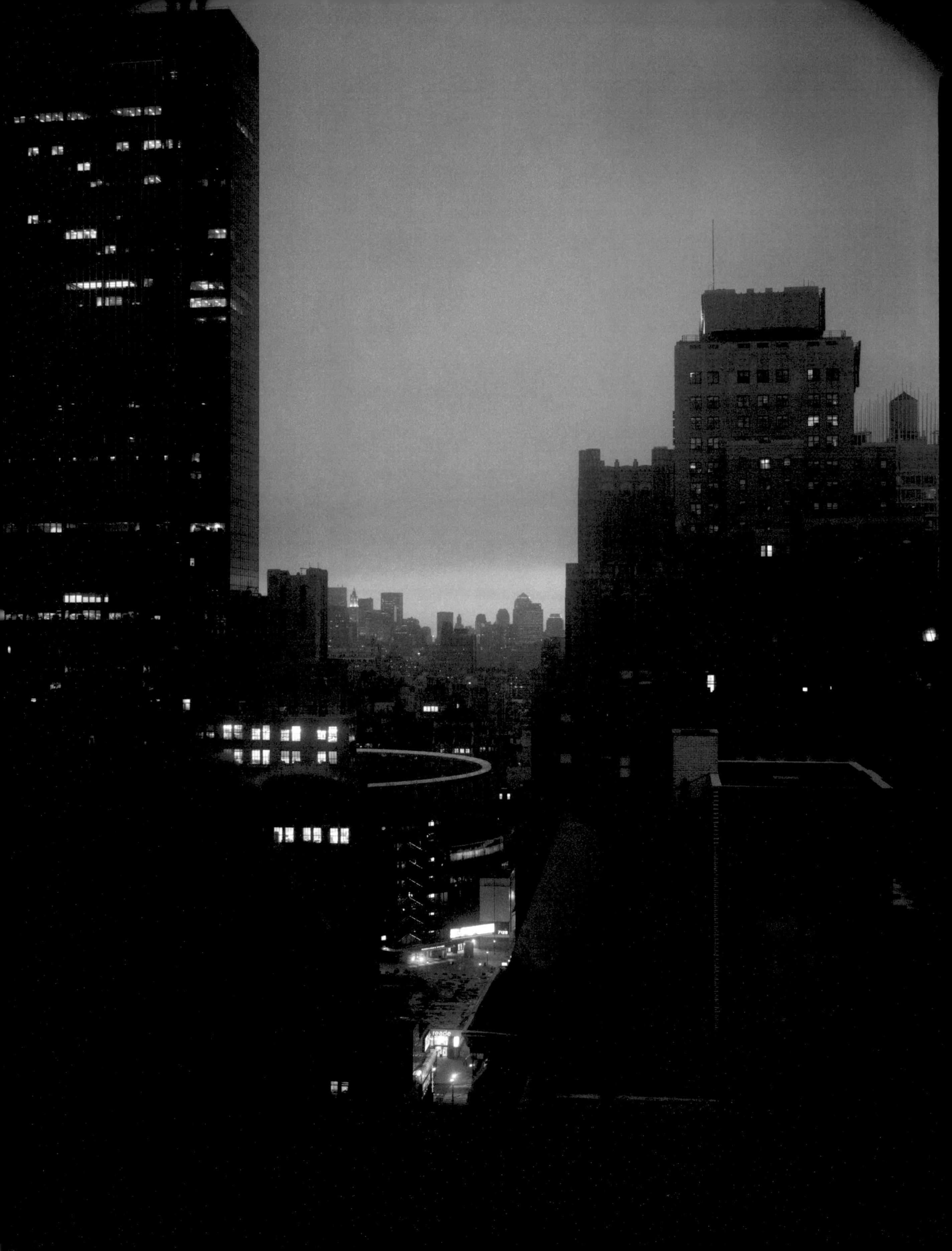

September 15, 2003

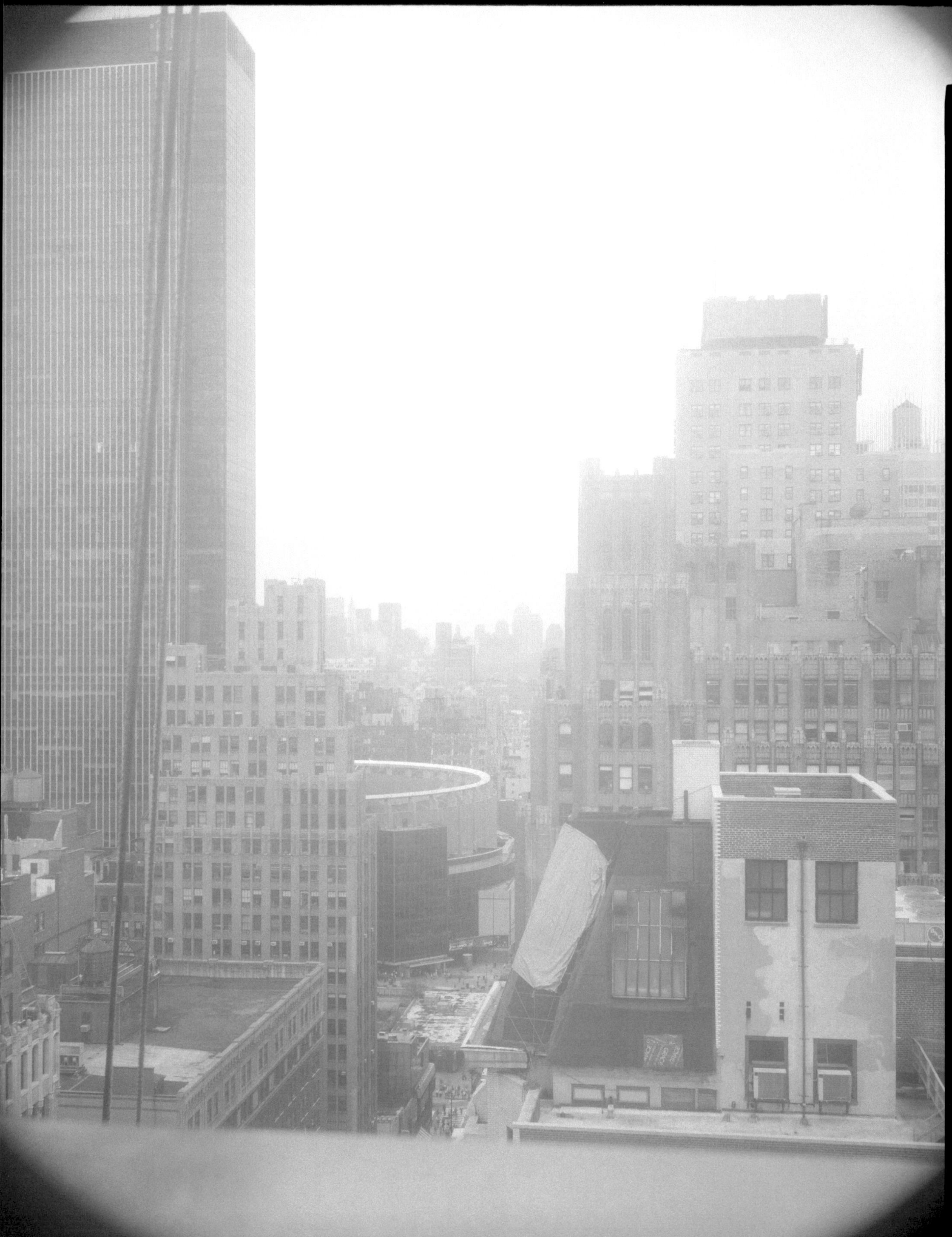

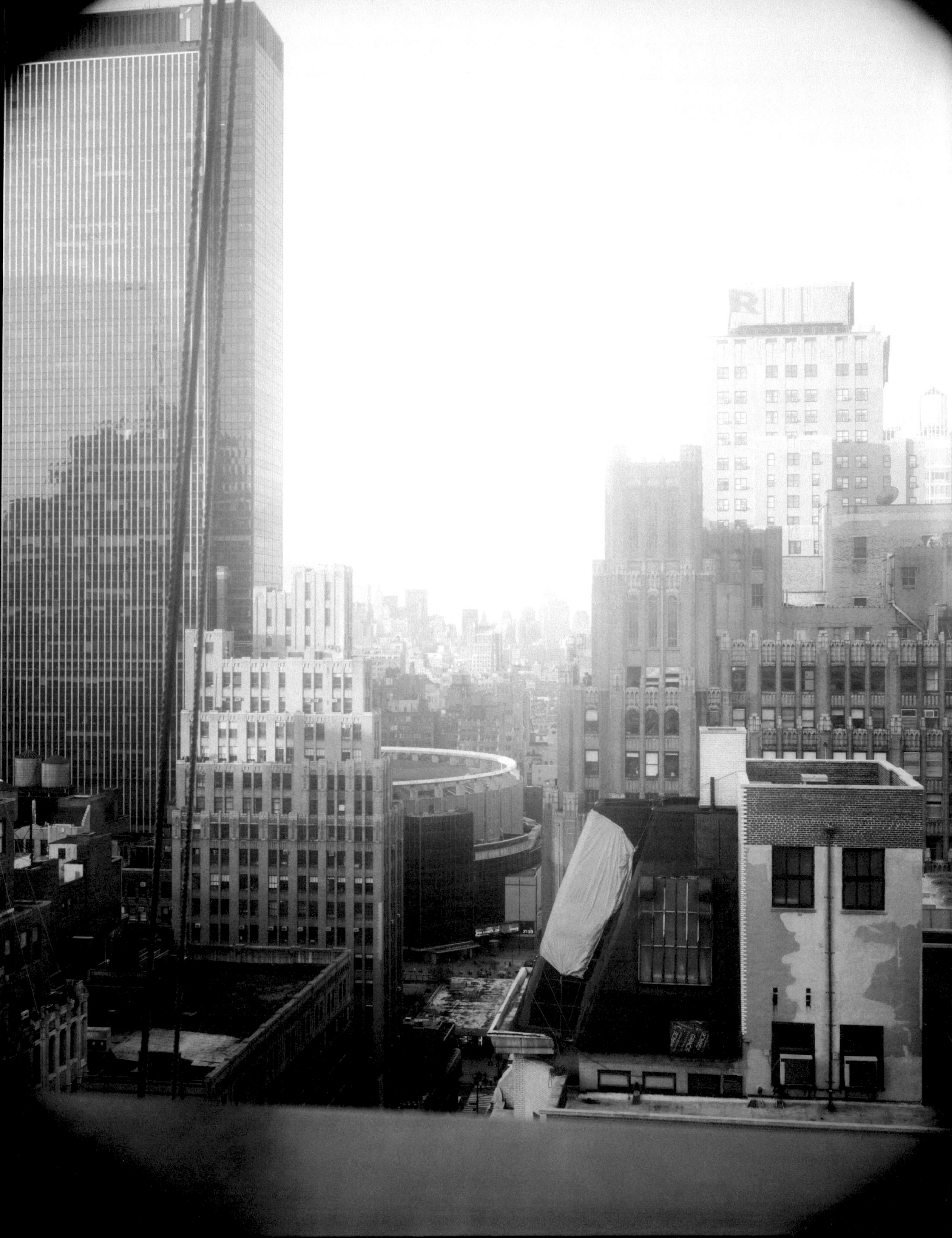

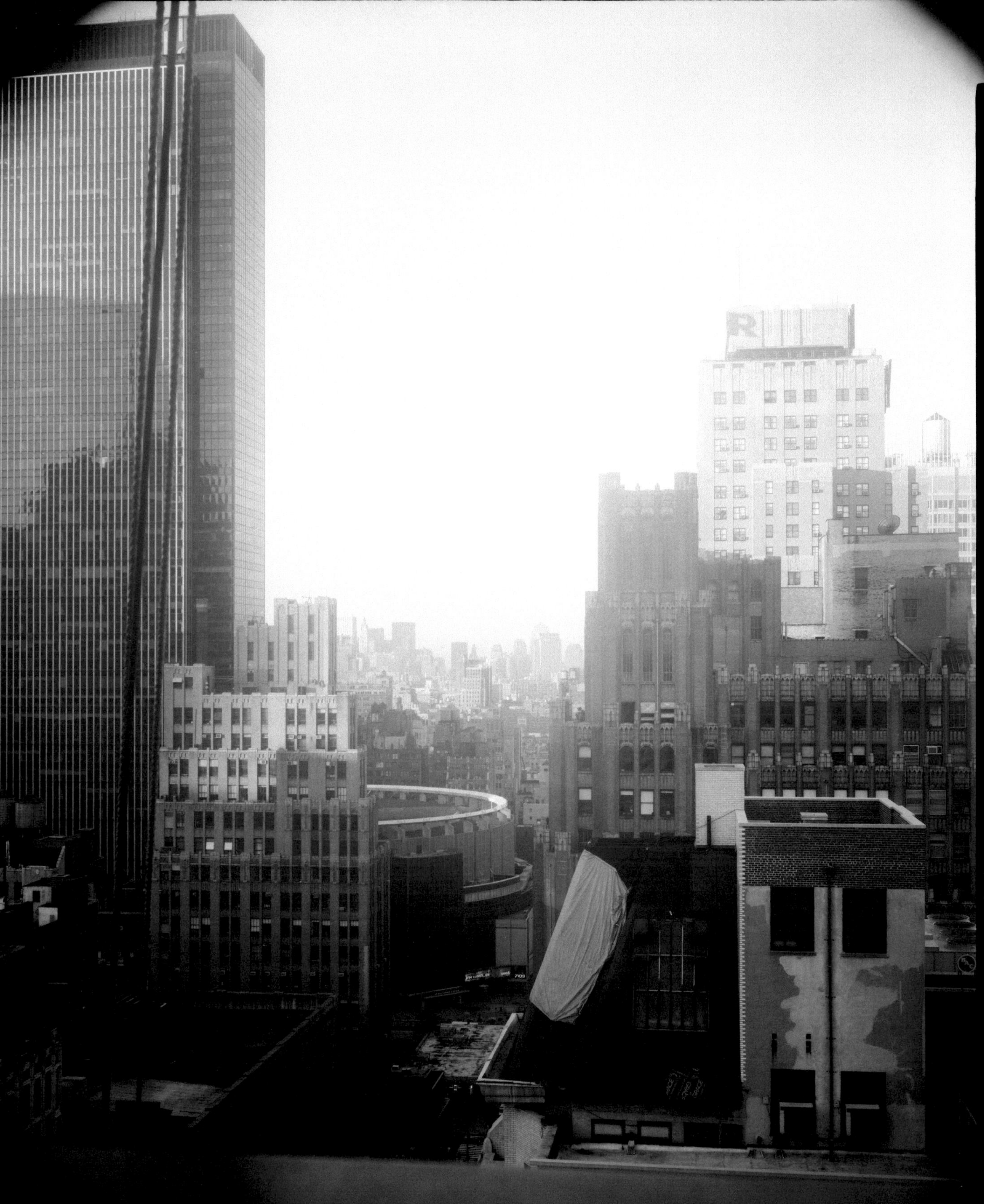

September 18, 2003

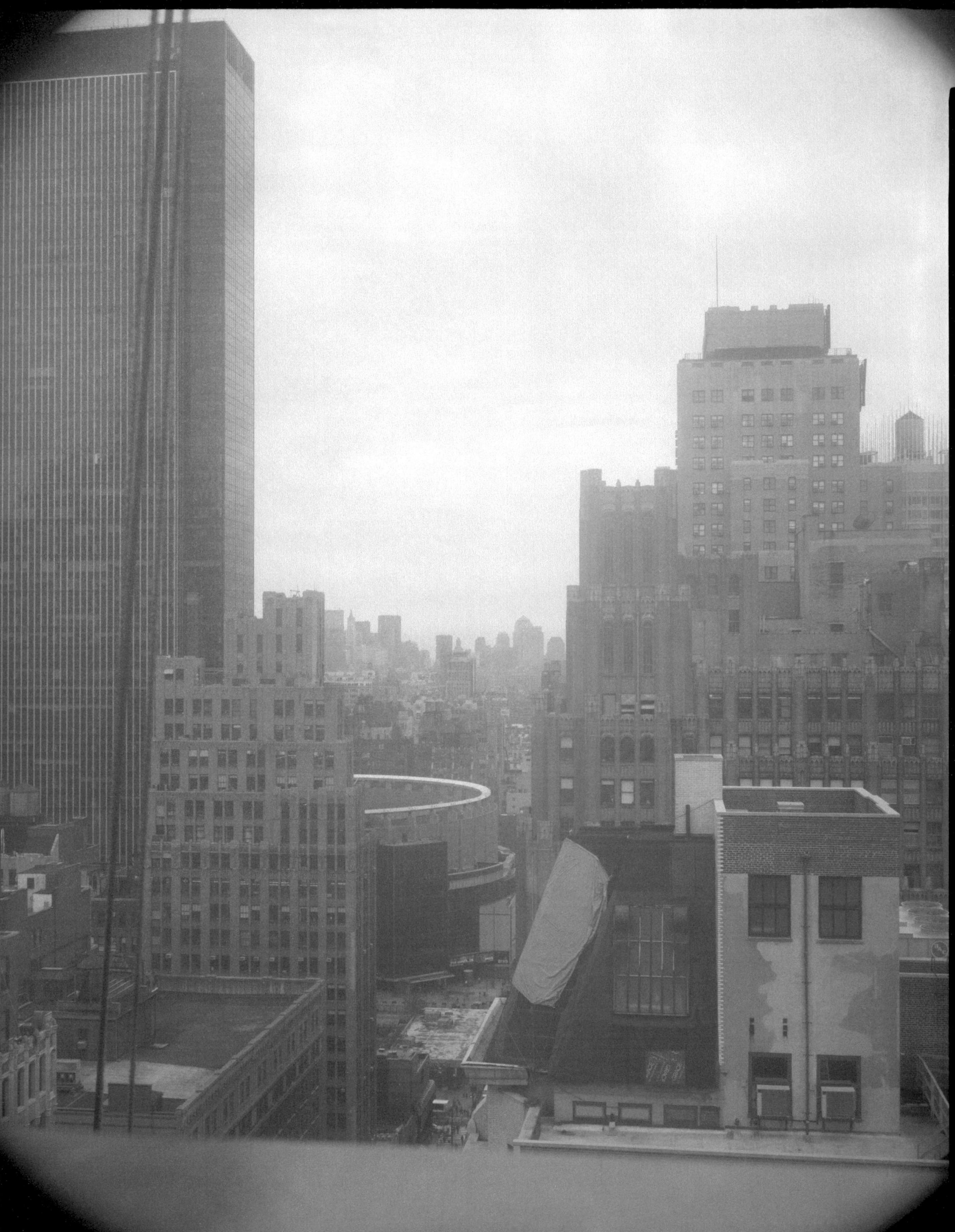

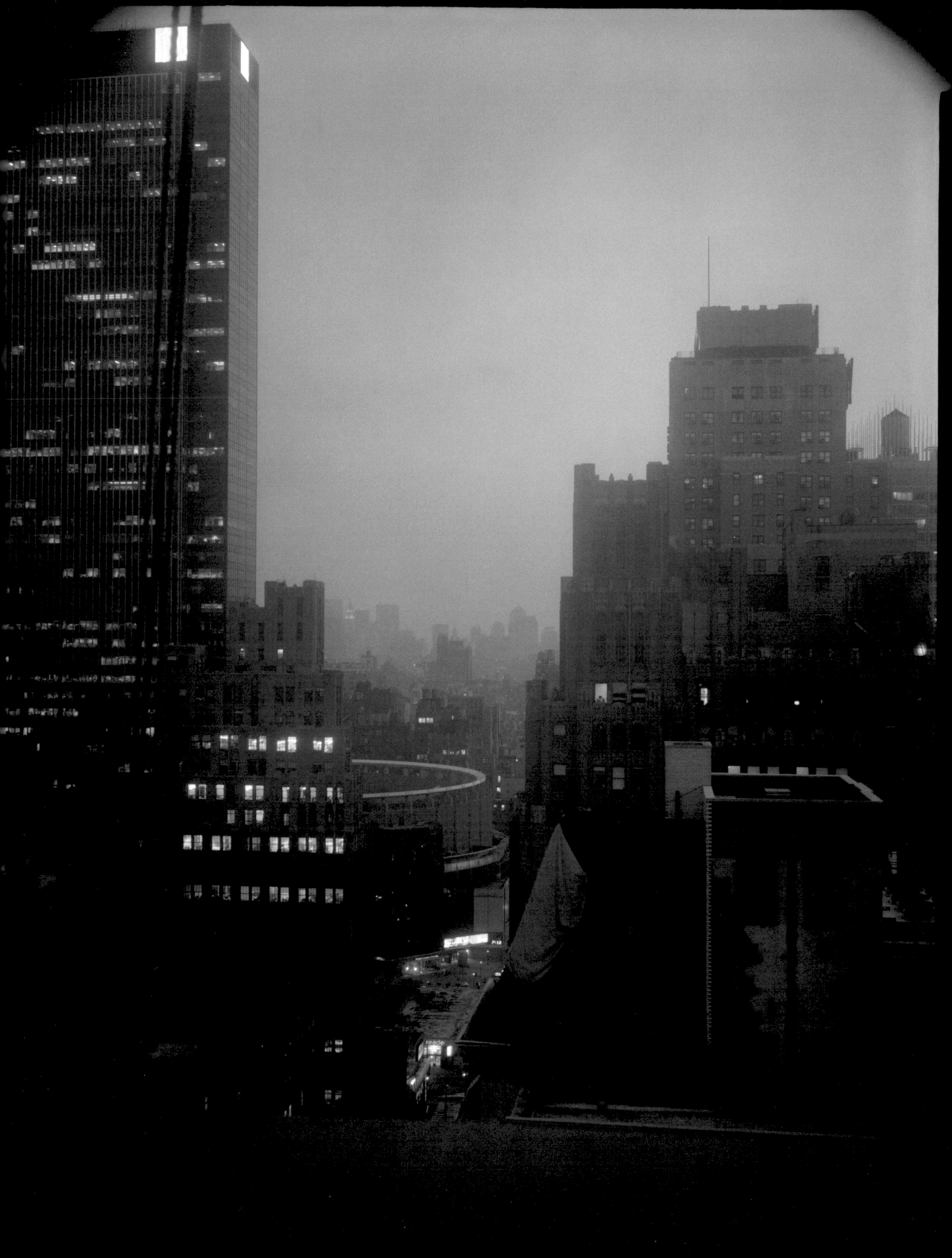

September 20, 2003

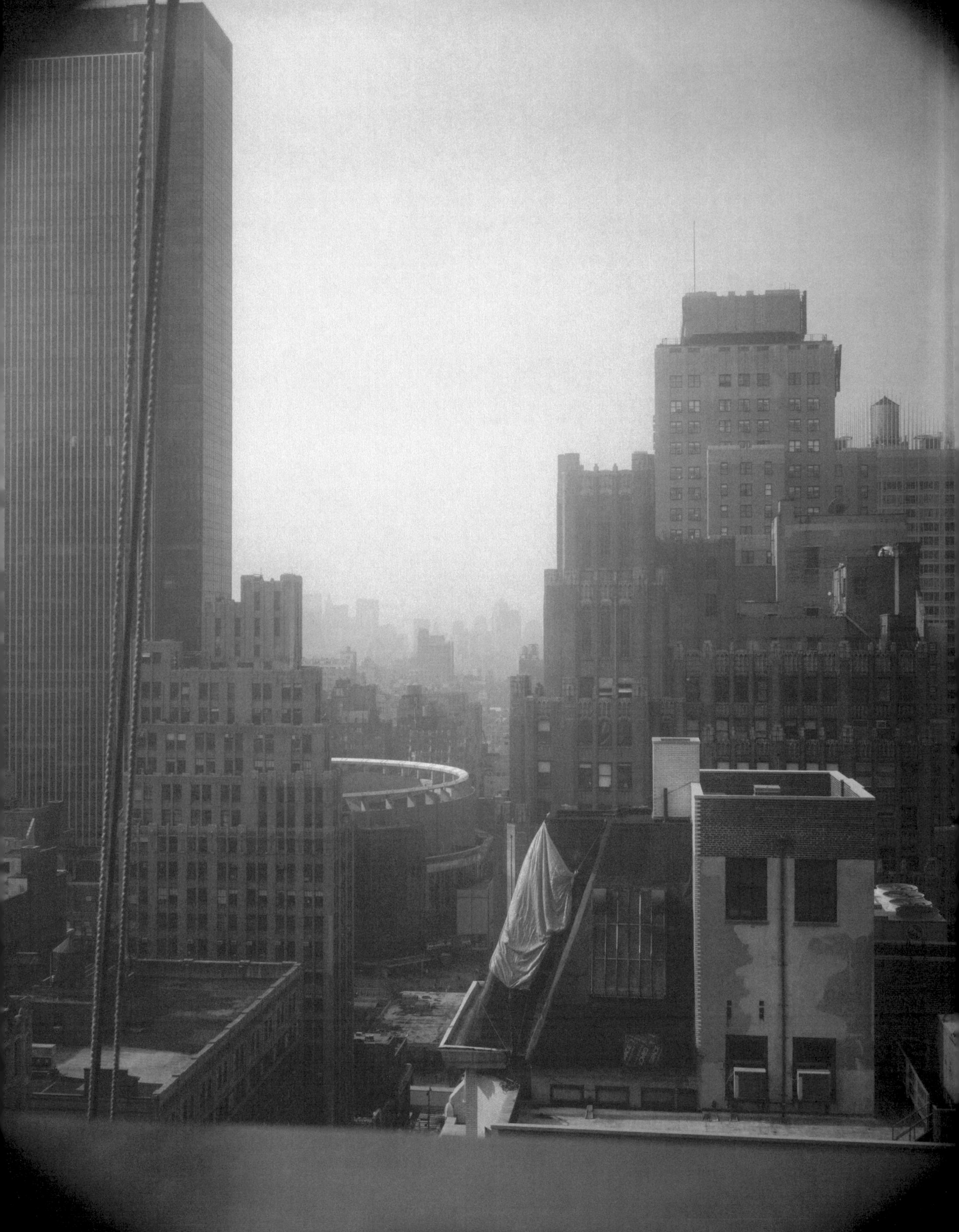

September 21, 2003

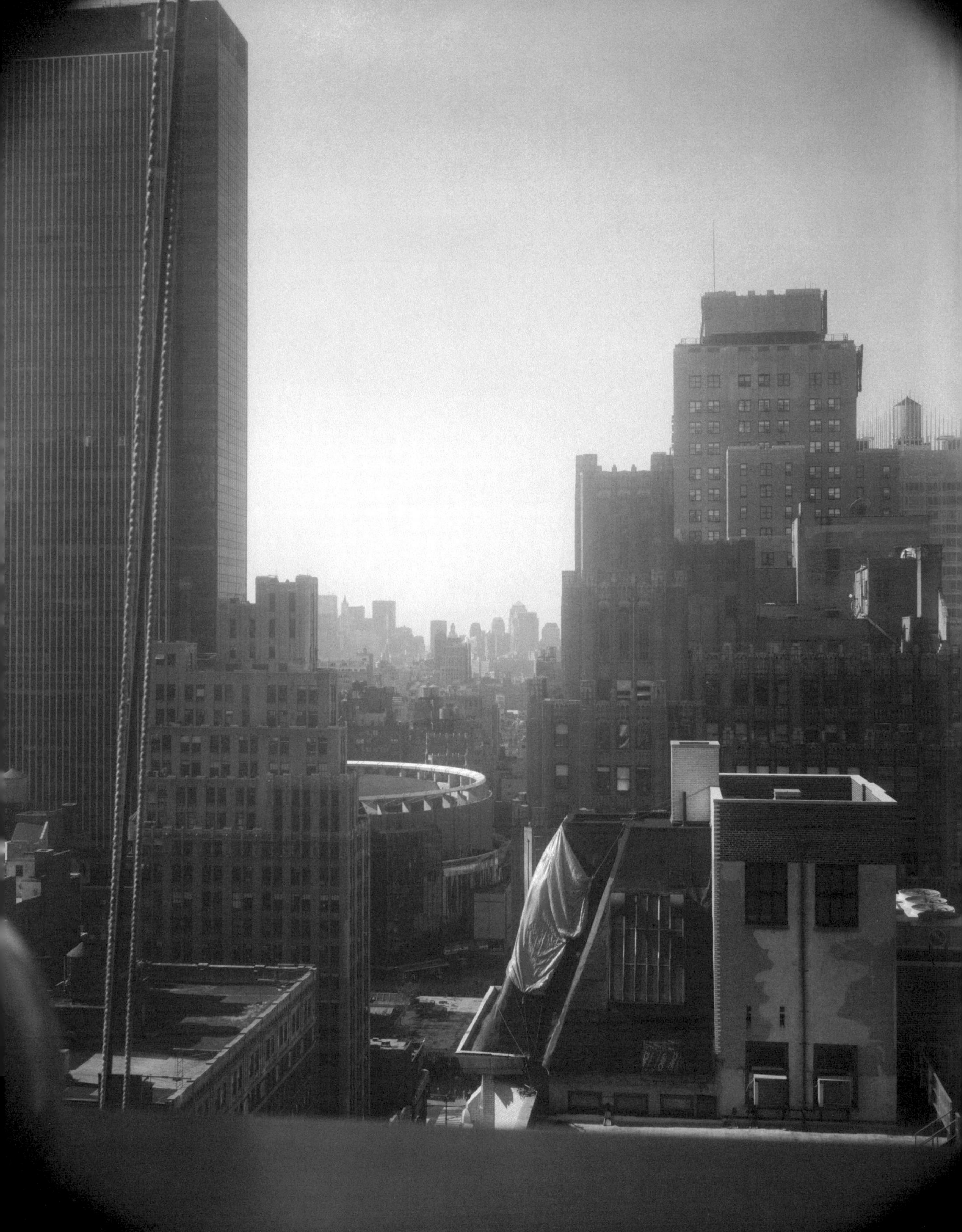

September 22, 2003

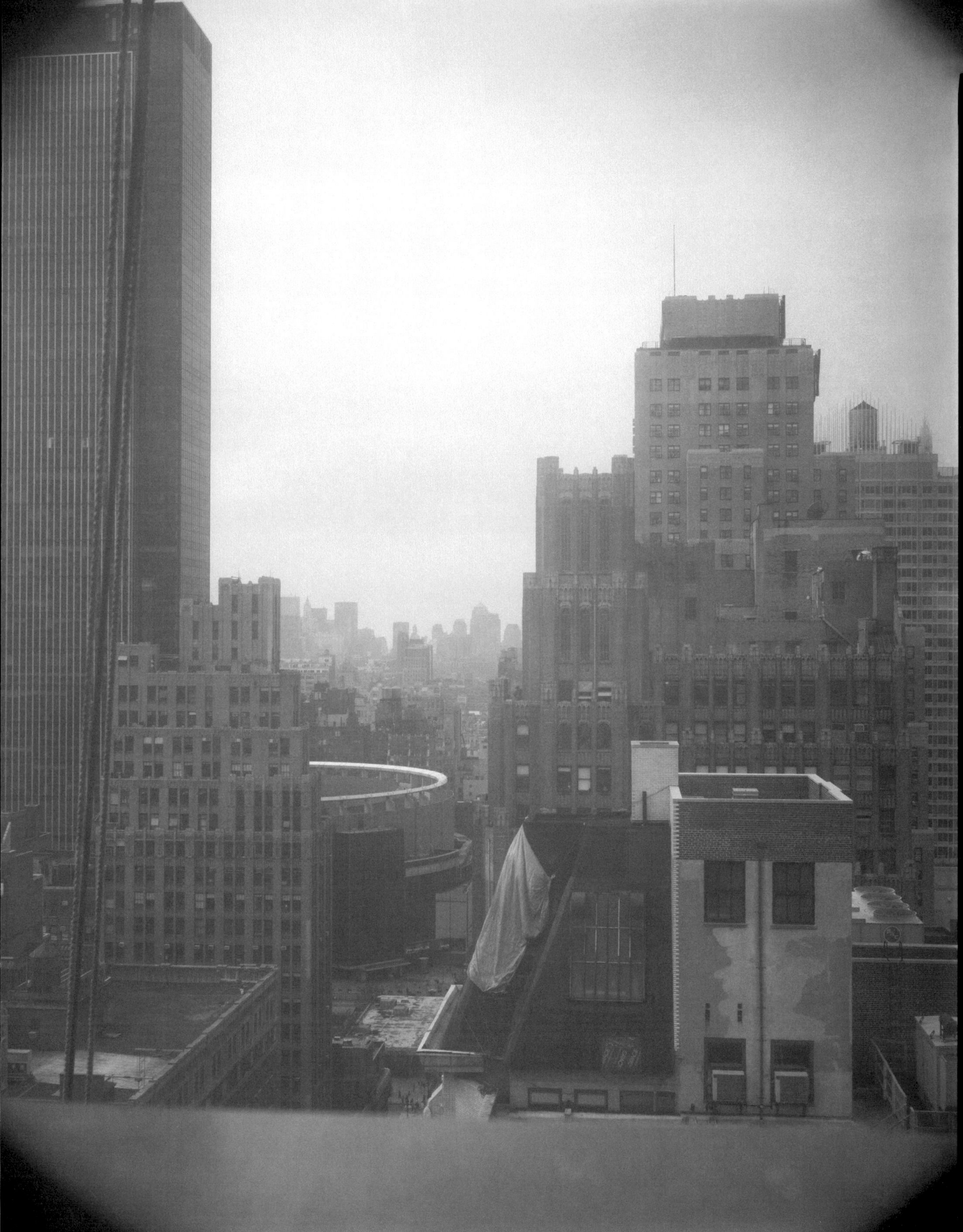

September 23, 2003

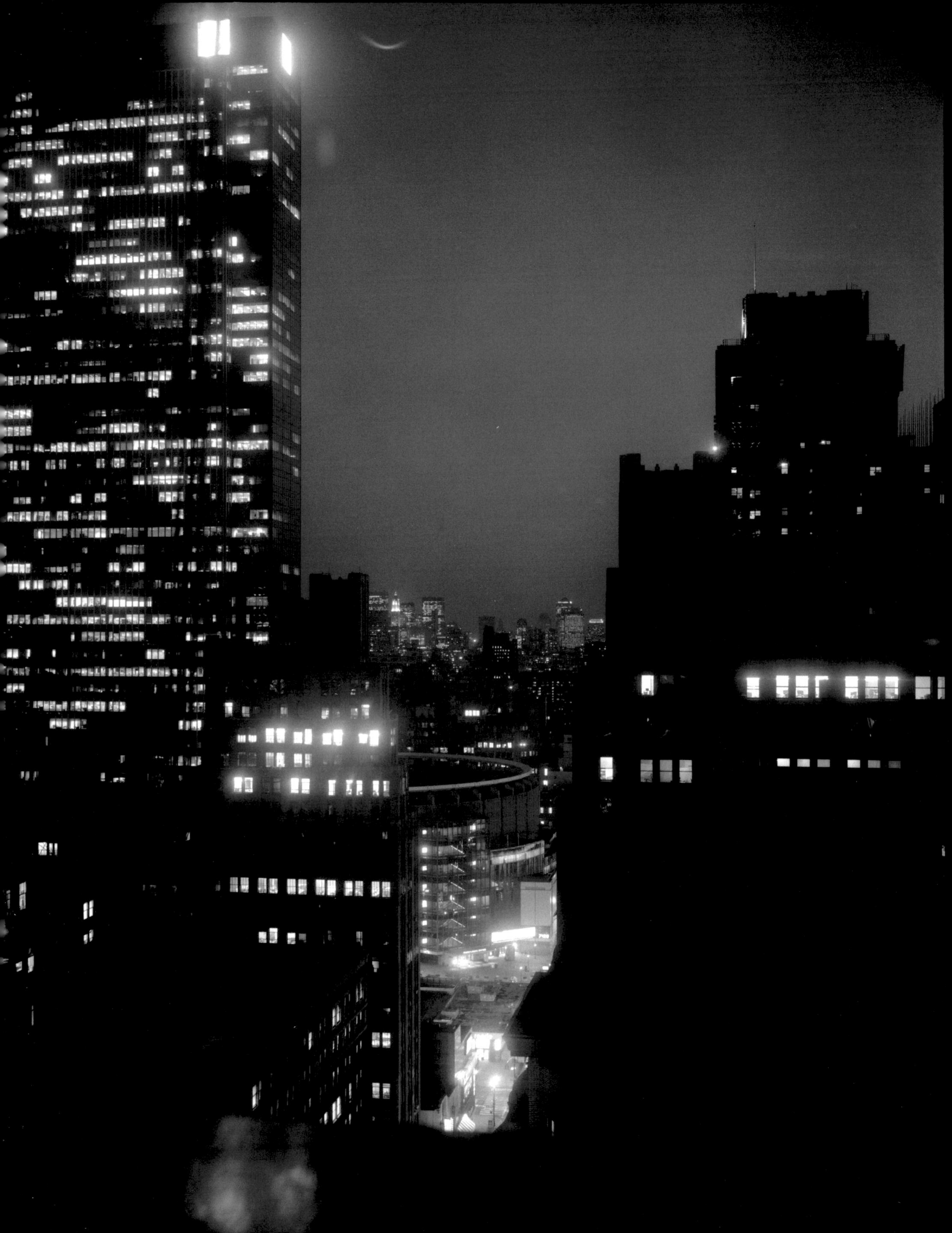

September 24, 2003

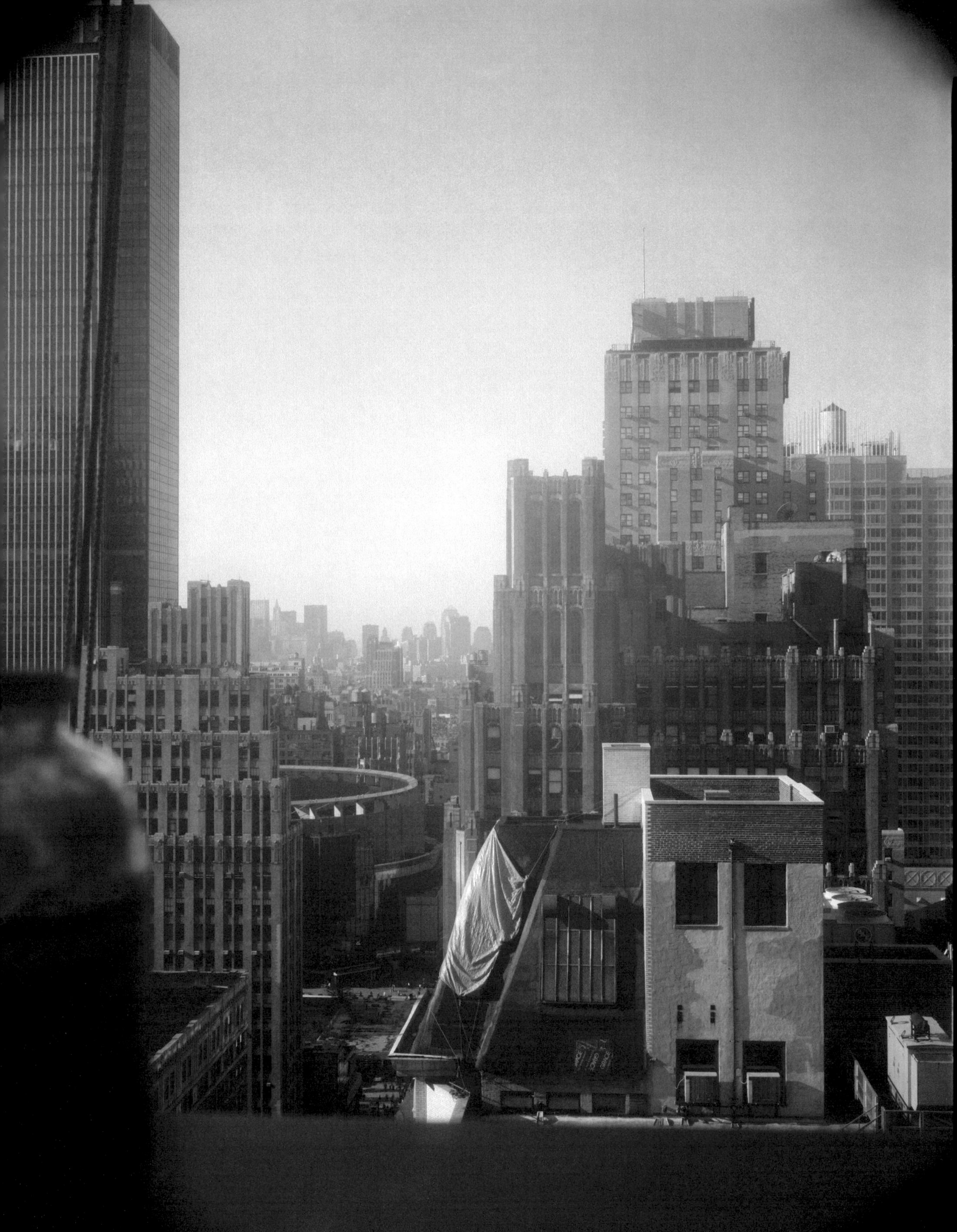

September 25, 2003

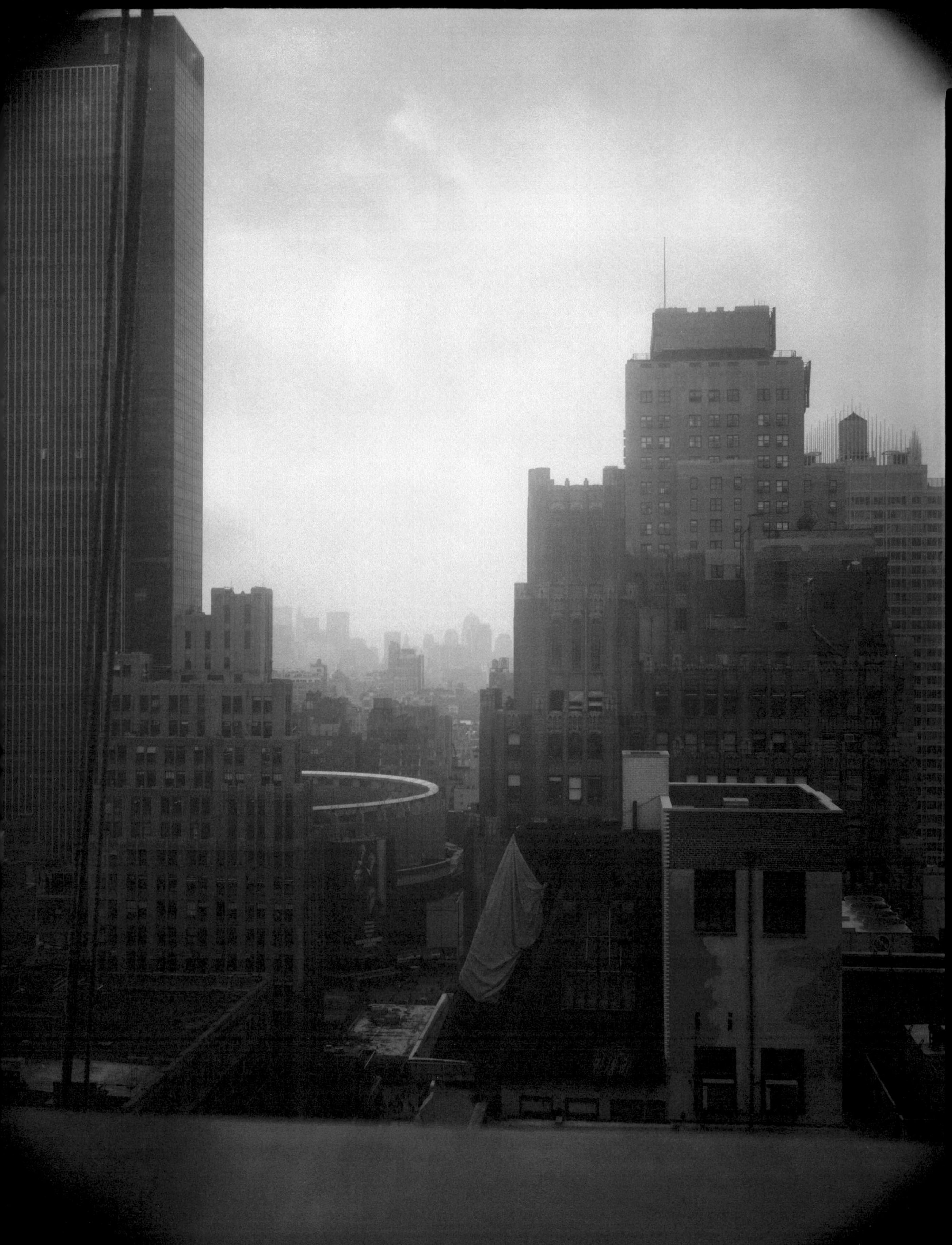

September 26, 2003

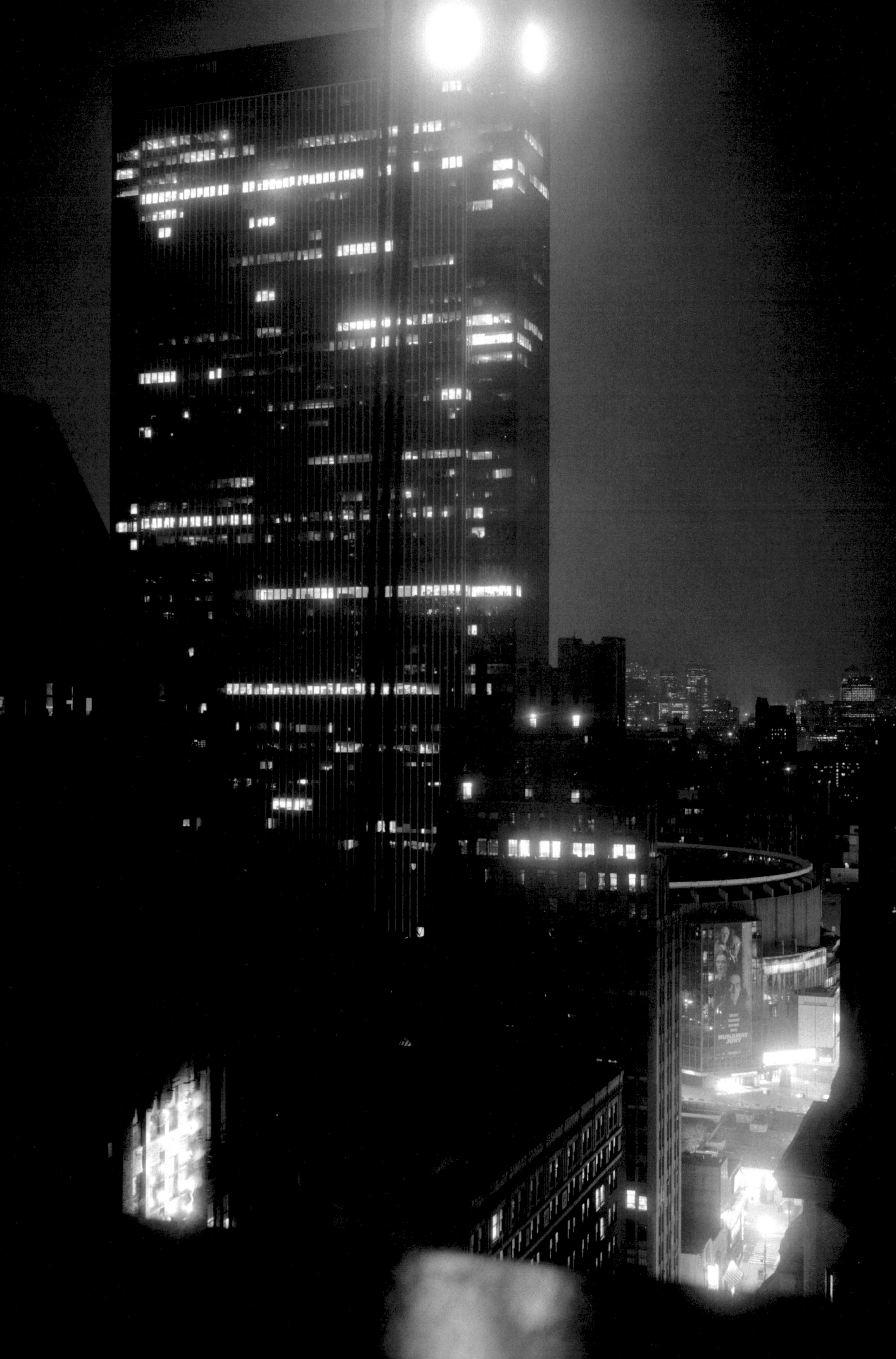

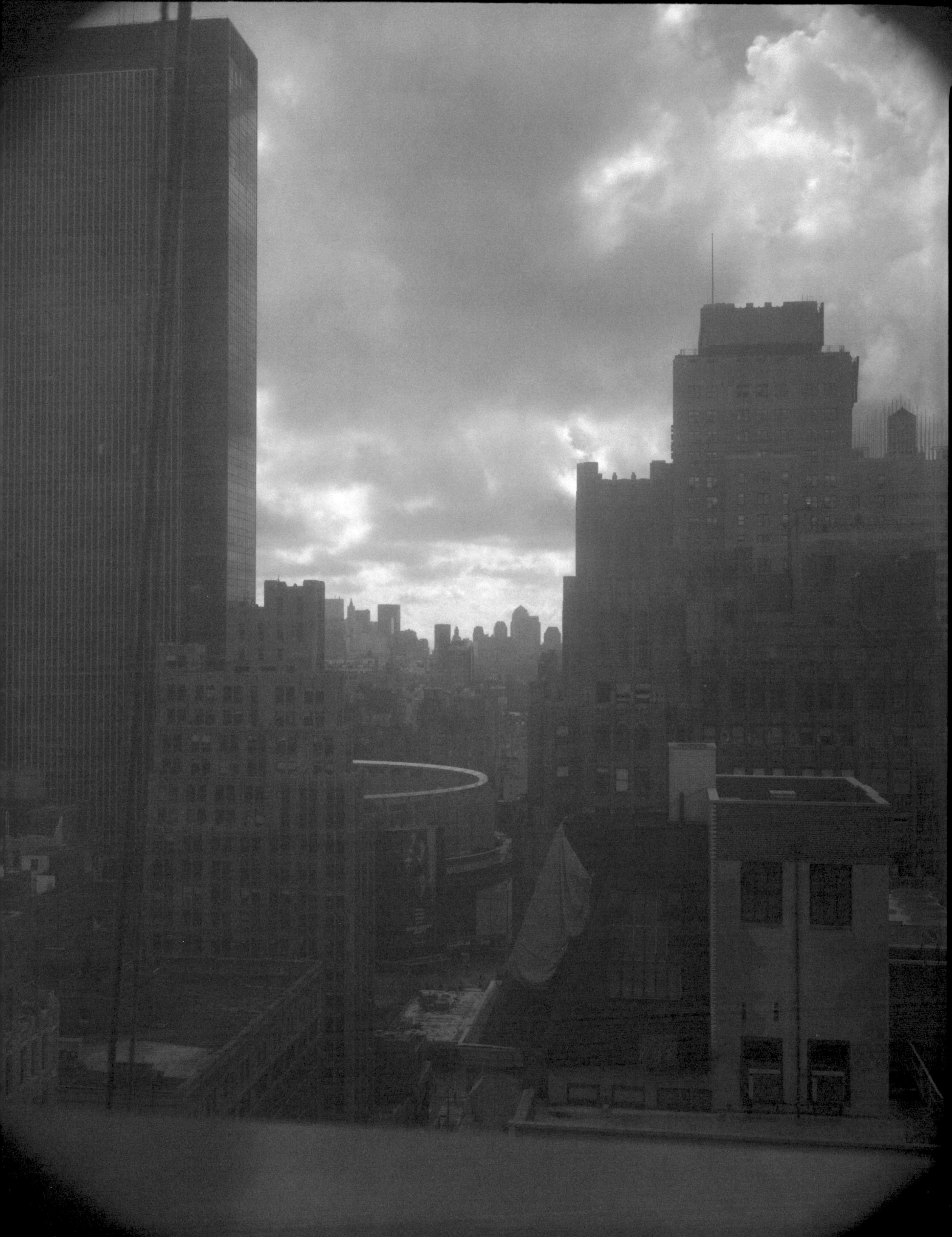

September 28, 2003

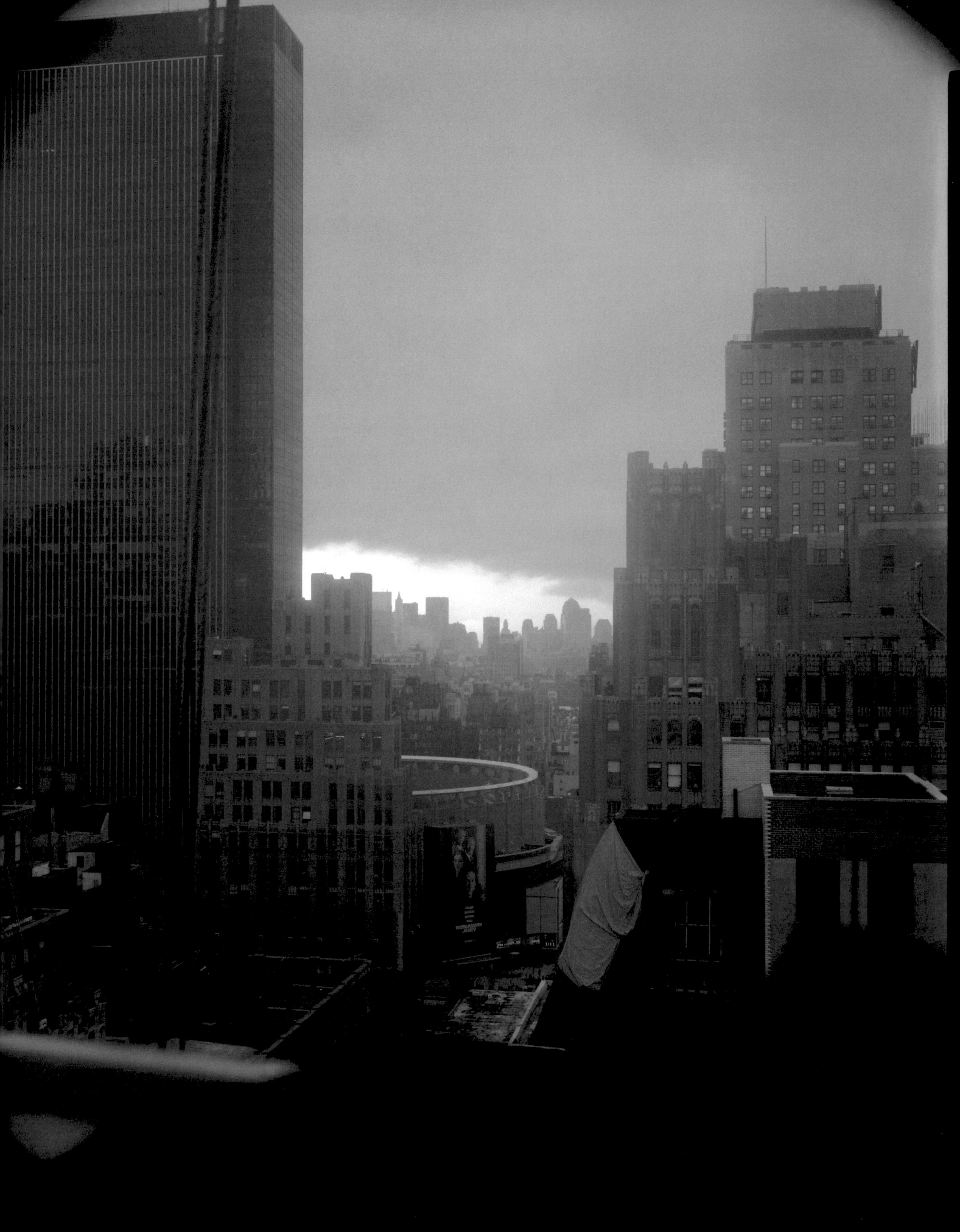

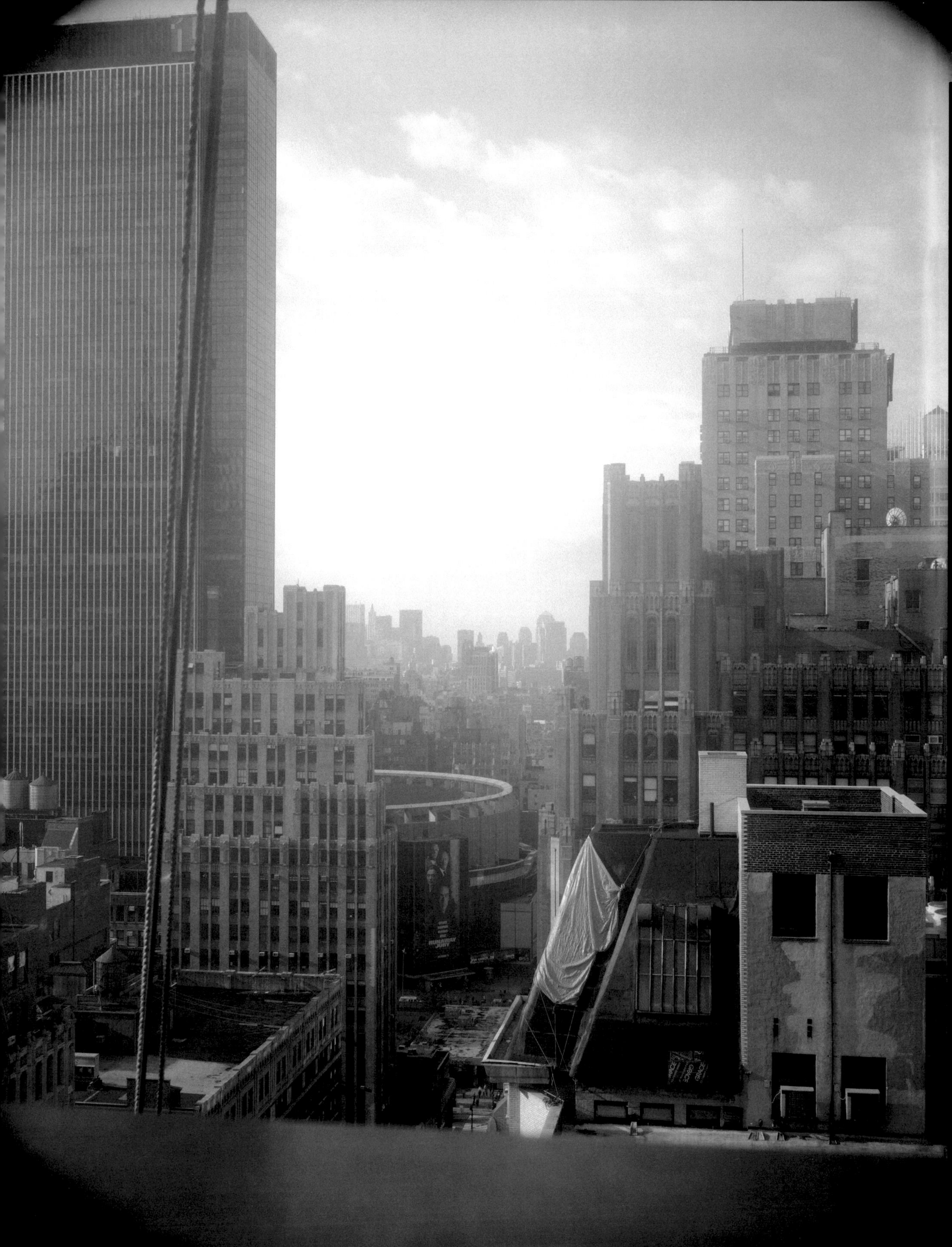

September 30, 2003

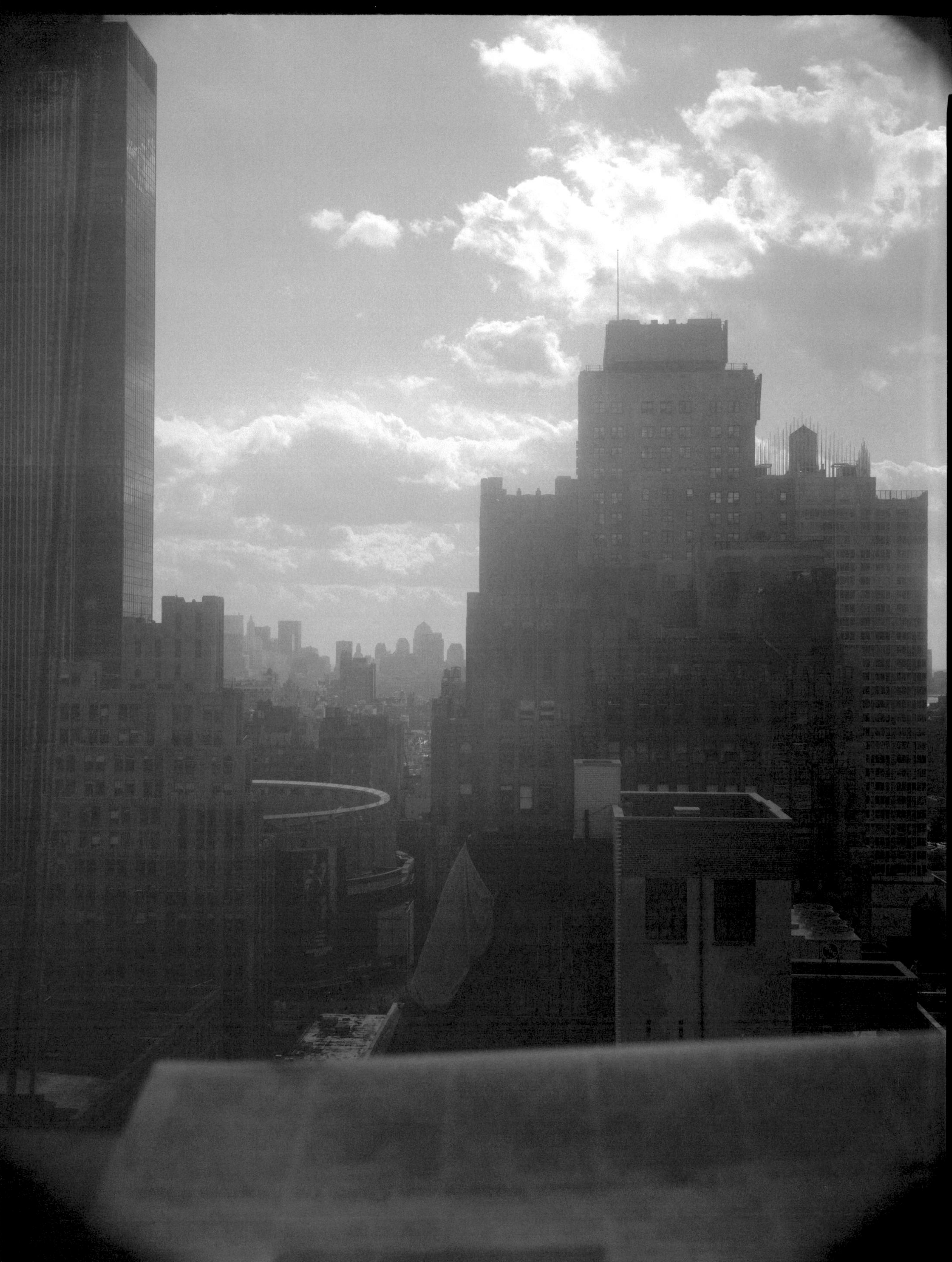

September 1, 2004

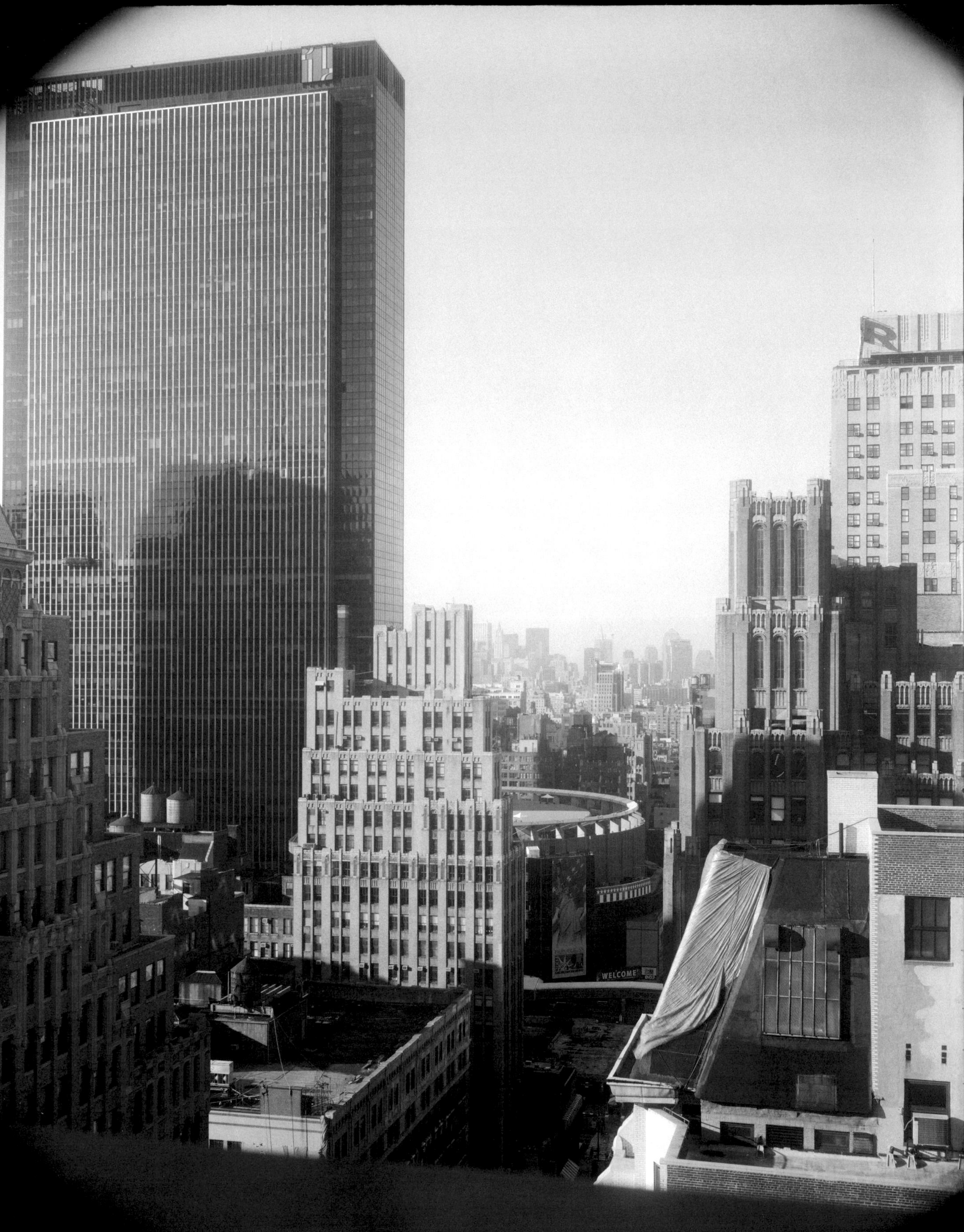

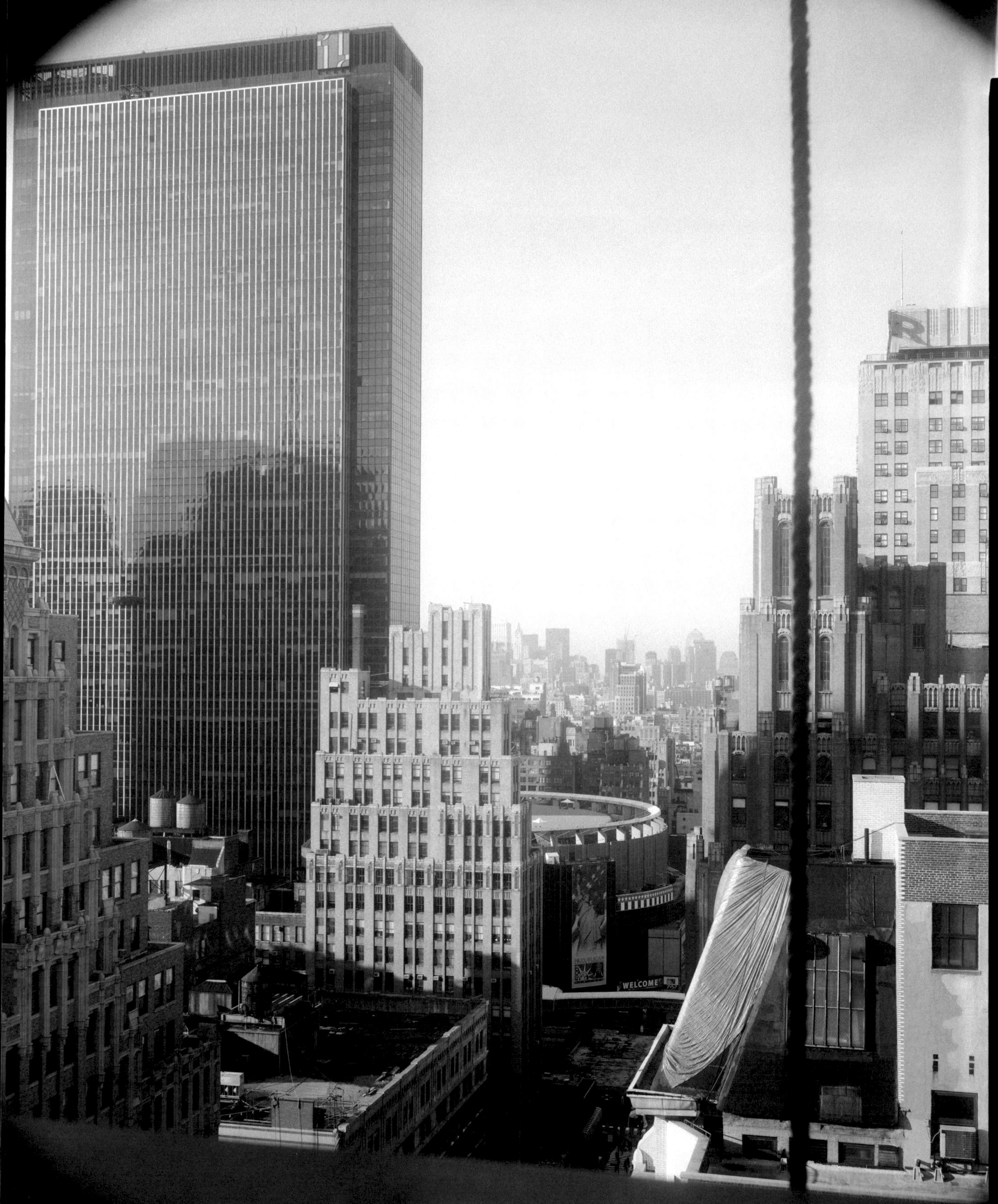

September 3, 2004

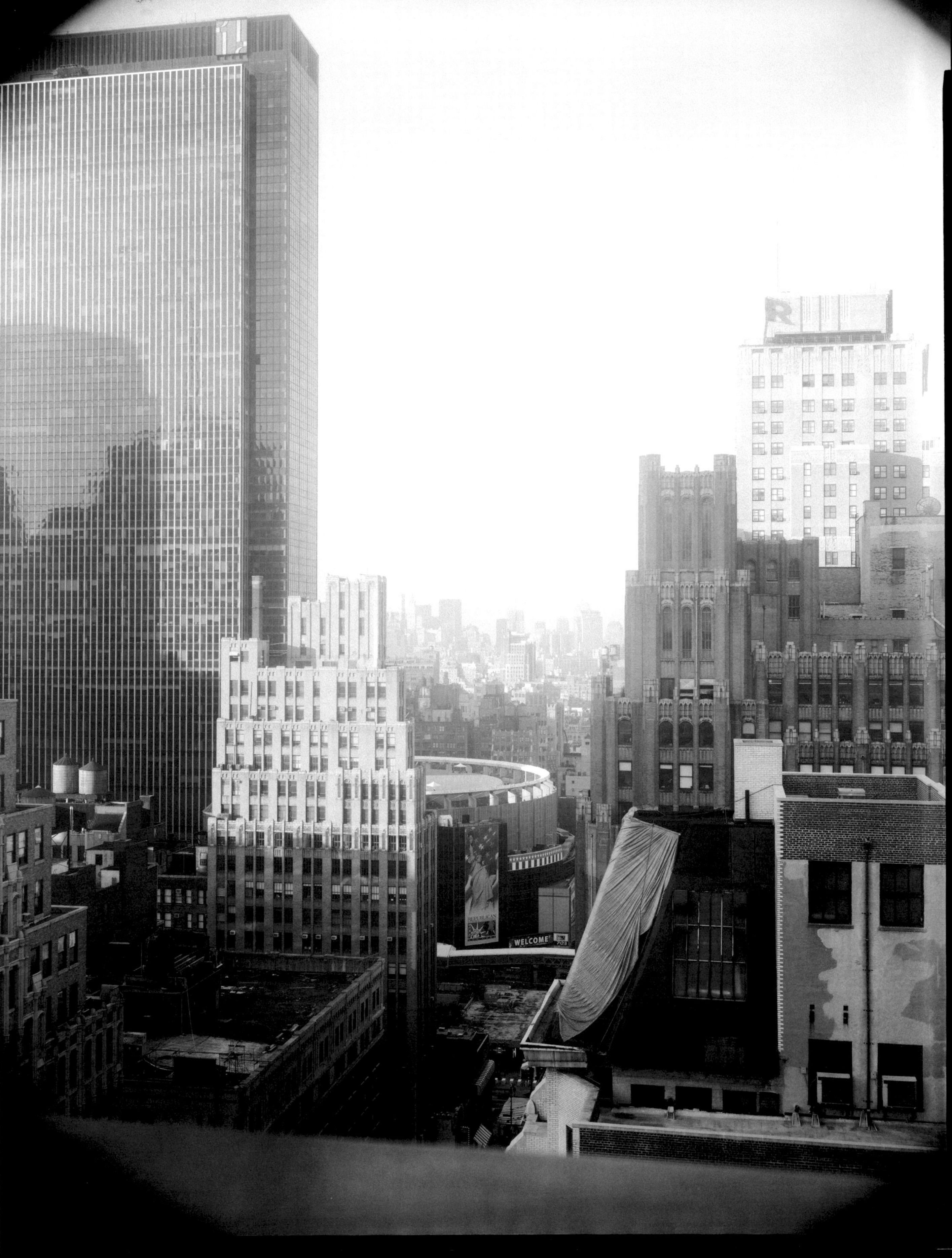

September 4, 2004

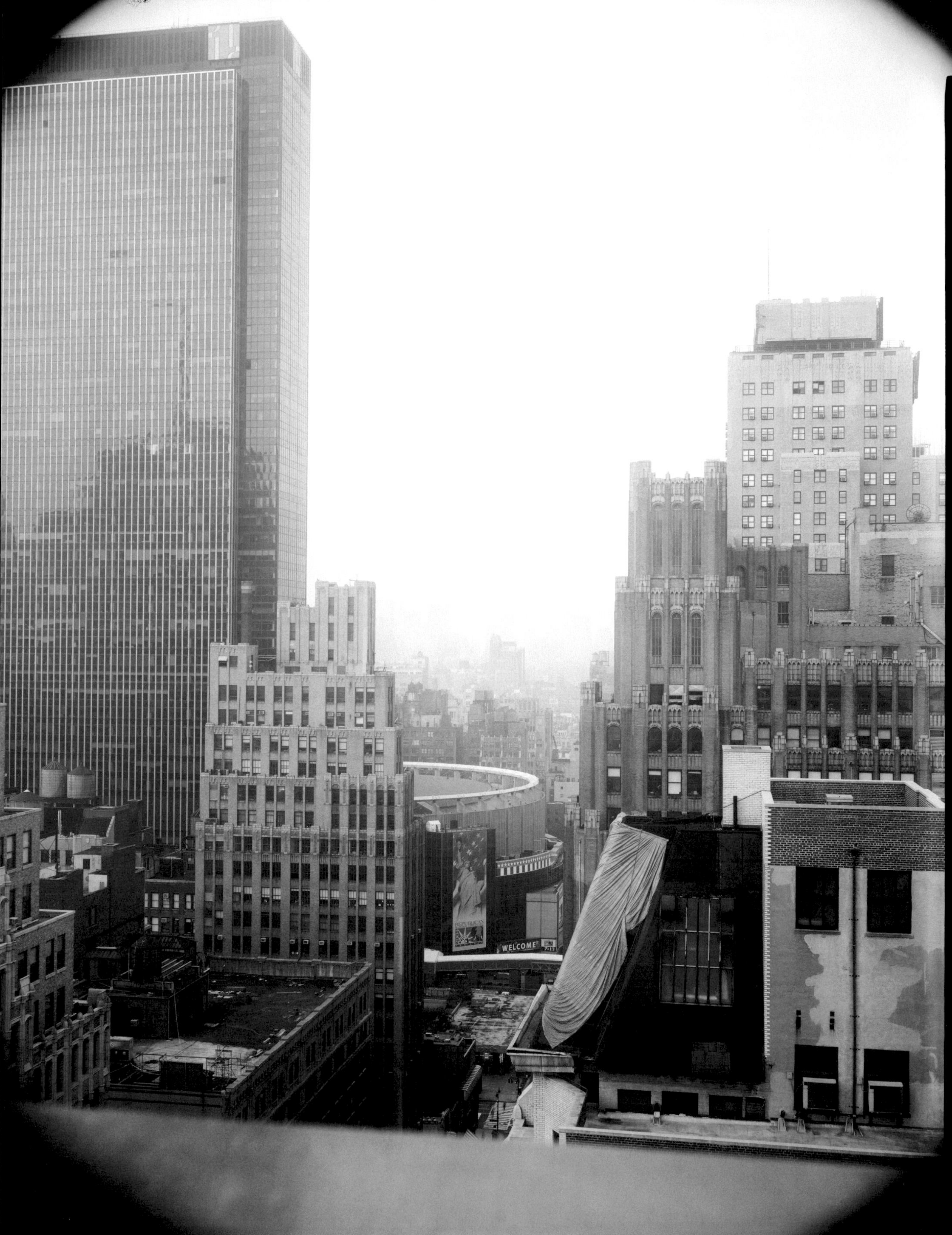

September 5, 2004

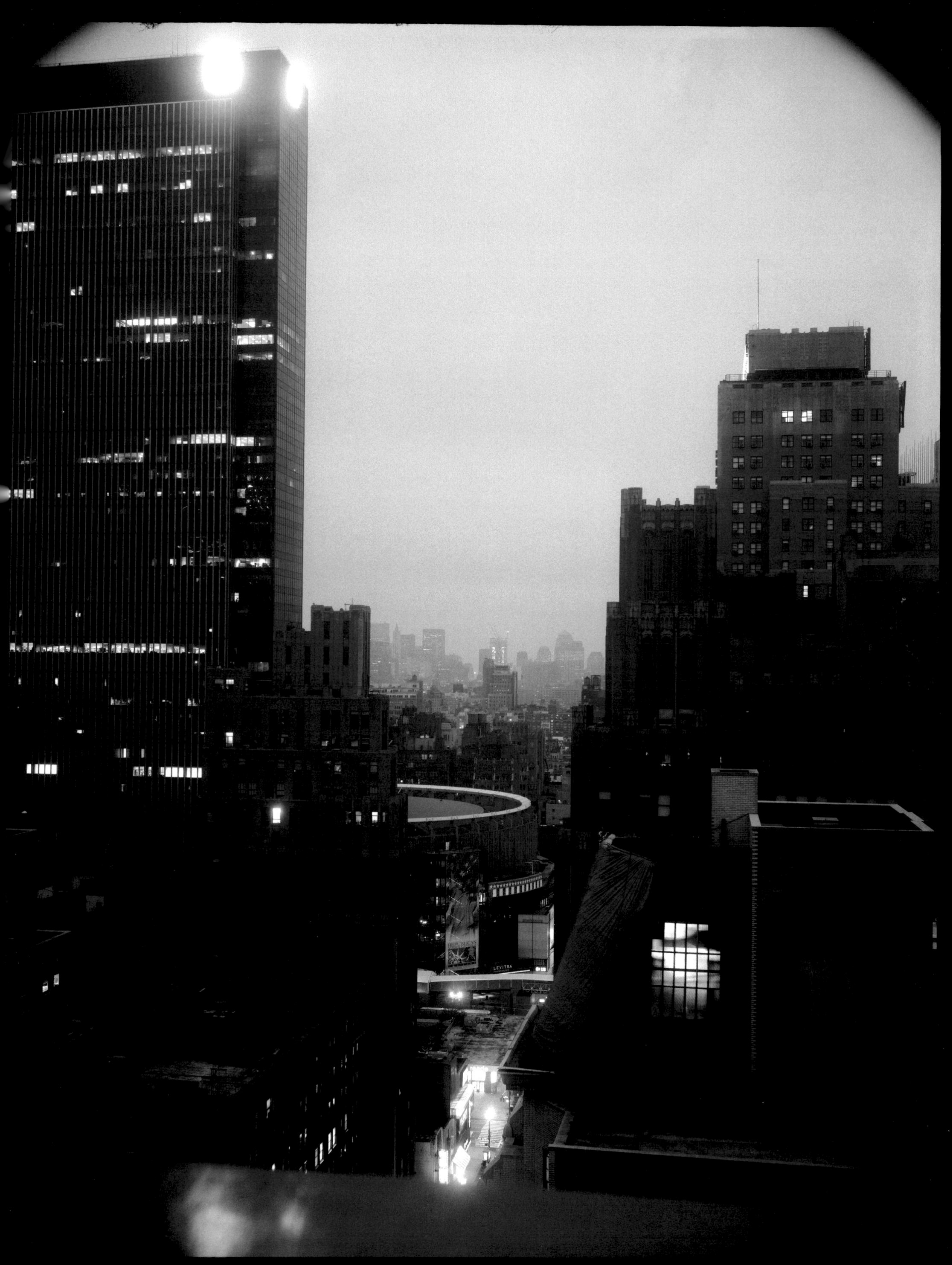
LEVITRA

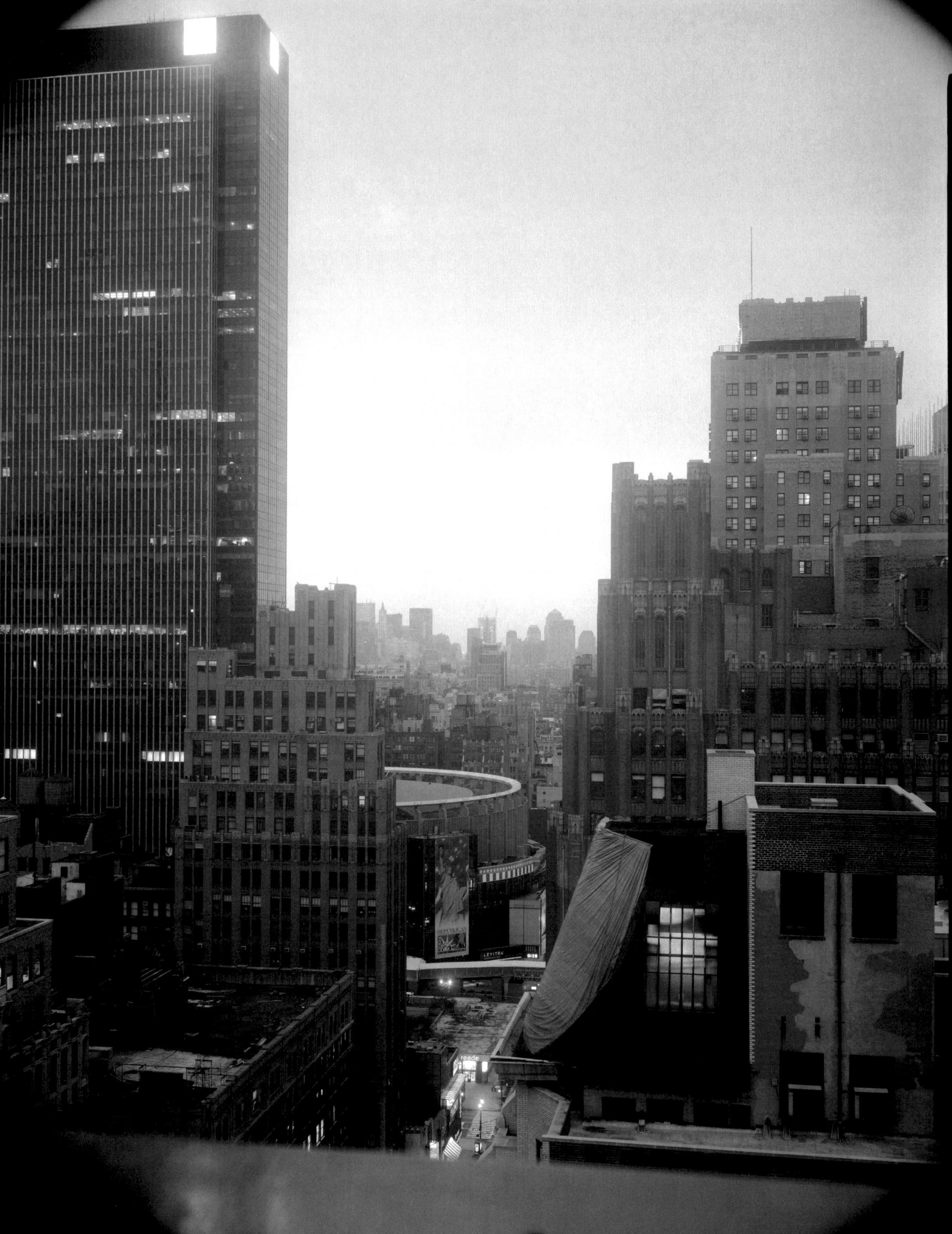

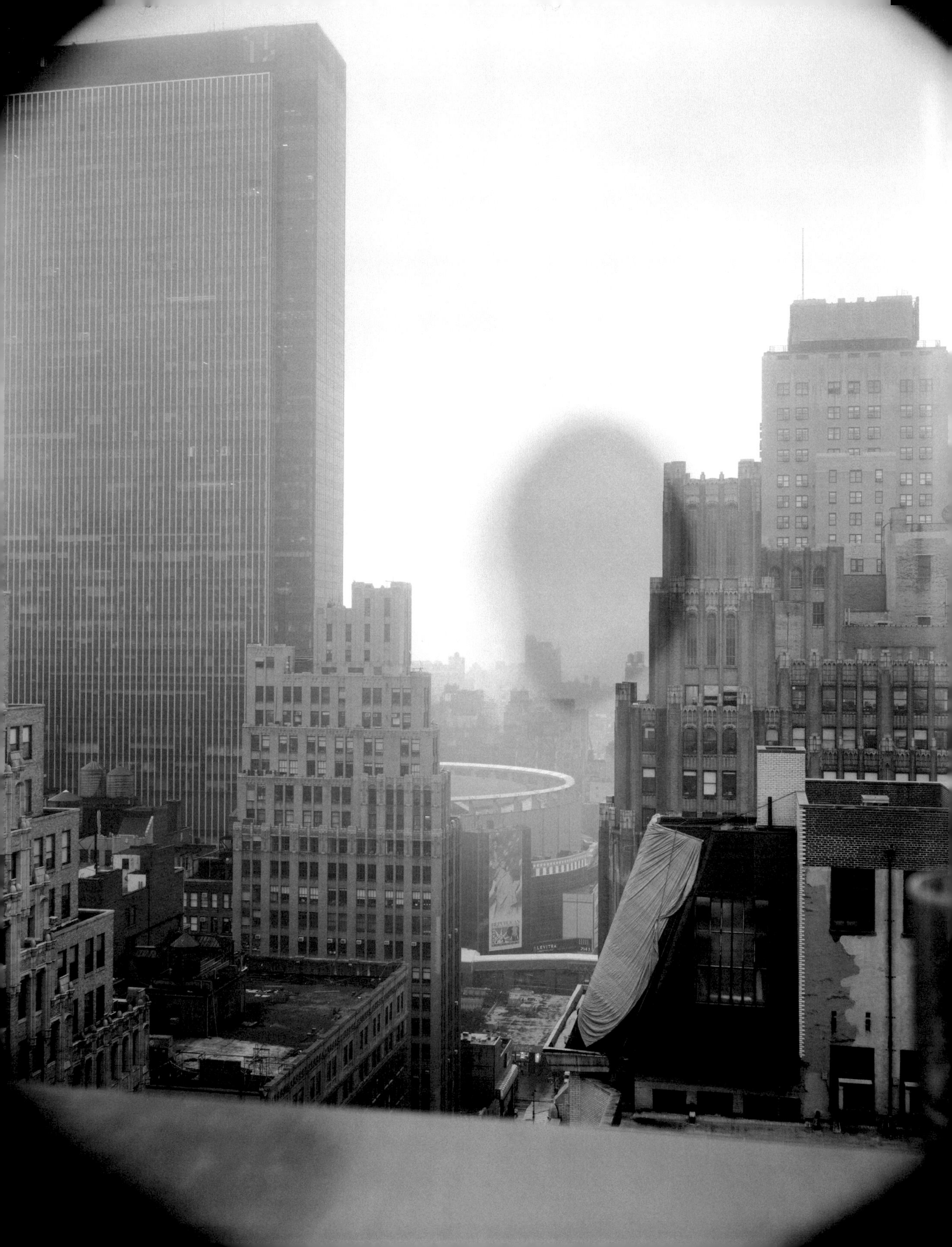

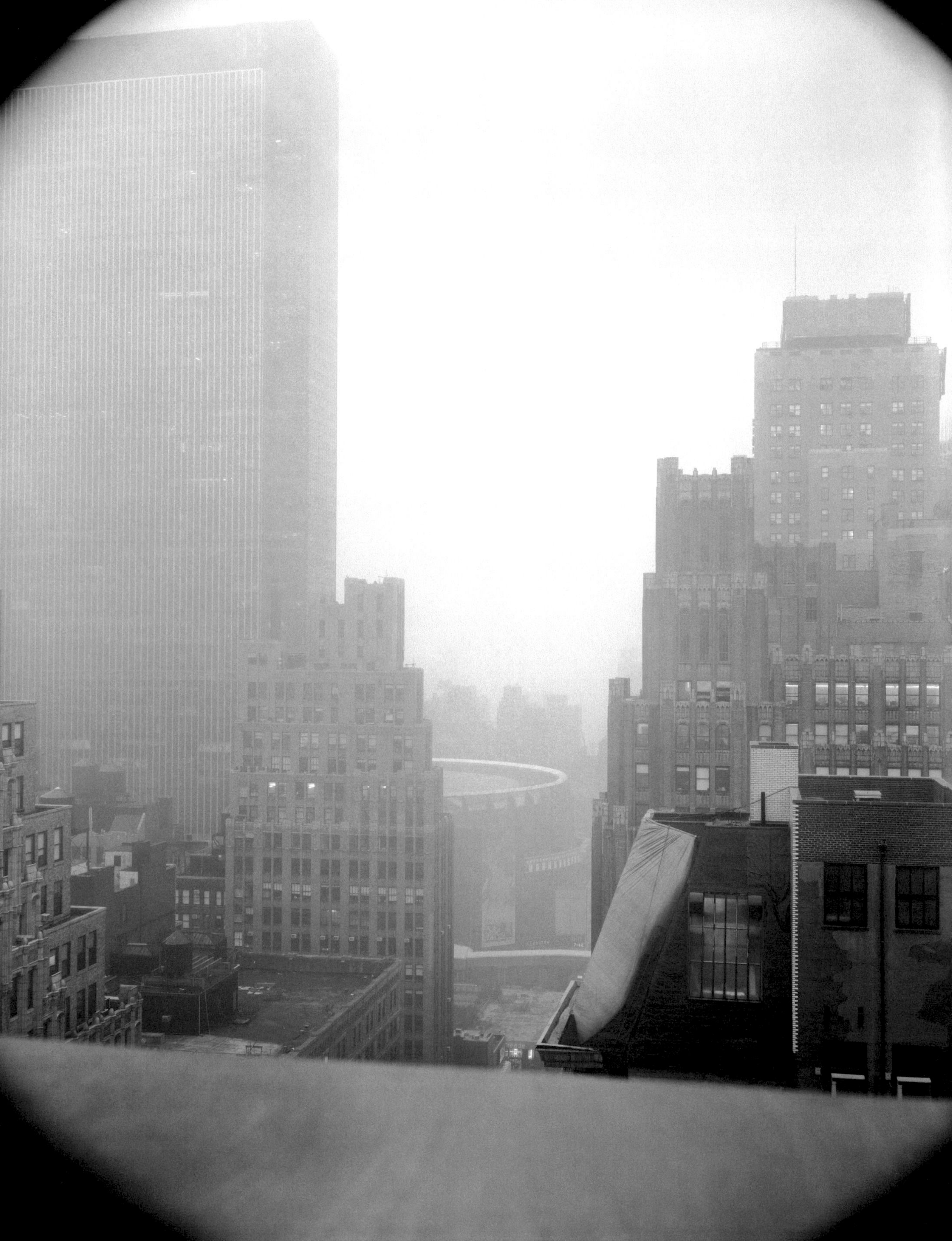

September 9, 2004

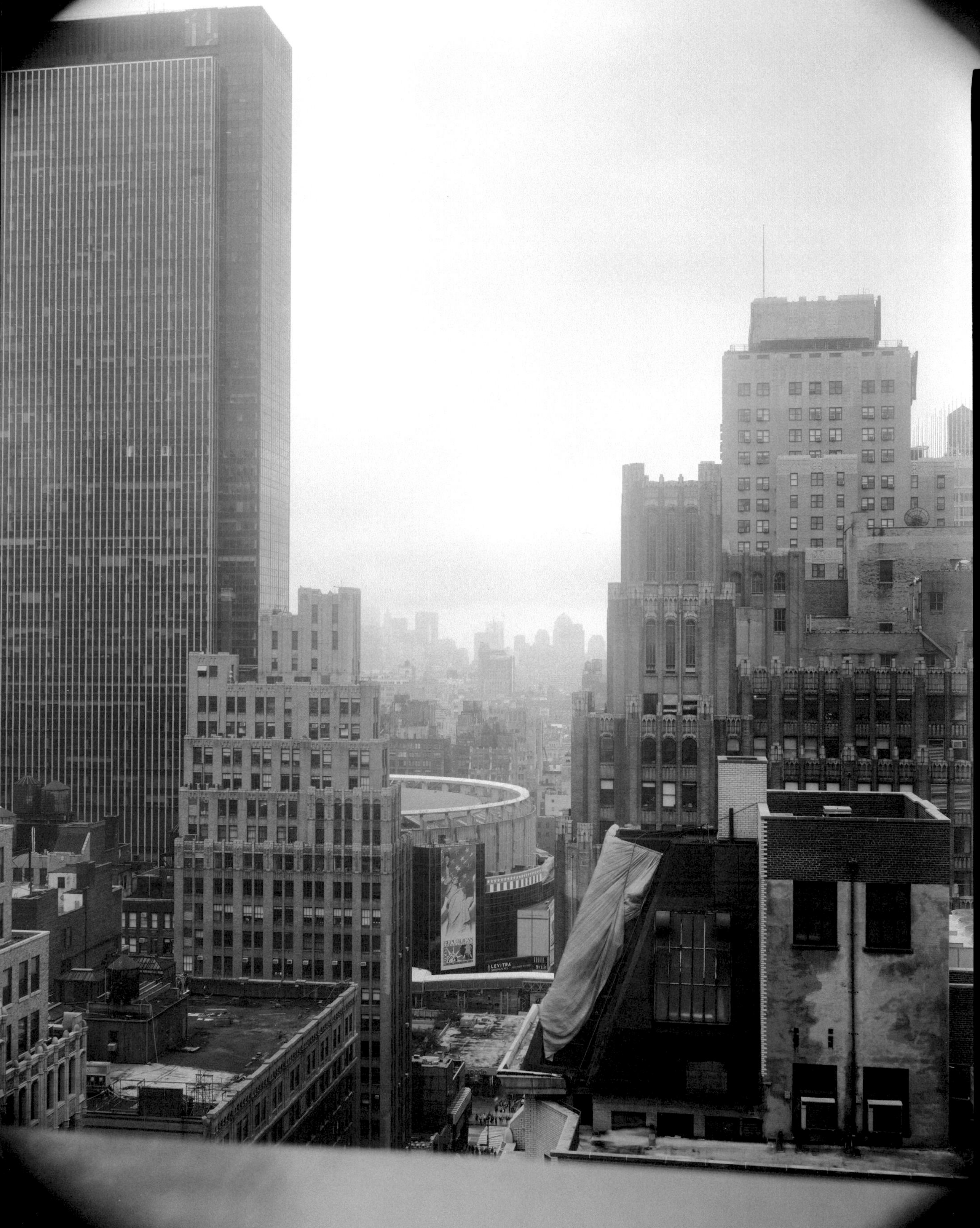

September 10, 2004

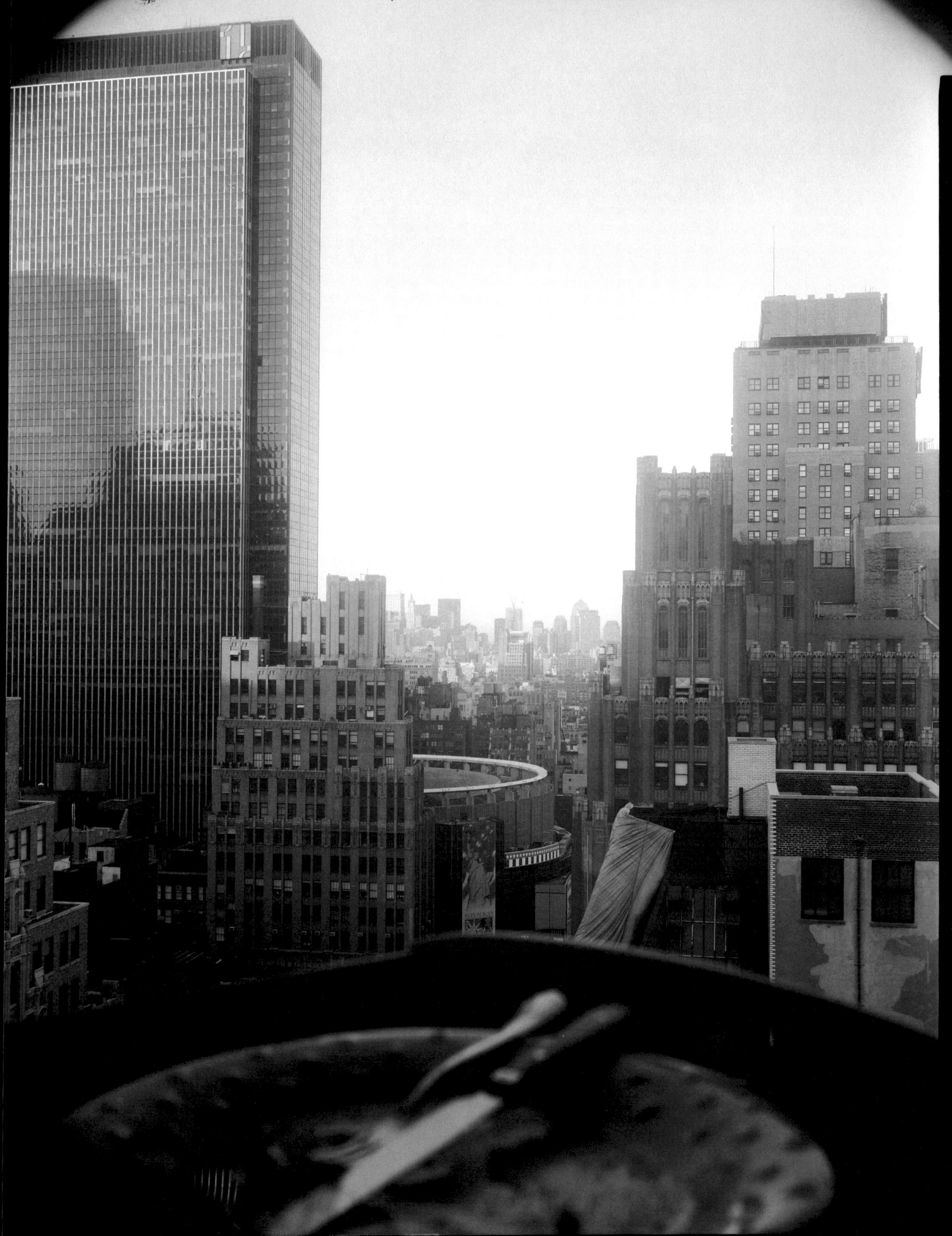

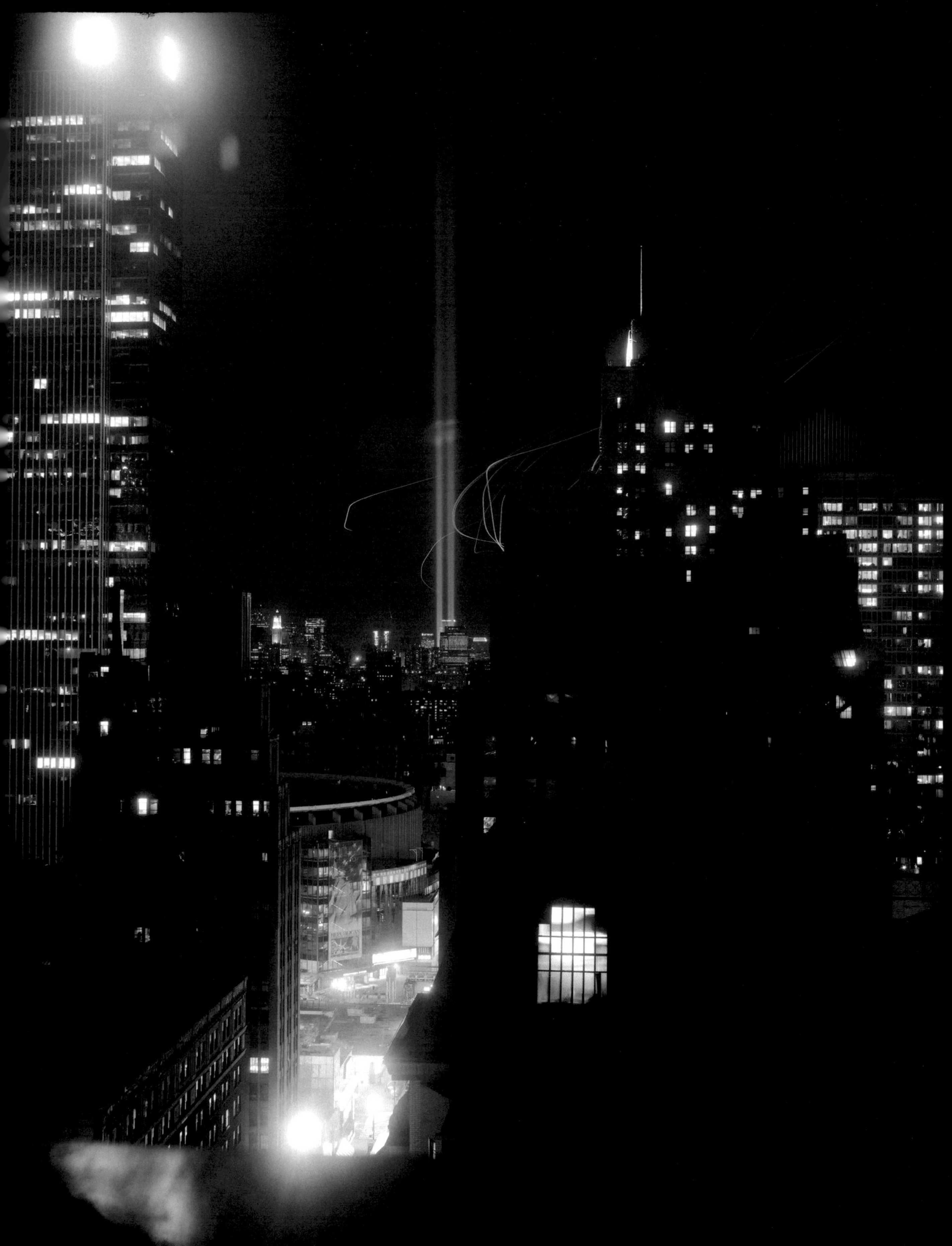

September 12, 2004

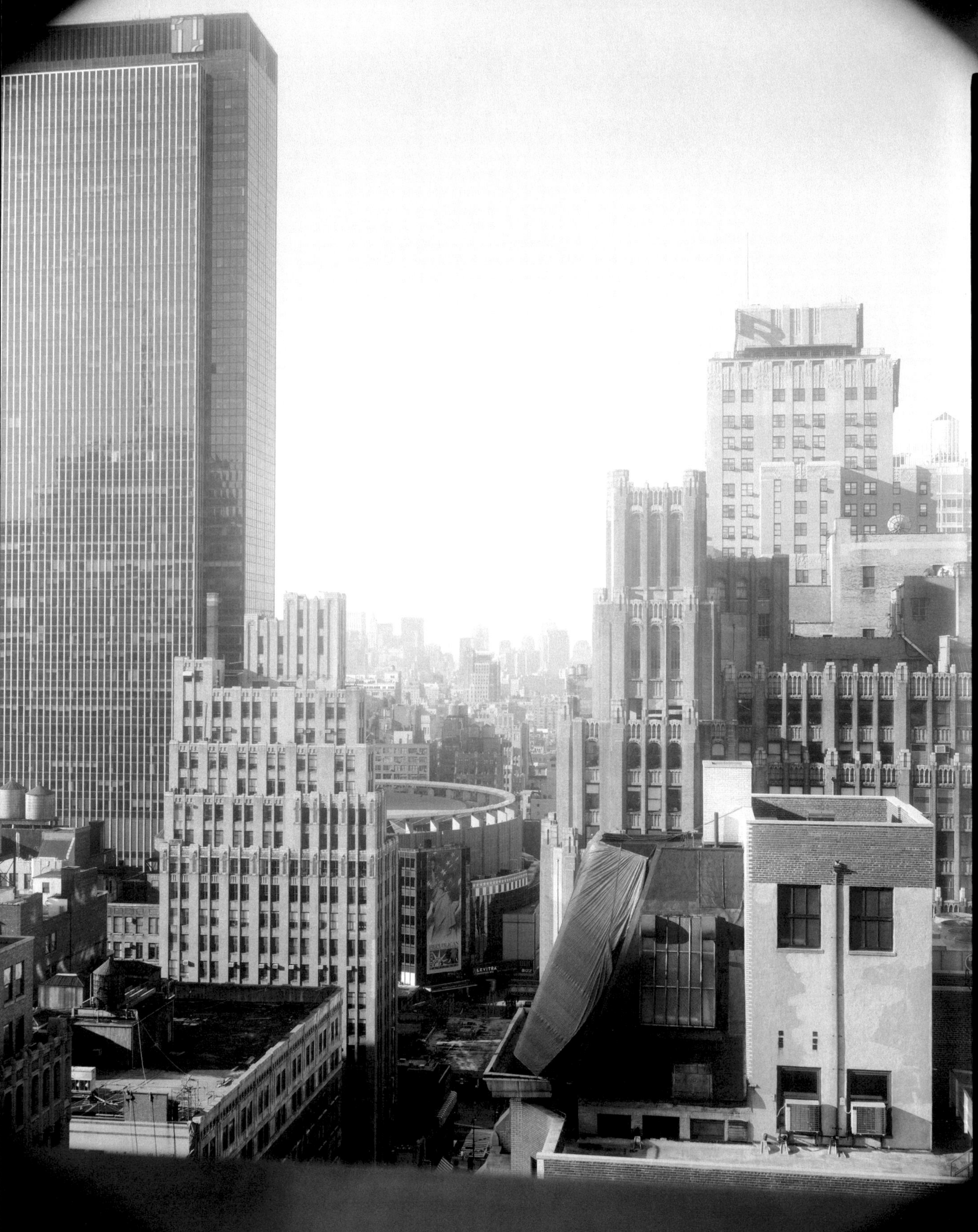

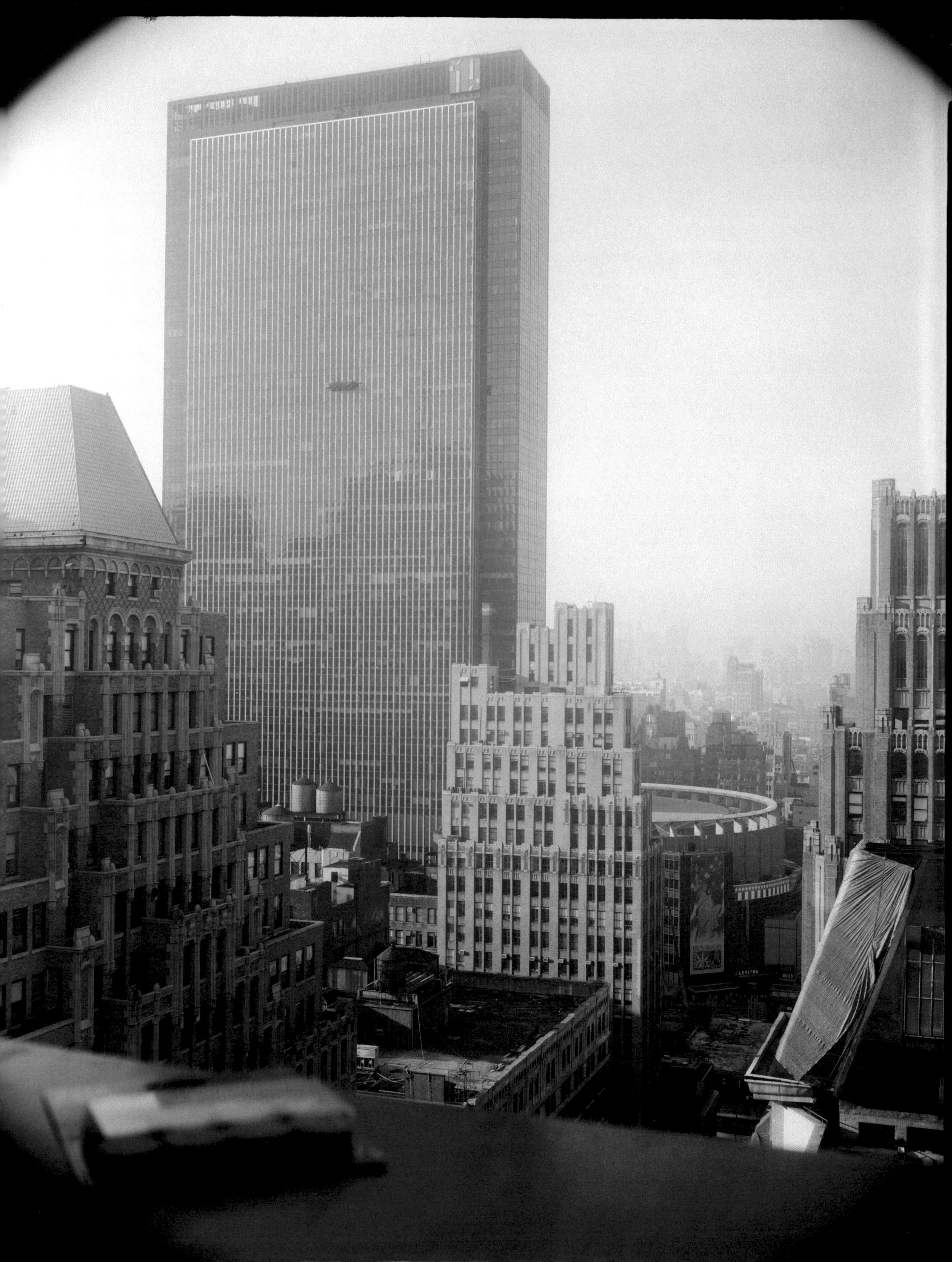

September 14, 2004

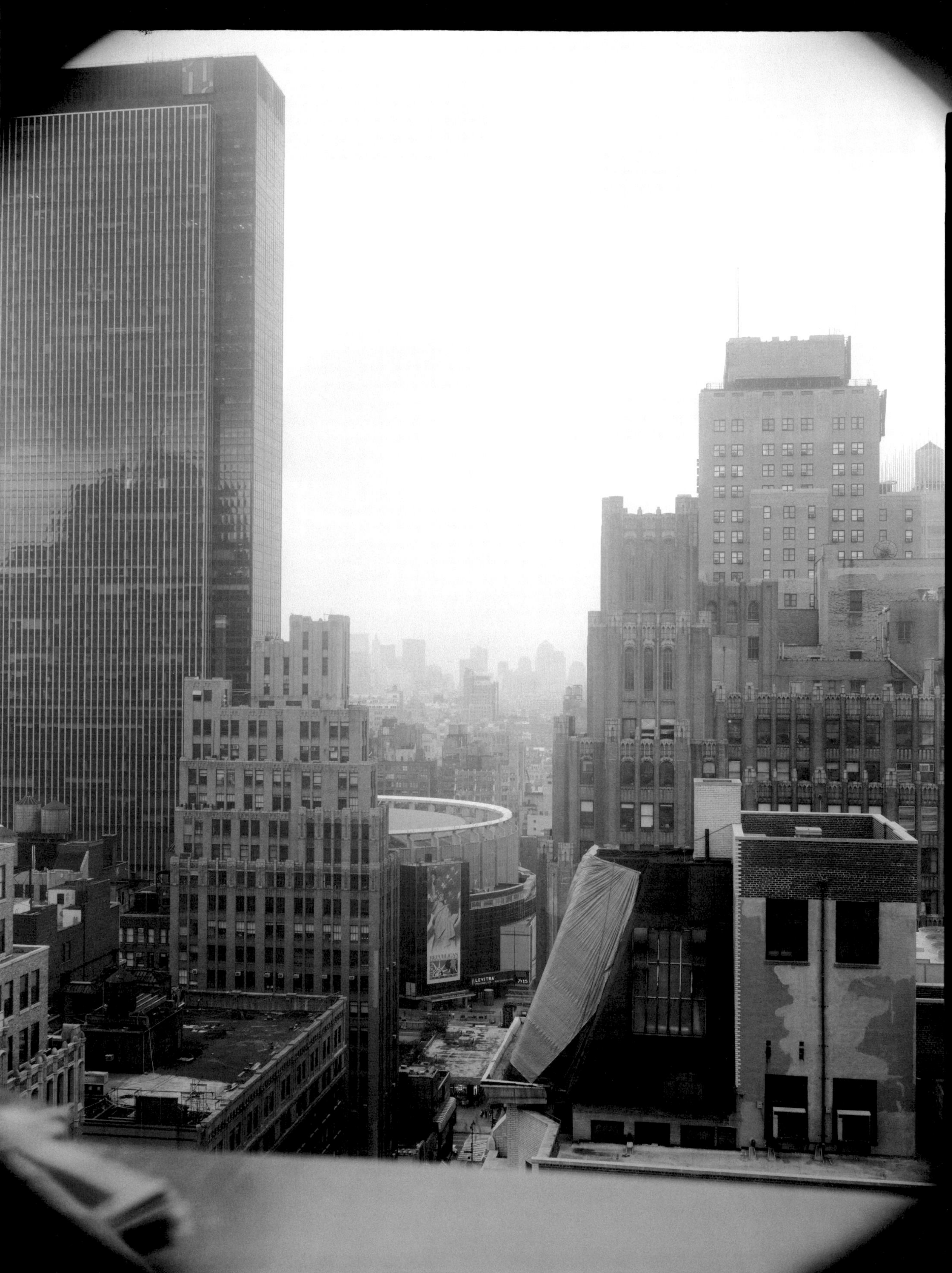

September 15, 2004

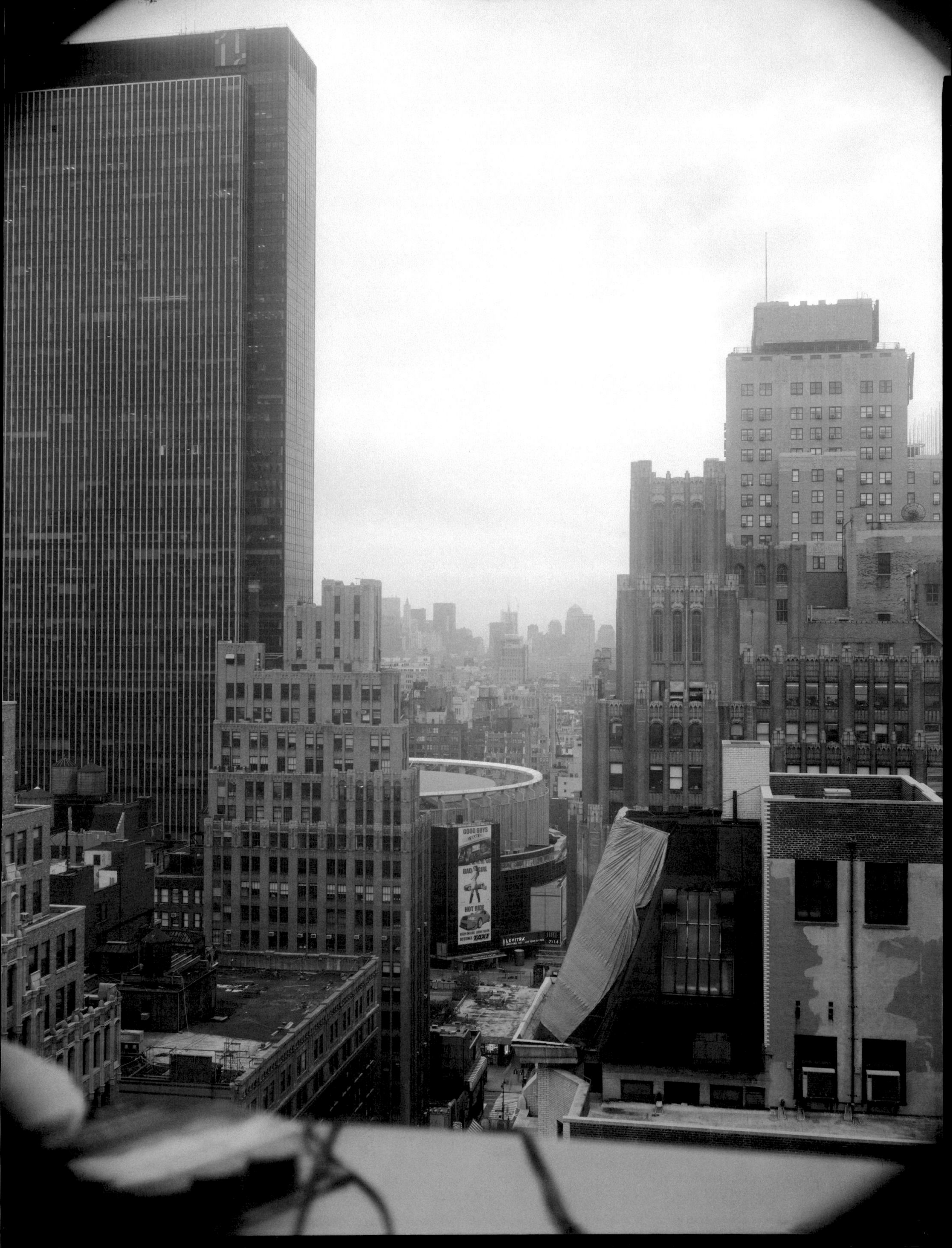

September 16, 2004

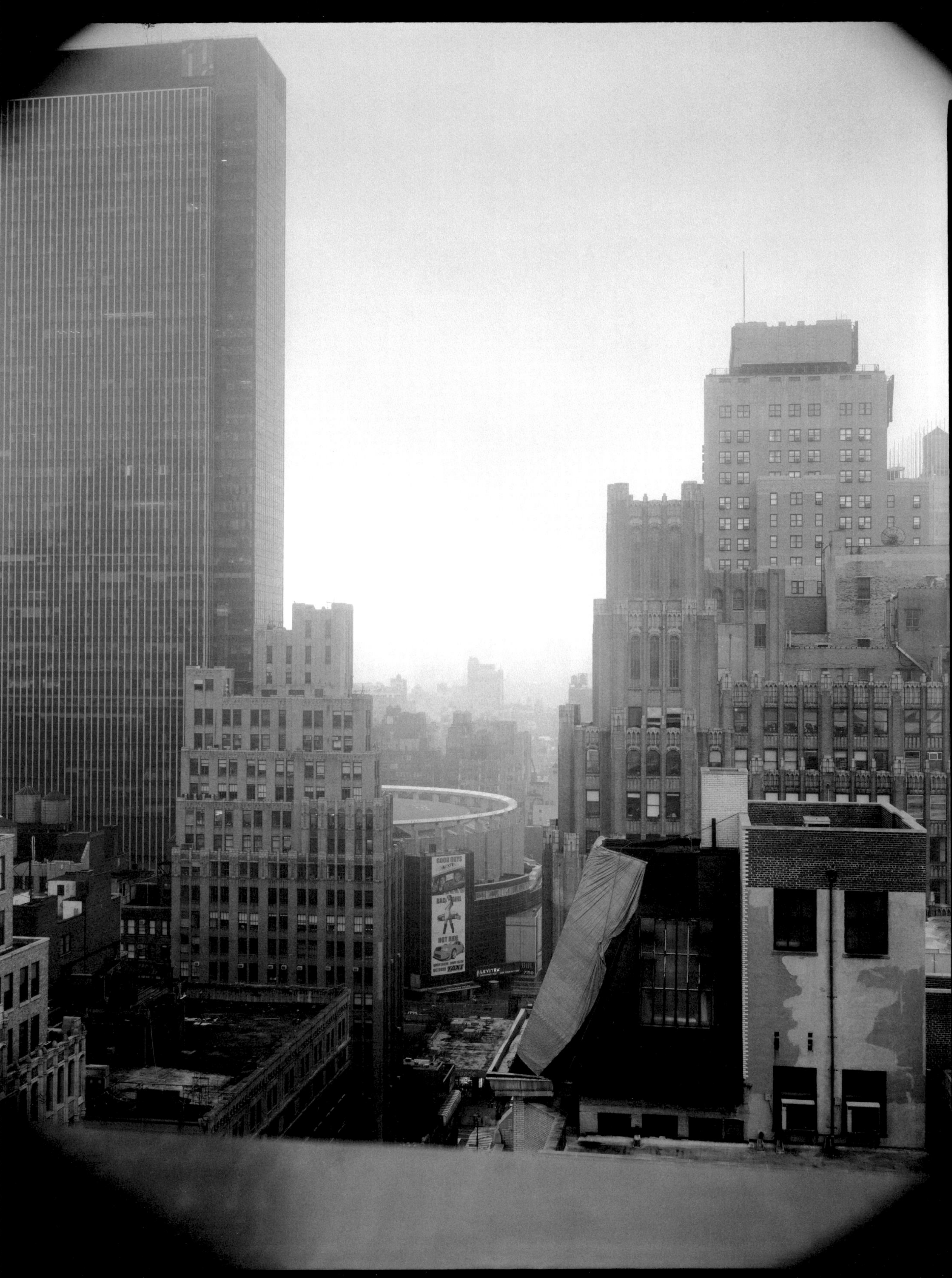

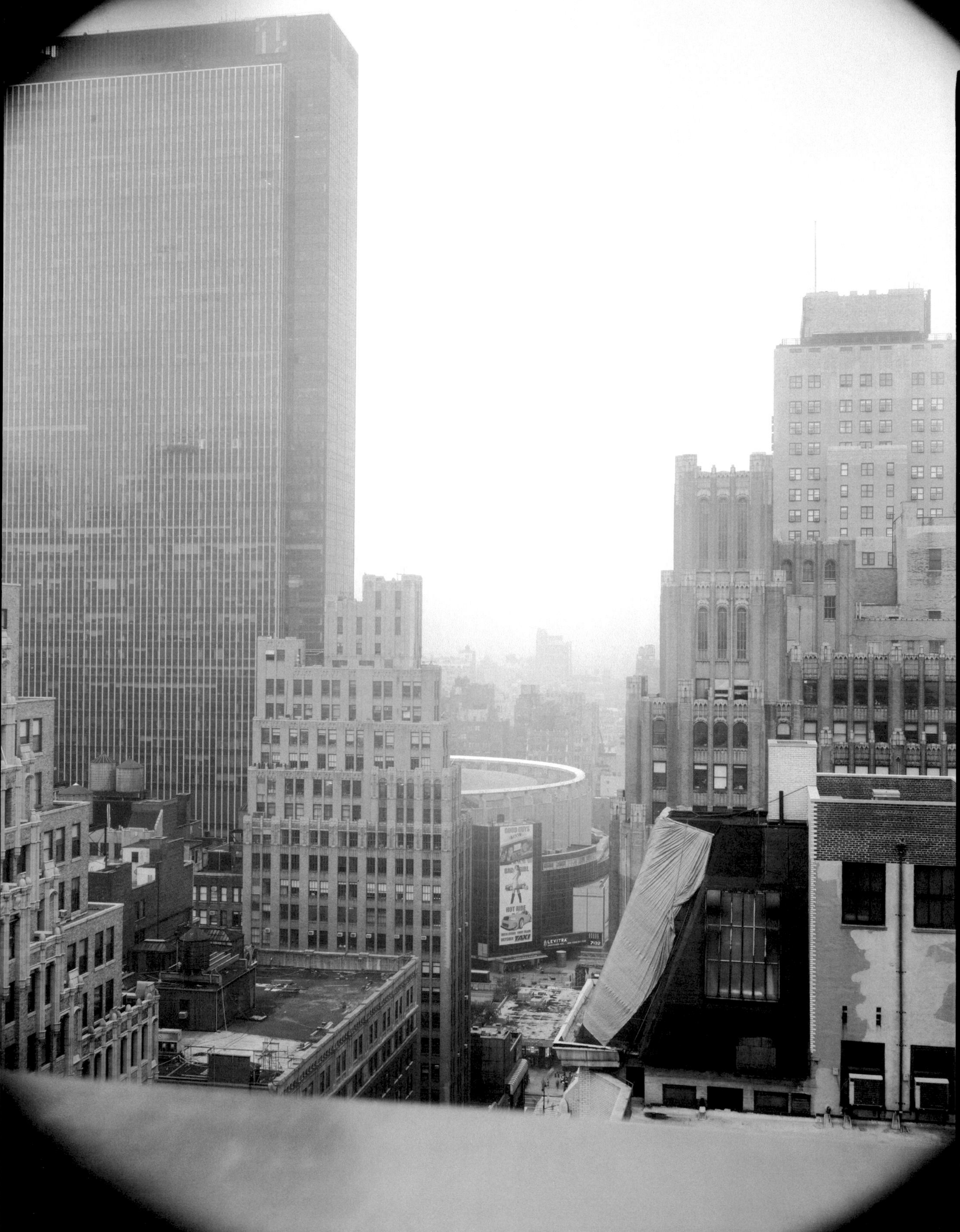

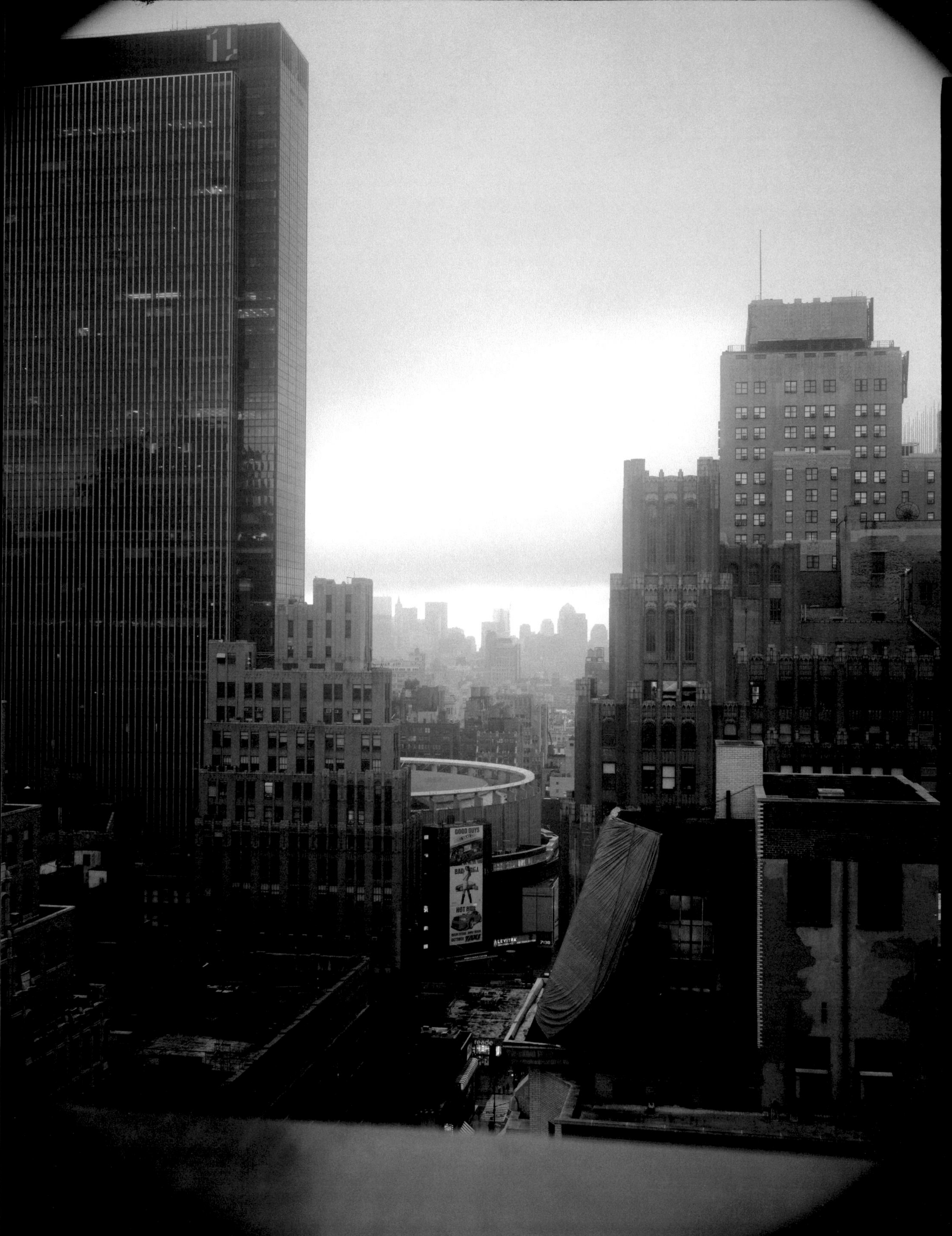

September 19, 2004

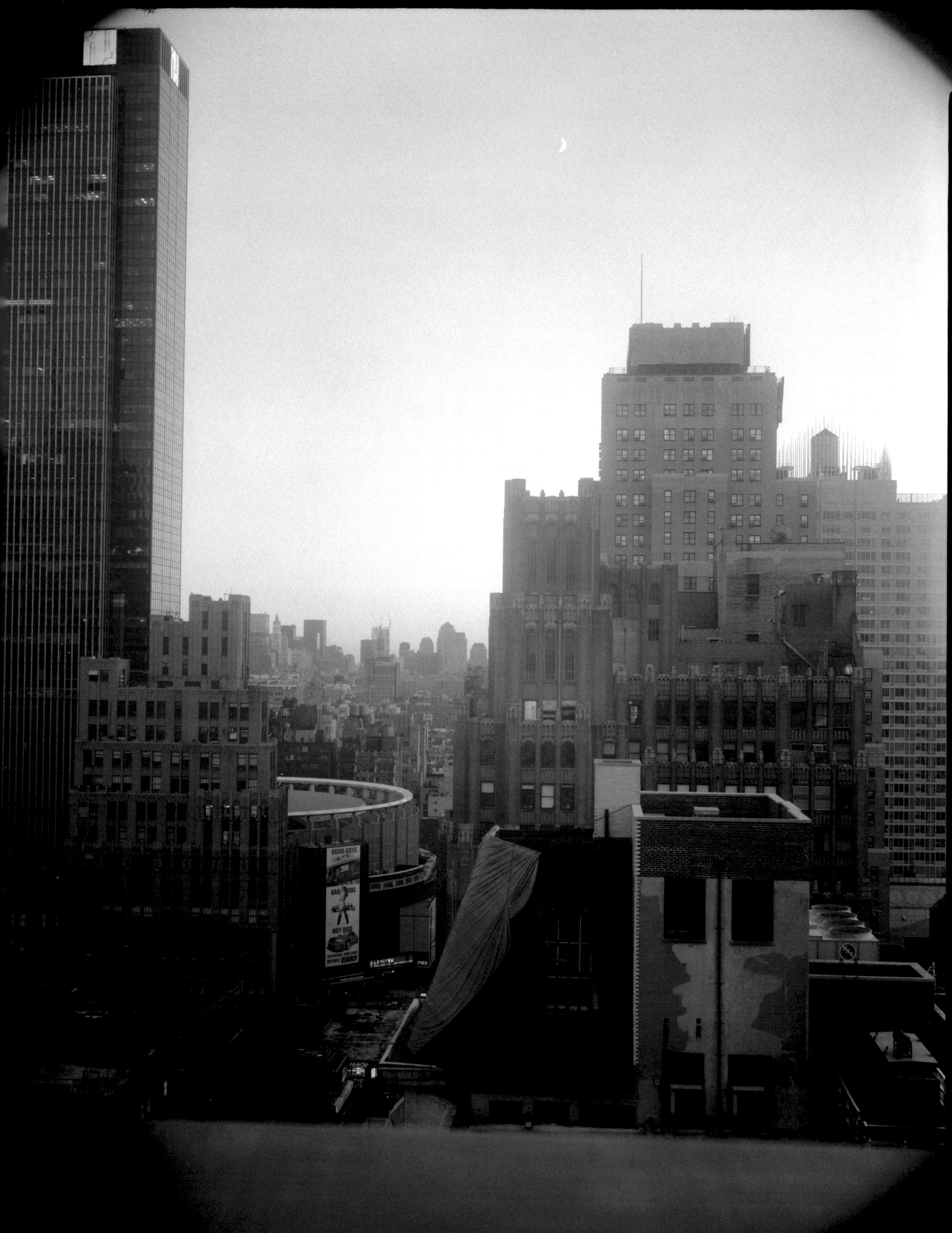
GOOD GUYS
BAD GIRL
HOT RIDE
OCTOBER TAXI
LEVITRA
7:02
reade

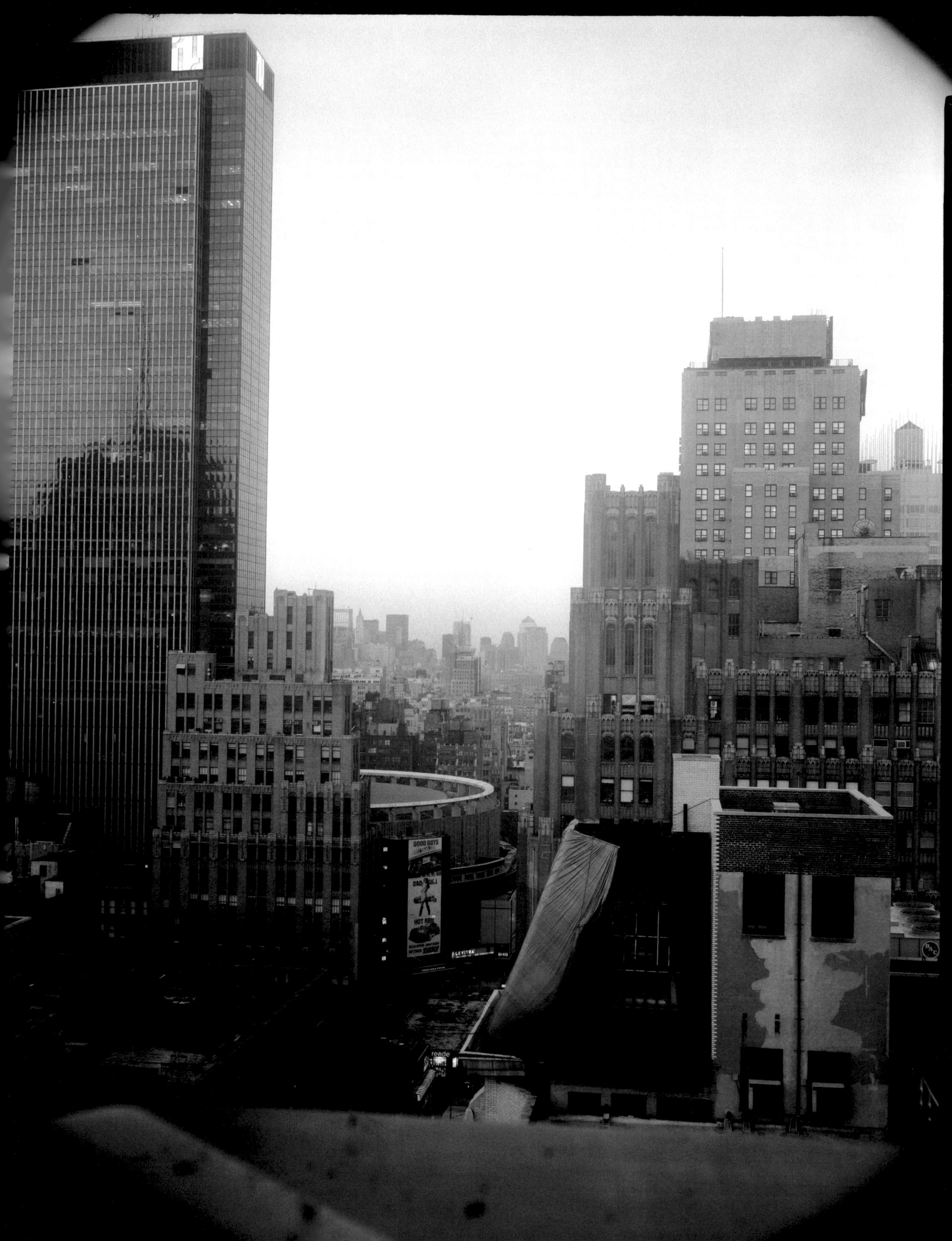

September 21, 2004

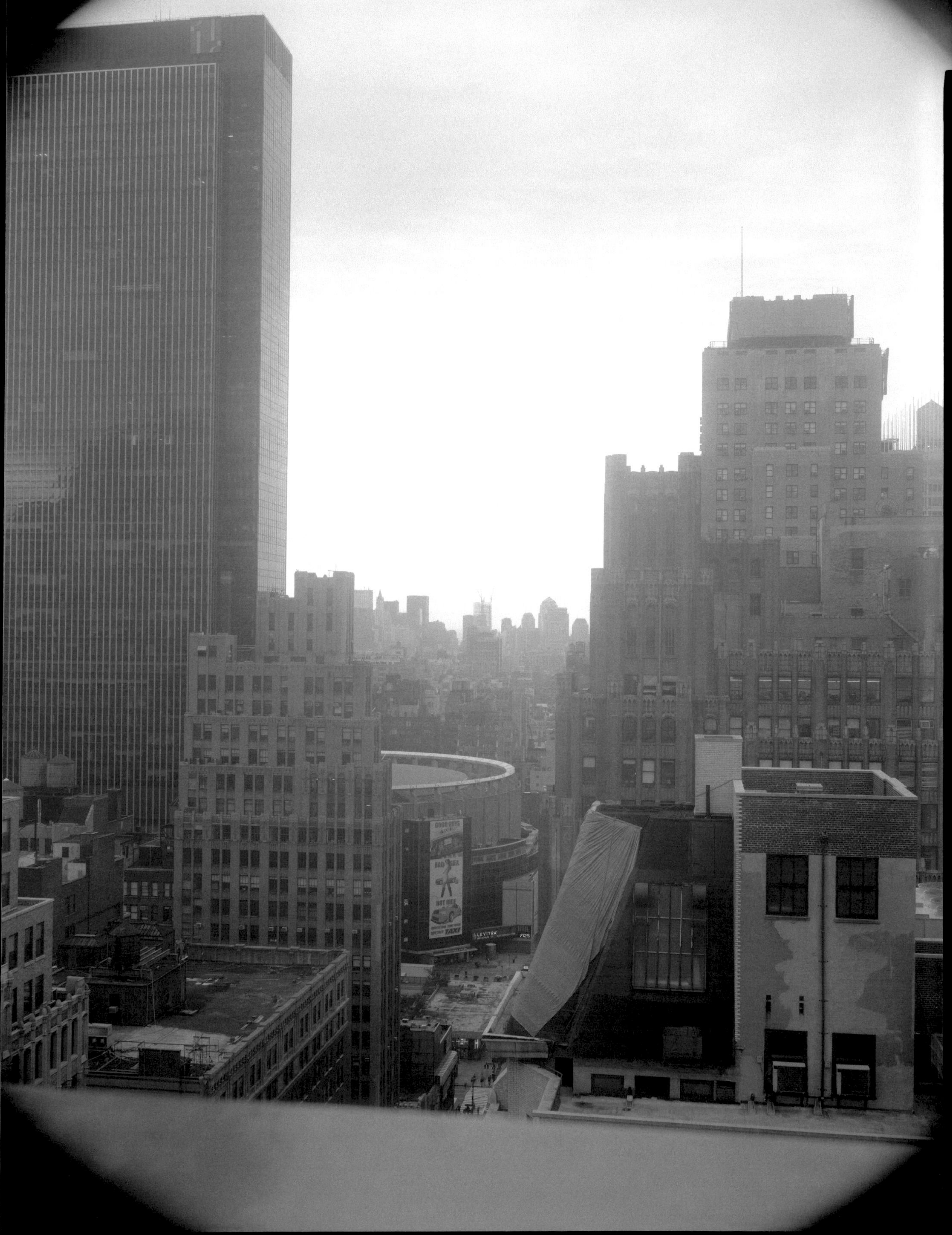

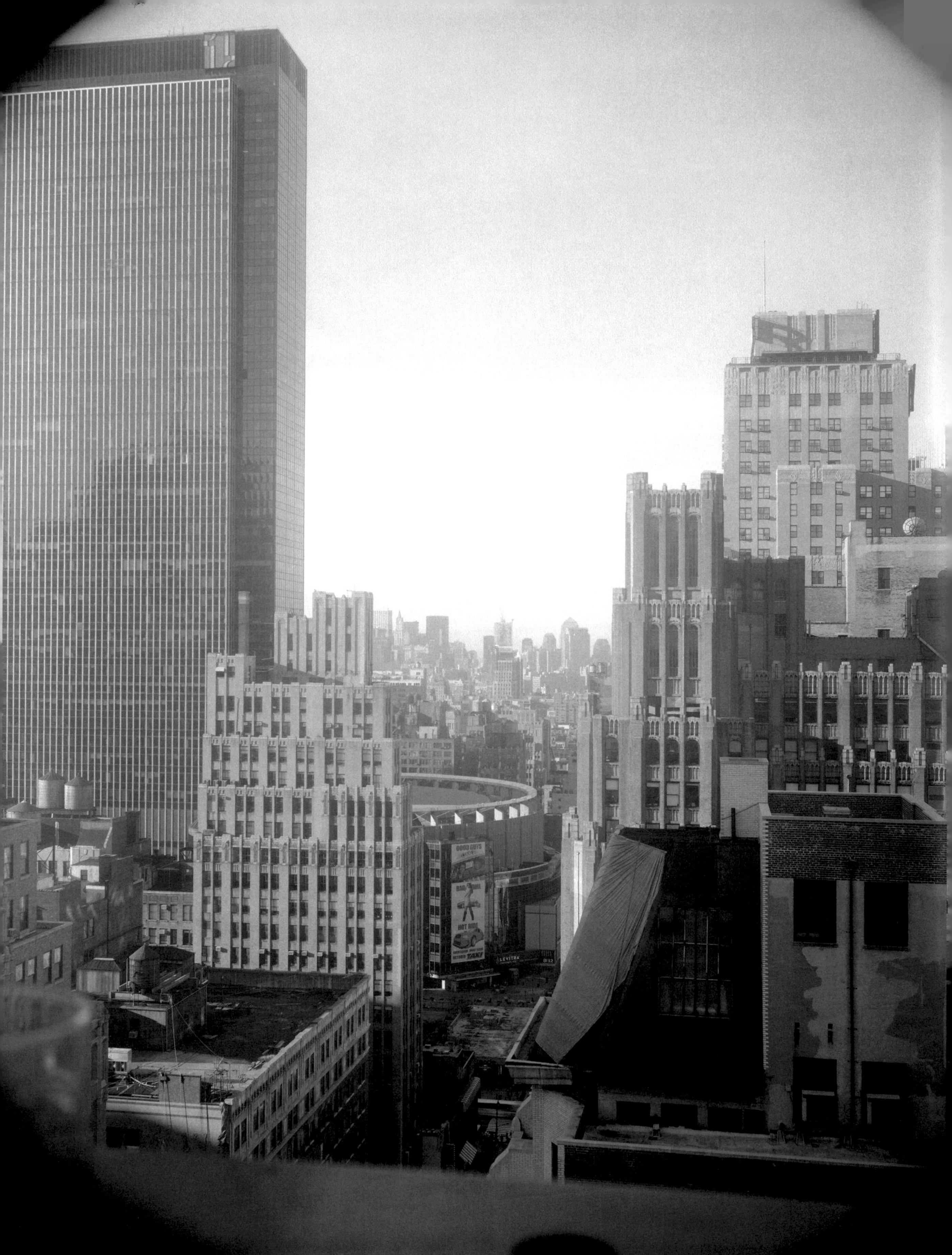

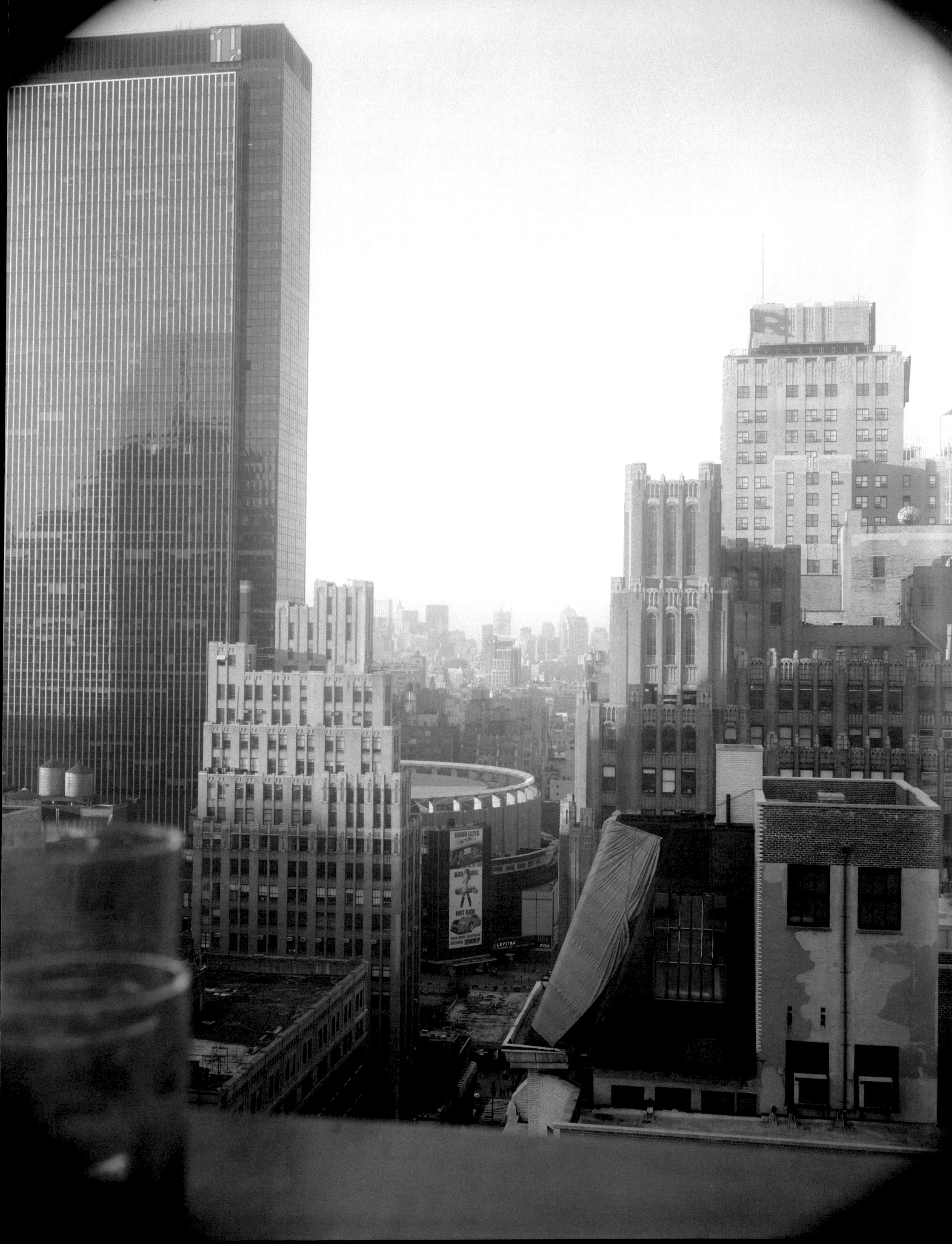

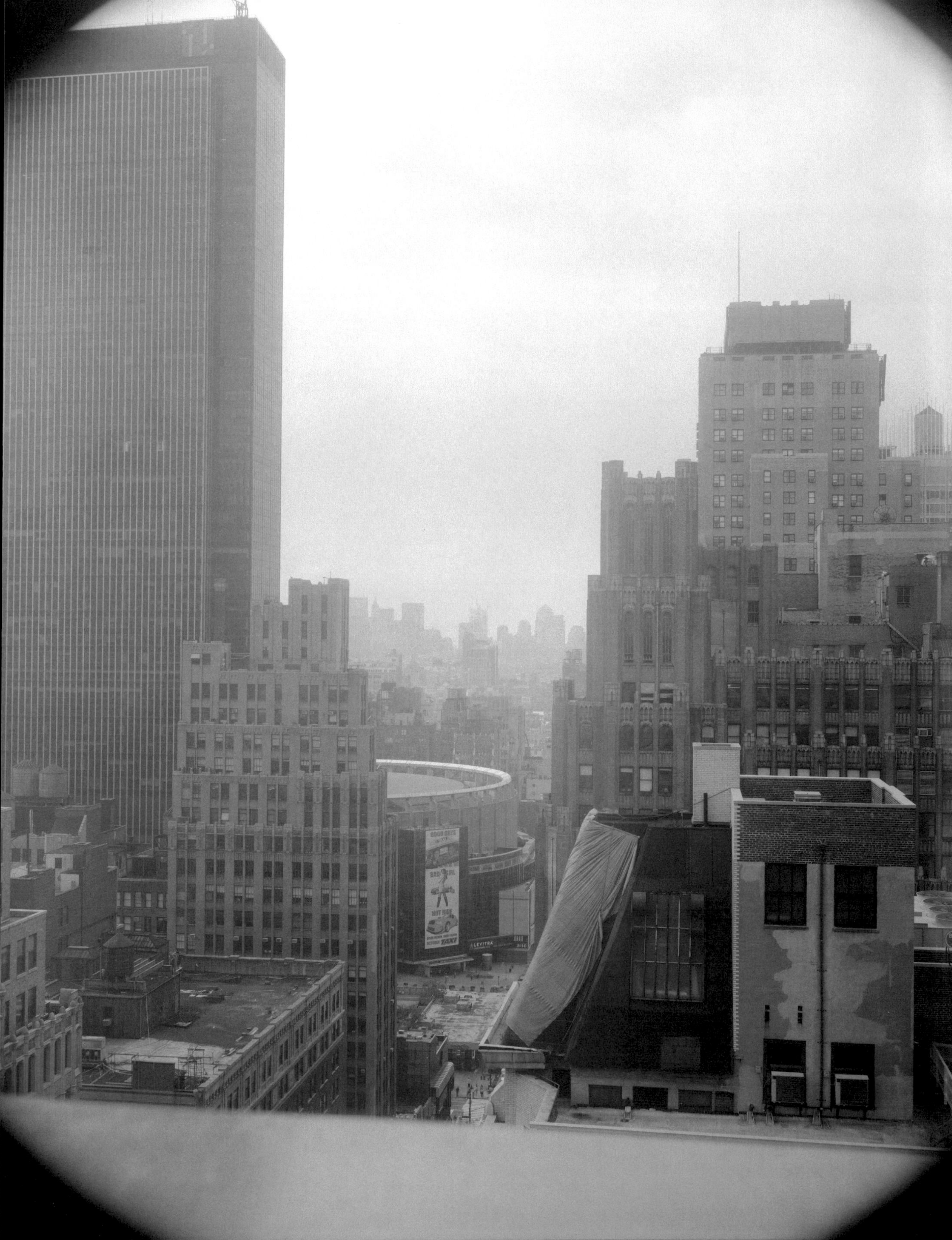
GOOD GUYS
BAD GIRL
HOT RIDE
TAXI
LEVITRA

September 25, 2004

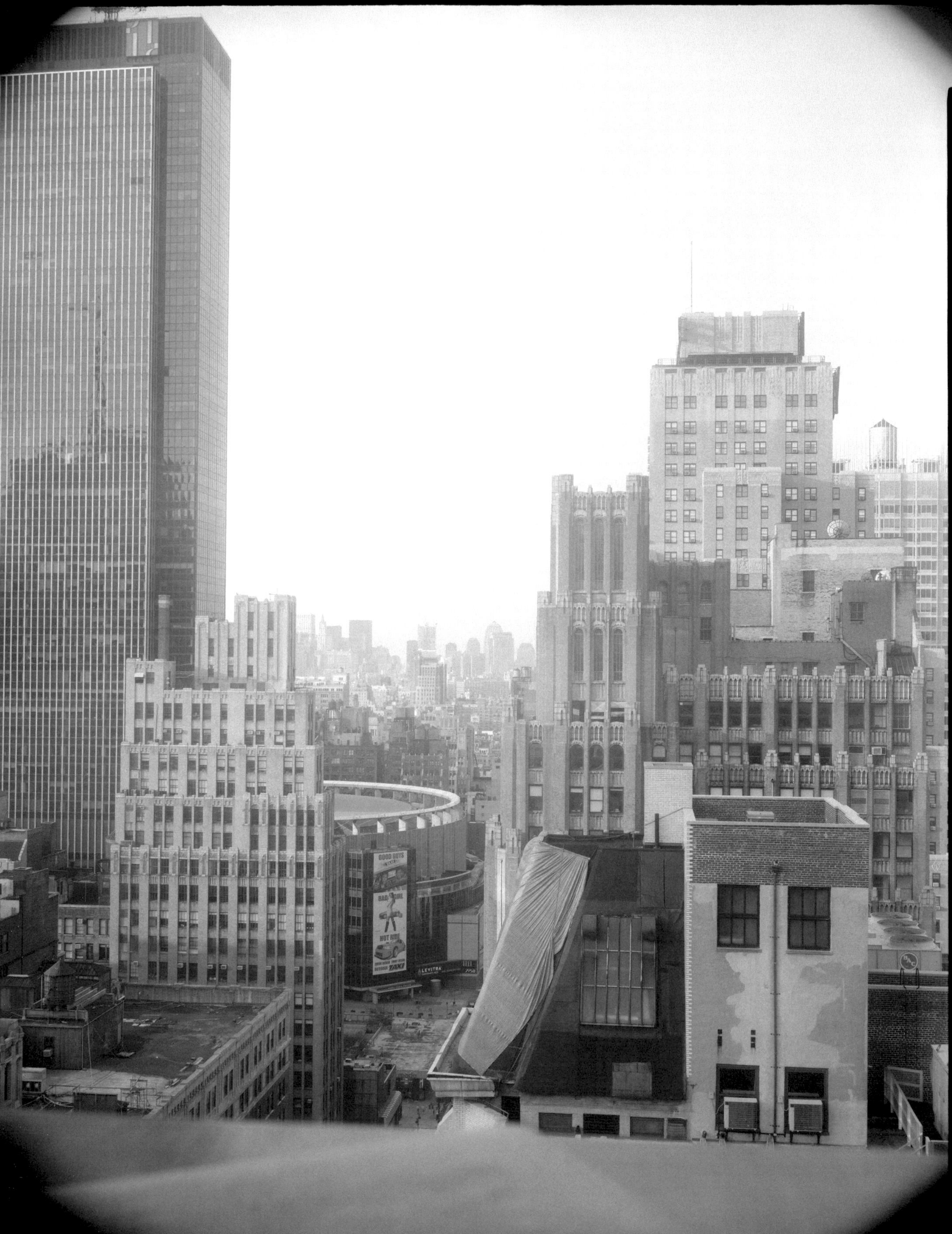

GOOD GUYS
BAD GIRL
HOT RIDE
TAXI
LEVITRA

September 26, 2004

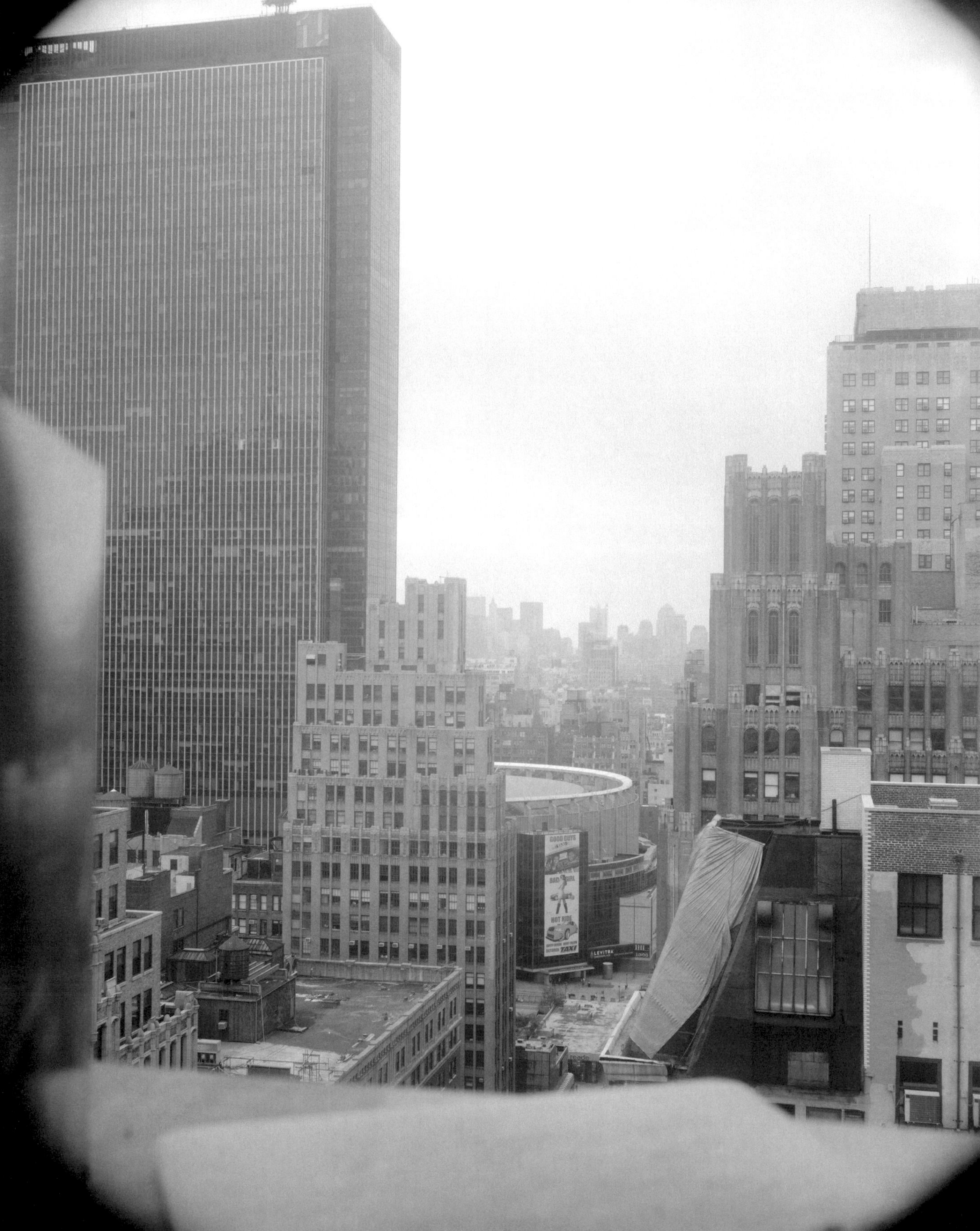
GOOD GUYS
BAD GIRL
HOT RIDE
TAXI
LEVITRA

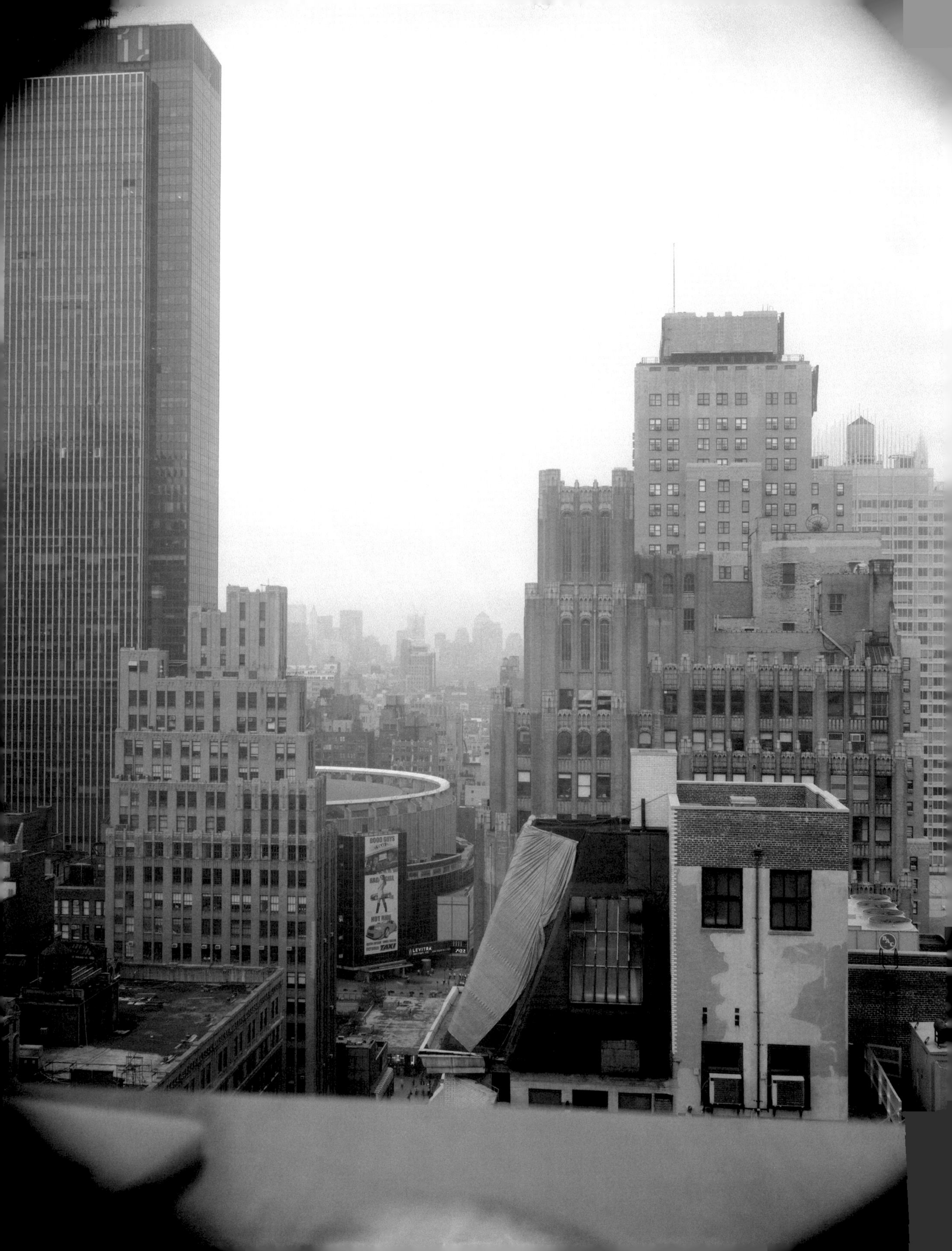

September 28, 2004

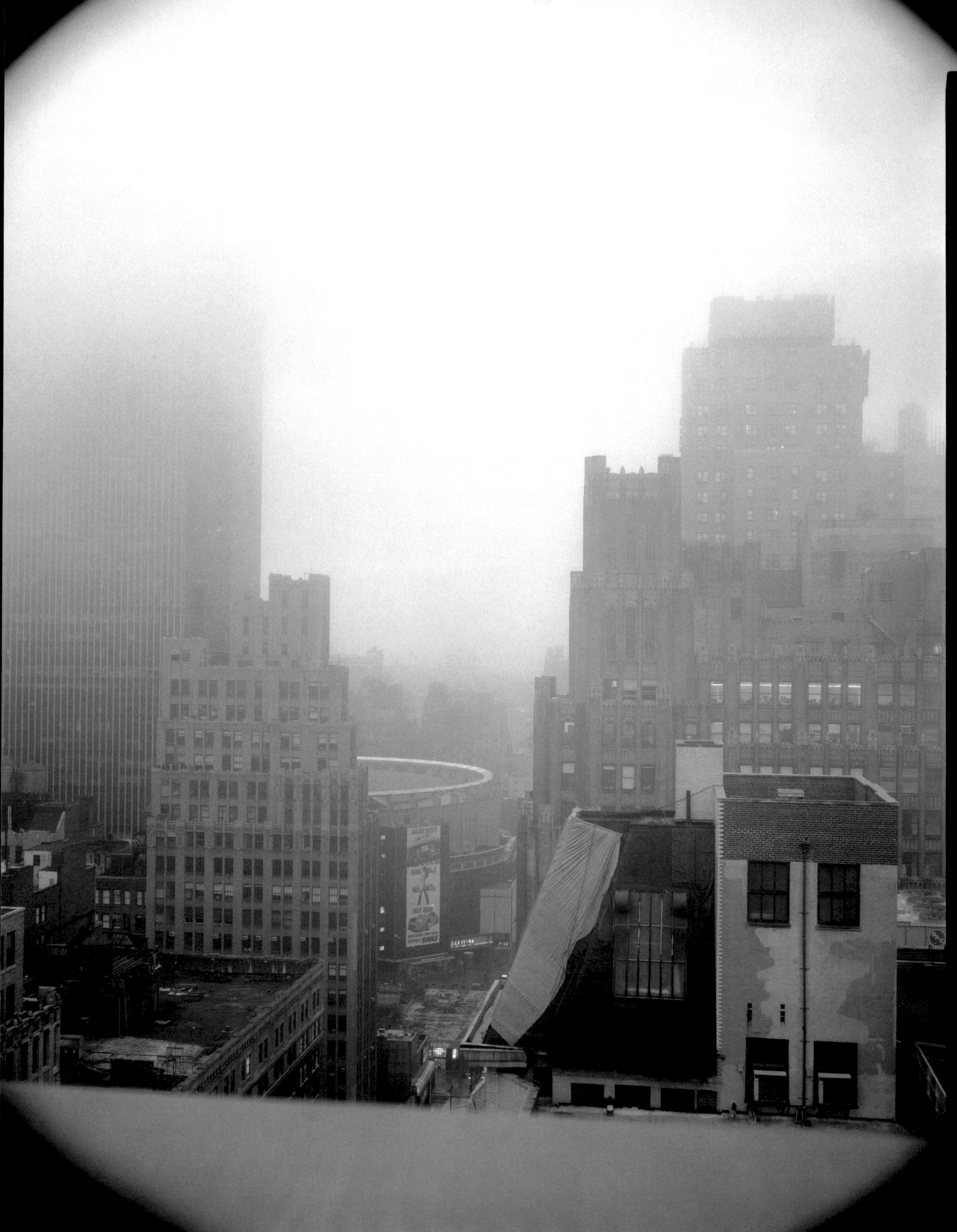

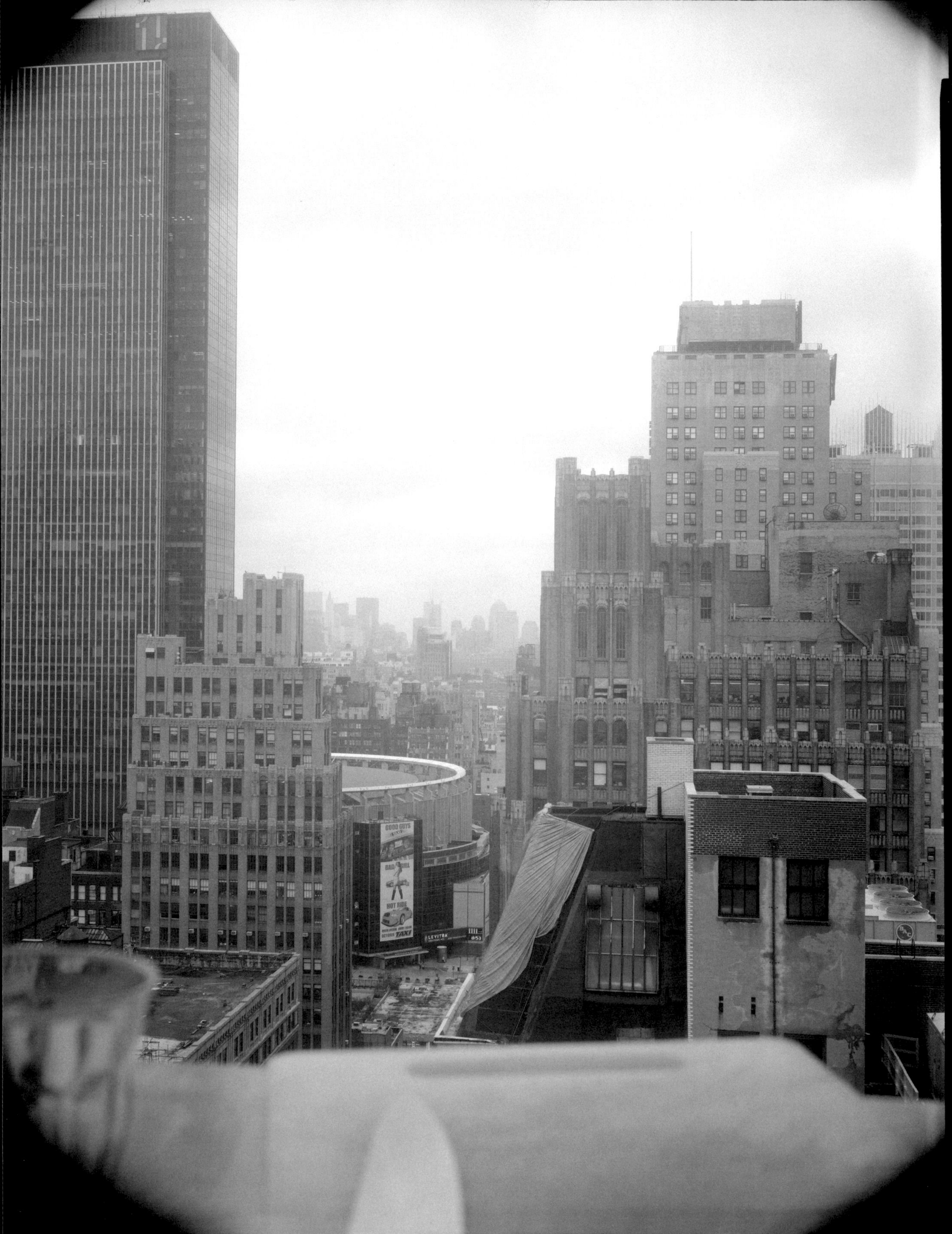

September 30, 2004

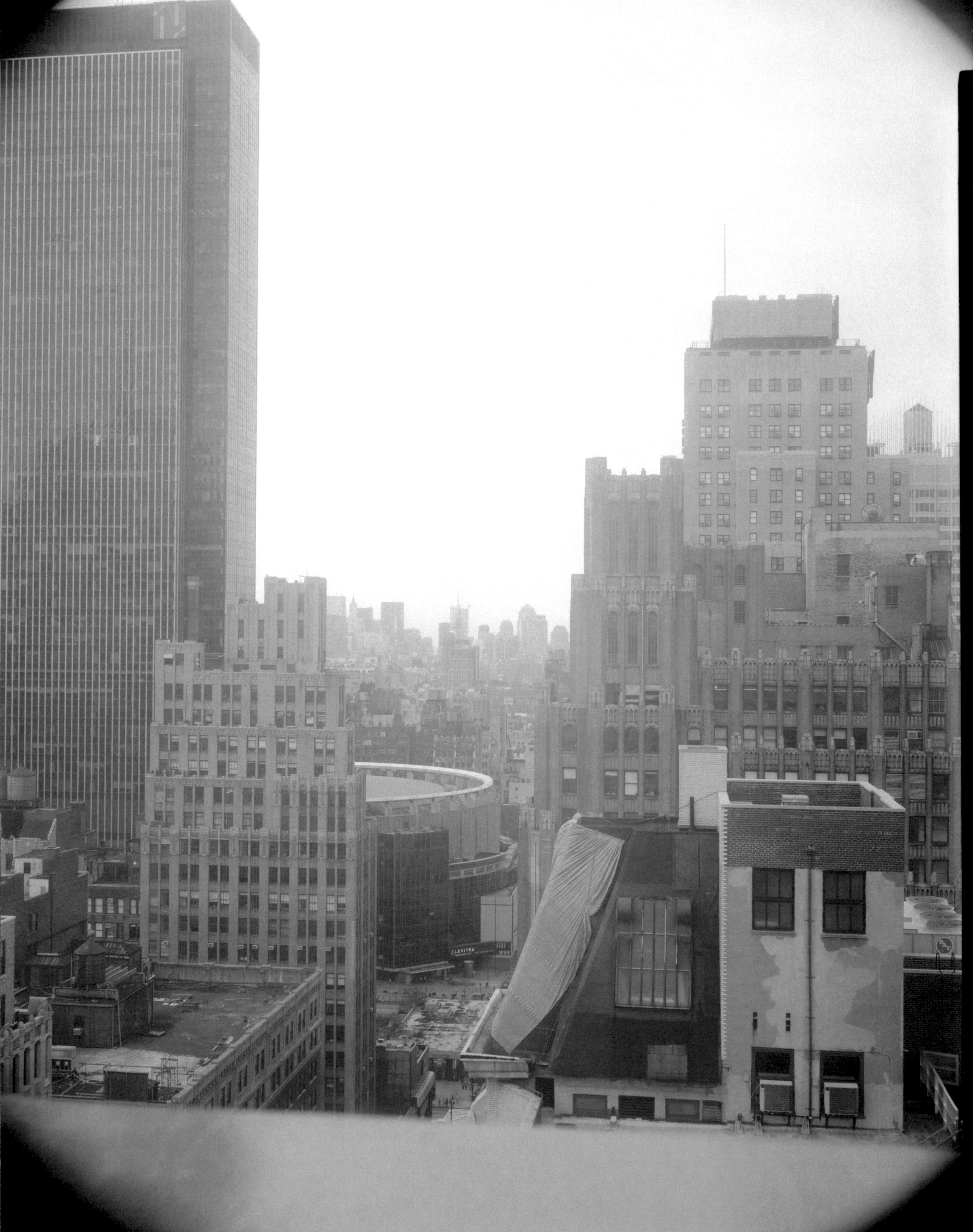

LEVITRA

September 1, 2005

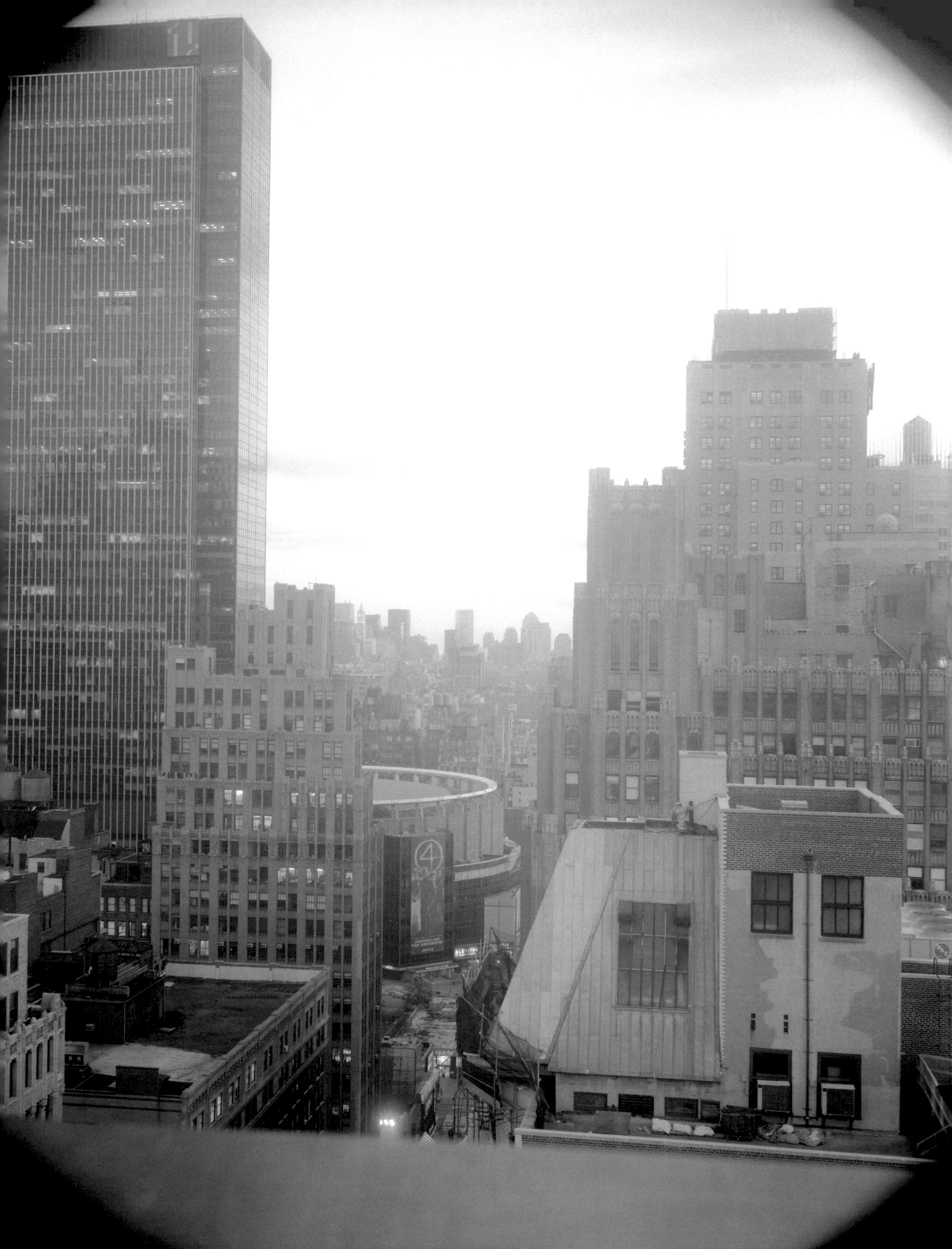

September 2, 2005

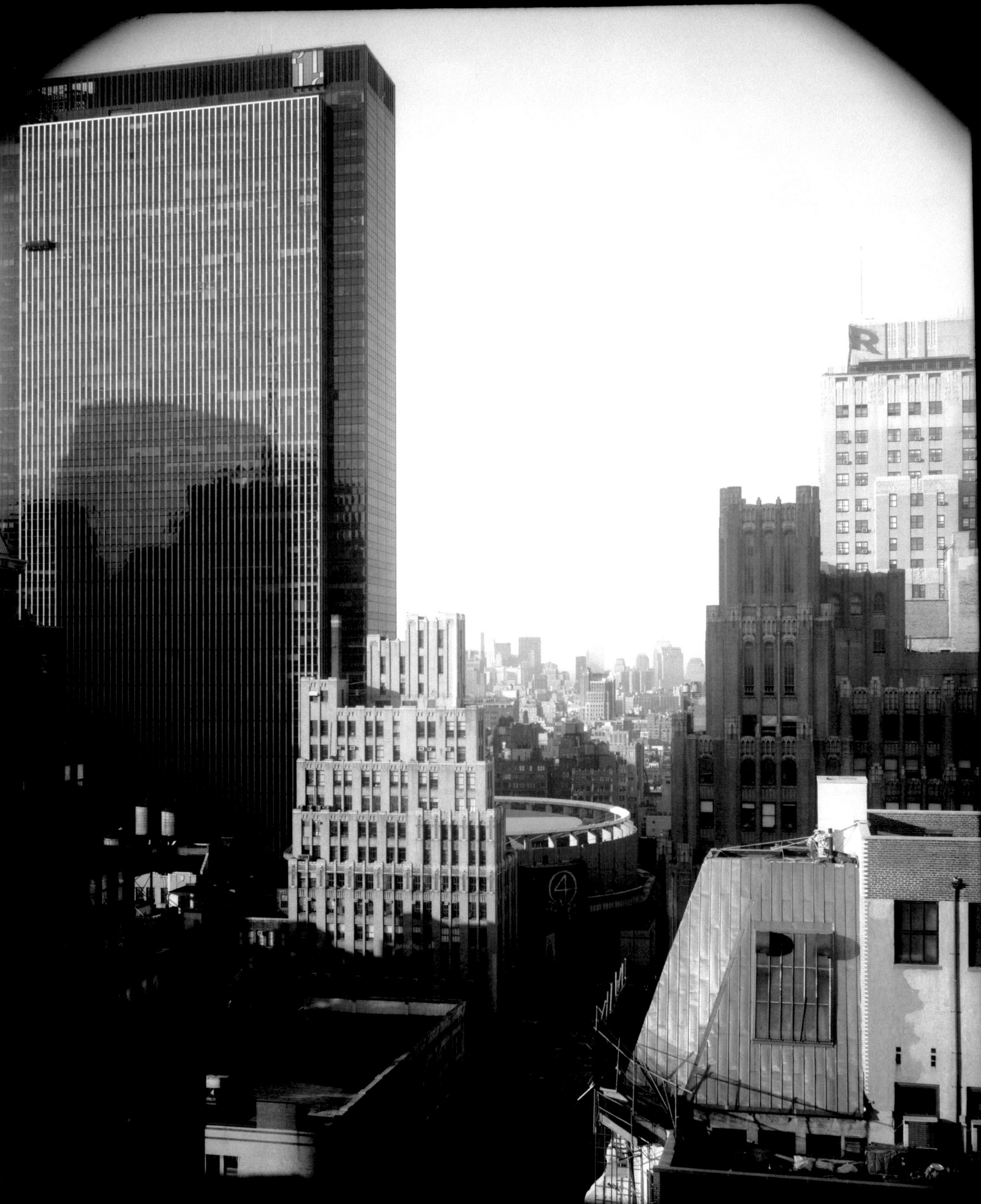

September 3, 2005

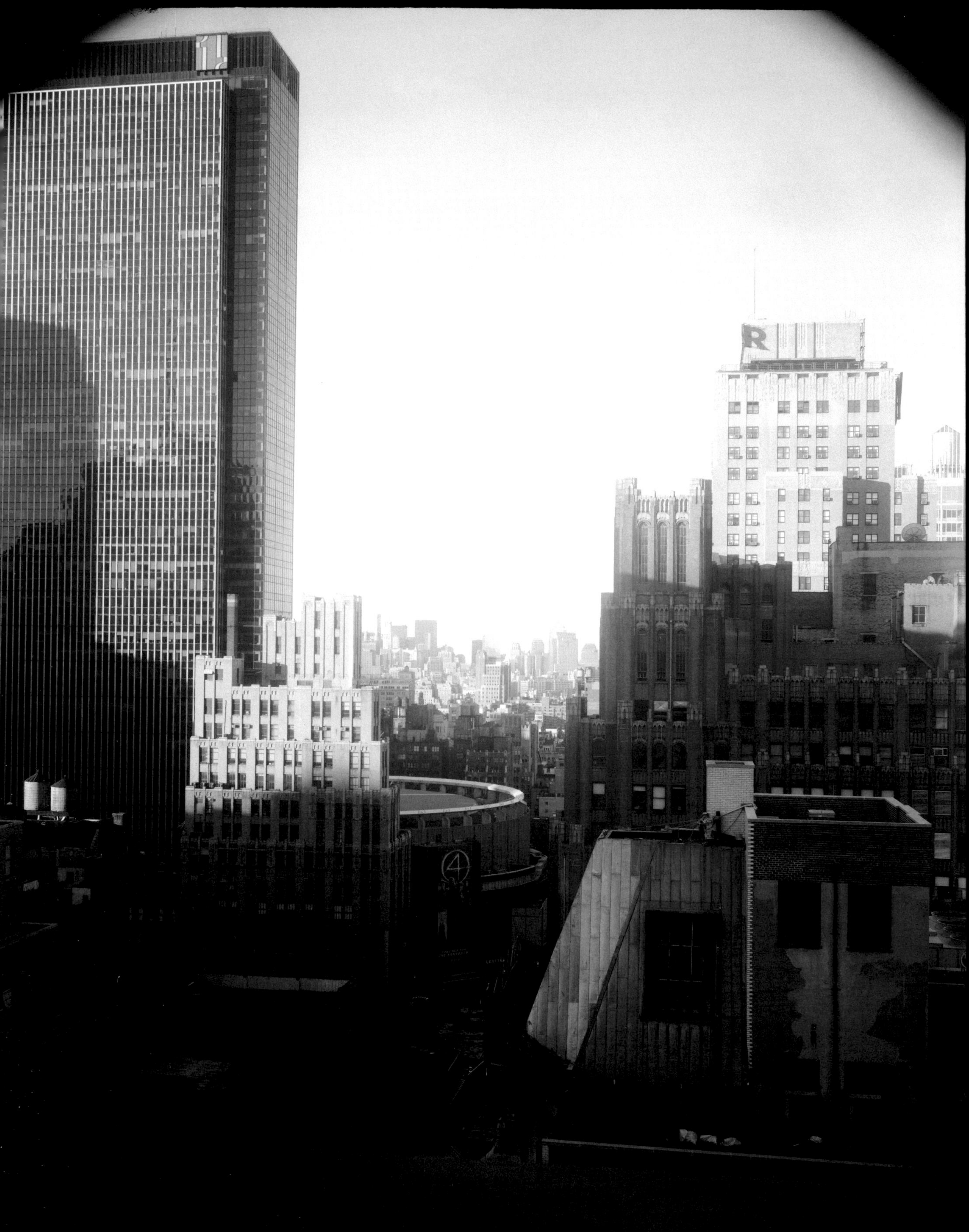

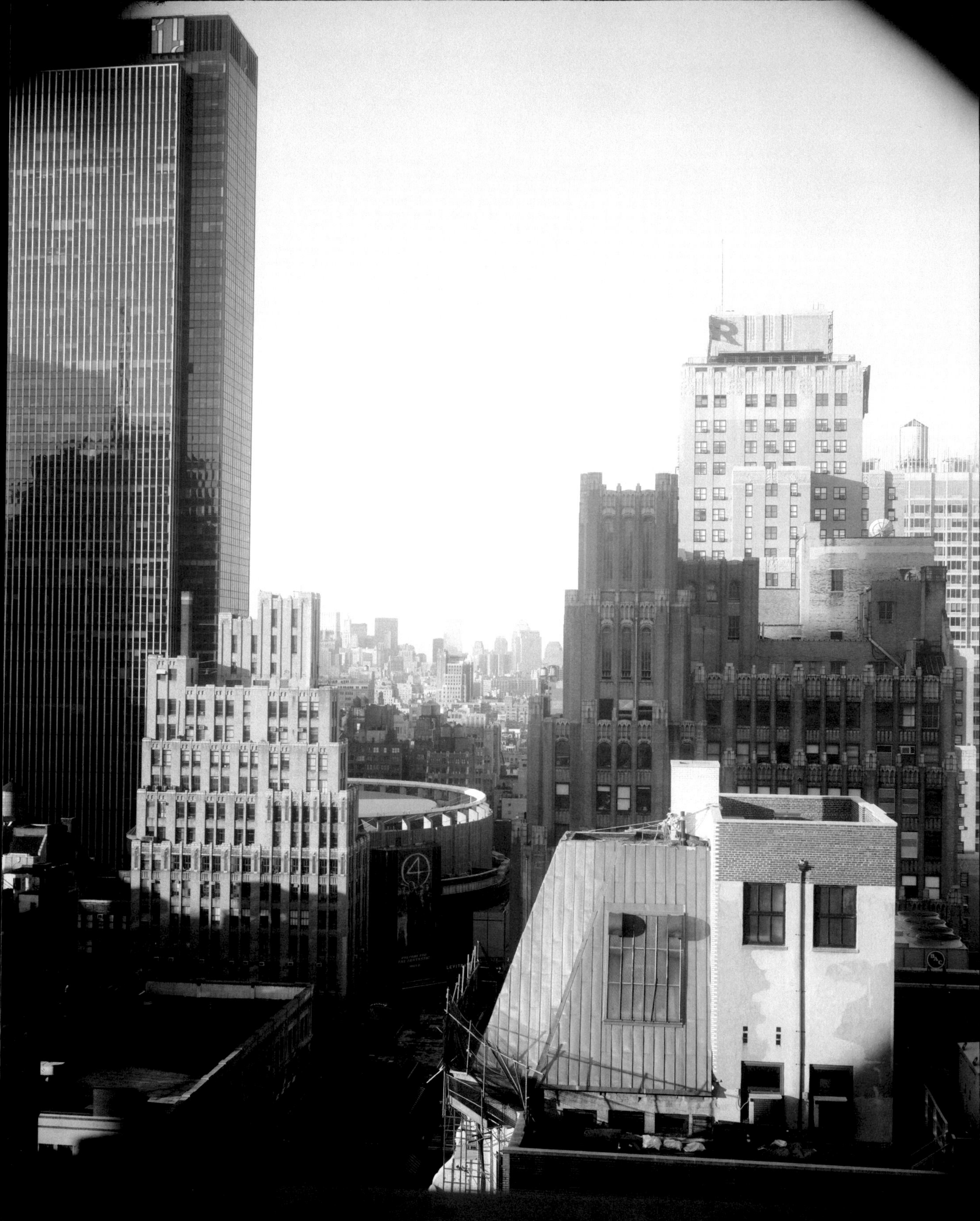

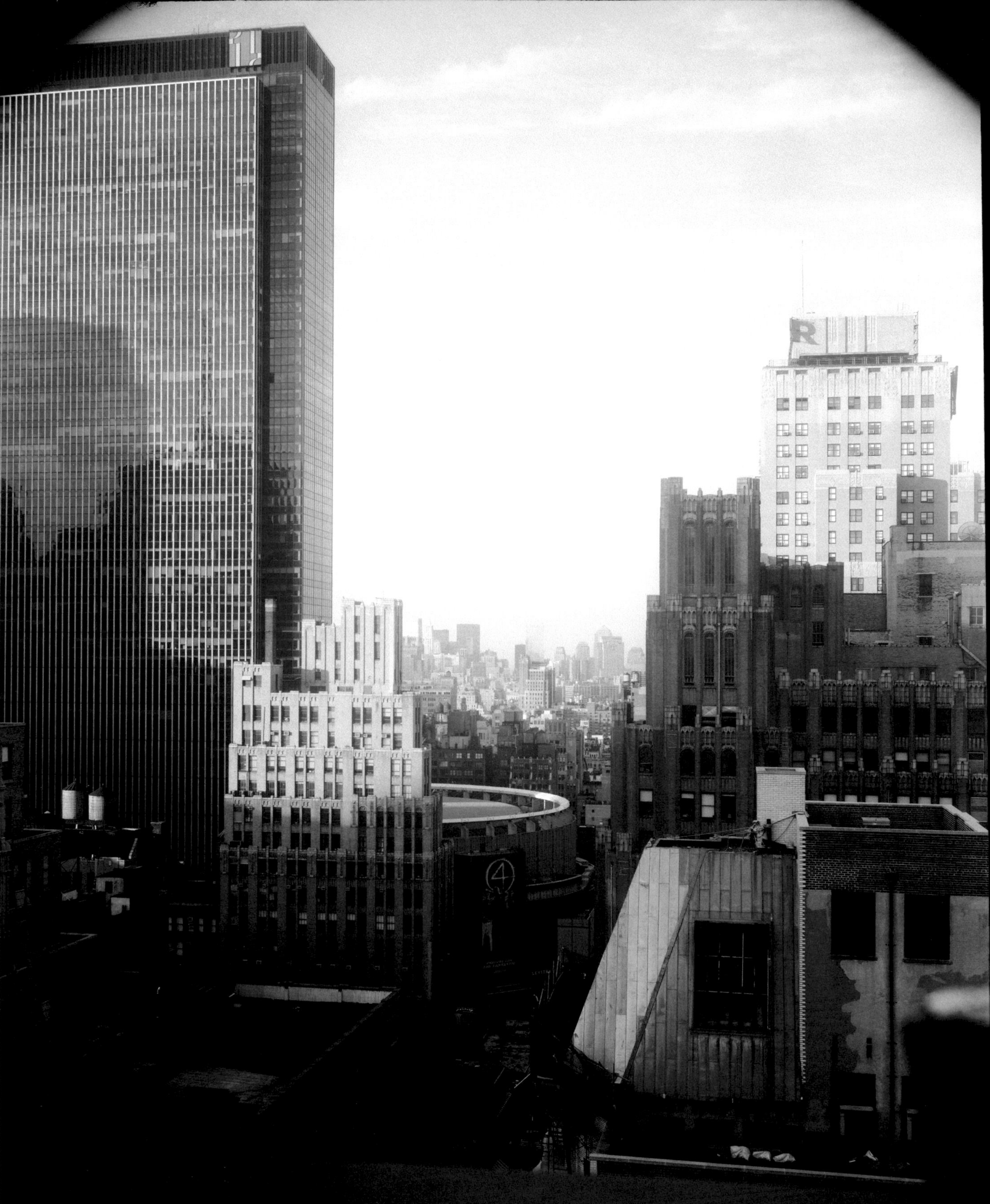

September 6, 2005

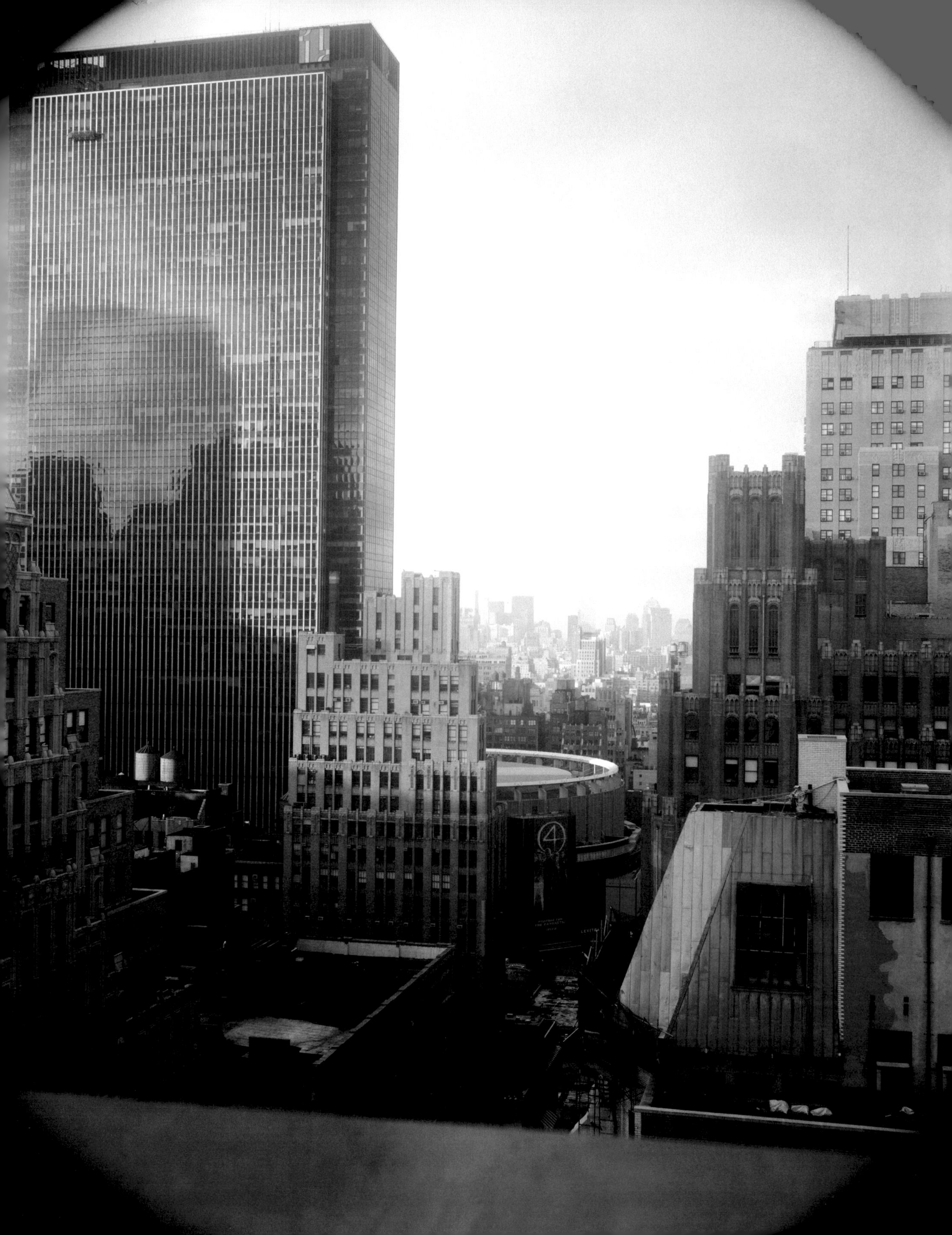

September 7, 2005

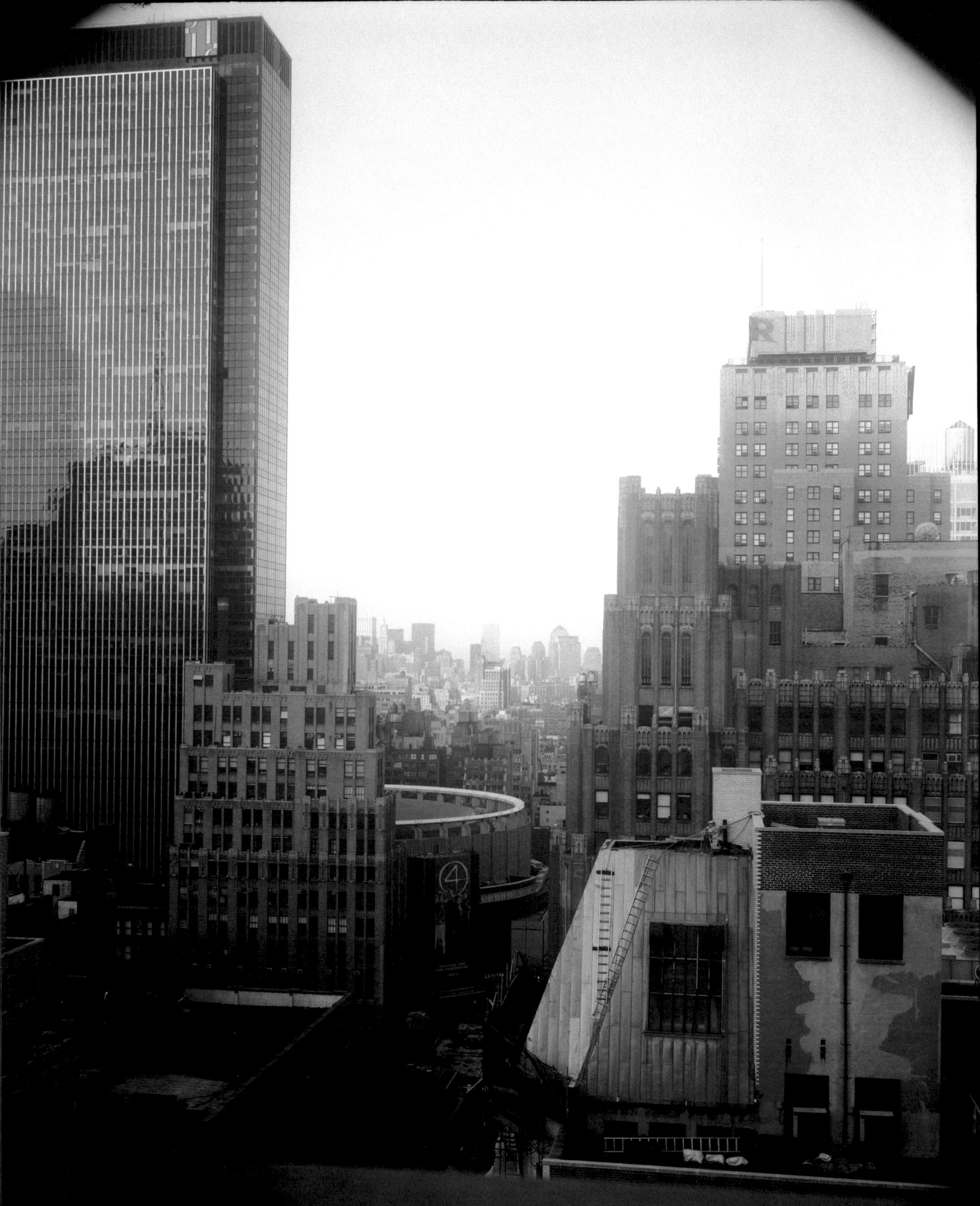

September 8, 2005

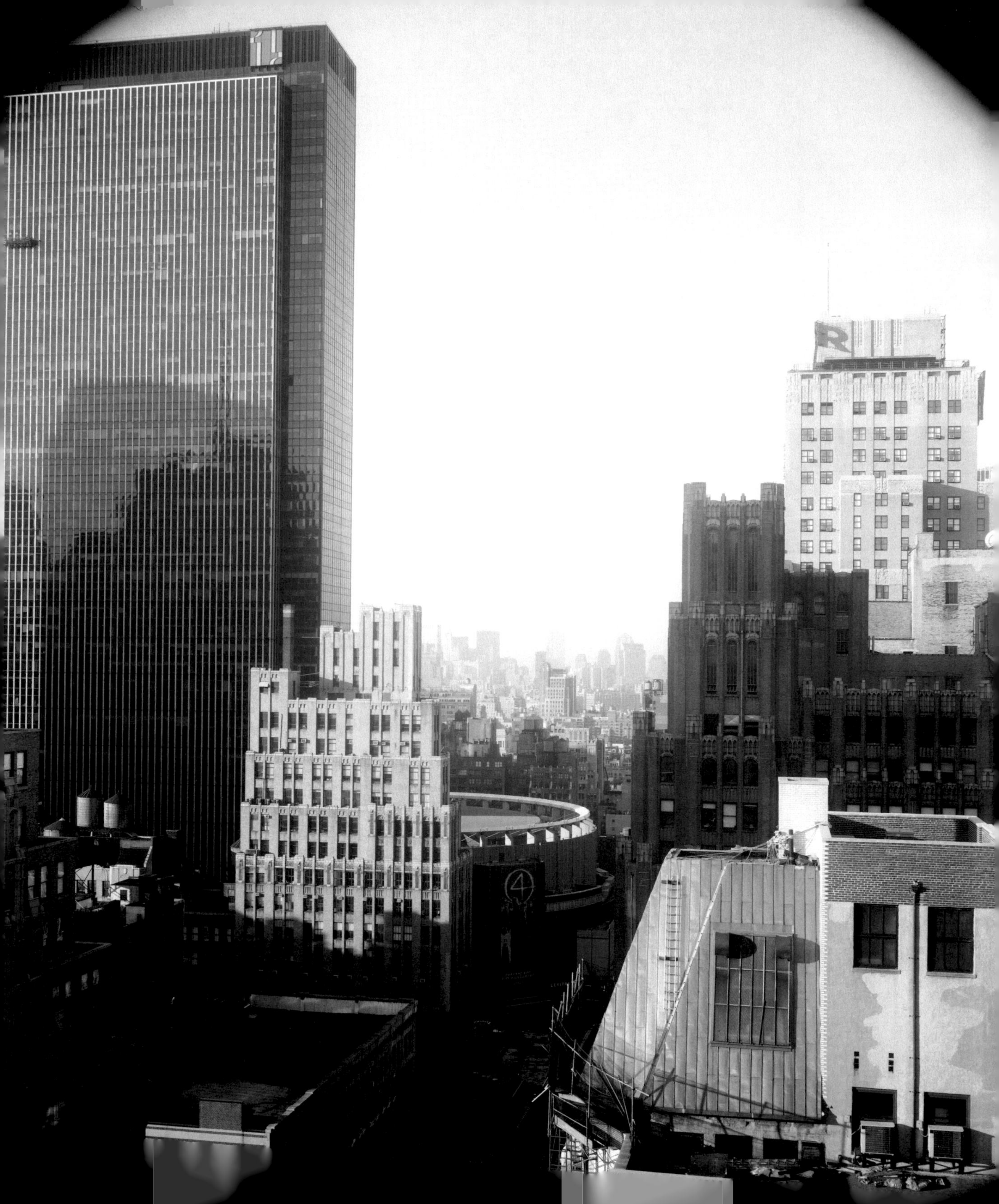

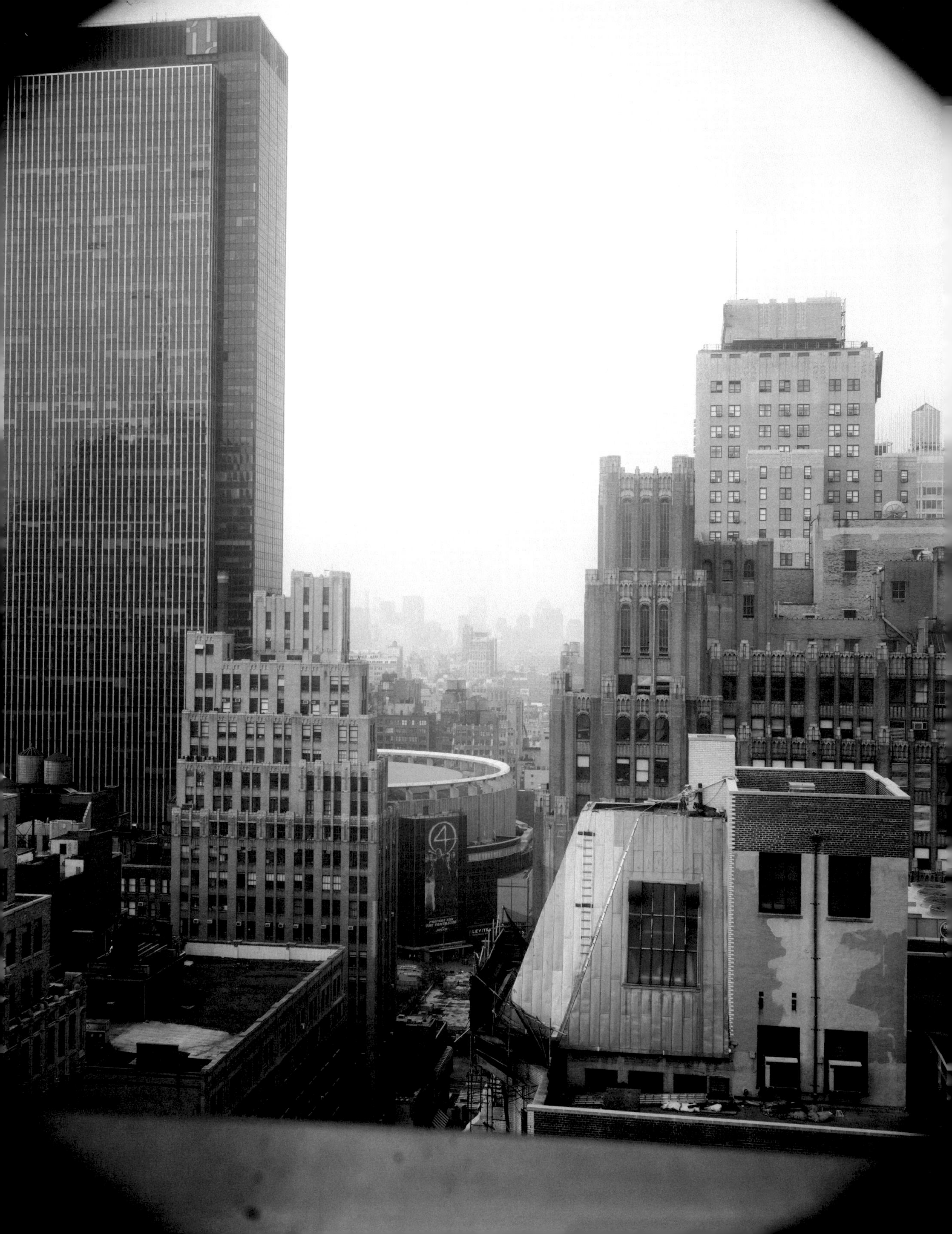

September 10, 2005

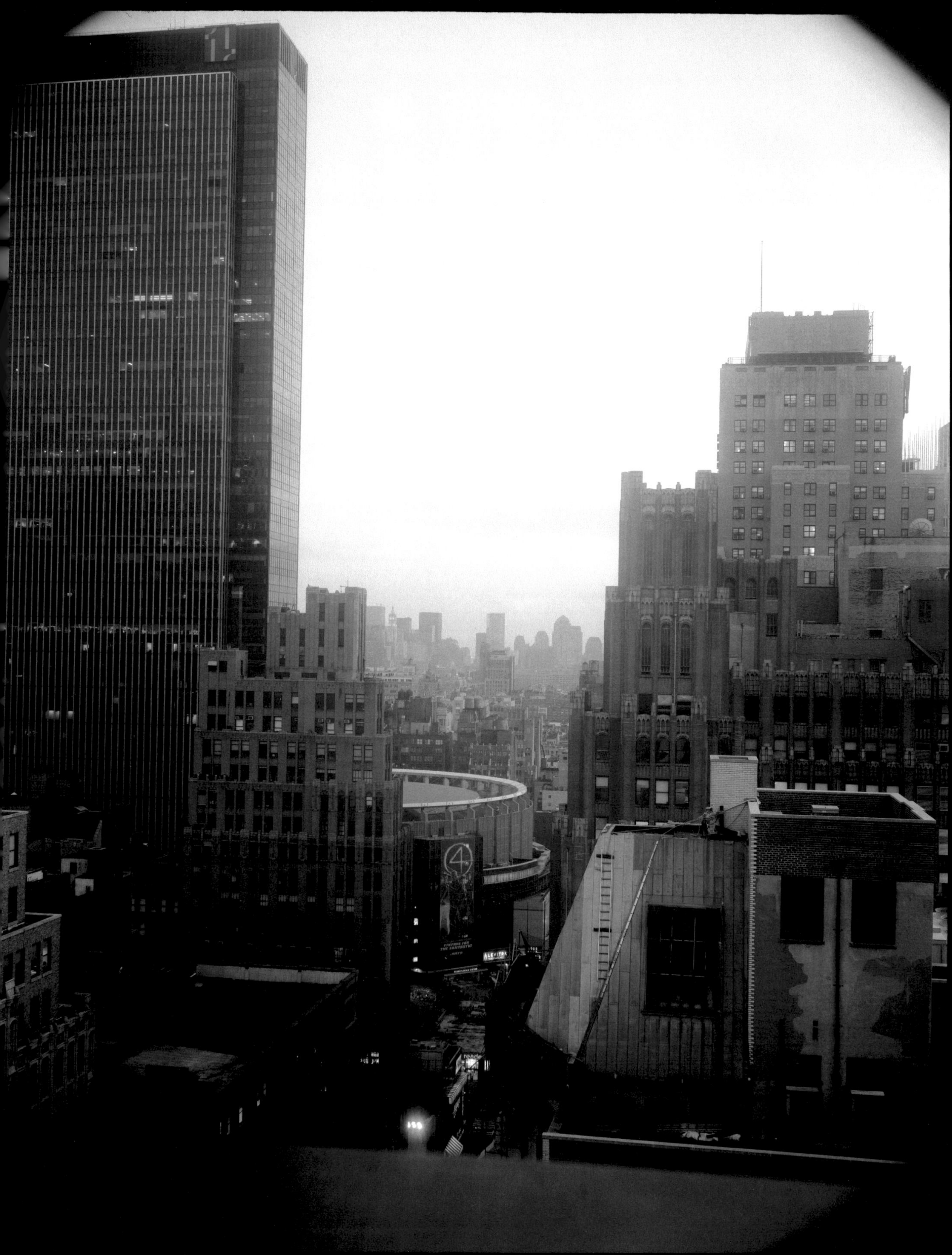

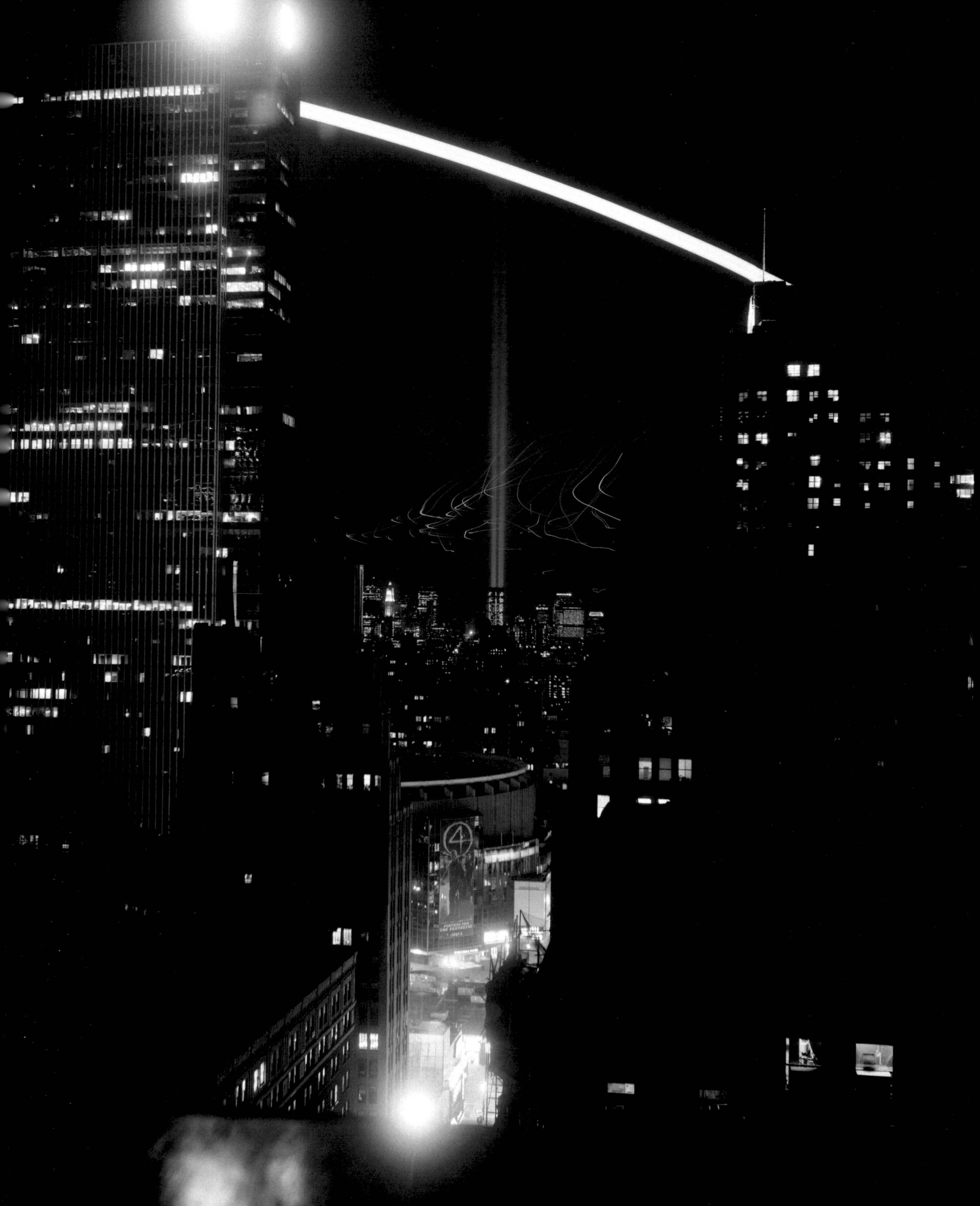

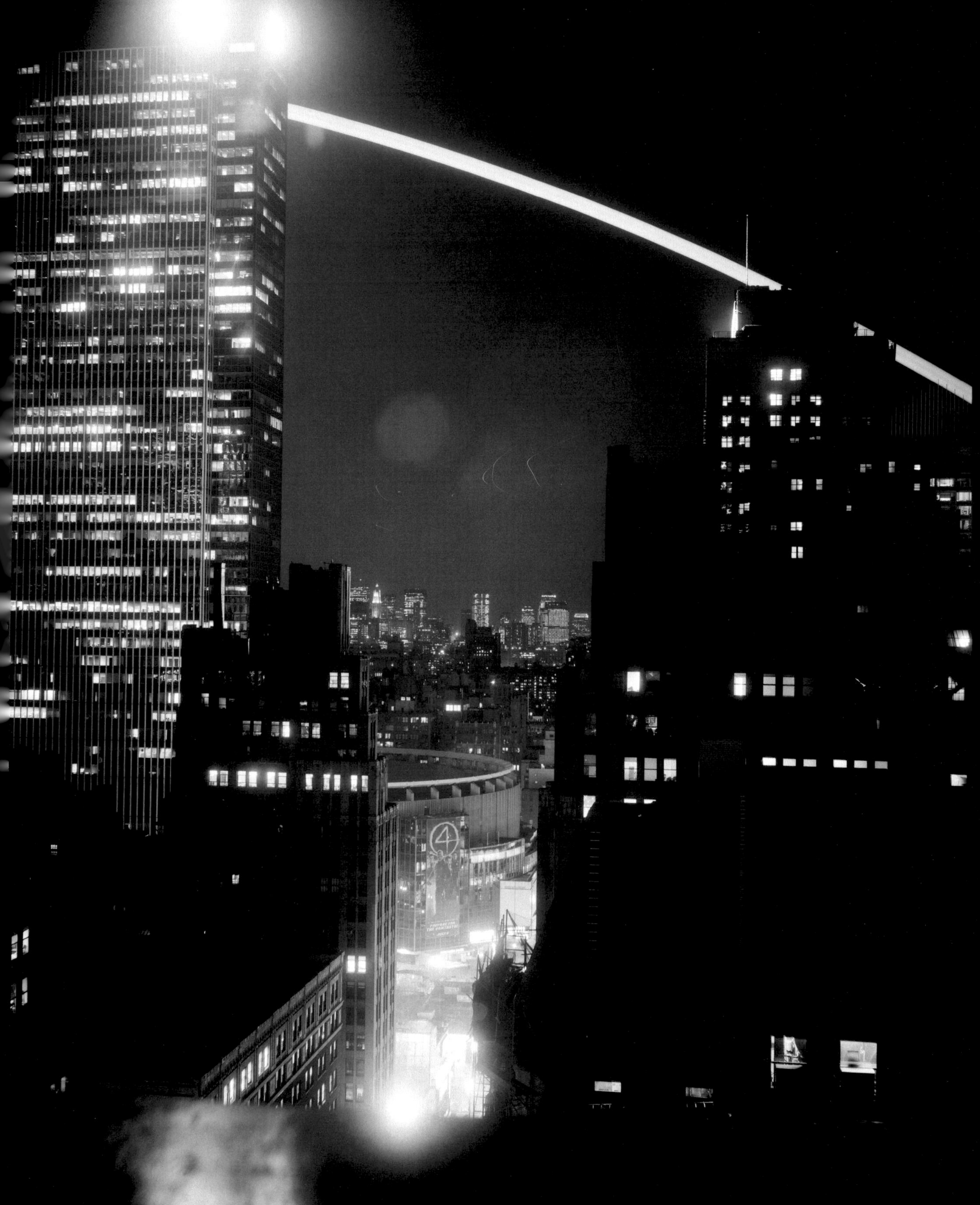

September 13, 2005

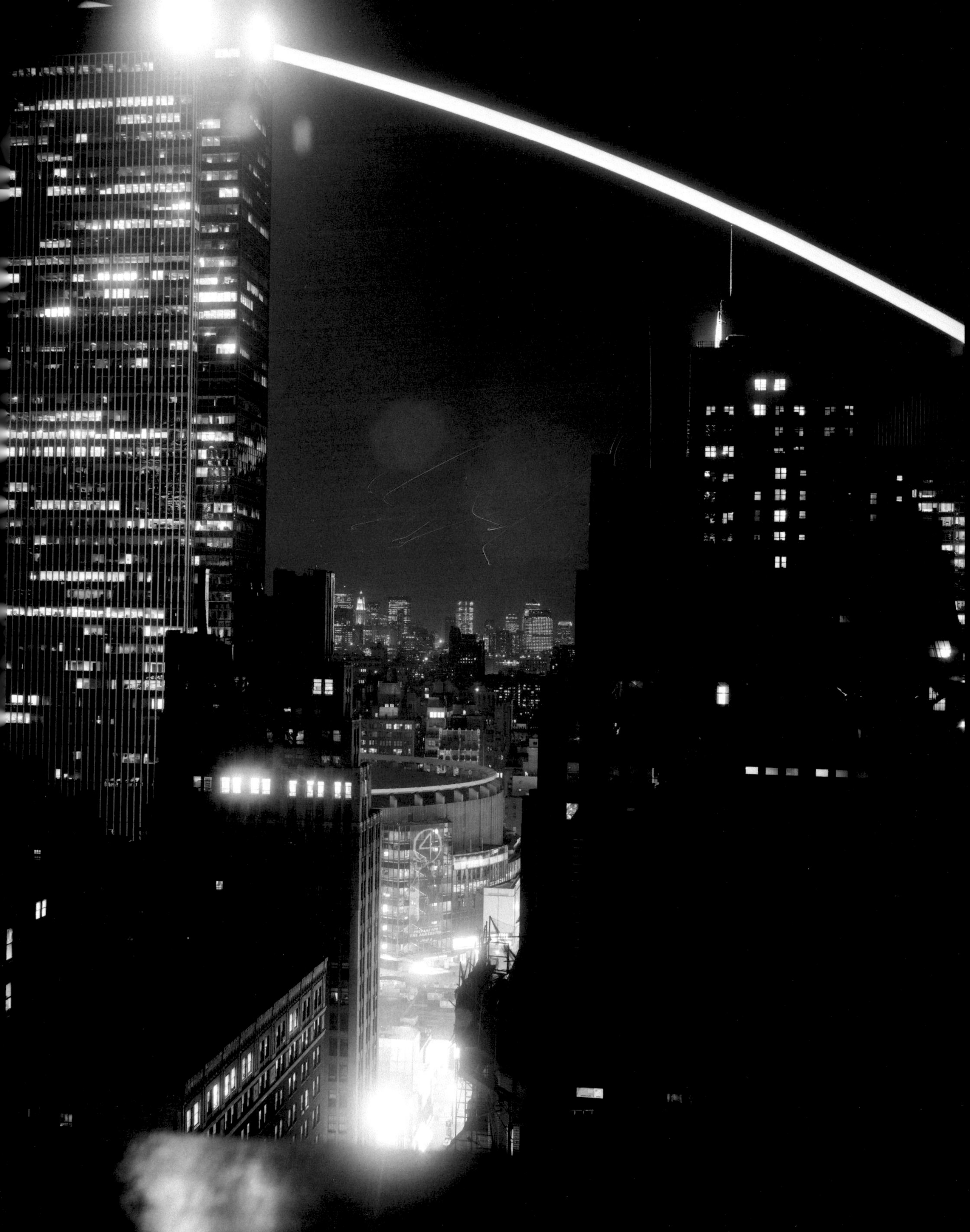

September 14, 2005

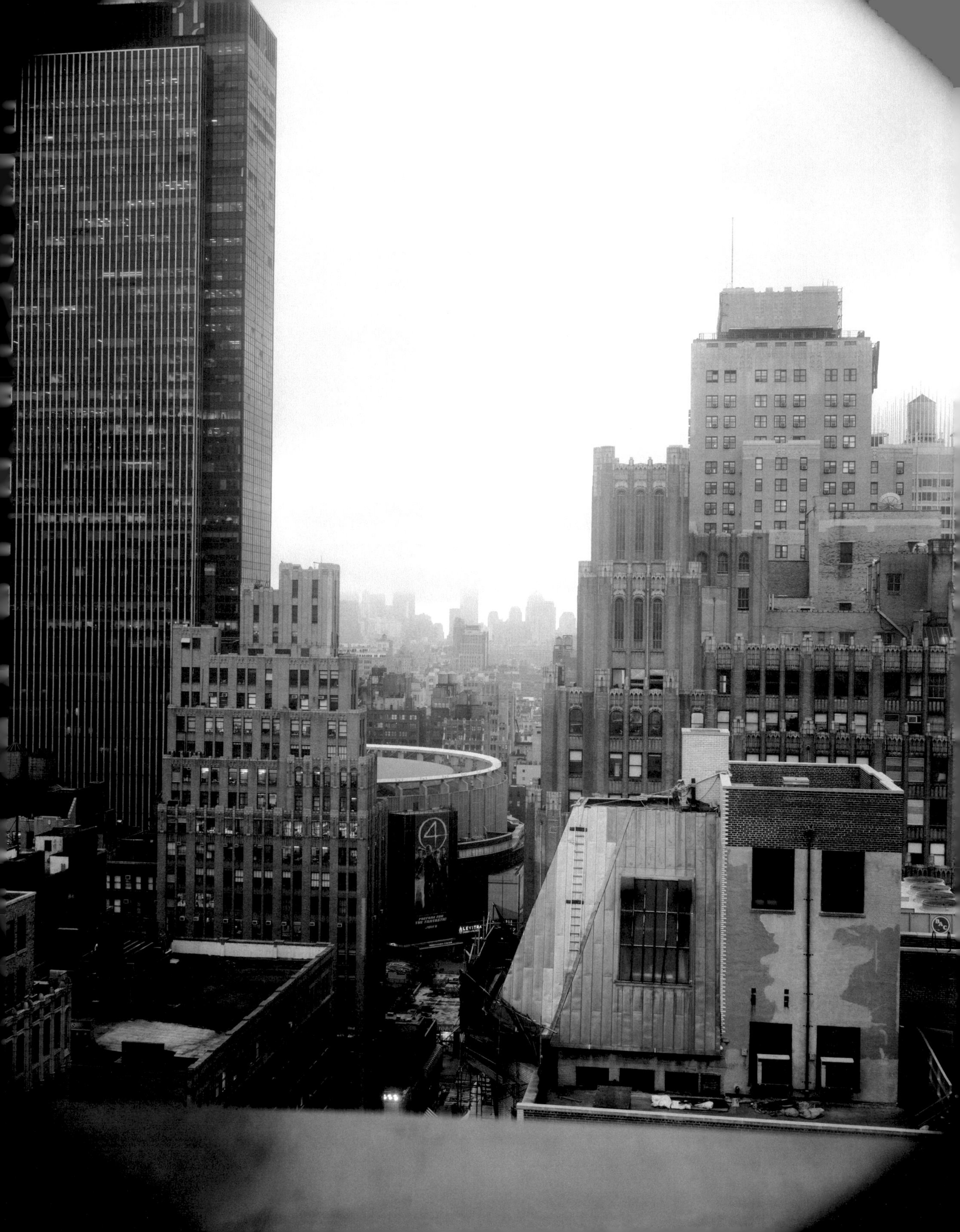

September 15, 2005

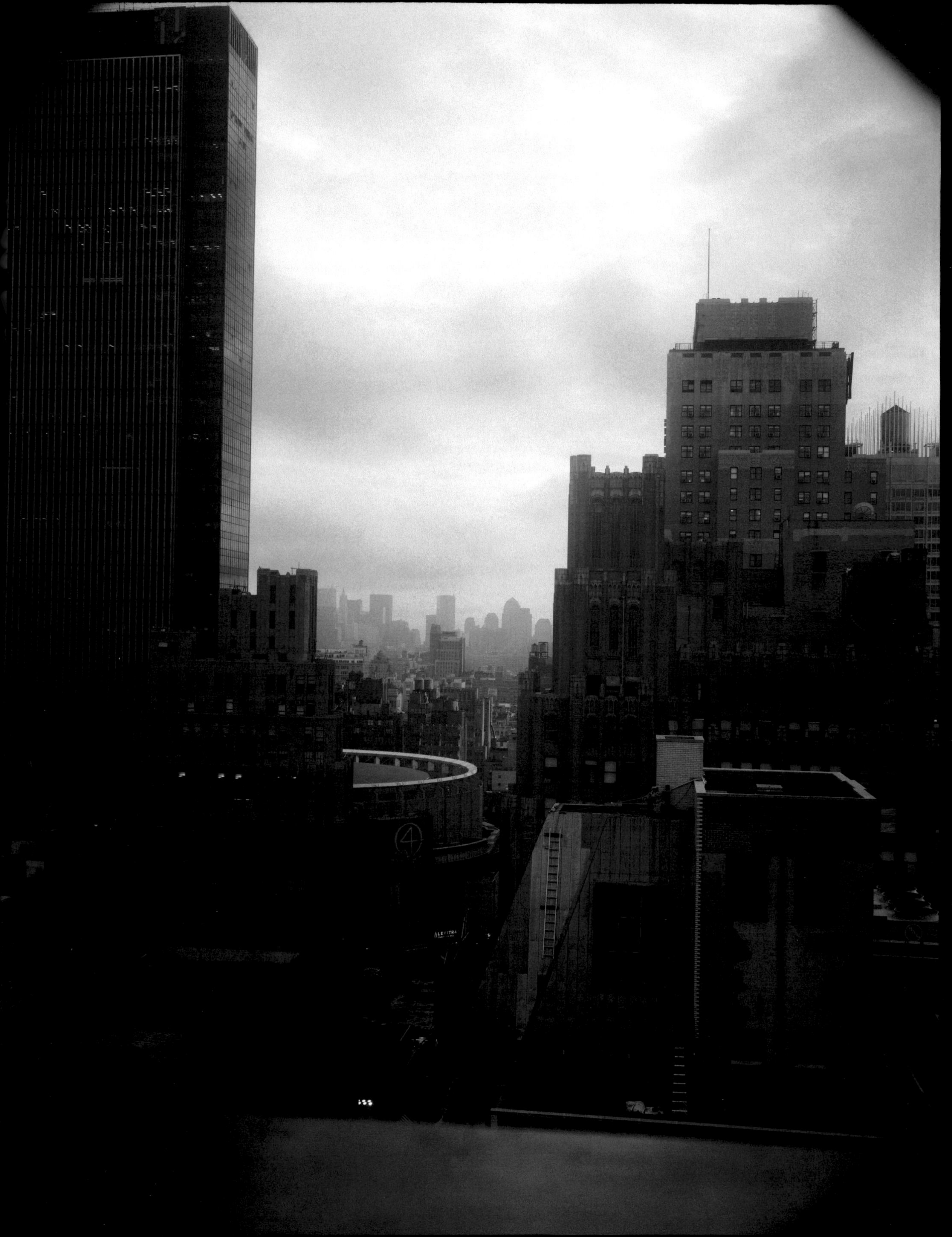

September 16, 2005

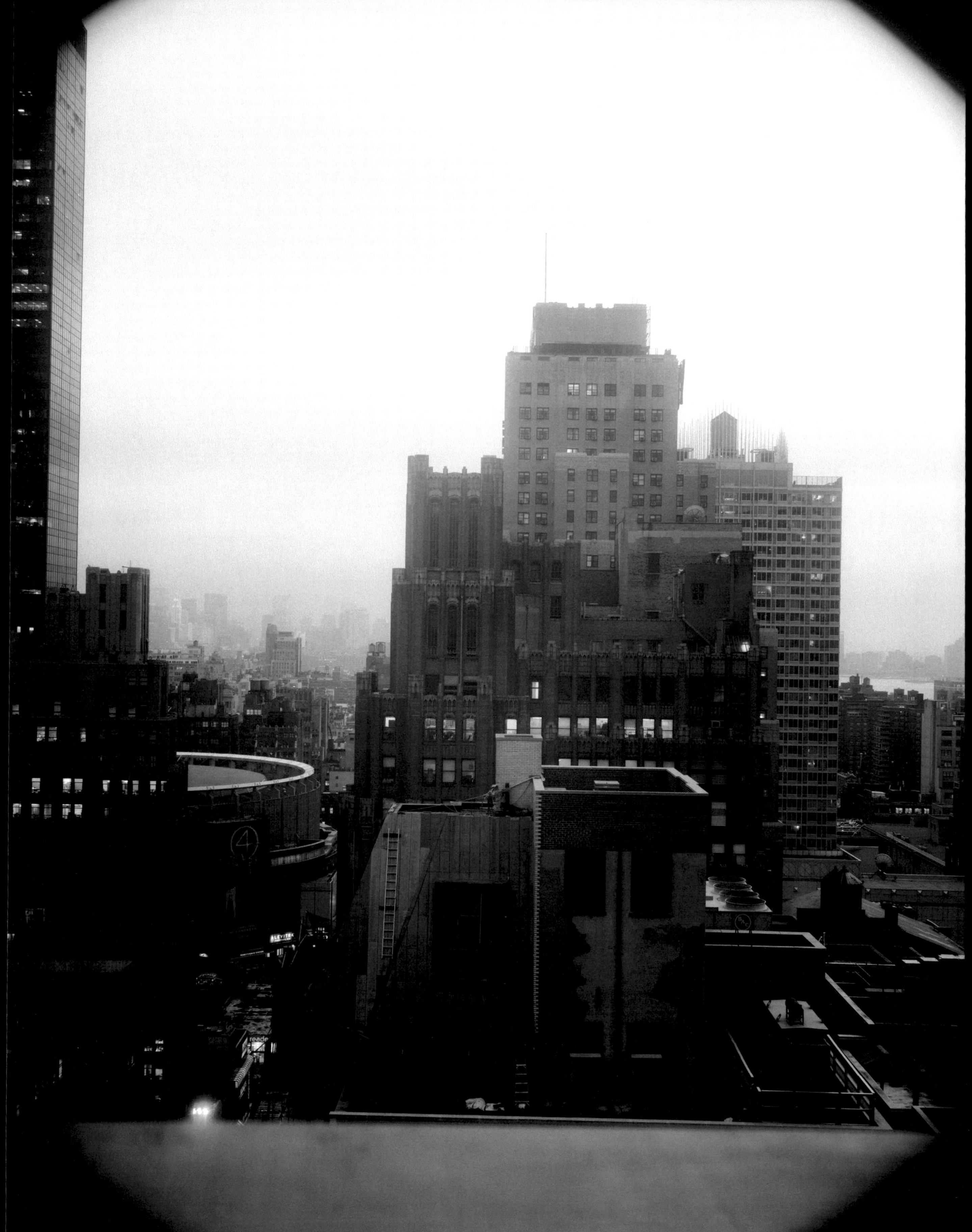

September 17, 2005

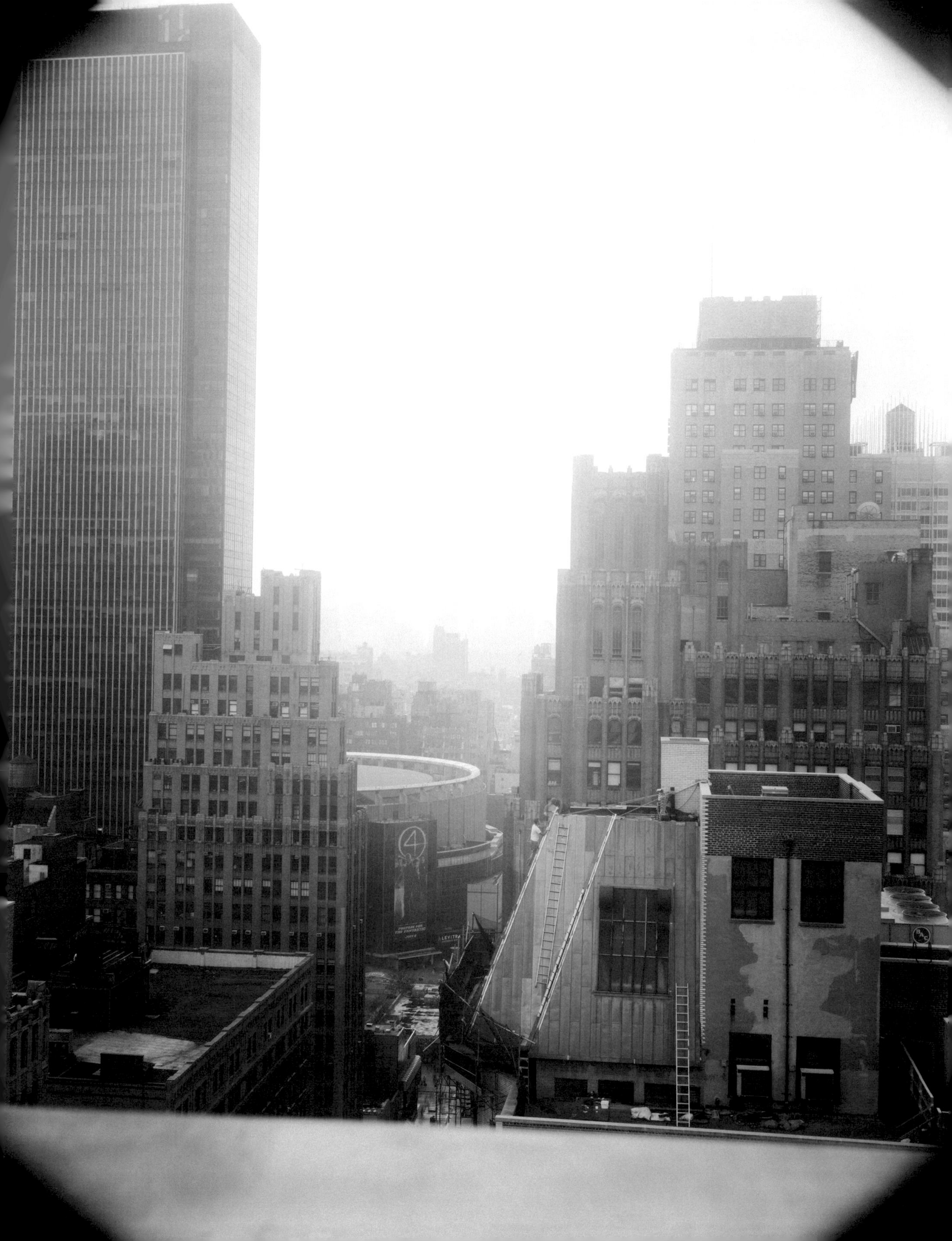

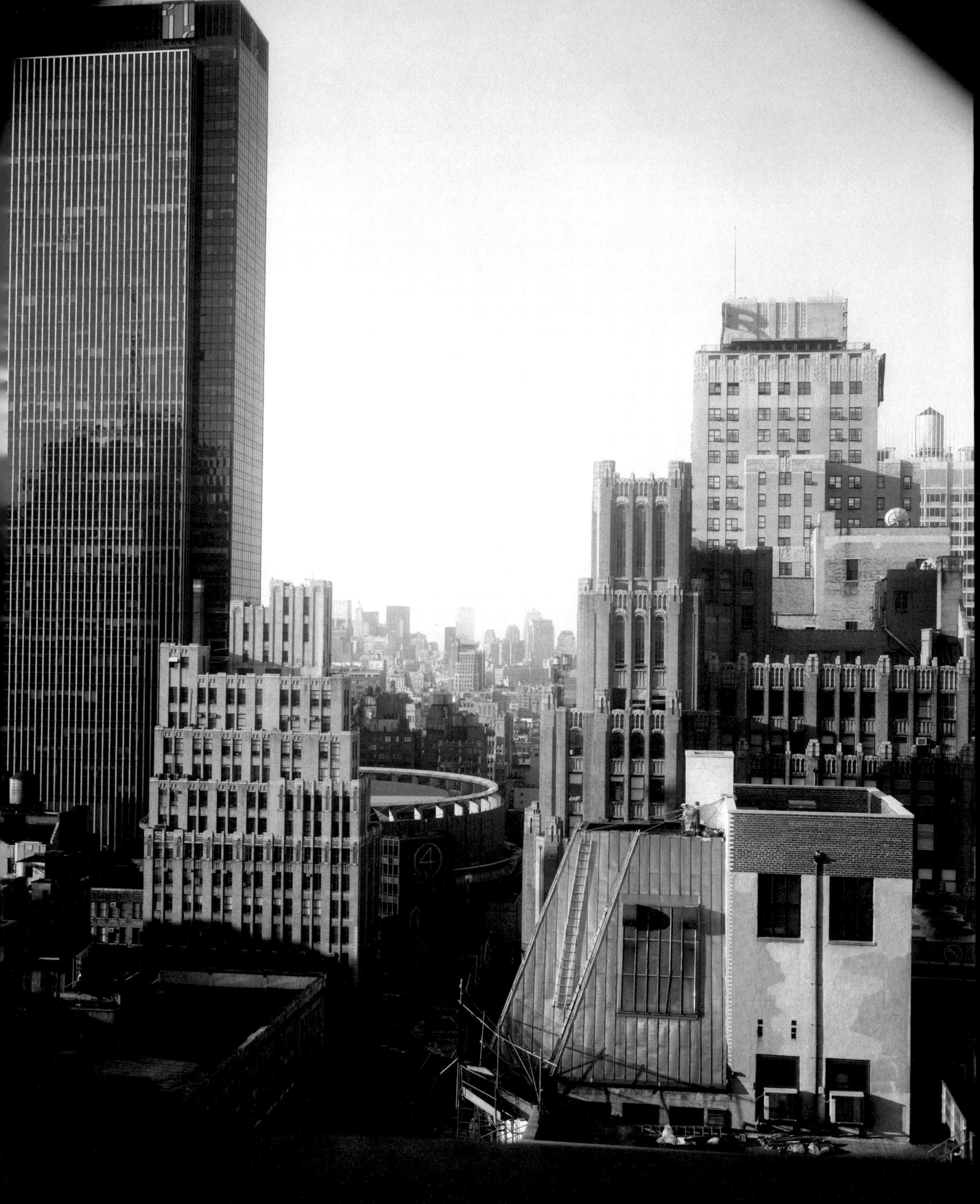

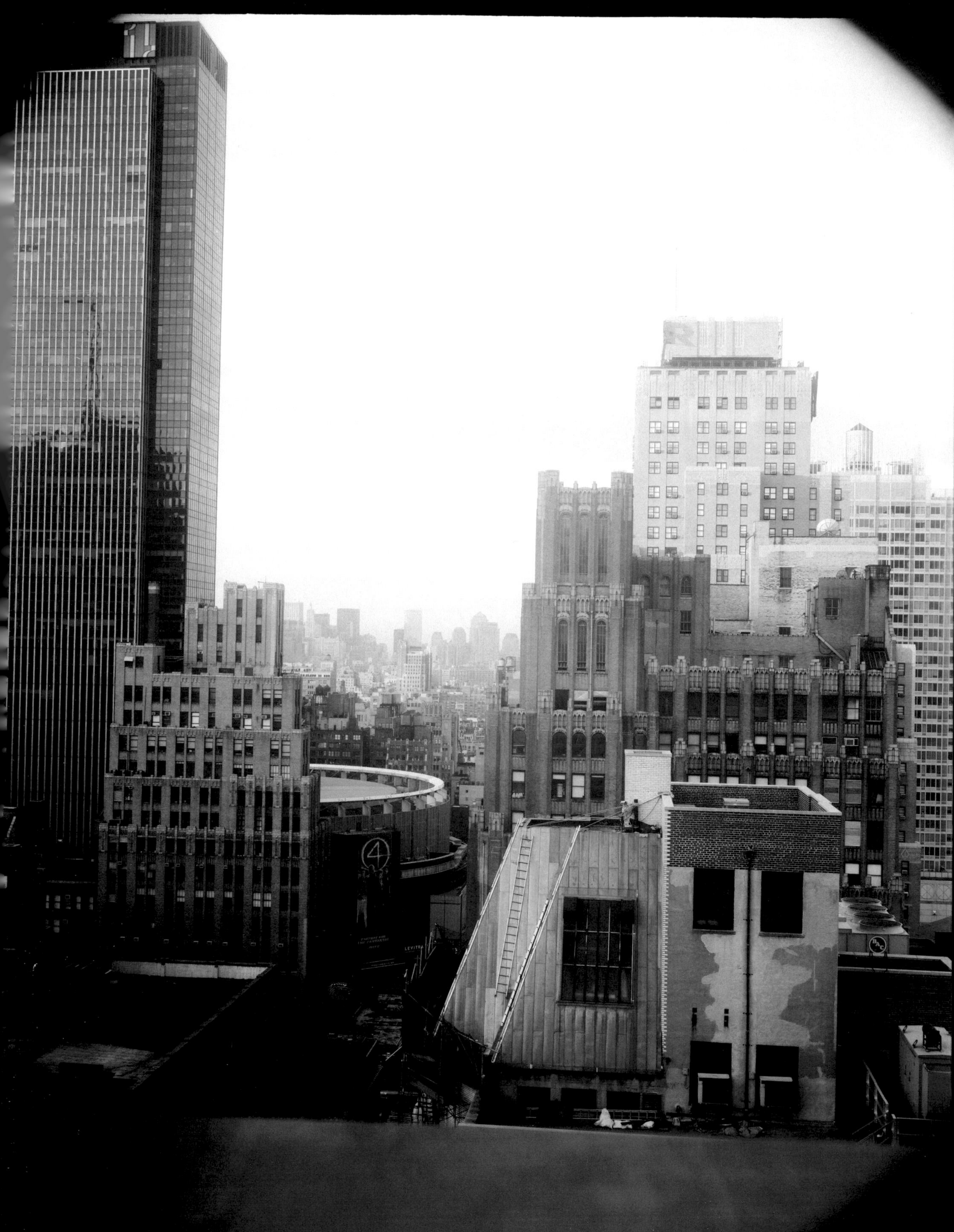

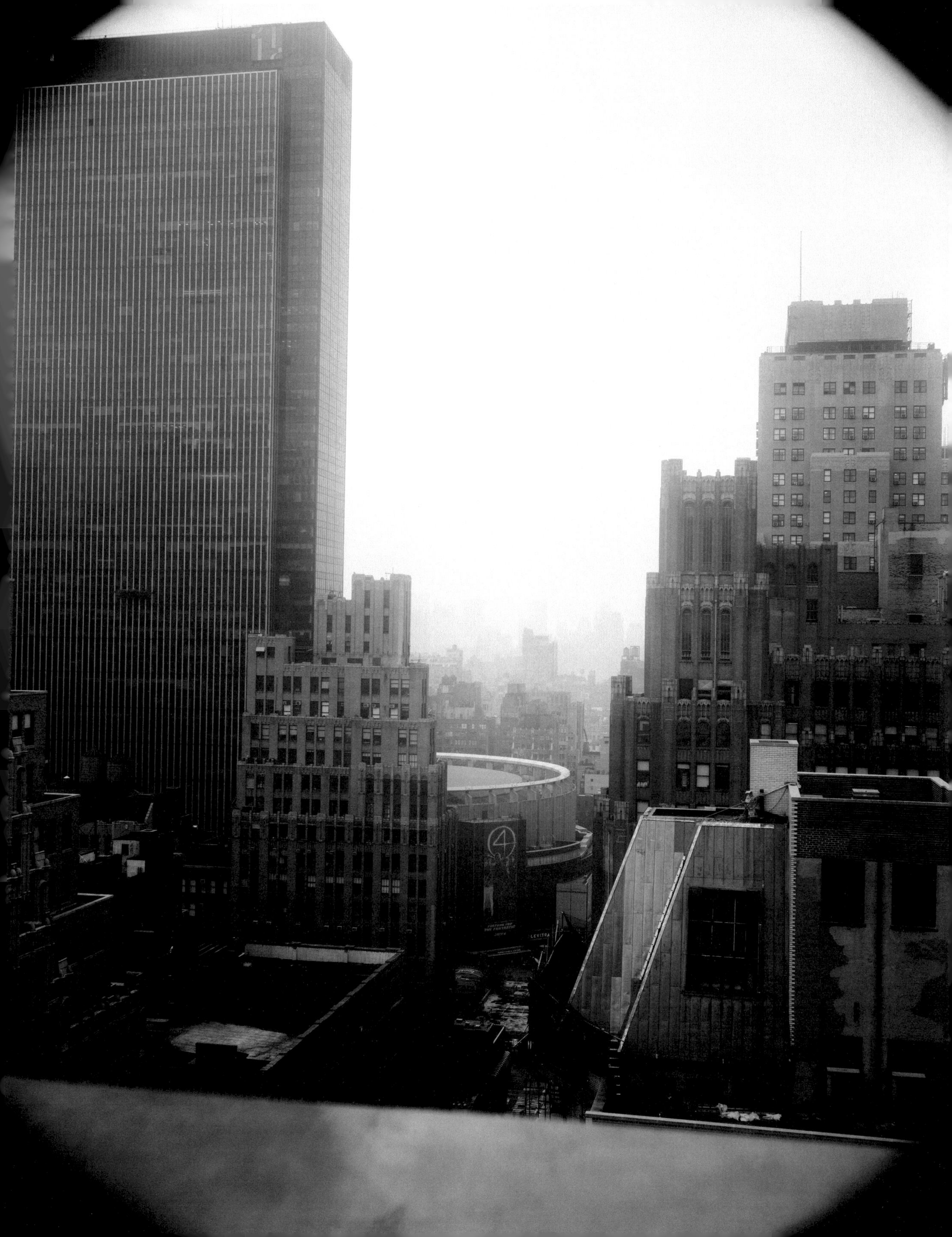

September 21, 2005

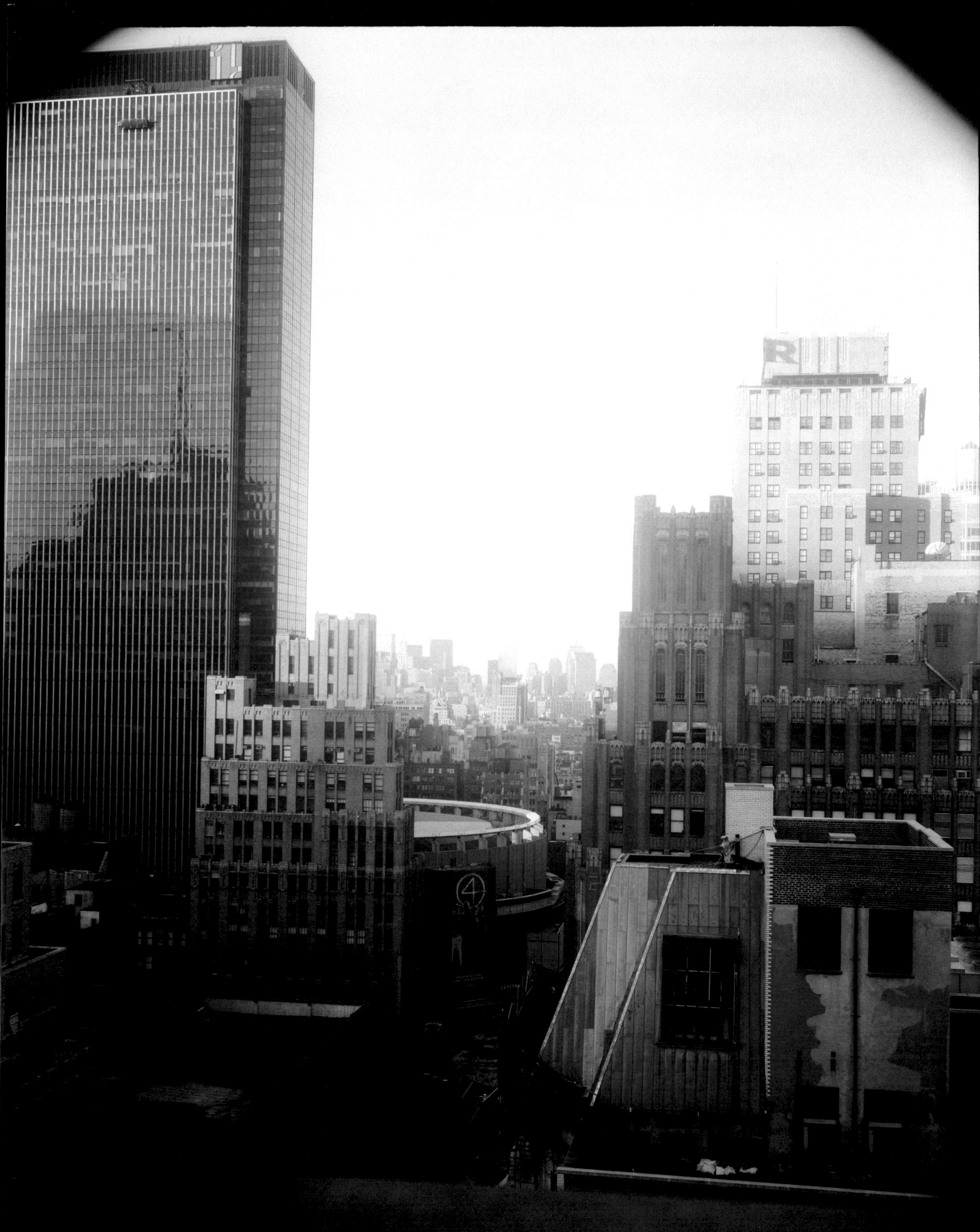

September 22, 2005

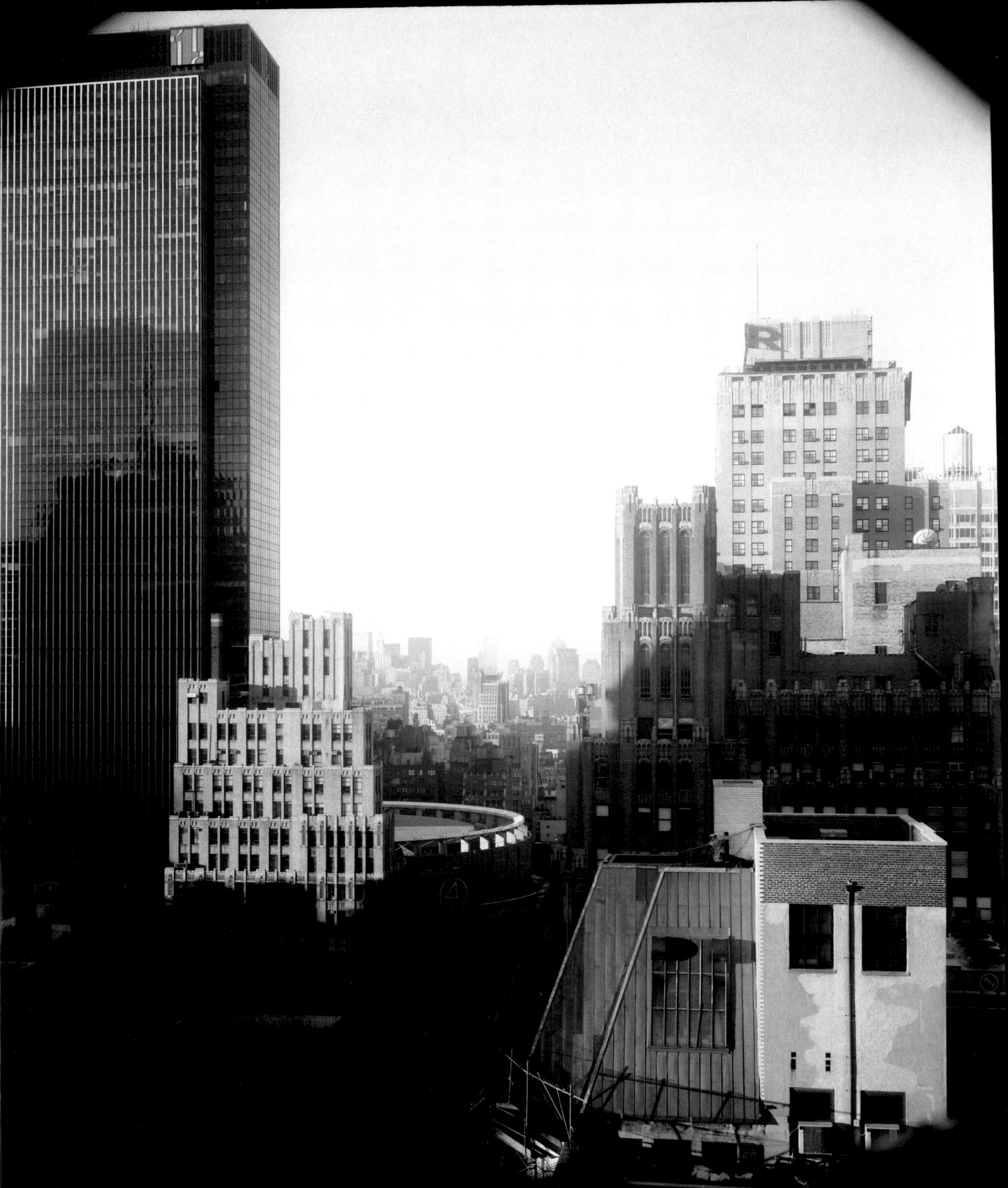

September 23, 2005

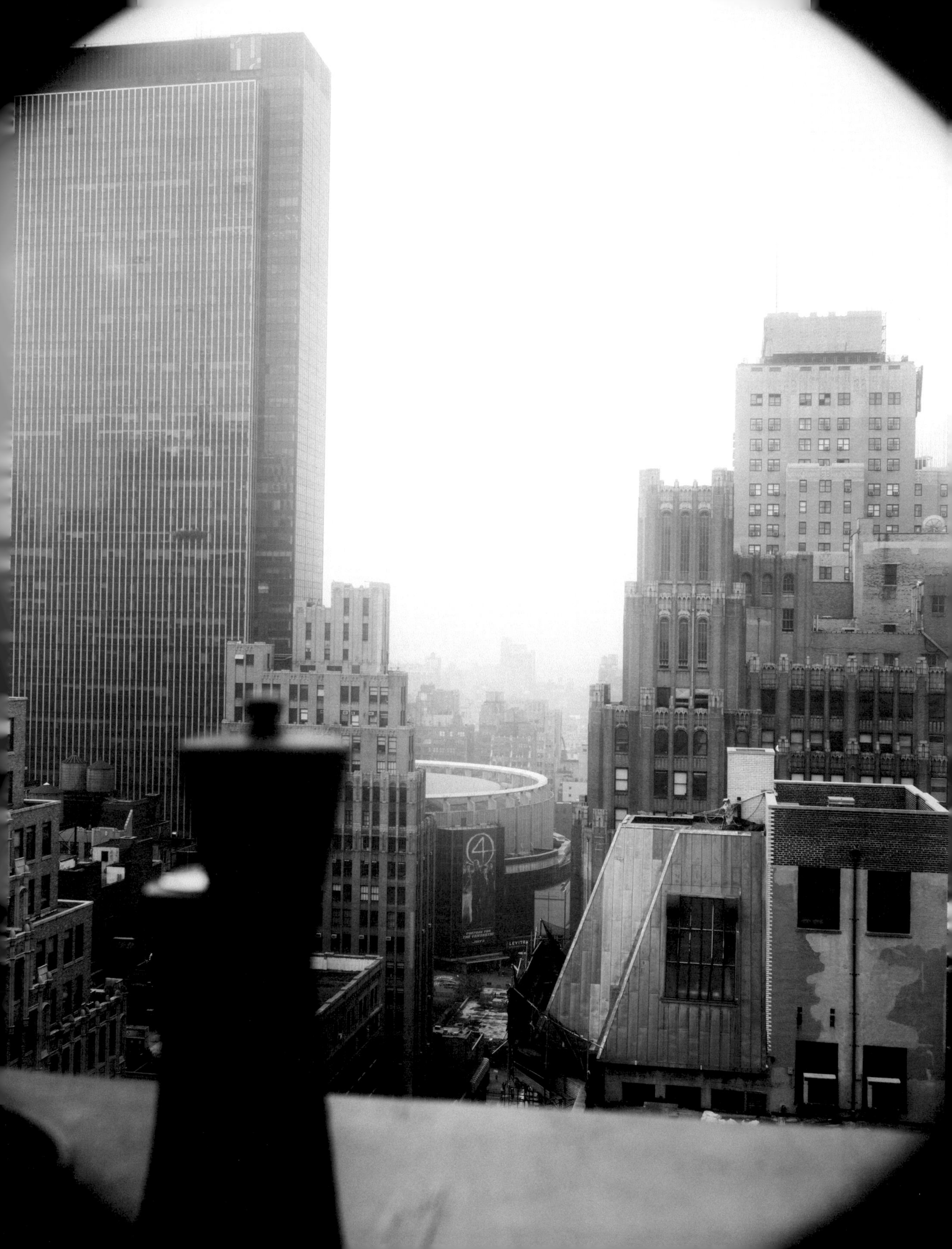

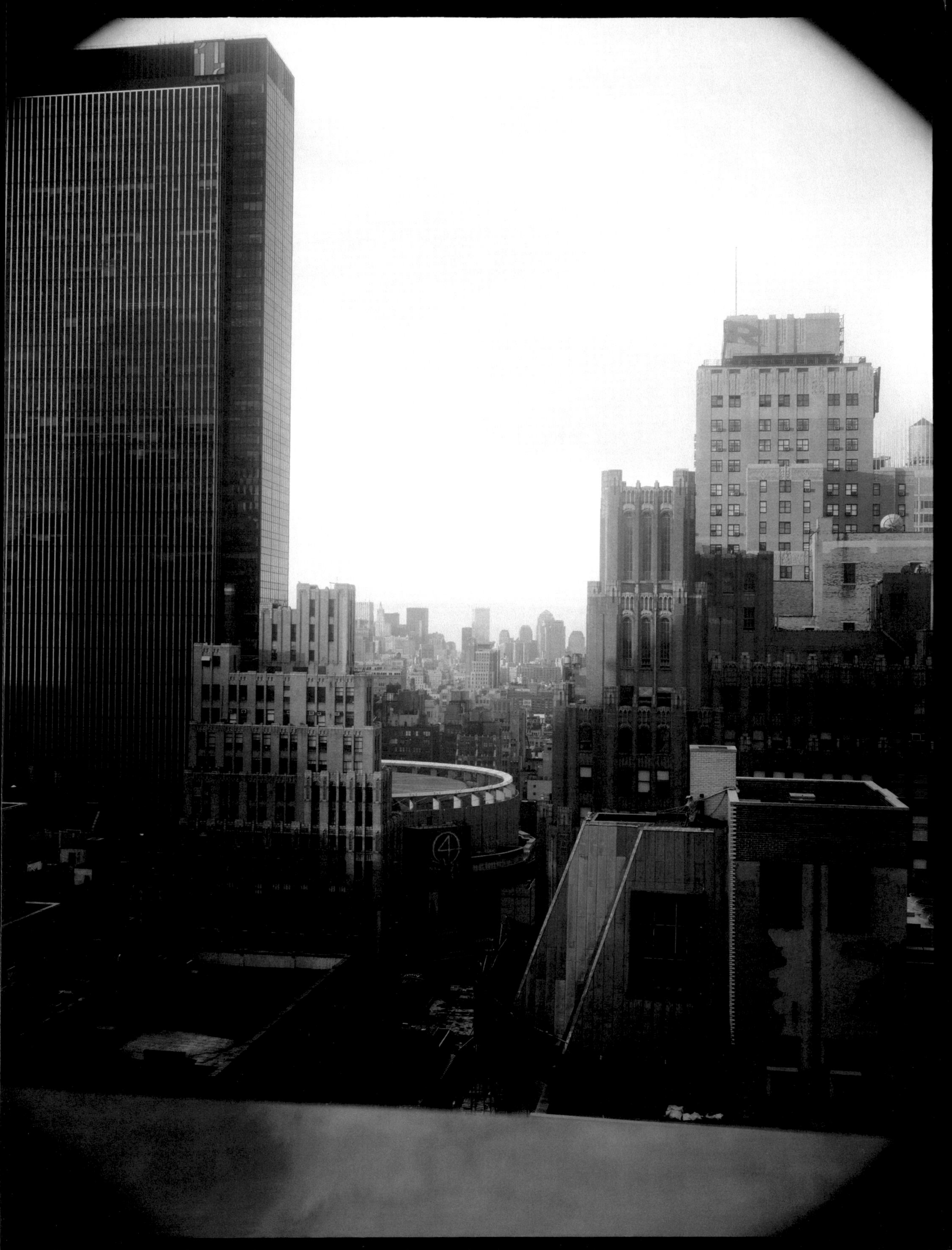

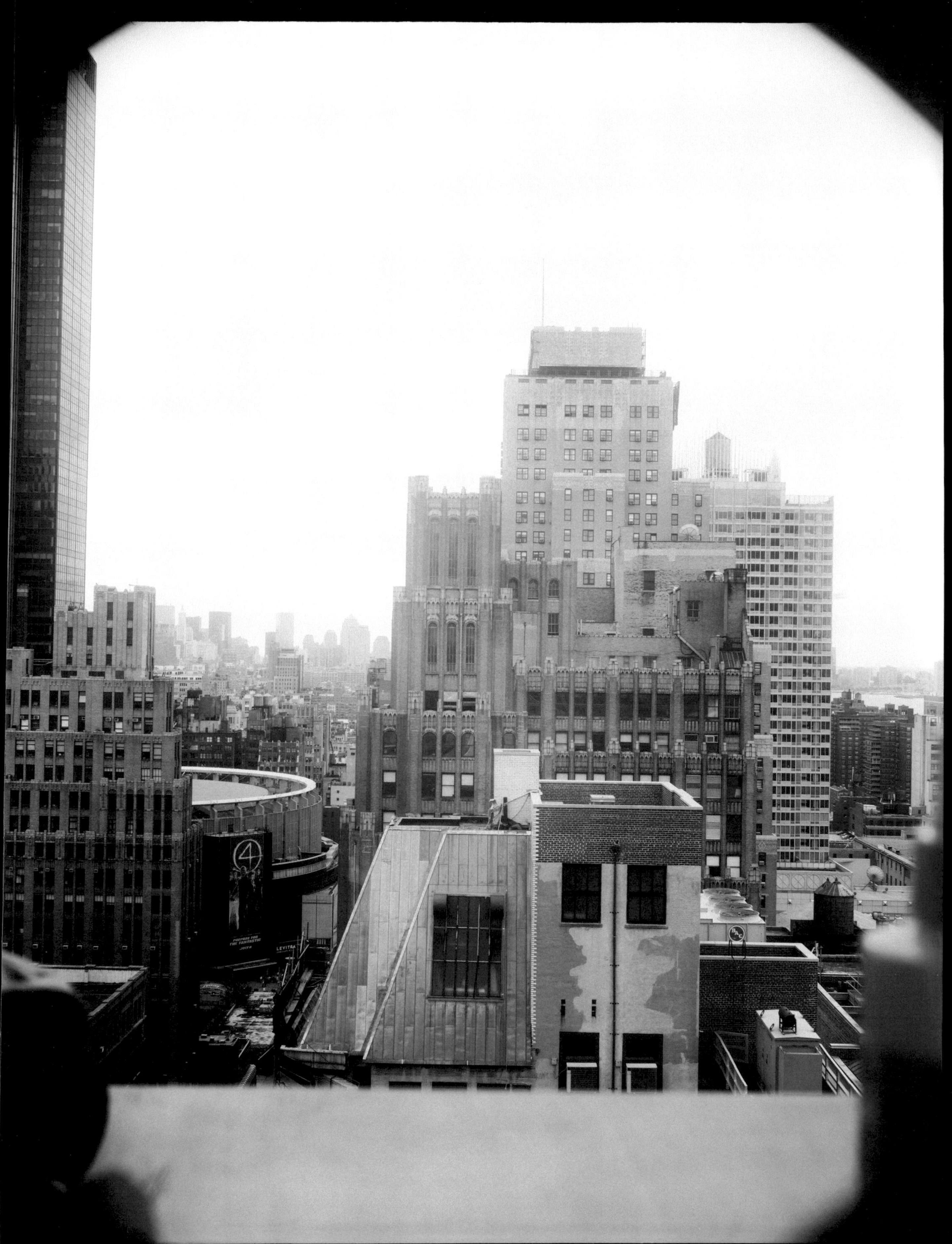

September 26, 2005

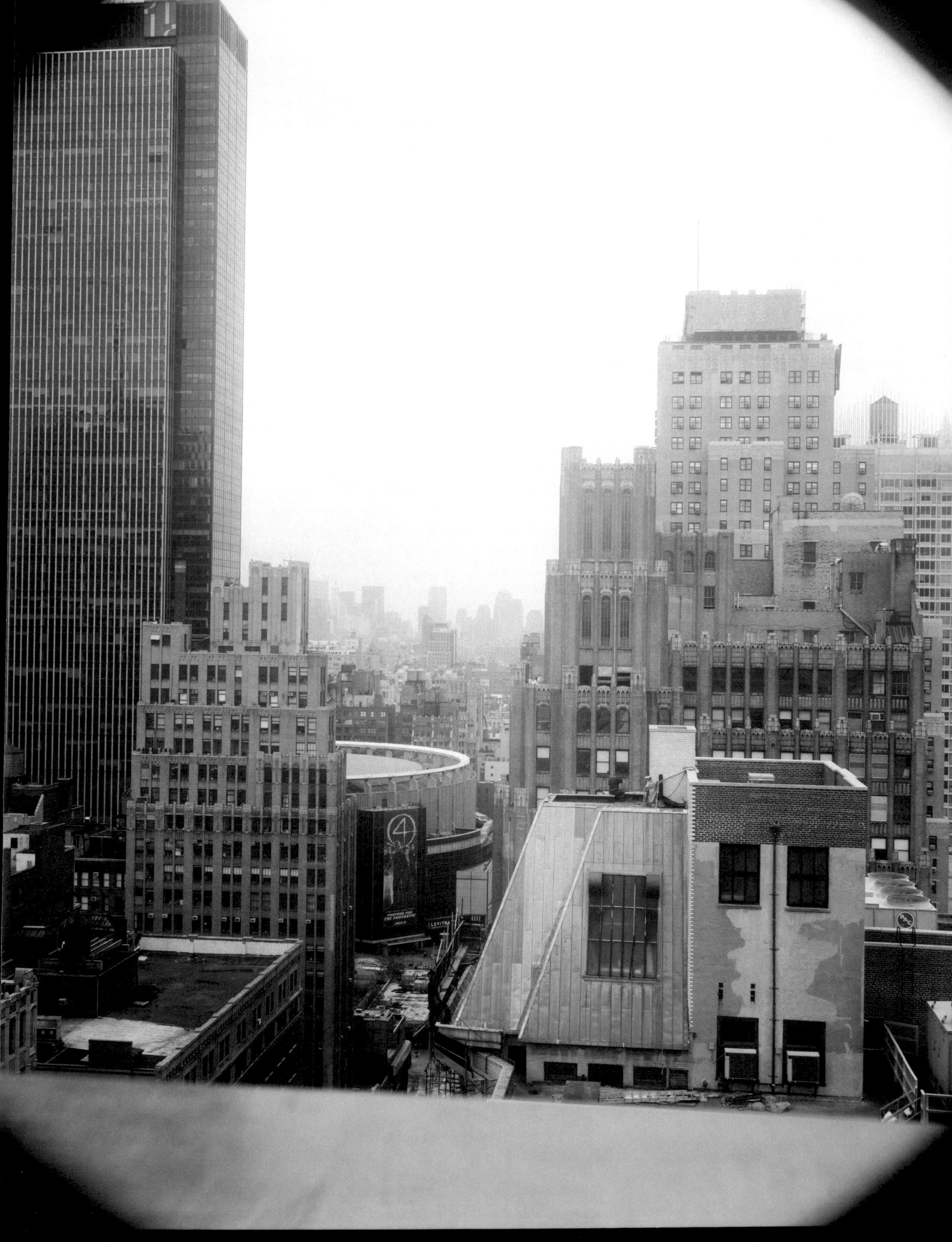

September 27, 2005

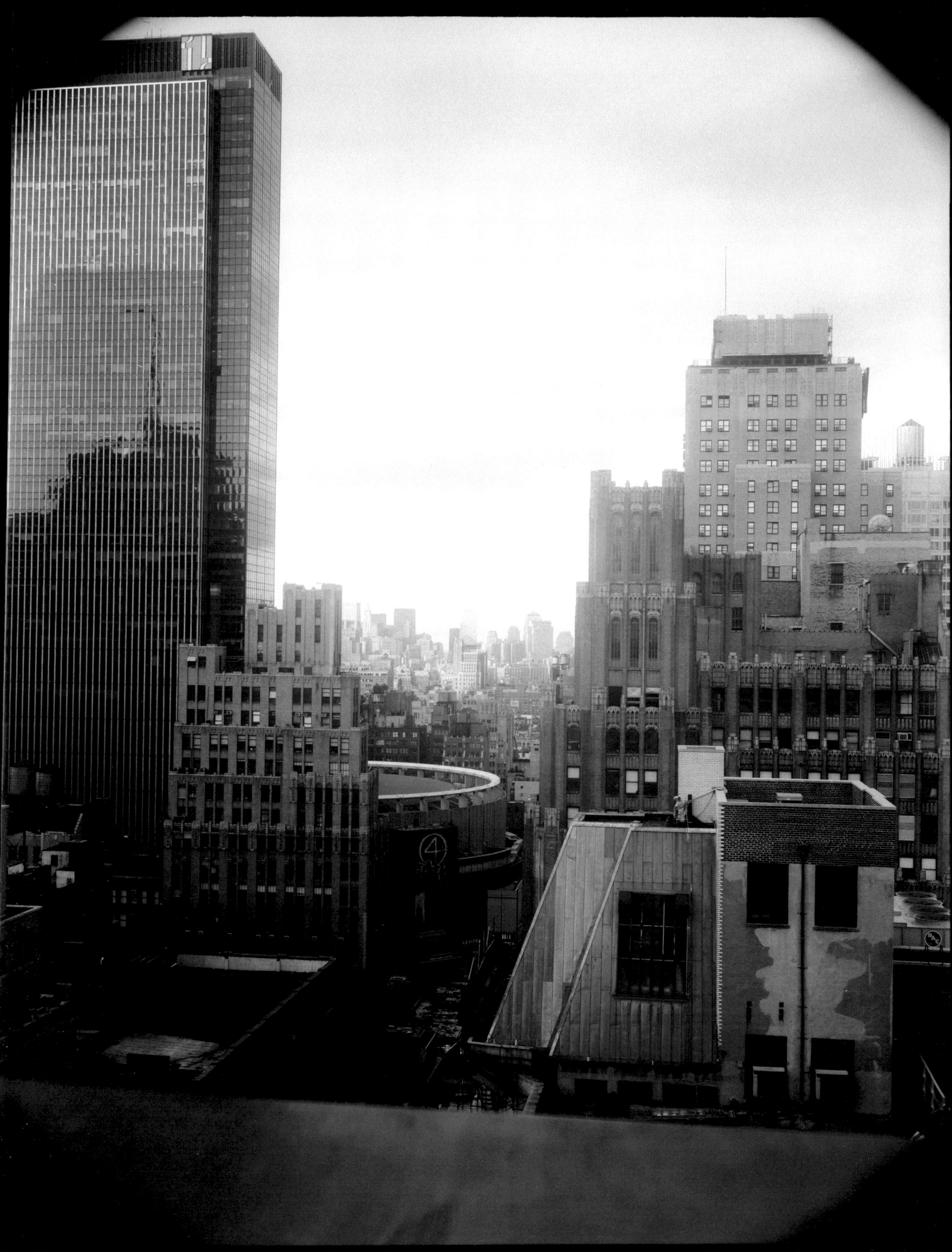

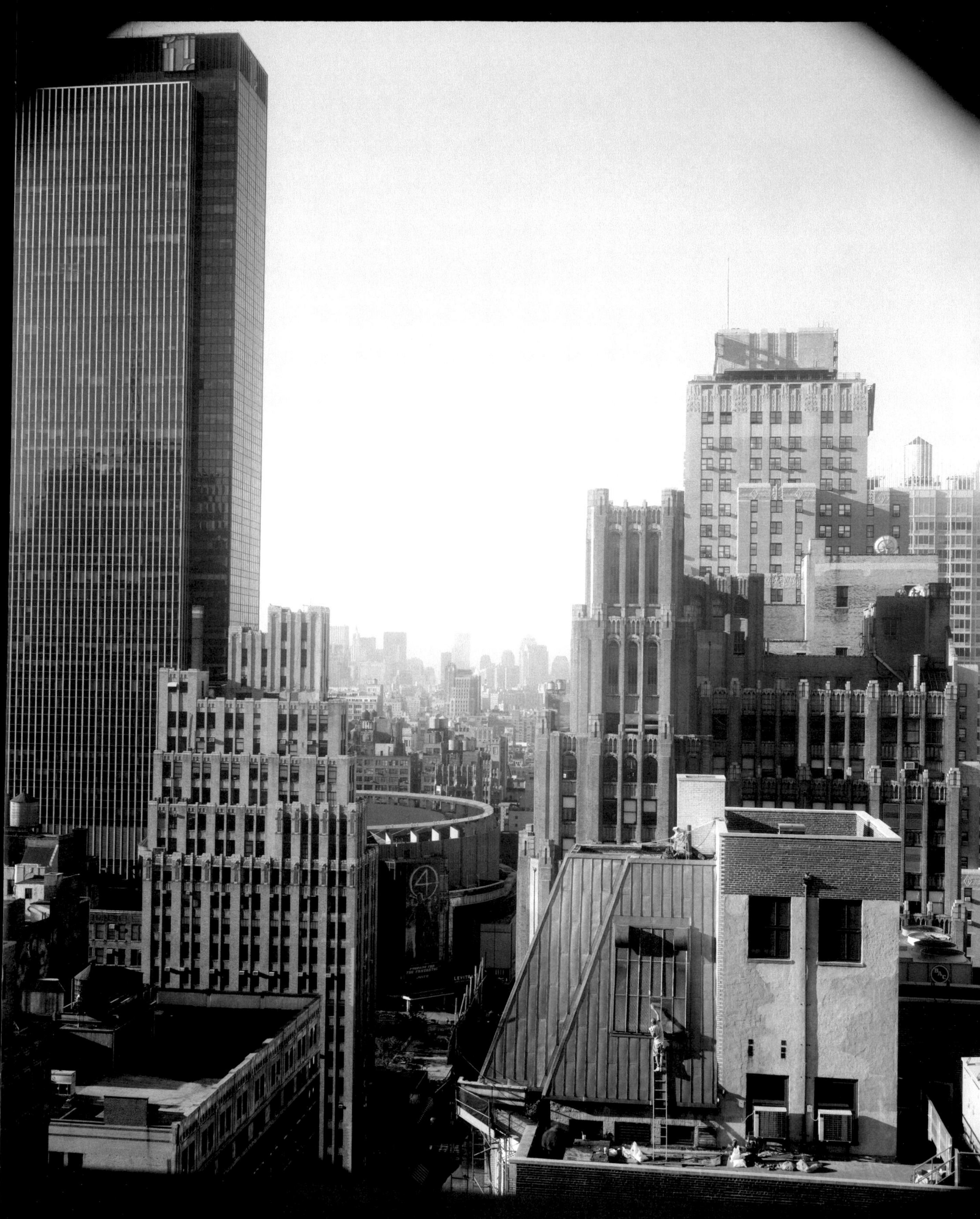

September 29, 2005

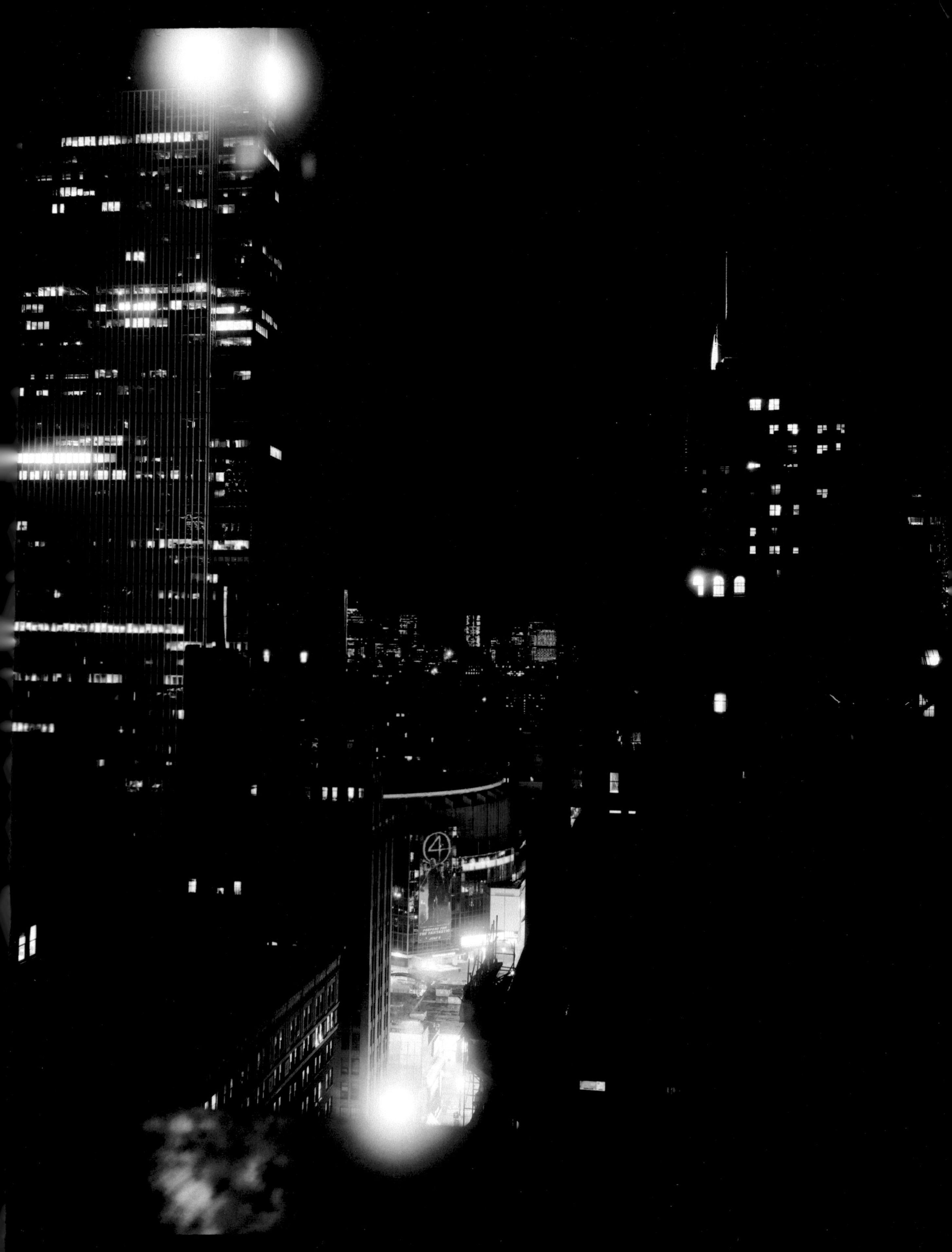

September 30, 2005

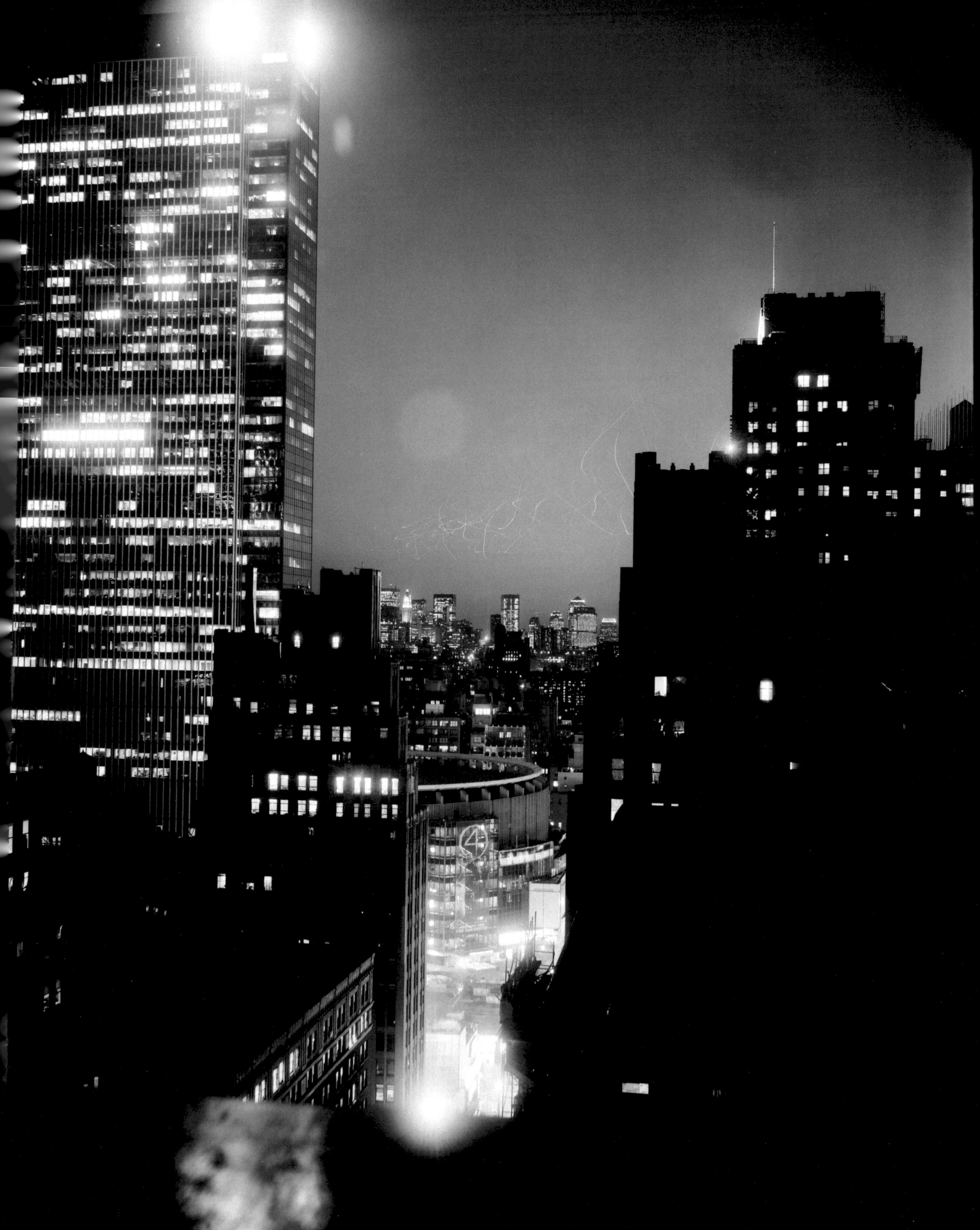

Window would not have begun were it not for
financial support from the DAAD in 1994–95, while I
was attending SVA. My artist's residency at Yaddo in
2003 was critical to the project's realization.
Later funding came from Hunter College in the form
of a 2005–2006 PSC-CUNY Research Award, as well as a
priceless sabbatical during spring term 2006.

My colleagues and collaborators at the EFA Studio
Center, the Visual Arts Program at MIT, Hunter
College's Art Department, Julie Saul Gallery,
Galerie Walter Storms and the Goethe Institute have
offered constant support and inspiration.

I am honored to work with Ludger Derenthal, whose
attention over a period of several years led to the
development of the exhibition concept. His vision
and perseverance made this massive installation a
reality, and this book would not be complete without
his insightful essay. Thanks, too to the Berlin
State Museums staff members who helped with the show.

A special nod to my father, who picked up a hammer
and helped assemble a staggering 1,000 light boxes.
Thank you to Karl Bichlmaier Co., which manufactured
the wooden parts for the installation, and to Tobias
Kugler for coordinating the entire process.

Prestel Publishing's Jürgen Krieger, Christopher
Lyon and Stephen Hulburt made this book braver and
better; and it simply would not have come together
were it not for the high standards and attention-
to-detail of Curt Holtz. Heartfelt gratitude goes to
publisher Jürgen Tesch, without whom *Eleven
Septembers* might never have happened.

The team at Karl Bayer Media demonstrated a rare
combination of generosity and professionalism in
making the reproductions for this book.

Friends and peers who have not tired of granting
me their time and thoughts include Rudolf Herz,
Felicitas Klein, Candida Höfer, Herbert Burkert,
Beth Noveck, Chris Pichler, Maya Ishiwata, Lynne
Cohen, Andrew Lugg, Albert Hien, Tuna Ciner and Susan
Wilmarth. My teachers and students, I can't thank you
enough. And I am grateful for my dear friends Peter
Axer and Jonathan Santlofer, who helped me bear
the weight of the project over the years; Jonathan
contributed not only a most wonderful centerfold
text, but a magical and contagious insight.

To Carole, who helps me hear, see, and feel.

Reiner Leist

Published on the occasion of the exhibition

Reiner Leist–Window
Museum für Fotografie
Staatliche Museen zu Berlin–Kunstbibliothek
September 8, 2006–January 7, 2007

Contributors:
Ludger Derenthal is the director of the Museum for
Photography in Berlin.

Jonathan Santlofer is an artist and writer who
lives in New York City.

First Edition 2006
© Reiner Leist and Prestel Verlag, 2006
© for text by Ludger Derenthal, Jonathan Santlofer
© for images by Reiner Leist, VG Bild-Kunst, Bonn

Prestel Verlag
Königinstrasse 9, 80539 Munich
Tel +49 (89) 38 17 09-0
Fax +49 (89) 38 17 09-35

Prestel Publishing Ltd.
4 Bloomsbury Place
London WC1A 2QA
Tel +44 (020) 7323-5004
Fax +44 (020) 7636-8004

Prestel Publishing
900 Broadway, Suite 603
New York, NY 10003
Tel +1 (212) 995-2720
Fax +1 (212) 995-2733

www.prestel.com

Library of Congress Control Number: 2006904844

British Library Cataloguing-in-Publication Data
A catalogue record for this book is available from
the British Library. The Deutsche Bibliothek holds
a record of this publication in the Deutsche
Nationalbibliografie; detailed bibliographical
data can be found under: http://dnb.ddb.de

Design and layout by Reiner Leist
Origination by Bayermedia, Munich
Printed by Offsetdruckerei Grammlich, Pliezhausen
Bound by Karl Dieringer, Gerlingen

Printed in Germany on acid-free paper
ISBN 3-7913-3679-7
978-3-7913-3679-4